Early Paleolithic in South and East Asia

World Anthropology

General Editor

SOL TAX

Patrons

CLAUDE LÉVI-STRAUSS
MARGARET MEAD
LAILA SHUKRY EL HAMAMSY
M. N. SRINIVAS

MOUTON PUBLISHERS · THE HAGUE · PARIS
DISTRIBUTED IN THE USA AND CANADA BY ALDINE, CHICAGO

Early Paleolithic in South and East Asia

Editor

FUMIKO IKAWA-SMITH

MOUTON PUBLISHERS · THE HAGUE · PARIS

DISTRIBUTED IN THE USA AND CANADA BY ALDINE, CHICAGO

Distributed in the United States of America and Canada
by Aldine Publishing Company, Chicago, Illinois
ISBN 90–279–7899–9 (Mouton)
0–202–90041–X (Aldine)
Jacket photo by Fumiko Ikawa-Smith
Cover and jacket design by Jurriaan Schrofer
Indexes by Society of Indexers, Great Britain
Printed in Great Britain at the University Press, Cambridge

General Editor's Preface

For more than a century opinion has alternated, according to "current" fossil and archaeological discoveries, on the question of where mankind first originated – Africa of Asia? In recent years most attention has been given to Africa, with exciting results. Since world events of the 1940's greatly hindered the international comparisons and interpretations of findings, without which paleoanthropology and prehistory are ineffective, minimal information has been forthcoming from Asia. The present book is the beginning of a fresh assessment by the scientific world of precisely that area which has for so long been neglected. A special conference, which was occasioned by an international congress of an unusually wide variety of scientists and scholars from every part of the world, was responsible for the development of this initiative.

Like most contemporary sciences, anthropology is a product of the European tradition. Some argue that it is a product of colonialism, with one small and self-interested part of the species dominating the study of the whole. If we are to understand the species, our science needs substantial input from scholars who represent a variety of the world's cultures. It was a deliberate purpose of the IXth International Congress of Anthropological and Ethnological Sciences to provide impetus in this direction. The *World Anthropology* volumes, therefore, offer a first glimpse of a human science in which members from all societies have played an active role. Each of the books is designed to be self-contained; each is an attempt to update its particular sector of scientific knowledge and is written by specialists from all parts of the world. Each volume should be read and reviewed individually as a separate volume on its own given subject. The set as a whole will indicate what changes are in store for anthropology as scholars from the developing countries join in studying the species of which we are all a part.

The IXth Congress was planned from the beginning not only to include as many of the scholars from every part of the world as possible, but also with a view toward the eventual publication of the papers in high-quality volumes. At previous Congresses scholars were invited to bring papers which were then read out loud. They were necessarily limited in length; many were only summarized; there was little time for discussion; and the sparse discussion could only be in one language. The IXth Congress was an experiment aimed at changing this. Papers were written with the intention of exchanging them before the Congress, particularly in extensive pre-Congress sessions; they were not intended to be read aloud at the Congress, that time being devoted to discussions – discussions which were simultaneously and professionally translated into five languages. The method for eliciting the papers was structured to make as representative a sample as was allowable when scholarly creativity – hence self-selection – was critically important. Scholars were asked both to propose papers of their own and to suggest topics for sessions of the Congress which they might edit into volumes. All were then informed of the suggestions and encouraged to re-think their own papers and the topics. The process, therefore, was a continuous one of feedback and exchange and it has continued to be so even after the Congress. The some two thousand papers comprising *World Anthropology* certainly then offer a substantial sample of world anthropology. It has been said that anthropology is at a turning point; if this is so, these volumes will be the historical direction-markers.

As might have been foreseen in the first post-colonial generation, the large majority of the Congress papers (82 percent) are the work of scholars identified with the industrialized world which fathered our traditional discipline and the institution of the Congress itself: Eastern Europe (15 percent); Western Europe (16 percent); North America (47 percent); Japan, South Africa, Australia, and New Zealand (4 percent). Only 18 percent of the papers are from developing areas: Africa (4 percent); Asia-Oceania (9 percent); Latin America (5 percent). Aside from the substantial representation from the U.S.S.R. and the nations of Eastern Europe, a significant difference between this corpus of written material and that of other Congresses is the addition of the large proportion of contributions from Africa, Asia, and Latin America. "Only 18 percent" is two to four times as great a proportion as that of other Congresses; moreover, 18 percent of 2,000 papers is 360 papers, 10 times the number of "Third World" papers presented at previous Congresses. In fact, these 360 papers are more than the total of *all* papers published after the last International Congress of Anthropological and Ethnological Sciences which was held in the United States (Philadelphia, 1956).

The significance of the increase is not simply quantitative. The input of scholars from areas which have until recently been no more than subject matter for anthropology represents both feedback and also long-awaited theoretical contributions from the perspectives of very different cultural, social, and historical traditions. Many who attended the IXth Congress were convinced that anthropology would not be the same in the future. The fact that the next Congress (India, 1978) will be our first in the "Third World" may be symbolic of the change. Meanwhile, sober consideration of the present set of books will show how much, and just where and how, our discipline is being revolutionized.

Other volumes closely related to the present book, on primatological, paleoanthropological, and archaeological topics as well as on more contemporary subjects of interest to Asia scholars, have also resulted from the Congress. They are all published in the series *World Anthropology*.

SOL TAX

Chicago, Illinois
September 2, 1977

Foreword

East is East, and West is West...Nevertheless they did meet in
Montreal, at the end of August 1973, for a conference on the East
Asian Paleolithic organized at McGill University by Fumiko Ikawa-
Smith.

To the European archaeologist, which I am, invited as an outsider
on the faint chance that, maybe, I could look at the problems with
a fresh eye, one fact is striking in the present state of our knowledge:
the East Asian Paleolithic is quite different from the Western one. By
Western I mean a zone which partly comprises India and may extend
quite far to the east in North Asia, as far as Teshik Tash, or even
the Chinese loess site of Shuitungkou. I have analyzed the material
from this last site, kept at the Institut de Paléontologie Humaine in
Paris, without much difficulty, using the Western approach. Not that
this material is quite like a Mousterian one, but nevertheless they
belong to the same general type of material culture. I suppose this
remark could be extended to Japan.

When it comes to other Eastern sites from Java, Borneo, the
Philippines, etc., things become different. The Patjitanian seems to
be a late "Acheulian-like" culture in a superficial way, owing more
probably to convergence than to direct derivation. But, for most of
Southeast Asia, the chopper tradition goes on and on until recent times
without much change. The great variety of tool types which is met
in the Western Middle and Upper Paleolithic seems to be lacking. Does
that mean that until protohistoric times these people vegetated at a
Lower Paleolithic level? Very probably not, the more so since at Niah
Cave modern-type man seems pretty early. But the lack of flint or
other suitable stone, and probably as Tom Harrisson, we believe,
hypothesized, the use of vegetal resources which were not available

to Western man (like bamboo) oriented their technology in quite a different way. Bamboo is a very versatile material which can be used for knives, bows and arrows, and spears (none of which need any stone blade) containers, construction material, etc. To work bamboo man needed only the simplest of tools, such as choppers and chopping-tools to cut them, and ordinary flakes to shape them. Unhappily, under tropical conditions bamboo does not keep, so it is quite possible that we shall never have, in these regions, more than the most basic tools.

This will make the study of Southeast Asia more difficult and less rewarding than the study of more lithic-minded countries. However, great progress has been made, and the comparison of the Eastern and Western Paleolithic may offer promising lines of work, provided one remembers that the differences are linked to very different environments rather than to differences in man himself.

FRANÇOIS BORDES
Professor of Pleistocene Geology and Prehistory
University of Bordeaux I

Table of Contents

Introduction:
The Early Paleolithic Tradition
of East Asia

FUMIKO IKAWA-SMITH

In most textbooks, the cultural remains of Pleistocene hunter-gatherers are discussed in terms of three periods or stages of development: the Lower, Middle, and Upper Paleolithic. It has been the general practice to use a different framework for the New World ("the Lithic Stage" or "the Paleo-Indian Period"), and still another set of terminology (the Early and Middle Stone Age) is used for Pleistocene assemblages of Africa. For Asia many scholars, including several contributors to this volume, have tried to work with the tripartite division of the Lower-Middle-Upper Paleolithic, even though it is fully recognized that the "Middle" and "Upper" Paleolithic of East Asia often bear little resemblance to the Middle and Upper Paleolithic assemblages of Europe or the Middle East.[1]

During the Conference on the Early Paleolithic of East Asia, held in Montreal, a debate, deadly serious to the extent of becoming humorous, took place over the advisability of applying the term "Upper Paleolithic" to assemblages outside Europe. Some participants maintained that it is patently obvious what is meant by the "Upper Paleolithic." It seems that some assemblages are called "Upper Paleolithic" when the tools share certain morphological characteristics with the Upper Paleolithic tools of Europe, but other assemblages are treated as "Upper Paleolithic" because they are thought to be comparable in age with the European Upper Paleolithic. In still others, the presence of *Homo sapiens sapiens* appears to be the deciding criterion. To some participants, what is meant by "Upper Paleolithic" did not appear clear at all.

Different criteria are used with reference to the "Middle Paleo-

---

[1] For India, division into the Early, Middle, and Late Stone Ages was suggested some years ago, but this scheme has not been widely used.

lithic" as well. For example, when P. I. Boriskovsky (this volume) speaks of the Middle Paleolithic of India, he calls our attention to the technological and typological similarities with the Mousterian of Europe and the Middle East. It is not known whether the "Middle Paleolithic" of India is really comparable in age with the Mousterian of the Middle East, and Boriskovsky, in any case, states that we cannot trace connections between the Middle Paleolithic of India and the Mousterian culture of any specific area. It seems that the "Middle Paleolithic" here is used in the morphological sense, with the Mousterian of Europe and the Middle East as the points of reference. The Cabalwanian pebble tools of the Philippines, which are called "Middle Paleolithic" by Robert Fox (this volume), show no morphological similarities with the Mousterian. In fact, these pebble tools occur in a formation assigned to the "Middle Pleistocene" in the local stratigraphic sequence. At the moment, there is no way to compare the "Middle Pleistocene" of the Philippines with the "Middle Pleistocene" of Europe, but the European Middle Paleolithic at any rate does not appear until the European "Upper Pleistocene" is well under way.

We think this is a very confusing state of affairs. The way around it, it seems to us, is to discard the tripartite division of the Paleolithic when we discuss Asian assemblages. We have not gone so far as to discard the term "Paleolithic" altogether as some workers have suggested (e.g. Solheim 1972).

We have thus called the volume *Early Paleolithic in South and East Asia*, dividing the Paleolithic assemblages of this vast area into "Early" and "Late" varieties. Even this division may not be called for in most of Southeast Asia, but in the northern regions, entirely different methods of tool manufacture, together with proliferation of specialized tool forms, appear between 30,000 and 20,000 years ago. These include parallel-sided blades, some of which are retouched into standardized forms, including many kinds of engraving tools (burins), scraping tools, and projectile points. There is a great deal of variation but, as a whole, these later tools are in sharp contrast to what Asiatic hunters and gatherers had used for thousands of years before, and continued to use in some areas until quite recently. The earlier and later toolmaking traditions appear to have overlapped in time in some places, such as Japan and perhaps in North China. It does not seem possible to divide the Pleistocene hunting-gathering cultures of East Asia into neat stages or periods. It seems easier to deal with the situation if we propose two broad toolmaking traditions: Early Paleolithic and Late Paleolithic. A number of subtraditions could certainly be recognized in each, especially for the Late Paleolithic tradition.

By proposing the Early Paleolithic tradition of East Asia, we are, in a sense, adhering to what is now often referred to as Movius' "two culture theory." A conference on the Asian Paleolithic cannot avoid the discussion of the proposition that the Paleolithic world was divided into two cultural areas, one in which fully bifacial handaxes predominated after a long initial "pebble tool" phase, and the other in which choppers and chopping tools continued until very late while handaxes were rare or absent. A. P. Khatri of the Indian Council of Scientific and Industrial Research, who was present at the conference, strongly argued against the proposition, based on his work on the Narmada River (Khatri 1963), and some of his arguments are echoed in Boriskovsky's paper in this volume. Certainly, bifaces have been reported from several sites in Asia since Movius presented his synthesis (1944, 1948), and both Bordes (1968, this volume) and Bartstra (1976, this volume) compare Patjitanian handaxes to European specimens. While it is probably true that the Paleolithic world was not composed of two mutually exclusive cultural spheres, there does not seem to be sufficient stratigraphic evidence from India (Sankalia, this volume) or anywhere else in Asia to justify the replacement, at this time, of the concept of separate technological traditions with a universal and unilinear evolutionary framework.

At the moment, therefore, we continue to postulate the existence in East Asia of a distinctive toolmaking tradition, with the Indian subcontinent and the desert-steppe zone of Inner Asia and Iran as the interface with the "western" tradition. We feel, however, that to call it the "chopper/chopping-tool" tradition probably overemphasizes the heavy tools, when in fact it was flakes that were numerically (and probably functionally as well) more significant in most of the assemblages. The importance of flakes is repeatedly brought up by various authors, and Aigner's summary (this volume, "North China") of the Choukoutien assemblages is of particular interest, since they are often thought of as the classic examples of the "chopper/chopping-tool" tradition.

GEOGRAPHICAL DISTRIBUTION

Movius' "chopper/chopping-tool culture" (1948) was represented by the Patjitanian of Java, the Anyathian of Burma, the Early Soanian of the Punjab (now Pakistan), the Choukoutienian of North China, and possibly the Tampanian of Malay Peninsula. A large number of additional assemblages are now added to Movius' list from continental and peninsular southern Asia and from China, as the papers by Boriskovsky, Sankalia, and Aigner in this volume indicate. Work by Robert Fox and his associates in the Philippines and by the Harrissons in Borneo and adjacent islands point to the likelihood that the Early Paleolithic toolmaking tradition was quite widespread in insular Southeast Asia and further into Oceania, which this volume does not cover.

Chard (1959) and MacNeish (1971, 1976), among others, suggested that the first migrants from Asia to the New World brought with them a tool kit similar to the ones known from Choukoutien and the Fenho Valley in North China. For a long time, the area between North China and the Bering Strait was a blank as far as the chopper-and-flake tool kits were concerned. Recent work in Mongolia and the Soviet Far East, as reported by Okladnikov and Derevianko in this volume, appears to fill part of the gap, although some scholars remain unconvinced that the specimens are artifacts (cf. Klein 1971; Powers 1973). A vast number of Early Paleolithic assemblages have been recovered since the 1960's in Japan, three of which are reported by Serizawa in this volume. Here again the materials are subject to controversy, and the papers by Ohyi and Ikawa-Smith outline some of the issues in the debate. Early Paleolithic specimens were recovered also from a stratified site in the Korean peninsula (Sohn, this volume), which lies between the Japanese archipelago and continental northeast Asia.

These assemblages from northeast Asia are of interest, not only for understanding the gradual expansion of human population into the New World, but also for understanding how and why the Early Paleolithic tradition of East Asia managed to be so conservative in its technological characteristics, insofar as can be seen in stone tools. It is often argued that the Paleolithic of South and East Asia remained unchanged because of the nature of resources available in the tropical forest. Derevianko (this volume) suggests that the Amur Basin at the time of the Early Paleolithic occupation was as mild as North China, but North China is hardly tropical in climate. As verified assemblages from northeast Asia increase, we need a model which can accommodate the Paleolithic populations in temperate and even cool regions of East Asia. To this date, no assemblage of the Early Paleolithic tradition has been reported from the Arctic parkland and tundra, although Mochanov (1973) suggests that his Duktai tradition of eastern Siberia represents a development out of this tradition after 30,000 B.P.

TEMPORAL RANGE

With the Pleistocene chronology of East and South Asia in its present state, it is difficult to say when the Early Paleolithic tradition began and when it ended. In Java, where some of the key formations are radiometrically dated, human fossils are not associated with indisputable artifacts. Jacob (this volume) reports that two kinds of early hominids, *Meganthropus* and *Pithecantropus modjokertensis*, occur in a formation dated to about 1.5 million years ago. Most authors feel that these specimens are morphologically similar to the Australopithecines of Africa (Howells 1973). If these Javanese hominids used tools as some of the African varieties seem to have, we have not yet identified them. The Trinil Bed which produced a number of *Homo erectus* specimens (or *Pithecanthropus erectus*, as Jacob and von Koenigswald prefer to call them in this volume) is given an age of between one million and 500,000 years, based on a new set of radiometric dates. This is not at variance with the previously reported date of 710,000 years on tektite samples. While von Koenigswald (this volume) believes that flakes collected at Sangiran were made by *Homo erectus*, many scholars remain unconvinced that they really are artifacts. On the other hand, the "Patjitan culture," which definitely represents human workmanship, cannot be dated at present and may actually be made up of a series of complexes (Bartstra 1976, this volume).

Flakes, cores, and a utilized pebble were found at Kungwangling (Lantian Locality 63706) just above the human skull. Aigner and Laughlin (1973) suggested that the associated fauna is comparable to the fauna of the Djetis Bed of Java, which could be about 1.5 million years old. A quartz pebble with flake scars has also been reported from the Nihowan Formation of North China near Peking (Gai and Wei 1974). The Nihowan is generally considered to be the "Villafranchian" of China. When these north Chinese specimens are corroborated by additional materials, and dates confirmed by independent dating methods, we may be able to say that the Early Paleolithic tradition began in East Asia as much as 1.5 million years ago.

Archaeological assemblages assigned with varying degrees of certainty to the "Middle Pleistocene" in various areas in East Asia include those from Chihchin (Kweichou Province) and Yungshan (Kiangsi Province) in South China (Aigner, this volume); Choukoutien Locality 1 and Locality 15 and K'oho in North China (Aigner, this volume); Filimoshki, Kumary, and Ust-Tu in the Amur-Zeya basin in the Soviet Far East (Derevianko, this volume); Ulalinka in the Altai region; Sain-Shand and Dalan-Dzagagad in Mongolia (Okladnikov, this volume); and the sites in Cagayan Valley on the northern Luzon in the Philippines (Fox, this volume). By far the best known is the Choukoutien Locality 1 assemblage, represented by thousands of artifacts and faunal remains. An age on the order of 0.4 to 0.6 million years has been suggested on the basis of faunal correlation (Butzer and Isaac 1975: 892). Aigner also remarks on the lithic technology of the Choukoutien assemblages on the one hand and the K'oho on the other. They may be examples of subtraditions within the East Asian Early Paleolithic tradition.

Some of the Early Paleolithic materials from Japan, such as those from the lower strata of the Hoshino and Iwajuku sites (Serizawa, this volume) may date to the Middle Pleistocene, but most of them are of Upper Pleistocene age, after the onset of the Last Interglacial. Among the most acceptable as artifacts are the Gongenyama I assemblages from the Kanto Plain north of Tokyo (Maringer 1956), which reportedly occurred in a horizon below the Hassaki Pumice dated to about 40,000 years ago, and the Horizon 15 assemblage of the Fukui Cave in Kyushu, dated by the radiocarbon method as being older than 31,900 years. The Sozudai assemblage, summarized by Serizawa (this volume) is younger than 130,000 B.P., but how much younger could not be determined by available data.

Recent work in the southern Kanto Plain near Tokyo, where archaeological horizons could be correlated with dated pumice and buried soil horizons, indicate that irregular flakes and heavy chopper-like tools continue to be used between 30,000 and 20,000 years ago (Ikawa-Smith i.p.). Some of the heavy tools have smooth, probably intentionally ground, edges. As in the Hoabinhian of Southeast Asia, edge-grinding appears in assemblages which are essentially the continuation of the Early Paleolithic tradition in other aspects of lithic technology. On the other hand, parallel-sided blades and functionally specific tools made in standardized forms began to occur in Japan about 20,000 years ago. Their appearance seems accompanied by marked population increase, at least if a sharp increase in the number of known sites is indicative. I would call them "Late Paleolithic" assemblages, which can be grouped into several subtraditions. Some of the Late Paleolithic subtraditions may be the results of local evolution from Early Paleolithic antecedents, and this may be demonstrated in techniques of flake detachment. However, chronometric and stratigraphic evidence available at this time tends to suggest that there was a period of a few thousand years when both Early and Late Paleolithic technological traditions coexisted in Japan.

The materials reported by Sohn in this volume appear to predate 30,000 radiocarbon years, but it is difficult to place them more precisely in a chronological framework until we know more about the geochronology of Korea.

In China, Aigner (this volume, "North China") notes that continuity in the lithic technology from Choukoutien to Hsiao-nan-hai, which probably dates to the Last Glacial (a Würm equivalent). Tingts'un and other assemblages in the Fenho Basin, which probably date to an earlier horizon of the Upper Pleistocene, are compared by Aigner to the K'oho assemblage of the Chinese Middle Pleistocene. Hsiao-nan-hai and Tingts'un appear to indicate the continuation of the Early Paleolithic subtraditions in North China into the Upper Pleistocene, although precisely what portion of the Upper Pleistocene we are referring to is impossible to specify at this time.

Various assemblages of the Ordos in northern North China and Inner Mongolia are even more difficult to date. We are told that Shuitungkou may not be an assemblage in the usual sense, but a collection of materials from different temporal horizons. In any event, the Shuitungkou materials, which Bordes (this volume) thinks are understandable by a "Western" approach, do contain a number of tools with standardized forms as Aigner's illustrations in this volume indicate. The same is true, it seems to me, of the materials recovered from the Shih-yu site in Shansi (Chia, Gai, and You 1972). These may be considered as Late Paleolithic manifestations in North China, which could be contemporaneous with the representatives of the Early Paleolithic tradition at Hsaio-nan-hai and elsewhere.

Flakes and pebble tools are reported from various localities in South China, in what is considered to be Late Pleistocene contexts. The assemblages which contain ground stone tools may turn out to be just as old in South China as in Japan or Australia.

We would include in our Early Paleolithic tradition the materials recovered from the Niah Caves in Borneo (Harrisson, this volume) and Tabon and Guri Caves on the Palawan Island of the Philippines (Fox, this volume), in spite of their young ages and their association, at Niah and Tabon, with anatomically modern hominids. The maximum age at these island sites appears to be about 40,000 years, and essentially the same lithic technology appears to continue into the Holocene.

CHOPPERS, FLAKES, AND NONLITHIC TOOLS

In this introduction I have not tried to delineate local subtraditions in flaking techniques, forms of the few standardized tools (such as the steep-back scrapers), and relative frequencies of core vs. flake tools. Relative frequency of core tools, or heavy-duty tools, probably is not a very good index of a cultural tradition. The ratio probably varies greatly from site to site, in part according to the kind of activities carried out by prehistoric people. It may also be influenced by the circumstances under which specimens were recovered. That the earlier descriptions of Paleolithic assemblages from East and South Asia tended to highlight choppers and chopping tools is possibly due to the fact that they often were collected from secondary deposits.

As many of the contributors point out, what characterizes this vast area and temporal span are the flakes, which are often amorphous and which were utilized with very little modification. Choppers, chopping tools, proto-handaxes, and even true handaxes occur with flakes in varying frequencies. Undoubtedly we are looking at the skeleton of the prehistoric people's tool kit. The flake tools may have served for cutting and scraping meat and vegetable materials, and heavy tools for chopping and smashing, but the daily tasks of obtaining foodstuff, preparing meals, keeping the shelter in order, and carrying out rituals surely would have required other tools and equipment made from bamboo, wood, bone, antler, shell, and other organic materials. The stone tools, in general, probably served to make these other artifacts.

The possible use of bamboo has been suggested by many authors, but we have virtually no hope of obtaining actual evidence. Fractured bone and antler pieces are known from North China, about half a million years ago, at Choukoutien Locality 1. Whether these were intentionally modified is still being debated (Aigner, this volume, "North China"). From about 40,000 years ago, bone tools are known from the Niah Caves in Borneo (Harrisson, this volume). The utilization of bone by early inhabitants of East Asia is of interest to New World prehistorians because, in Arctic North America, where bones are better preserved, some of the early inhabitants appear to have relied heavily on bone as the raw materials for toolmaking (Irving, this volume; Bryan, this volume).

We suspect that the apparent simplicity and similarity in stone tools in East and South Asia is deceptive and it probably masks a great diversity in local cultural traditions and adaptive strategies. Tools made of nonlithic materials, using these simple stone tools, may have been quite complex and highly varied. The Early Paleolithic tradition stretches from tropical and subtropical forests, through upland karst areas, to temperate woodland and grassland, with a number of micro-environments in each of them. Requirements for extractive tools would have been very different. In addition to functional differences, there may have been stylistic differences in form and decoration of nonlithic tools, such as wooden spears, bamboo knives, snares, and traps.

We have long admired *Homo erectus* living near the glacial front in North China, but we are also learning that life in the tropics is not an easy existence either. Hutterer (1976) has recently shown a highly complex and dynamic mosaic of adaptive strategies in the tropical forests. Harrisson (this volume) argues that *Homo erectus* was incapable of penetrating tropical forest, while Sankalia cites evidence that the forest was not a hindrance to early man in India. We need to know more about the nature of the forests in each case, but it is very unlikely that South and East Asia was a "stagnant" culture area during Paleolithic times as was long claimed.

We must agree with Movius (this volume) when he says that in the past three decades "scarcely anything substantial has been added to our general understanding of the fundamental problems of the core and flake assemblages of South and East Asia." It is precisely because nothing comparable to his classic papers (1944, 1948) has appeared in the intervening three decades that the Montreal conference was called in August, 1973, as a pre-Congress conference of the IXth International Congress of Anthropological and Ethnological Sciences in Chicago. We hoped to come closer to a better understanding of the problems by updating each other's knowledge. For, unlike the prewar days, much of the work is now carried out by local scholars and the results published locally as well, in most cases in native languages. If we have made a little progress in overcoming the communication barrier, both in data and in theoretical approach, we feel we have accomplished a great deal.

The Montreal conference was made possible by the generous support of the Canada Council (Ottawa) and McGill University in Montreal, Canada. The Ford Foundation also provided travel grants for some of the participants. We are grateful to the organizers of the IXth International Congress of Anthropological and Ethnological Sciences for providing the opportunity for calling the conference and the forum for discussion at the Chicago meeting. Finally, we should like to express our appreciation of the lively participation by the late Tom Harrisson at the Montreal conference; we mourn his tragic death in a road accident in Thailand in January 1976.

REFERENCES

AIGNER, JEAN S., WILLIAM S. LAUGHLIN
    1973   The dating of Lantian Man and the significance for analyzing trends in human evolution. *American Journal of Physical Anthropology* 39 (1): 97–110.
BARTSTRA, GERT-JAN
    1976   *Contribution to the Study of the Palaeolithic Patjitan Culture, Java, Indonesia*, part one. Leiden: E. J. Brill.
BORDES, FRANÇOIS
    1968   *The Old Stone Age.* New York: McGraw-Hill.
BUTZER, KARL W., GLYNN LL. ISAAC, *editors*
    1975   *After the Australopithecines.* World Anthropology. The Hague: Mouton.
CHARD, CHESTER S.
    1959   New World origins: a reappraisal. *Antiquity* 33: 44–48.

CHIA, LAN-P'O, PEI GAI, YU-ZHU YOU
1972   Report on the excavation of the Late Palaeolithic site of Shih-yu, Shohsien, Shansi. *K'ao-ku Hseh-pao* 1: 39–58. (In Chinese.)

GAI, PEI, QI WEI
1974   Discovery of a stone artifact from the Lower Pleistocene, Nihowan. *Vertebrata PalAsiatica* 12 (1): 69–74. (In Chinese.)

HOWELLS, WILLIAM
1973   *Evolution of the Genus Homo.* Reading, Mass.: Addison-Wesley.

HUTTERER, KARL L.
1976   An evolutionary approach to the Southeast Asian cultural sequence. *Current Anthropology* 17 (2): 221–242.

IKAWA-SMITH, FUMIKO
i.p.   Chronological framework for the study of the Palaeolithic in Japan. *Asian Perspectives* 19 (1).

KHATRI, A. P.
1963   Mahadevian: an Oldowan pebble culture in India. *Asian Perspectives* 6: 186–197.

KLEIN, RICHARD G.
1971   The Pleistocene prehistory of Siberia. *Quaternary Research* 1 (2): 133–161.

MACNEISH, RICHARD S.
1971   Early Man in the Andes. *Scientific American* 244 (4): 36–45.
1976   Early Man in the New World. *American Scientist* 64: 316–327.

MARINGER, JOHANNES
1956   Einige faustkeilartige Geräte von Gongenyama (Japan) und die Frage des japanischen Paläolithikums. *Anthropos* 51: 175–179.

MOCHANOV, Y. A.
1973   "Early migrations to America in the light of a study of the Duktai Paleolithic culture in Northeast Asia." Paper presented at the IXth International Congress of Anthropological and Ethnological Sciences, Chicago.

MOVIUS, HALLAM L., JR.
1944   Early man and Pleistocene stratigraphy in southern and eastern Asia. *Papers of the Peabody Museum of American Archaeology and Ethnology* 19 (3).
1948   The Lower Palaeolithic cultures of Southern and Eastern Asia. *Transactions of the American Philosophical Society*, n.s. 38 (4): 329–420.

POWERS, WILLIAM R.
1973   Palaeolithic Man in Northeast Asia. *Arctic Anthropology* 10 (2).

SOLHEIM, WILHELM G., II
1972   An earlier agricultural revolution. *Scientific American* 226 (4): 34–41.

TAKAMIYA, HIROE, TAMAKI MORIKATSU, KIN MASANORI
1975   Artifacts of the Yamashita-cho Cave site. *Journal of the Anthropological Society of Nippon* 83 (2): 135–150. (In Japanese.)

TOKUNAGA, S.
1936   Bone artifacts used by ancient men in the Riukiu Islands. *Proceedings of the Imperial Academy* 12 (10): 352–354.

PART ONE

Insular Southeast Asia

New Finds of Lower and Middle Pleistocene Hominines From Indonesia and an Examination of Their Antiquity

TEUKU JACOB

HOMININE ANTIQUITY

All fossil hominines of Indonesia were discovered in the Pleistocene beds. The oldest ones came from the Lower Pleistocene Puchangan formation of Perning (Mojokerto) and Sangiran (Surakarta). The antiquity of these specimens was dated by the K/Ar method at Kepuhklagen (Waringinanom, Surabaya), near Perning, north of Mojokerto, and at Kebonduren (Kedungbrubus, Gunung Butak area), north of Charuban, East Java. The samples from Perning consisted of pumice obtained just a few meters below the site where the juvenile skull of *Pithecanthropus modjokertensis* was found in 1936. The samples from Kebonduren consisted of andesite from the formation below and some distance from the site of the juvenile mandible of *P. erectus* found in 1889. Both samples gave a result of respectively 1.9±0.4 and 1.91 million years (Jacob and Curtis 1971; Curtis, personal communication 1972). It can therefore be concluded that *P. modjokertensis* both from Perning (East Java) and Sangiran dome area (located in the counties of Sragen and Karanganyar, Central Java) are

I appreciate the support received for the research reported above from the Department of Education and Culture, Jakarta, Gadjah Mada University and its College of Medicine, Yogyakarta, and the Wenner-Gren Foundation for Anthropological Research, New York. A Ford Foundation grant has made it possible for the author to present this report at the Conference on the Early Paleolithic of East Asia, Montreal, August 1973.

I also express my thanks to Mr. Johannas, Director, Mr. Darwin Kadar, Paleontology Section, and Mr. T. Soeradi, Museum and Documentation Section, Directorate of Geology, Bandung, for the permission to study their collection of human fossils. Identification of most of the animal fossils reported was made or confirmed by Dr. D. A. Hooijer, Museum of Natural History, Leiden.

Lastly, I have used the research facilities of the Indonesian Paleoanthropological Research Project.

at least 1.5 million years old. Thus they lived in the upper Lower Pleistocene and in the lower Middle Pleistocene.

The next oldest fossils came from the Kabuh formation of Middle Pleistocene age. Their antiquity was dated by the same radiometric method based on hornblendes extracted from pumice from the layers below, at, and above the levels of the sites where skull caps were found in 1963 at Tanjung (Sangiran 10) and in 1965 at West Puchung (Sangiran 12). The average of the four dates obtained is 830,000 years (Curtis, personal communication 1972).

K/Ar dates were also obtained from tektites thought to be associated with the Kabuh formation of Sangiran and they gave an antiquity of 710,000 years (von Koenigswald 1968a). Another date obtained from leucite from the Muria volcano in north Central Java from the level above that of pithecanthropines gave a date of 0.5 ± 0.06 million years (von Koenigswald 1964).

Consequently it is reasonable to conclude that *P. erectus* lived in the Middle Pleistocene roughly between one million and half a million years ago. This would be valid for *P. erectus* from Sangiran, Trinil, and Kedungbrubus.

There have been no successes as yet in radiometrically dating the hominines of the Upper Pleistocene. Solo man is thought by some authors to be only 15,000 years old because of the supposedly associated Magdalenian artifacts. The presence of a crane (*Grus grus*) humerus among the animal fossils places the hominine in a cold period comparable to the climate of present North China where the bird still lives; it was concluded that it must be during the Würm glaciation (von Koenigswald 1951).

It is interesting to observe, however, that the Ngandong skulls show numerous primitive characteristics peculiar to *Pithecanthropus* (Weidenreich 1951; Jacob 1967). Stone balls similar to those reported from Ngandong were also found in Sangiran (Jacob 1964) where fossil finds consist only of Lower and Middle Pleistocene hominines. At Sambungmachan, east of Sragen, comparable stone balls were also found recently. None of them have been subjected to a thorough study.

In 1969 a skull was discovered in the Kabuh formation at East Puchung, Sangiran, which displays remarkable morphological similarities to Solo man (Sartono 1973; Jacob 1973). The cranial capacity is 1125 cc., the vault bones are very thick (at some points no diploetic structure is observed), the heavy and anteriorly convex supraorbital torus shows signs of breakdown in the middle and downwards and backwards winging at its lateral ends, the temporal lines are well marked, flatness of the vault (instead of a depression) is evident parasagittally, and the mastoid processes are well developed. Only the occipital torus is not sharp at its lower border and no triangular prominence is formed at inion as in Solo man, but the external occipital crest is present. The specimen has facial bones. From the features displayed we can infer that its lower jaw should be comparably heavy and robust with strong lateral tori or a thick base. The cheek bones are much heavier than the cheek bone of *Pithecanthropus erectus* or *Pithecanthropus pekinensis* (Jacob 1966, 1973; Weidenreich 1943).

Another skull cap was found at Ngadirojo, Sambungmachan (Sragen), early in 1973 in the lower Kabuh beds. It is associated with an antler fragment of *Cervus zwaani*, a horn core of *Bibos palaeosondaicus*, and a molar of *Stegodon trigonocephalus*; at some distance other animal fossils were discovered. The skull cap was found just above the black clay in the calciferous sandstone of the boundary beds between the Puchangan and Kabuh formations. This strongly cemented sandstone forms a tough endocast which holds the skull cap together. The skull also demonstrates surprising nonmetrical and metrical morphological similarities to Solo man. The cranial capacity is 1035 cubic centimeters, the supraorbital torus exhibits supraglabellar disintegration and marked winging at the lateral ends, the temporal lines are well developed, flatness of the vault is present parasagittally, the forehead is more curved and the vault higher than in *P. erectus*, the mastoid processes are strongly developed, and the lower border of the occipital torus is sharp with the presence of a triangular prominence and external occipital crest. It is unfortunate that the anterior portion of the nuchal plane is freshly broken, as are both the left orbital roof and the sphenotemporal area of the skull base. The spinous foramen is present on the left, although slightly damaged, but the oval foramen, which is characteristic of Solo man, is freshly damaged.

These two latest skulls point out that the antiquity of Solo man is greater than hitherto supposed. Close affinities also exist between *P. modjokertensis* and *P. soloensis* (Solo man) as suggested by the size and shape of several morphological traits. The two skulls mentioned above resemble *P. modjokertensis* too in several metrical characteristics. Furthermore, I think that some of the variable mandibles which have been found at Sangiran might belong to Solo man.

From the above it seems to be justifiable to suppose that Solo man lived from 1,000,000 to 200,000 years ago. It might have evolved from *P. modjokertensis* at the beginning of the Middle Pleistocene.

Table 1.   Fossil hominines from the Lower Pleistocene of Java

Site	Number[a]	Fossil	Year of discovery
			1936–1941
Perning	1	Calvaria	1936
Sangiran	1	Mandibular fragment	1936
	4	Calvaria	1938–39
	5	Mandibular fragment	1939
	6	Mandibular fragments	1941
	7	Teeth	1937–41
			1960–present
Sangiran	9	Mandibular fragment	1960

[a] Numbers are given in chronological order of discovery at the individual sites.

FOSSIL FINDS

Hominine fossil finds from the Lower Pleistocene are given in Table 1. Only one fragment was found in the last twenty years. Some isolated teeth might have also come from the Puchangan formation but we are not certain. Hominine fossils from the Middle Pleistocene are given in Table 2. From this table it is clear that most of the recent finds came from the Kabuh formation. And hominine fossils from the Upper Pleistocene are given in Table 3. No fossils were reported from the Upper Pleistocene in the last four decades.

In our recent research animal fossils were also found and most of them came from the Kabuh formation where most of our work has been concentrated. Of the animal fossils from the Puchangan formation of Sangiran and Sambungmachan we have: *Sus* sp., *Hippopotamus sivalensis, Cervus zwaani, Rhinoceros sivasondaicus, Tapirus indicus, Bibos palaeosondaicus, Archidiskodon planifrons, Stegodon trigonocephalus, Felis* sp., *Macaca* sp., *Presbytis* sp., *Pongo* sp., *Hylobates* sp.

From the Kabuh formation of Sangiran and Trinil we have the following fossils: *Sus brachygnathus, S. macrognathus, S. verrucosus, Hippopotamus sivalensis, Axis lydekkeri, Cervus palaeomendjangan, Duboisia santeng, Bibos palaeosondaicus, Bubalus palaeokerabau, Rhinoceros sivasondaicus, Tapirus indicus, Stegodon trigonocephalus, S. hypsilophus, Elephas hysudrindicus, Felis tigris, Cuon sangiranensis, Ursus malayanus, Acanthion brachyurus, Pongo pygmaeus, Hylobates* sp., *Presbytis aygula, Macaca fascicularis, Crocodilus ossifragus, Gavialis bengawanicus, Batagur siebenrocki,* and *Trionyx trinilensis.*

We have only a small quantity of animal fossils from Ngandong,

Table 2.   Fossil hominines from the Middle Pleistocene of Java

Site	Number	Fossil	Year of discovery
			1890–1941
Kedungbrubus	1	Mandibular fragment	1890
Trinil	1	Molars	1890
	2	Calotte	1891
	3	Femur	1892
	4	Femoral fragment	1900
	5	Femoral fragments	1900
	6	Femoral fragment	1900
Sangiran	2	Calotte	1937
	3	Calotte	1938
	7	Teeth	1937–41
			1952–present
Sangiran	8	Mandible	1952
	10	Calotte, cheekbone	1963
	11	Teeth	1963
	12	Calotte	1965
	13	Skull fragments	1965
	14	Skull base fragments	1966
	15	Maxillary fragments	1968–1969
	16	Teeth	1969
	17	Calvaria	1969
	18	Skull fragments	1970
	19	Occipital fragment	1970
	20	Skull fragments	1971
Sambungmachan	1	Calotte	1973

mainly of *Bubalus palaeokerabau*, *Bibos palaeosondaicus*, *Stegodon trigonocephalus* and *Sus* sp. More intensive studies on the faunal remains from all formations and from exactly known beds are needed in the future.

From the lists of hominine fossils presented above we noticed that during the Lower Pleistocene there lived two varieties of hominines, Meganthropus and *P. modjokertensis*. Close comparison of the two is impossible because Meganthropus remains comprise only two mandibles and teeth and no skull bones, while of *P. modjokertensis* we have skulls, mandibles, and teeth, but no mandibles were found in association with the skulls. Therefore, only the mandibles can be compared. In Meganthropus the jaw is very robust and its base is also thick, whereas in *P. modjokertensis* only the alveolar process is thick. The mandibular corpus in the latter is strengthened by the strong lateral tori and transverse tori on the inner aspect of the symphysis (von Koenigswald 1968b). It can be inferred that a Meganthropus skull should have a stronger supraorbital torus and occipital torus and an extensive nuchal area. Temporal lines should be very well marked and

Table 3.   Fossil hominines from the Upper Pleistocene in Java

Site	Number	Fossil	Year of discovery
			1889–1933
Wajak	1	Skull, neck vertebra	1889
	2	Skull fragments, jaws, teeth, femur, tibia	1890
Ngandong	1	Calotte	1931
	2	Frontal bone	1931
	3	Calotte	1931
	4	Parietal fragment	1931
	5	Calotte	1932
	6	Calotte	1932
	7	Calvaria	1932
	8	Parietal fragment	1932
	9	Tibia	1932
	10	Tibia	1933
	11	Parietal bones	1933
	12	Calotte	1933
	13	Calotte	1933
	14	Calvaria	1933

the cheek bones more robust than in Sangiran 17 or Sangiran 10.

The teeth are larger in Meganthropus, especially the cheek teeth of which we have evidence. This fact reflects the difference in diet. It is disputable whether Meganthropus has a closer affinity to *Australopithecus* or *Pithecanthropus*. There is no evidence of Meganthropus above the boundary beds of the Kabuh formation. *P. modjokertensis* in the meanwhile, as mentioned earlier, evolved into *P. soloensis*.

In the Middle Pleistocene we have Meganthropus, *P. erectus* and *P. soloensis*. Of *P. erectus* we have available skulls, mandibles, teeth, and thighbones, while of *P. soloensis* we have skulls and teeth. Facial skeletons of the latter are more complete than those which we have of the former. Most of *P. erectus* specimens came from the middle layers of the Kabuh formation, whereas remains of *P. soloensis* are of slightly earlier antiquity.

P. erectus has a smaller cranial capacity, low skull vault, more receding forehead, and less developed neck and chewing muscles. Cheek-bones are smaller in *P. erectus* and therefore it is assumed that mandibles of *P. soloensis* should be more robust. No difference in tooth size is evident.

The supraorbital torus in *P. soloensis* is disintegrated in the supraglabellar region and anteriorly convex. Postorbital constriction is more marked in *P. erectus*. At inion a triangular prominence invariably develops in *P. soloensis* and continues downwards as the external occipital crest. Some similarities are found on the base of the skull but there are also dissimilarities which we will not go into here. The mastoid process is larger in *P. soloensis* (Jacob 1967, 1973).

Of course questions could be raised whether the differences between *P. erectus* and *soloensis* are not simply due to sex or age. This problem should certainly be investigated further as new finds are made, but at the moment I am inclined to think that they are separate groups and not just females and males or juveniles and adults of the same group. Both sexes are represented among the finds of both groups; for example, Sangiran 2 is a female *erectus* and Sangiran 10 a male; and Ngandong 6 and Sangiran 17 are male *soloensis* and Ngandong 1 and Sambungmachan 1 female. Different age groups are also represented among the available finds; for example, Sangiran 10 is an *erectus* young adult, while Sangiran 12 is an old one; and Ngandong 12 is an old *soloensis*, while Ngandong 2 is a juvenile.

In the Upper Pleistocene of Indonesia we have *P. soloensis* and *Homo sapiens* separated by a relatively wide time gap. There is no problem in identifying the Wajak fossil remains as *H. sapiens*; however, it is slightly difficult to compare them to extant races (Jacob 1967). Races of *H. sapiens* as they exist today in Southeast Asia seem to have appeared during the post-Pleistocene period (Jacob 1972). Fossil links should be searched for between Solo and Wajak men to correlate them.

As of now, we have to rely on multiple hypotheses, such as correlating Solo man and the supposedly Neanderthal Mapa skull from China, and this to Wajak, or correlating Wajak and the Australoids, and these to Solo. Similarities between the Australoids and Solo man are primarily owing to their massive chewing apparatus as adaptation to similar diet.

Of Solo man from Ngandong we have skulls and tibiae. As described earlier, the skulls are very similar to Sambungmachan 1 and Sangiran 17, especially Ngandong 1 and 7 to Sambungmachan. Radiometric dating of Ngandong should be attempted further in order to correlate the groups in time. But even if the Ngandong remains are only 200,000 years old, it is not surprising at all that no remarkable changes had occurred in their morphology during approximately one million years.

SUMMARY AND CONCLUSIONS

All hominine fossils of Indonesia came from the Pleistocene. The oldest dated remain is of 1.9 million years' antiquity from the Puchangan formation of Perning, Mojokerto. Finds of comparable age from Sangiran are Meganthropus and *P. modjokertensis*.

The next oldest remains came from the Kabuh formation of Sangiran; their average date is 830,000 years. The average date obtained from tektites of Sangiran is 710,000 years. No dates are available for the Upper Pleistocene.

Most of the new finds of the last two decades came from the Kabuh formation. One of these is Meganthropus but most are *P. erectus* remains. Two finds are extremely interesting because they resemble *P. soloensis* in many respects, both metrically and nonmetrically; one of them was recovered from the boundary beds between the Puchangan and Kabuh formations. In some respects they resemble *P. modjokertensis* and this leads us to the conclusion that *P. modjokertensis* evolved into *P. soloensis* at the beginning of the Middle Pleistocene and survived into the Upper Pleistocene.

Mandibles are difficult to classify because not one has been found in association with skulls. Since it is a very variable bone, it shows many variations in size and shape.

Some differences between Meganthropus and *Pithecanthropus*, and among *P. modjokertensis, erectus,* and *soloensis* were discussed; differences between *erectus* and *soloensis* are not due to sex and age.

Plate 1a, b.   Skull cap of *Pithecanthropus soloensis* from Sambungmachan, Central Java, Indonesia; a: viewed from the right; b (opposite): from above.

REFERENCES

JACOB, T.
  1964 *Fosil-fosil manusia dari Indonesia.* Jogjakarta: Universitas Gadjah Mada.
  1966 The sixth skull cap of *Pithecanthropus erectus. American Journal of Physical Anthropology* 25: 243–269.
  1967 *Some problems pertaining to the racial history of the Indonesian region.* Utretcht: The Netherlands.
  1972 Evolution of man in Southeast Asia. *Regional Seminar on Southeast Asian Prehistory and Archaeology.* Manila.
  1973 Palaeoanthropological discoveries in Indonesia with special reference to the finds of the last two decades. *Journal of Human Evolution* 2: 473–485.

JACOB, T., GARNISS H. CURTIS
  1971 Preliminary potassium–argon dating of early man in Java. *Contributions of the University of California Archaeological Research Facility* 12: 50.

SARTONO, S.
  1973 On cranial measurements of *Pithecanthropus erectus* (*Pithecanthropus* VIII). *Publikasi Teknik Seri Paleontologi* 4.

VON KOENIGSWALD, G. H. R.
  1951 "Introduction," in *Morphology of Solo man.* By Franz Weidenreich, 211–221. Anthropological Papers of the American Museum of Natural History 43: Part 3.
  1964 Potassium–argon dates and early man: Trinil. *Report of the 6th International Congress of Quaternary Research 1961* 4: 325–327.
  1968a "Das absolute Alter des *Pithecanthropus erectus* Dubois," in *Evolution und Hominisation.* Edited by Gottfried Kurth, 195–203. Stuttgart: Gustav Fischer.

1968b Observations upon two *Pithecanthropus* mandibles from Sangiran, Central Java. *Proceedings of the Koninklijke Nederlandse Akademie van Wetenschappen*, series B, 71: 99–107.

WEIDENREICH, FRANZ

1943 The skull of *Sinanthropus pekinensis*: a comparative study on a primitive hominid skull. *Palaeontologia Sinica*, n.s. D, 10 (127).

1951 *Morphology of Solo man*. Anthropological Papers of the American Museum of Natural History 43: Part 3.

Lithic Industries of
Pithecanthropus erectus *of Java*

G. H. R. VON KOENIGSWALD

The finest natural exposures of Lower and Middle Pleistocene deposits in Java can be found around Sangiran, about fifteen kilometers north of the town of Surakarta in Central Java. Here in a circle of about four or five kilometers diameter around a dome-shaped tectonic structure, a section about 120–150 meters high can be studied. Known for a long time, a few bones had been reported long ago and a rich Pliocene assemblage of marine molluscs had been described, collected from the *Turitella* beds which form the very base of the section. The importance of the region for the stratigraphy of Java and the early history of man had not been recognized before 1934, paradoxically the very year the Geological Survey dismissed half of its staff for so-called economic reasons.

Remains of fossil vertebrates, reptiles, and mammals are abundant but scattered through the sediments. Two main units can be distinguished. First there is a lower unit at the base with a volcanic conglomerate followed by about sixty to eighty meters of black clay. The clay is full of freshwater mollusks (*Melania*, *Paludina*) and apparently laid down in a rather deep lake. Only near the bottom is there a marine intercalation, about one meter thick. The fauna of the lower layers is the Djetis Fauna, the fauna of the Javanese Villafranchian. The upper unit consists of fluviatile layers, volcanic tuffs, sandstones, and conglomerates, and contains a typical Trinil Fauna of exactly the same composition (with many specimens of the Axis deer, *Axis lydekkeri*) as described by Stremme from Trinil, the famous type site of *Pithecanthropus erectus*.

The first skulls of *Pithecanthropus erectus* came to light in Sangiran in 1937 and 1938; additional finds were made by Teuku Jacob and Sartono after World War II. So far five *P. erectus* skulls have been published from these layers and there are fragments of more. New potassium–argon datings, based on volcanic tuffs, gave an average of 830,000 years (according to a communication from Jacob); a date based on tektites was 710,000 years.

At the site of Trinil no traces of industry have ever been observed. At Sangiran, stone implements are limited to the upper, fluviatile part of the section; in the lower part there was not enough transport and the mammalian remains are from bodies which drifted into the lake. The first flakes, apparently the work of man, were recognized even in 1934, together with tektites, "glass meteorites," which were found here for the first time together with fossils and which are very valuable for dating, as we will see in a moment.

The industry from Sangiran has been collected from the surface, as have most of the fossils, and so my American friends were skeptical, although in 1939 I had already described a small series as the products of *Pithecanthropus*. For a test excavation in 1935 I had chosen a not too favorable locality which had yielded fossils and implements directly under the surface. As the native population collected everything (and asked money for it!), there was little chance to find specimens *in situ*. But after World War II van Heekeren collected some implements from near the top of the sequence in the so-called Notopuro Beds (van Heekeren 1957: 44).

The industry is a clear flake industry. The implements are seldom larger than 5 or 6 centimeters; the materials used are chalcedony, agate, jasper, silicified wood, and silicified limestone. They are shiny, lustrous, and very well patinated, and so differ from the Neolithic implements which are not rare in the Gunung Kidul, the "Southern Mountains," a region just south of Surakarta. Roughly half of the flakes still have part of the original cortex preserved, a sign that small pebbles have been used as raw material. Flaking is rare but many flakes have been used. The angle of percussion is variable, in many cases about 60 degrees. Bipolar flakes occur and there are also a few implements worked from both sides. (For some examples, see Figure 1.)

While there is a great variety of forms, there is no really fixed typology. Dr. Asok K. Ghosh of the University of Calcutta, with his wide knowledge of the Indian Paleolithic, very kindly helped us to classify the assemblage of flakes collected in Sangiran between 1934 and 1941. As part of my collection was lost during the war in the Pacific, the percentage of various groups certainly is not representative for the assemblage as a whole. Also, one must not forget that there is no living floor in Sangiran, that the industry is irregularly distributed, and that all our implements have been picked up from the surface.

We can distinguish more elongated blades, flakes with a fair number of pointed flakes, several types of scrapers, single- and double-edged as well as nosed scrapers. There are even some borers, fine and crude,

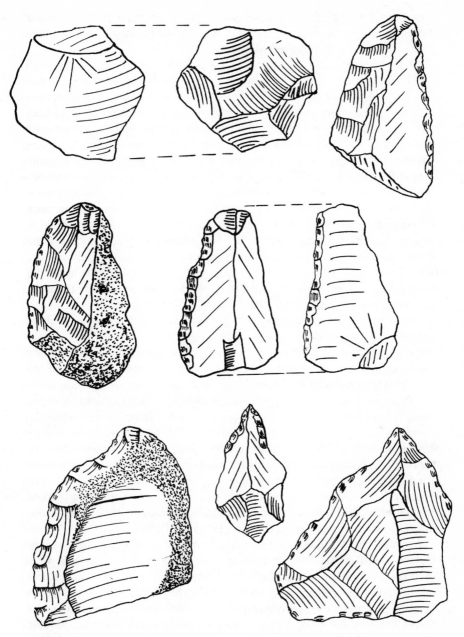

Figure 1. Used flakes from the middle Pleistocene of Sangiran, Central Java (after von Koenigswald and Ghosh 1973)

and even four small "bifaces," a somewhat strange element in our collection. For a detailed description we must refer to our joint publication (von Koenigswald and Ghosh 1973).

That we are right to associate the Sangiran Flake Industry with *Pithecanthropus erectus* has become evident by recent discoveries made by Maringer and Verhoeven (1970) on the Island of Flores east of Java. From beds which have yielded the same primitive elephant (*Stegodon*) as Sangiran and, most important, even tektites – there has been only one fall of tektites, covering the whole area between Thailand–Philippines, Java–Borneo–Flores–Australia at the same moment – they have found on the surface and in excavations exactly the same type of industry near Mengeruda and Olabula. Unfortunately no human skeletal remains came to light. The implements have been fabricated from different volcanic rocks; some chopper-like types are larger than in Sangiran. There are abundant elongated and pointed flakes and there are also specimens worked from both sides, a type which we have also seen in Sangiran and suspected that it might be younger. This assemblage from Flores is additional proof that the flake culture from Sangiran really is of Middle Pleistocene age.

On the island of Celebes, van Heekeren has discovered a flake culture near Tjabengè, which is similar, practically identical, to our industry on Java. All finds are surface finds; the fossil mammals are endemic and not comparable with Javanese species. Tektites, which are such a great help on Flores, are, at least so far, absent.

Pithecanthropus erectus from Java is closely related to *Sinanthropus* from China (we are using the classical names here as they indicate fixed species). So it is not surprising that both forms have a very similar industry. The implements from Location 1 at Choukoutien are more crude as they are made from quartz, a material not very suitable for flaking. We find here a mixture consisting mainly of flakes, even bipolar flakes, and some crude choppers. Scrapers, points, beaked implements, and cores can be distinguished. A review of the Choukoutien Culture has been given by Movius (1948).

In India the Madras Culture with abundant handaxes and cleavers has no counterpart further east, as already stated by Movius, who distinguishes between Handaxe and Chopping-Tool Cultures. Bifaces are indeed rare in China and the Patjitan Culture in Java with handaxes is perhaps Upper Pleistocene. In Choukoutien and Indonesia, worked flakes are perhaps more typical than chopping tools. So for the Middle Pleistocene in Indonesia and China we would be confronted with a flake tradition, while in Europe and Africa (Olduvai) we already have typical bifaces (handaxes). It seems as if we had, on both sides of the Indian Ocean, different ancient cultural traditions, perhaps indicating an independent start of cultural activities in both regions.

REFERENCES

MARINGER, J., TH. VERHOEVEN
1970   Die Steinartefakte aus der *Stegodon*-Fossilschicht von Mengeruda auf Flores, Indonesien. *Anthropos* 65: 229–247.
1970   Die Oberflächenfunde aus dem Fossilgebeit von Mengeruda und Olabula auf Flores, Indonesien. *Anthropos* 65: 530–546.
MOVIUS, HALLAM L., JR.
1948   The Lower Palaeolithic cultures of southern and eastern Asia. *Transactions of the American Philosophical Society*, n.s. 38 (4): 329–420.
VAN HEEKEREN, H. R.
1957   *The Stone Age of Indonesia*. Verhandelingen van het Koninklijk Instituut voor Taal-, Land-, en Volkenkunde 21. The Hague: Martinus Nijhoff.
VON KOENIGSWALD, G. H. R., A. K. GHOSH
1973   Stone implements from the Trinil Beds of Sangiran, Central Java. *Proceedings of the Koninklijke Nederlandse Akademie van Wetenschappen*, series B 76: 1–34. Amsterdam.

The Patjitan Culture: A Preliminary Report on New Research

G. J. BARTSTRA

1.   From July to October 1972 we conducted new research concerning the Paleolithic Patjitan culture[1] in East Java (Indonesia). This research was performed in cooperation with the National Archaeological Institute of Indonesia, Department of Prehistory, in Jakarta, and was financed by WOTRO, the Netherlands Foundation for the Advancement of Tropical Research, and the University of Groningen.

The results are rather interesting and justify a short account. However, the remarks here are very preliminary; the preparation of a definitive report has to await the analysis of the collected material.[2] A first account of our fieldwork was presented at a seminar held in Yogyakarta in October 1972, on the occasion of the tenth anniversary of the National Palaeoanthropological Research Project in Indonesia.

2.   On October 4, 1935, G. H. R. von Koenigswald and M. W. F. Tweedie discovered primitive stone implements in the bed of the Baksoko River, in the vicinity of the village of Punung, on the south coast of East Java. The Baksoko flows through the *Gunung Sewu* "Thousand Mountains," a part of the *Gunung Kidul* "Southern Mountains," and empties into the Indian Ocean. The upper course of the river lies in a region with volcanic, clastic deposits, while the lower course is situated in a karst region with numerous, beehive-shaped mountains (cone karst). According to the discoverers, the artifacts are primitive and rather crude. Von Koenigswald (1936) describes them as "Chelléen" and he says the implements come not only from the riverbed, but also from a boulder conglomerate in the bank of the river.

[1]   The spelling of this name in the Indonesian language is Pacitan. It is, however, preferable to retain the traditional spelling for archaeological use.
[2]   Since this report was written in 1973, much new research has been done. In the light of the new material, I have changed some of my conclusions (see Bartstra 1976).

This Paleolithic culture has become known in the literature as the "Patjitan culture" or the "Patjitanian," named after the little town of Pacitan. A few years afterwards, in 1938, the region was visited by members of the Joint American Southeast Asiatic Expedition for Early Man: Teilhard de Chardin, De Terra, and Movius. Teilhard de Chardin (1937, 1938) described the terraces of the Baksoko River. He discerned three of them, at two, ten, and twenty-five meters above the present riverbed (see Figure 1).

De Terra (1943) also distinguished river terraces, but only two. According to his interpretation, the so-called two-meter terrace is not a real terrace because in the wet monsoon periods it is subjected to inundation. So he notes a high terrace at twenty meters and a low terrace at ten meters. The first one has nearly disappeared; occasionally one may discover the "dissected remnants of flat benches." De Terra picked up artifacts both in the riverbed and on the ten-meter bench. He did not find them at twenty meters because of the rainy weather, which made searching impossible on the muddy slopes. Finally, according to De Terra, the terraces of the Baksoko are quite young ("Ngandong" and "post-Ngandong age"); they rest on Tertiary volcanic deposits. In the latter ones the silicified tuff and the fossil wood also occur; these served prehistoric man as the raw material for the implements that he used as he roamed over the region.

Movius (1944, 1948) made the first detailed studies of the artifacts themselves, based on von Koenigswald's collection of more than 2,000 items. According to Movius, the Patjitanian forms part of the "chopper/chopping-tool complex" in East Asia. Movius himself was the first to announce the existence of that complex; he did so after studying the Paleolithic assemblages of the Far East. There we find very characteristic core tools, which are nearly absent in the more western traditions (chopper, chopping tool, handadze); the biface and the Levallois technique do not occur at all. There are handaxes within the Patjitanian. According to Movius, however, there are only very few of them; furthermore they are totally different from the western bifaces; they are made with a "longitudinal flaking technique."

After the war, the Baksoko region was visited several times by van Heekeren (1955, 1972) and Soejono (1961) who made several new discoveries. In the first place, artifacts were now found on the highest Baksoko terrace. According to van Heekeren, more than one hundred items made from silicified limestone were found. A second important discovery was the finding of Paleolithic implements outside the valley of the Baksoko, in the area surrounding the little village of Tabuhan. Some rivulets flow there in a typical karst landscape. Boulder benches in the bed, and a meter above it, contain stone artifacts.

The fieldwork of Sartono (1964) in the Thousand Mountains is very

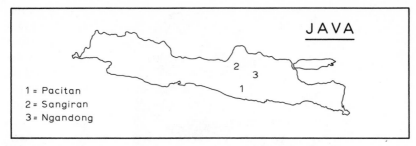

Figure 1. Map of Java with the Paleolithic sites of Ngandong, Sangiran, and Pacitan (drawing by J. M. Smit)

important from a geological point of view. We are now able to correct many of the former, prewar observations.

Finally, it should be kept in mind that at no time in the entire history of Patjitanian research were systematic excavations ever carried out in the Baksoko terraces. The collected artifacts are all surface finds.

3. We started our fieldwork in July 1972. At first we made reconnaissance expeditions to get an impression of the morphology and geology of the region and to check the various remarks of former investigators. The explored region stretches around the village of Punung, the base camp of our team, and occupies more than 300 square kilometers. During this fieldwork about forty more or less prolific Stone Age sites were discovered.

By the middle of August we had started several excavations. In the Baksoko terraces we dug six pits, which gave us an impression of the terrace stratigraphy and the spread of the artifacts. At the same time parts of the explored region were mapped and a dozen valley profiles were made. We took about 300 black-and-white photos and an equal number of color slides. During out explorations and excavations we collected more than 1,500 artifacts and about fifty soil and stone samples. All this material will be analyzed both in Indonesia and in Holland.

The research was done in cooperation with the National Archaeological Institute of Indonesia, Department of Prehistory, in Jakarta. The never-ceasing interest of its director, Dr. D. P. Soejono, resulted in the composition of a cooperative field team. The members were Messrs. Basoeki, Soeroso, H. Sukendar, G. W. Ording, and myself. Very fruitful discussions in the field were possible as a result of visits from Dr. Soejono, Dr. van Heekeren, Dr. T. Jacob, Dr. H. T. Waterbolk, Dr. W. C. Mook, Dr. D. A. Hooijer, A. G. Thorne, M.A., and some members of the above-mentioned seminar in Yogyakarta.

Figure 2.   A Patjitanian handaxe (drawing by J. M. Smit)

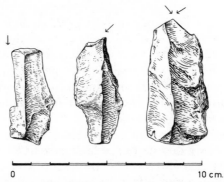

Figure 3.   Gravers from the Baksoko high terrace (drawing by J. M. Smit)

Finally, we acknowledge the support of Bapak Bupati at Pacitan, and of Bapak Camat, Bapak Lurah, and Bapak Partoredjo at Punung.

At the time this article was written, the investigations into the Patjitan culture were not completed. They were continued in the course of the following year.

4.   Very soon after we began our explorations, we found that there is indeed a terrace system in the valley of the River Baksoko. We distinguished a high terrace, a middle terrace, and a low terrace not only in the valley of the Baksoko but also near other more northerly rivers. It is possible that within that threefold terrace system one may discern different levels – for instance, the low terrace could consist of two levels – but this question has not yet been resolved. It is

important, moreover, that this extended terrace system occurs only in the valleys with volcanic, clastic bedrock and not in the karst region.

All the terraces are typical erosion terraces. The fluviatile deposit, consisting of a base boulder gravel and red loam above it, is very thin and lies mostly with a marked unconformity on the Tertiary sediments. The high terrace slopes perceptibly toward the river; this suggests that it is, most probably, a polygenetic terrace. This slope makes the assessment of an altitude difficult. In general we find the high terrace at about twenty meters above the present riverbed, the middle terrace at about ten meters, and the low terrace between two and five meters.

5. Not only the present riverbeds but also the three terraces yield Stone Age artifacts. Previous literature has always referred to the Patjitanian as a single, uniform culture. Now it is possible that this assumption will have to be revised. At present we cannot be certain, but some artifacts seem to be cruder and more primitive than others and the former are found *in situ* in the highest gravel layers.

Most important, moreover, is the finding of very advanced tools on small flakes: scrapers, borers, and gravers. Those are found even in the high terrace. The artifacts show that the Patjitanian culture does not at all match its inherited image of gigantolithism: large and massive cores and flakes. The latter occur, of course, but our excavations revealed in the whole assemblage a larger amount of small implements. And these small ones have always escaped the attention of those seeking artifacts in the riverbed and in the gravel layers on the valley slopes (see Figure 3).

The handaxes are also very interesting. We collected quite a number of them, some of which are very beautiful specimens. Sometimes they hardly differ from the West European bifaces and many of them were not prepared with a longitudinal flaking technique (see Figure 2).

In summary one may say that our research around Punung can result in the identification of a number of successive stone industries (together forming the Patjitan culture), which can partly be correlated with different river terraces. A further stage, in which comparisons can be made with other, more distant stone industries, e.g. Sangiran and Tjabengè, will also be interesting.

6. One of the main purposes of our entire research project was to get a possible dating of the Patjitanian. To date the culture means to date the different terraces in which the industries are found. We can try to do this by means of paleontological, absolute, archaeological, and geological dating.

a. The first method is of no use. There are no fossils in the gravel and loam layers of the high and middle terraces in the valleys around

Punung that are contemporaneous with the construction of the benches. Occasionally one may find shells, but these are petrified and derived from the Tertiary limestone formation. Also the fossil wood, that is present in large quantities in the river gravels, comes from Tertiary, volcanic sediments.

Only the low terrace contains a few vertebrate fossils. These fossils appear to be of a recent fauna, which suggests that the low terrace is quite young. This conclusion is reinforced by the archaeological dating.

The absence of fossils in the high and middle terraces can be explained by the very strong lateritization of the soil, which has not yet occurred on the low terrace.

The presence of Pleistocene vertebrate fauna in the fissures in the limestone hills is very interesting, but it is not yet possible to correlate these deposits with the terraces.

b.   The second method, absolute dating, does not seem to be very promising. So far we have not discovered charcoal layers or primary tuffs in the terrace sediments.

c.   The third method must be handled with caution. One gets into a logical vicious circle if one dates the terraces with the artifacts; the ultimate aim, one must remember, is to date the artifacts with the terraces. Only in a very broad sense can the implements tell us something. For instance, we find rolled Neolithic axes in the low terrace. This points to a recent construction of that terrace which fits excellently with the results of the above-mentioned paleontological dating.

In the high terrace we find a rather advanced industry with flake tools. The impression that the assemblage gives us is certainly not crude, primitive, and old. That impression is reinforced by the results of dating the high terrace by means of the fourth method.

d.   Dating by means of geomorphological events may be of use in the Punung area. Epeirogenesis must have contributed greatly to the construction of the river terraces there. Possibly climate also played a significant role, but that is still unclear at this stage of research. The uplift of the Southern Mountains caused the rivers to incise and deepen their valleys. As far as we can now determine, these movements must have begun in the beginning of the Young Pleistocene, which should mean that the terrace system of the Baksoko River and of the other, more northerly rivers is not older than the Early Pleistocene. That means, moreover, that the Patjitan culture might be the work of Solo man, namely *Homo soloensis*.

REFERENCES

BARTSTRA, G. J.
1976   Contribution to the study of the Palaeolithic Patjitan Culture, Java,
       Indonesia, part one. Leiden. E. J. Brill.
DE TERRA, H.
1943   "Pleistocene geology and early man in Java," in Research on early
       man in Burma. By H. De Terra and H. L. Movius. Transactions of
       the American Philosophical Society, n.s. 32 (3). Philadelphia.
MOVIUS, HALLAM L., JR.
1944   Early man and Pleistocene stratigraphy in southern and eastern Asia.
       Papers of the Peabody Museum of American Archaeology and
       Ethnology 19 (3).
1948   The Lower Palaeolithic cultures of southern and eastern Asia. Trans-
       actions of the American Philosophical Society, n.s. 38 (4): 329–420.
SARTONO, S.
1964   Stratigraphy and sedimentation of the easternmost part of Gunung
       Sewu (East Djawa). Publikasi Teknik Seri Geologi 1. Bandung.
SOEJONO, R. P.
1961   Preliminary notes on new finds of Lower Palaeolithic implements
       from Indonesia. Asian Perspectives 5: 217–232.
TEILHARD DE CHARDIN, P.
1937   Notes sur la paléontologie humaine en Asie Méridionale. L'Anthro-
       pologie 47: 23–33.
1938   Deuxièmes notes sur la paléontologie humaine en Asie Méridionale.
       L'Anthropologie 48: 449–457.
VAN HEEKEREN, H. R.
1955   New investigations on the Lower Palaeolithic Patjitan culture in
       Java. Berita Dinas Purbakala 1. Jakarta.
1972   The Stone Age of Indonesia. Verhandelingen van het Koninklijk
       Instituut voor Taal-, Land-en Volkenkunde 61. The Hague: Martinus
       Nijhoff (second revised edition).
VON KOENIGSWALD, G. H. R.
1936   Early Palaeolithic stone implements from Java. Bulletin of the Raffles
       Museum, series B, 1: 52–60.

Plate 1.   One of the excavations in the high terrace of the river Baksoko (photo G. W. Ording)

Plate 2.   The valley of the river Baksoko. In the background the high terrace (photo G. W. Ording)

Present Status and Problems for Paleolithic Studies in Borneo and Adjacent Islands

TOM HARRISSON

Archaeological and related research of the past two decades, backed by C^{14} datings, has shown that man was at the Niah Caves in Sarawak, Borneo, by 35,000 or more years B.P.; at the Tabon Caves in west Palawan, southern Philippines, before 30,000 B.P.; in the east, even at an altitude of 1,800 meters, in the highlands of New Guinea by 26,000 B.P.; and reached the Australian continent by 23,000 B.P. at the latest (Brothwell 1960; Fox 1970; Allen 1972; Mulvaney 1969; respectively). All these were evidently *Homo sapiens*, who apparently replaced *H. erectus* in Java about this time (van Heekeren 1972: 10), perhaps by direct evolution (see Pilbeam 1970: 183 on archaic *H. sapiens soloensis*). This early hominid island material, first recognized by Dubois in 1890, is now generally regarded as all *H. erectus* and includes the mainland China cave material. *H. erectus*, a fully Early Paleolithic man, has not yet been recorded on any of the islands except Java. The important question is whether this lack of evidence arises from inadequate searching or because no Early Paleolithic man lived on the islands.

1. PROBLEMS OF TIME AND SPACE

During the last (Würm) glacial period lowered seas extended along mainland Southeast Asia from the Mekong to Singapore eastward as far as Palawan and Borneo, in "Sundaland." Celebes remained cut off further east of Borneo by deep water – "Wallace's Line." Previous glacials had similar effects, though scale and exact sequences have yet to be determined for the archipelago. Even the precise sea levels of some later Sundaland changes are far from finally settled (see, for example, for Borneo: Haile 1968 contesting Wall 1967; Sabels 1966; cf. Petersen 1969; Ashton 1972; Tate 1971).

After twenty years of fieldwork in Borneo, I have lately surveyed prehistoric evidence for the island as a whole (Harrisson 1970). Subsequently, I focused attention especially on the period from 10,000 to 40,000 B.P., employing the term "pre-Neolithic" to cover island uncertainties for the Mesolithic, "Hoabinhian," and other better established continental (only) time boundaries. It now proves possible to extend this retrospective by reexamining the earlier material, before 40,000 B.P., with the benefit of valued help from Drs. Kenneth Oakley, Don Brothwell, and J. A. Sutcliffe at the British Museum (Natural History); Dr. D. A. Hooijer of Leiden; Prof. H. Movius of Harvard; Lord Medway, who worked with us at Niah and then went on patiently studying the cave fauna for some years; and, as always, Barbara Harrisson at Cornell University. The uncoordinated data have hitherto been scattered mainly in Dutch and Asian publications. This contribution seeks to meet the problems raised and attempts some provisional answers, taking Borneo as one huge unit, but recognizing the complexity of inter-island and mainland relationships from the past.

2.   TEKTITES AS EARLY PALEOLITHIC "SITE MARKERS"

Since Ralph von Koenigswald in Java, encouraged by Otley Beyer's early Philippine work, correlated the large Southeast Asian tektite shower and the fossiliferous Trinil beds, these little tektites with their low specific gravity have been widely regarded as prime clues for the Middle Pleistocene, and by interpolation the Early Paleolithic. A Trinil tektite has been potassium–argon dated circa 710,000 B.P. (von Koenigswald 1968 and personal communication in 1973; Zahringer 1963). *Homo erectus* is found at Trinil, along with rich proboscidean and other fauna which prehistorians have usually described as "extinct." In fact, of the forty mammal species well identified in Trinil, twenty-five (mostly smaller and often arboreal) are still extant in the region (63 percent), while only 37 percent (*all* large and terrestrial) are extinct. The five nonhominid primates (including three apes) are all extant today, though two no longer occur in Java (see section 4).

Closely similar tektites occur quite commonly in one Borneo locality only – within about twenty miles of Brunei Town in the coastal northwest, scattered mainly through sand and gravel beds along the sea beach and lower tidal rivers (Wilford 1961; Tate 1970, 1971). One found *in situ* at Bufir quarry is dated 730,000 B.P., very close to Trinil

(Zahringer 1963). It has therefore been widely assumed that this so-called "Jerudong formation" must be Middle Pleistocene. As Museums and Archaeological Adviser to the Brunei Government, I have kept watch on Bufir quarrying and other operations over several years. Nothing remotely of a fossil or artifact nature appeared. As recently as the authoritative second Hull–Aberdeen Symposium on Malaysian Ecology, the distinguished plant ecologist, Dr. Peter Ashton (previously a Brunei forester), emphasized that the Jerudong beds could be safely dated circa 700,000 B.P., "owing to the presence of tektites at their bases" (Ashton 1972: 41). This view was accepted by all present.

New C^{14} analyses of wood from the Jerudong beds and the research of Brunei's State Geologist, Dr. R. B. Tate (1971), have shown, however, that this correlation is erroneous – with significant possible repercussions for other areal interpretations of Paleolithic events generally. The following table shows the relevant Borneo figures. Those from Brunei are all taken geologically from the Jerudong formation except number 11, excavated in the immediate vicinity at our prehistoric open site of Kota Batu. Numbers 2 and 4 are with the deepest skull at Niah. Two interesting dates from Sabah, further north, indicate major late erosion high on Mount Kinabalu (the highest peak in Southeast Asia – number 12) and eruption age from *below* a lava flow at Tawau (number 10) – there are no longer active volcanos in Borneo. These figures indicate massive land and water interchange activities which are certainly not solely characteristic of

Table 1. "Tektite bed" and relevant dates from northern and southern Borneo (1963–1972)

Numbers	Years B.P.	Place	Material	Reference
1(a)	730,000	Brunei	tektite	Zahringer 1963; Tate 1971
(b)	710,000	Java	tektite	Zahringer 1963
2	41,500±1,000	Niah	charcoal	Harrisson 1970: 40
3	>40,200	Brunei	wood	Tate 1971: 111
4	39,600±1,000	Niah	charcoal	Harrisson 1970: 40
5	37,500±2,400	Niah	shell	Harrisson 1970: 40
6	32,630± 700	Niah	charcoal	Harrisson 1970
7	>31,600	Brunei	wood	Tate 1971: 111
8	30,000 $\{^{\pm 2,600}_{1,900}$	Brunei	wood	Tate 1971: 111
9	29,000±2,300	Brunei	wood	Tate 1971: 111
10	27,000± 500	Sabah	charcoal	Harrisson and Harrisson 1971: 8
11	14,350± 350	Brunei	charred wood	Harrisson 1972: 10
12	7,980± 100	Sabah	wood	Harrisson and Harrisson 1971: 8
13	6,700± 160	Brunei	wood	Tate 1971: 111
14	5,850± 110	Brunei	coral	Tate 1971: 111

more recent times and generally complicate detailed interpretation. In particular, the Brunei tektites have clearly been washed down (or up) from elsewhere. The same could be said as readily of pollen (so that Schuster's 1911 Trinil flora, showing close affinities with today's montane plants and long taken as evidence for marked lowland climate change, may indeed have come down from far higher elevations (cf. Muller 1972; van Heekeren 1972: 8). In brief, tektites can no longer be accepted, without support, as date indications at open sites in this region.

In this connection, too, we have to recognize that even in Java the rich finds of fossil hominids which undoubtably will be augmented, have never been directly correlated with artifacts of any kind. Most of those deposits were "caused by volcanic or stream action" (van Heekeren 1972: 32). So far, Niah has the oldest dated *direct* correlations in the islands, though these are far from extensive as we move back towards circa 40,000 B.P.

3. "CHOPPERS" AND OTHER TOOLS

3.1. *Stone*

As now abundantly demonstrated for Borneo and Palawan, the same early tool forms continued in later use over millennia, *without* those late Paleolithic and "Mesolithic" evolutions familiar on the Asian mainland and elsewhere (Fox 1970). These later forms, therefore, naturally have much in common with those considered Early Paleolithic in the chopper/chopping-tool system, so well described first by Movius (1948, 1958; cf. van Heekeren 1972). This tradition has even locally survived almost into historic times, with surface and early Neolithic parallels at Niah Caves and in Sabah (Harrisson and Harrisson 1971), as well as in New Guinea (Allen 1972) as far eastward as New Britain (Shutler and Kess 1969).

Until Niah, all chopper types in the area had been presumed to be Early Paleolithic. The only ones previously published from Borneo were six of mixed sizes found in a riverbed near Martapura, southeastern Borneo (Kalimantan). But these fit perfectly with the series excavated at Niah (see Table 2), and also with Tabon, Palawan, examples from after 20,000 B.P., which I examined there (cf. Fox 1970: Figure 7n. with van Heekeren 1972: Figure 13). For that matter, a large quartzite flake from about the 30,000 B.P. level at Niah (trench E/B3(c) on 26.2.58) almost diametrically fits over and matches one found in "Middle Pleistocene" setting on the Baksoko River, Java (as cal-

Table 2. "Choppers" excavated at the Niah Caves (1954–1967)

Approximate age (of deposit) in years B.P.	No. of tools	Subcaves involved	Remarks
40,000–20,000	9	West Mouth and Angus	+1 of more friable stone
20,000–5000	6	West Mouth and Angus	including one of flattish fossil coral
Later than 5000	3	West Mouth, Kana and Jeragan	1 from guano swamp gulley

culated by van Heekeren 1972: Figure 12; the correspondence will be demonstrated visually here).[1]

Through the courtesy of the present curator of the Sarawak Museum, Mr. B. Sandin, I have, for study purposes, duplicate casts of eighteen choppers he excavated at Niah. If we classify these for age by broad depth-correlation and C^{14} associations, the time spread of this series can be factually demonstrated.

There is no regular difference or development discernible between the oldest and youngest examples in the deposit. Evidently, either a simple, rather distinctive, and consistent way of monofacially flaking largish pebbles continued over great periods of time or the same pieces were used and reused, worked and reworked through countless generations. In any case, it seems too dangerous to decide where to set boundaries in time for morphological concepts, even as between "chopper" and "flake," in island Southeast Asia, let alone to use them as phase evidence until we have many more well-dated, excavated horizons guaranteed free of possible pollution or dilution.

The same considerations apply to a 130 by 100 millimeter chopping tool from a solid chunk of quartz found in the Sematan Bauxite Mine deposits, southwest Sarawak, in 1958, now in the Sarawak Museum (a cast is in the British Museum, number 5456b). This looks like an "early" and "different" handaxe, although it is worked more on one side than the other side, and with a little of the *beaked* effect characteristic of Niah chopping tools. The "feel" is not very *Homo sapiens*.

---

[1] Baksoko flake 78×43×14 mm., Niah 79×44×16 mm., same shape and make. (Borneo choppers are illustrated in Harrisson 1958a: Figure 1; 1958b: 579–80; 1959a: Figure 2; Solheim 1958: Figure 3; cf. Harrisson and Reavis 1966: Figure 2; Harrisson and Harrisson 1971: Plate 36 and Figure VI/7; Shutler and Kess 1969: Figures 5 and 6.)

Table 3.   Classification of 206 bone artifacts, excavated at Niah, from 1954 to 1959, by approximate depth/age (based on Harrison and Medway 1962a: Tables I–XIV)

1962 Code Numbers	Group of categories	Number of categories in group	Number of tools studied	Distribution by calculated age (years B.P.)		
				1,000– 8,000	8,000– 16,000	16,000+
A–B	Elaborate carvings and accessories	2	7	6	1	0
C–G	Rings, beads, pendants	5	54	53	1	0
H–K	Ornamental plugs, clips, etc.	4	26	26	0	0
L–N	Turtle and tusk tools, drifts and rods	3	29	14	11	4
O–R	Awls, points, gauges, spatulas	4	87	17	51	19
	Total	18	203*	116	64	23

* Three undetermined for age.

3.2.   *Bone*

No certain Early Paleolithic bone (or shell) tools are known for Borneo or its surroundings, though abundant after 40,000 B.P. at Niah, where we have classified them in some detail (Harrison and Medway 1962a): 206 bone and tooth artifacts classified and illustrated in eighteen categories (Plates I to IX) were excavated there up to 1959. Most of the deeper work was done from 1960 to 1967, but enough shows in the 1962 study to permit reanalysis of the raw data by depth/age, not specifically calculated before. The results appear open to reasonable projection back past 40,000 B.P., which is rather striking for strict bone "tools."

We can properly regard A to K in Table 3 as ornaments or "extras" of various kinds (43 percent of the total) – largely connected with the great Neolithic cemetery in the West Mouth and smaller burial grounds in the Gan Kira and Lobang Toland mouths of Great Cave (B. Harrisson 1967). L to N can be considered "marginal tools," some of them anomalous, soft, and only a few with clearly defined function (14 percent). O to R are all unmistakably pure tools (43 percent). Clearly, the ornamentals are overwhelmingly in the younger levels, the marginals being almost evenly divided between younger and older levels and the pure tools heavily more numerous in the older levels. This trend is the more striking because so much less excavation came at the deeper levels and because bone deteriorates and is often lost with age.

The final and most emphatic category, spatulas (R), covers the only

Table 4. Niah bone artifacts by age/depth, as percentage of each main group

| Age (approximate) in years B.P. | Main groupings; occurrence by depth as percentage of each group | | | |
	(A–K) Ornamental	(O–R) "Pure" tools	(L–R) All tools	(A–R) All artifacts
1–8,000	98	20	26	57
8–16,000	2	58	54	32
16,000+	0	22	20	11
Total	100	100	100	100

artifacts never found in the Neolithic or other late settings, settings with a ratio of eight to one in favor of those older than 16,000 B.P. (full details in Harrisson and Medway 1962). They *outnumber* choppers from the same period and deep excavation phase (cf. Table 2).

3.3. *Wood*

Unlike bone and shell, wood does not seem to survive more than 3,000 years under cave conditions in Borneo, though it lasts much longer in alluvial and peat deposits (cf. Table 1). It is easy and natural to postulate early wood use, especially where good stone is scarce (as in much of Borneo), but difficult to prove it. Indeed, the failure of wood to appear at all in pre-Neolithic Niah is rather surprising, for excellent workable wood is available all around. Was bone perhaps an adequate substitute?

In any case, given the existing evidence it is difficult to follow Dr. W. G. Solheim's imaginative new rearrangement of all Southeast Asian Stone Age sequences. Based on two Thai cave deposits (both less than 15,000 years old), he proposes to rename the Early Paleolithic simply "Lithic." But from 40,000 B.C. to 20,000 B.C. this becomes the "Lignic," "the period when wood tools proliferate." None have been found in the Thai caves either, but the presence of charred bamboo is mentioned (Solheim 1972: 38–39). This bamboo surely provided easily made preceramic cooking (and water) vessels to a people which had numerous quartz fire strikers (deep levels at Niah), as well as providing direct vegetable food. Bamboo is still extensively used for these purposes in the Borneo interior, as well as for making a multitude of other relatively pliable products, such as baskets, hats, mats, musical instruments, and fences, though we are now long past that phase according to Solheim's succession (having also gone through his "Crystallitic" and "Extensionistic").

I prefer the concept that hardwoods, bone, and other materials were extensively used to supplement and elaborate simple stone-cutting tools right through the Paleolithic (cf. "Paleolignic"). This is related to the very slow and narrow elaboration of lithic types, which caused Movius long ago to write off the whole area, in effect, as being culturally backward. In forested lands, especially, stone was only the primary coarse tool. Wood, bone, and shell did the finer work, especially where stone was so scarce that it clearly had enduring value and was persistently reused (as above), until marine transport became effective between and within the islands to enable interchange not only of techniques, but also of actual tools and materials. This came late in Borneo (Harrisson 1970). Looked at this way, the very slow, painful evolution of Early Paleolithic stone typologies is not necessarily indicative of "cultural levels" as a whole.

A recent rediscovery of relevance here was made in February 1973 in the little-known and unpublished collections of the Capuchin Mission at Tilburg, Holland, mostly from the middle Kapuas district of Kalimantan Barat. With the kind help of Father Gregorius van der Boom, we located there as item A.VI.420, an astonishing kind of "handaxe," 164 by 98 millimeters, which was thought to be, and looks as if it was, shaped from a finely use-worn brown stone. With a pronounced sharp cutting edge at one side and a good grip at the other, flaked and worked all over bifacially, it proved to be of ironwood (*Eusideroxylon zwagerii*). Details of provenance, etc., are being sought and the piece will be fully published presently. But it suggests at least the possibility of a promising and potentially self-datable clue to the lithic riddle.

4.   BORNEO "FOSSILS" WHICH ARE REGARDED AS EARLY

Two fully fossil and several "semi-fossil" teeth and other bones have been described from Borneo, the former both casual native finds of very doubtful provenance, the latter nearly all associated with Sarawak and Brunei caves, sometimes under puzzling circumstances. All are large mammals (proboscidea, rhinoceros, orangutan). The two fossil proboscidean teeth are both of forms unknown in any extinct island fauna, but known from the mainland. The others are of still extant species; one is the lower jaw used in the Piltdown forgery.

As these, particularly the first two, constitute the *only* pre-Niah Bornean evidence for fossil or cave faunas of sorts commonly regarded as Pleistocene, with some strong Early Paleolithic hominid associations elsewhere, and as they have not been previously reviewed collectively or at all critically, it is necessary to consider them afresh.

Table 5. Analyses of "fossil" teeth from Borneo (tabulated from Dr. Oakley's unpublished data)

Species	Locality	Results					
		F (per-cent-ages)	100F/ P_2O_5	$CaCO_3$ (per-cent-ages)	Fe (per-cent-ages)	N (per-cent-ages)	U_3O_8 (parts per million)
Elephas maximus	Brunei ("cavern")	0.6	0.2	—	—	2.4	9
Stegolopho-don lydekkeri	Brunei ("jungle")	1.75	5.1	5.8	2.95	0.69	15
Elephas clifti	India (Upper Sawalik beds)	2.21	6.3	3.6	0.8	0.13	12

This has been possible thanks to the help and active cooperation of Kenneth Oakley, D. A. Hooijer, and Lord Medway, the leading scholars in this mammal field. In addition, Dr. Oakley has generously supplied his previously unpublished analyses of material relevant to Borneo, which are shown in Table 5.

4.1. The Samarinda Palaeoloxodon

Like every item considered in this section, the Samarinda *Palaeoloxodon* has a checkered record since it fell into *Homo sapiens* hands, firstly regarding the actual island discovery, and secondly regarding its subsequent treatment and identification in a western museum. Hooijer's initial paper (1952) describes it as *Palaeoloxodon* cf. *namadicus*, as he was doubtful about precise identity from the one tooth. He now advises (personal communication 1973) that we can drop the "cf." It really is *namadicus*, a widespread early post-Villafranchian elephant of the generally Middle Pleistocene *Stegodon-Ailuropoda* fauna known from South China, Indo-China, upper Burma, and Java. Although *Palaeoloxodon* itself is common in India, it was not previously recorded east of Malaya, where it is known from the Kinta Valley along with hippopotamus, extinct deer, and the extant Javan rhinoceros (Medway 1972).

This massive, beautifully preserved, bluish-white and dark brown molar was "found" behind the seashore near Samarinda in East Kalimantan, 350 miles northeast of the Martapura stone tools (section 3); it originally belonged to the Sultan of Kuti, who left it to a Dutch Borneo administrative officer, whence it passed to the head of a Haarlem girls' school and then into the private Teyler Museum there in 1911. It lay there for decades unobserved, until the present conservator, Dr. C. O. van Regteren Altena, noticed it and called in Dr. Hooijer. I had the pleasure of reexamining it with both gentlemen in 1973.

Zoographical considerations apart, two disturbing features are the lack of even faint geological information or association and the evident value of this handsome lump as a charm and status symbol in a Sultanate which had rich overseas trade links, India included, for centuries before (see Appendix).

4.2.   *The Brunei* Stegolophodon

Everything about this single, heavily broken, fossil molar is more or less curious. It was obtained by a famous commercial collector in Borneo, A. H. Everett (who has been linked with the Piltdown forgery, see section 4.4), from a Muslim Brunei native who said he found it "in the jungle" in 1885. The original supposedly passed to the Zoological Society of London, but in 1958 could not be traced there (Harrisson 1958b: 559). A *cast* (poor, as it turns out) was placed in the British Museum (Natural History Number M. 2498). It was first described as *Mastodon latidens* by Lydekker (1885) with a good illustration (reproduced in Harrisson 1958b: Plate 3).[2] But in 1936 Osborn, using the British Museum cast, surprisingly deduced from it – in his tome on the *Proboscidea* (1936: 700) – a new species, *Stegolophodon lydekkeri* (still unique to Brunei), supplemented by his own poorer version of Lydekker's woodcut. In January 1973, incited by me, Dr. J. A. Sutcliffe of the British Museum and Lord Medway located the missing original in South Kensington (British Museum Number 7225), originally registered in 1898, but since confused with, indeed positively displaced by, its own cast! I reexamined it shortly thereafter and was surprised at how broken it was. No wonder Medway now finds that Osborn's "description is faulty in several points." He considers the tooth taxonomically close to the well known *Stegolophodon latidens* of Burma's Upper Irrawaddy fauna, but is not sure the differences "might be within the range of variation of one species" (Medway, personal communication 1973).[3]

The genus *Stegolophodon* is not otherwise recorded for the islands or east of the Irrawaddy. Dr. Oakley's analysis of the tooth is consistent, of course, with a venerable antiquity, but does not fit equi-

---

[2]   Lydekker later (1886: 74–77) listed the Brunei cast along with ten other items in the British Museum which he regarded as certainly *M. latidens* (five casts), all from India or Burma. He stressed that these were so close to *M. cautleyi* and *Elephas clifti* "that it is frequently a matter of extreme difficulty to refer individual teeth to their respective species."

[3]   Compare the words cited in fn. 2, from Lydekker 1886.

valent Upper Sawalik material from India (Table 5). Unfortunately, Burmese material has not been tested.

The tooth's presence in Brunei, again without any supporting data, is certainly remarkable even zoographically. But, whereas in eastern Kalimantan geological searches have not been at all intensive, in Brunei over past decades oil and government geologists, as well as archaeologists, have combed this small state without finding another mammal fossil or any possibly related human artifacts, only the unhappily situated tektites (section 2). Indeed, no stone tool of any kind has yet been located *in situ* in Brunei (Harrisson 1971). These considerations cannot exclude the fair chance for a genuine local occurrence, but equally may be taken to add some weight to Ralph von Koenigswald's view (1958) that this and others occurring casually in the islands were probably brought from the mainland by Chinese traders (1958; see section 5).

4.3.   *The Brunei* Elephas

This species has never been proven to have been wild in Borneo and has not been excavated at Niah. The published semifossil tooth, also in the British Museum (Number M.10237), is another proboscidean molar from Brunei – again, unfortunately, with a puzzling proven-ance. The British Museum registered it as from a "cavern" in the Belait district. This is about the flattest part of western Borneo, with neither limestone nor a single cave, there being only two sandstone caves, both tiny, known in all of Brunei.[4] Presented in 1910, it is recorded as originating from "the Resident, B. O. S. Storey" (cf. Hooijer 1972a). This must have been B. O. Stoney, briefly seconded from Malaya, who was Acting Resident for ten months in 1909 (Brunei Government 1968: 284). Hooijer (1972a) positively identified it as typical *E. maximus*, the Indian Elephant. Although not previously recorded in a prehistoric context in Borneo, it is extant wild in Sumatra (not Java); but in Borneo supposedly all are feral and now local to northeast Sabah only.

Hooijer reports a U_3O_8 determination of nine parts per million, indicating the Pleistocene, instead of what he regards as the earliest

[4]   The absence of caves, and specifically of a single limestone cave, in the Belait district (or elsewhere in Brunei) largely reflects the "lateness" of most of this terrain (cf. section 2), as first analyzed by Wilford (1961), and on this point confirmed by my years of cave search through west and north Borneo (Harrisson 1970). For this paper latest information was checked with P. M. Shariffudin, Curator of the Brunei Museum, and Dr. R. B. Tate, Brunei State Geologist, both of whom agreed on this lack of caves (communication of March 1973). The two little sandstone caves are nearly 100 miles outside the Belait district and archaeologically insignificant, as is normal for sandstone in Borneo.

known date for human introduction, A.D. 1750. Actually Magellan's crew, circumnavigating the globe in A.D. 1521, were met on landing by the Sultan of Brunei's splendidly equipped domesticated elephants (Harrisson and Harrisson 1971: 29–31). Oakley's analyses suggest rather an early Holocene date (personal communication 1973). The nitrogen figure of 2.4 percent may be compared with 2.5 percent for bone from Toge Cave, Flores, correlated by C-14 with 3,550±525 B.P. (van Heekeren 1972: 141), and in contrast to a much higher figure for recent Sarawak bone (4.6 percent, see section 5).

Either, then, strong local traditions of elephants as fairly recent live imports are wrong or the "cavern" and its single tooth, still unsupported at Niah, are "wrong." In this connection it must be made clear that such teeth have had local value of a high order since the first Chinese trade contacts. So much so that since the establishment of the richly endowed Brunei Museum in the fifties, we have never been able to find one trace of the old sultanate elephant herd. Not a tusk or tooth survives even in the royal collections. There must have been a market of long standing for this commodity. (The dollar traffic in *Homo erectus* fragments, lately even in forged fragments, illustrates how such fashions can develop locally.)

4.4. *Sarawak "Semi-Fossils" (Rhino and Ape)*

There are three other lots which have been seriously discussed in print as archaeologically relevant and/or potentially Pleistocene:
1.   Two rhino molars sent to England by the first white Rajah of Sarawak in 1869 (the year A. H. Everett arrived there), identified as *R. sondaicus*, otherwise unrecorded in Borneo (Busk 1869); subsequently proved by Hooijer to be the extant *R. sumatrensis* (Medway 1965: 80).
2.   Two rhino molars and other bones from the Bau Caves, southwest Sarawak, almost certainly collected by A. H. Everett and now in the British Museum. Referred to as *R. sondaicus* again by Lydekker in 1886, but lately proved to be *R. sumatrensis* by Medway (1965: 80).
3.   Orangutan teeth, jaws, and other bones from the Bau Caves and elsewhere in Sarawak brought back to the British Museum by A. H. Everett in 1875. One of these has an "undiminished" nitrogen content of 4.6 percent, very close to that of the Piltdown forgery's lower jaw, which it closely resembles in other ways (de Vries and Oakley 1959; Harrisson 1959b).

None of these can any longer be treated seriously as fully Pleistocene or relevant. Their associations with the same men who collected the Brunei *Stegolophodon* tooth are further disturbing. In 1958, before the Piltdown exposure, I wrote, concerning *Stegolophodon*, that "in my considered opinion, Everett's material of a prehistoric character cannot be accepted on present evidence." The evidence for these three lots is no more reassuring. In this connection, also, it is perhaps important that in 1878, the great American naturalist William Hornaday visited Everett in the field at Bau and described, among other treasures seen in his collection, "one skull of a *Simia Wormbia* in a fossil state" (Hornaday 1885: 478). Perhaps this ape wonder will turn up one day, out of previous confusion also. . . ?

4.5. *Fossil Conclusion*

We are left with the extraordinary situation that no true fossil relevant to the Paleolithic at any stage has yet been found satisfactorily *in situ* anywhere in Borneo. Only two proboscidean teeth, from opposite sides of the island, can possibly predate the older nonfossil bone in Niah Caves (section 5). Neither of these relates closely to any Javan or other known island form. Yet further east, from the Celebes, is an abundant and proven fossil mammal Middle Pleistocene fauna, though unsafely correlated with hominid activity (van Heekeren 1972). This may be partly a problem of land bridges *before* the later Sundaland. But we cannot *assume* that there is no equivalently rich fauna parallel to Java or Celebes in Borneo. It may be only a question of proper search (see section 6). On the other hand, we cannot simply "expect" to find hominid-related life in any one place. We must really *find* it. If too much is expected, weak evidence is readily elevated to acceptance as authentication of preconceptions.

Meanwhile, it is necessary to face the fact of a widespread tradition for trading (and even faking) in elephant and other large teeth, whether fossil or not being unimportant if they appear strange and rare. This is reflected even among the animists of the interior, where the shaman's esoteric gear consists mainly of curious teeth, misshapen horns, crystals, stones, and strangely shaped roots – including the Tilburg "wooden axe" (section 3.3). On the coast, with no transport problem, much larger items were esteemed, even up to the level of the Sultanates (section 4.1).

Inevitably this interest was exploited, if not actually instigated, by those great traders and travelers of the coastlands, the Chinese, who started active business in Brunei waters at least as early as the T'ang dynasty (A.D. 618–907; cf. Cheng 1969). The implications reach beyond Borneo and have to be considered. The essential facts, first recognized by von Koenigswald, are stated in an Appendix although we may note here that he specifically suggested that the Brunei *Stegolophodon* was a druggist's import (von Koenigswald 1958: 547).

5. FOSSIL EVIDENCE AND *MANIS PALAEOJAVANICA*

In view of the somewhat depressingly negative effect of the preceding discussion, it is important to recognize that nonfossil bone may well be at least Late Paleolithic, as demonstrated fully at Niah, and perhaps earlier, under even better "sealed" cave conditions. Material cannot now be discussed as new simply because it looks so. The presence at Niah of complete and completely unfossilized *Manis palaeojavanica* bone from well over 30,000 B.P. astounded everyone. It had only been known before from "Early Paleolithic" levels, fully fossilized, in Java (Harrisson, Hooijer, and Medway 1961). This huge scaly anteater, larger than any extant, was one of the marker fossils for potential *H. erectus* horizons there. Had it been a fossil found in another Borneo context, erroneous date conclusions could have very naturally been reached. The deepest *M. palaeojavanica* at Niah is close to the deepest *H. sapiens* (Brothwell 1960).

6. POST-JAVA

One cannot be certain that any Early Paleolithic or associated Pleistocene life was present in Borneo. Java is the nearest point. But then, the same can be said for Bali or Sumatra, alongside Java, and that gap was demonstrably bridged with ease in those times. *Homo erectus* and his associates can hardly have deliberately bypassed Sumatra. The situation then becomes explicable in terms of a failure to find evidence through inadequate research or some other ecological factor affecting zoographic patterns within the region. The first of these will be discussed in the following section, the second in more detail in a later paper. Needed at this stage is a brief summary of the comparative situation for other Pleistocene mammals.[5]

A. 1. Of twenty-one mostly small- or medium-sized, often arboreal, and carnivorous mammal species fossil in Java's Trinil (with *H. erectus* cf. *Meganthropus*), fourteen still exist in Borneo now, though only twelve remain extant in Java.

2. Of these fourteen Borneo extants, eleven also occur in the Niah Paleolithic deposits and three more in later subsurface deposits.

3. The other seven of the twenty-one have never been recorded in Borneo, past or present.

[5]   The following summary is a reanalysis primarily from data in Medway (1966, 1972), along with van Heekeren (1972). Both these lucid authors give full bibliographies of primary source studies, mainly by von Koenigswald, Hooijer, and, in the case of Niah, also by Medway himself and his father, the Earl of Cranbrook (see Harrisson 1970).

B. 4.   Of eighteen larger and wholly nonarboreal, mostly herbivor-
ous mammal species fossil at Trinil, only four are still in Java,
only two in Borneo.
5.   One of these two occurs in the Niah Holocene, plus two more
there which are now extinct on both islands.
6.   Fourteen large Javan Pleistocene forms are thus unrecorded
at any time in Borneo.
C. 7.   On the other hand, ten mammalian genera occur in the older
Niah deposits which have *not* been found at Trinil (or elsewhere).
8.   Of these ten, seven actually inhabit Java today.
9.   Two of the ten are large and all are characteristically shade
and forest animals (five are nocturnal).
D. 10.   An additional seven genera occur only in the Holocene levels
at Niah, all of these surviving in Borneo.
11.   None of these seven occur in Java.
12.   These seven are all medium-sized rain forest mammals, five
of them wholly or normally nocturnal, while two are wholly, and
three partly, arboreal.
E. 13.   The two fully fossil mammals recorded (each by one molar
without provenance) from Borneo are of genera never recorded
from Java or elsewhere off the present mainland (cf. section 4).
F. 14.   Five of the Trinil fossils are arboreal, higher, nonhuman
primates, all of which are still extant, though two not in Java.

It is relevant, too that *Stegodon trigonocephalus* of Trinil and other
Java sites is found in geological horizons, again *east* of Borneo, beyond
"Wallace's Line" in Celebes, and again southeast on Timor and
Flores, while *Archidiskodon*, a typical Lower Pleistocene proboscidean in Java, also occurs in the same places (Hooijer 1972b, and
personal communication 1972). These outlying occurrences have been
explained by an early land bridge northward to China through the
Philippines (Medway 1972). No associated hominid material is known
and all the artifacts from these large islands are acceptable within
the time span of *H. sapiens* since 40,000 B.P.

In view of these and other apparent zoographical anomalies, it is
possible that a significant segment of the larger, terrestrial, herbivor-
ous mammal fauna failed especially to populate effectively heavily
humid, forested terrain, including much of Borneo and Sumatra.
Perhaps *H. erectus* was primarily dependent on these and had eco-
logically similar habits, ill-adapted to the equatorial jungle which
H. sapiens slowly mastered with new techniques of craft and wit.[6]

[6]   In one view, the fully developed handaxe, so notably missing on the islands
generally, was a major tool facilitating development of human potentials. But if
alternative materials were (as here suggested) more important than stones, particularly
for primitive jungle life, the reverse interpretation could apply: axeless men were more
experimental and adaptive through other media, even if the remaining remnants do not
fit any accepted western cultural classification or earn those men of long ago high marks
by the usual categories of modern archaeology.

7. WHERE TO LOOK NOW (AND NEXT)?

None of the foregoing should be taken as "defeatist." But to plan an orderly search for the Early Paleolithic in and beyond Borneo, the ground must be cleared of old debris. If, then, the ultimate results prove mainly negative, that in itself will be important for the understanding of human evolution. And if the results are positive, they may prove surprisingly rewarding and fresh.

Specifically, for Borneo – and the same considerations can apply to most other Indo-Malaysian islands – it may be necessary to locate, by palynology and informed deduction, areas of possible past savannah, in this case perhaps more likely in southeastern Kalimantan than in the north and west (cf. Ashton 1972; Muller 1972). Clearly a fuller search of suitable, known geological formations is also overdue, notably in Kalimantan, which has been described as the "East Borneo Vacuum" for research (Harrisson 1970: 43).

The coastal lowlands must have offered alternative food and mobility attractions compared with the rugged interior. But here locating ground undisturbed by massive erosion, which continues right into the Holocene, is a real difficulty, as we have already seen with the Brunei tektites (section 2). The bed of the Riam Kandan River near Martapura in the southeast clearly merits direct reexamination as the only located open site which has produced pre-Neolithic artifacts (section 3; van Heekeren 1972: 46) – the Sematan "handaxe" land has been totally removed by bauxite mining.

Site identification is a great difficulty in all these jungle territories. Only in limestone outcrops can the sites be readily mapped and their caves explored (Harrisson and Harrisson 1971). Although Professor von Koenigswald argued against caves as shelters for Asian Paleolithic man (1956: 28), Niah experience, backed by Tabon in the Philippines (Fox 1970), makes this view open to doubt. But if Early Paleolithic man was also a cave dweller equatorially, it is again difficult to find accessible caves which have not been disturbed by Pleistocene submergences or very recent major human disturbance for the recovery of guano, edible nests, mica, or cement. It seems necessary to explore the archaeologically untouched limestone of interior Kalimantan (e.g. Kapuas, upper Bahau). (Niah was either drowned or cut off before the Würm glacial.) But there are other Niahs, no doubt, on this and other islands, and also in Malaya, where the whole Paleolithic rests on the very crude Tampan tools unassociated with any animal or human material.

8. CONCLUSIONS

1. For Borneo (as also in varying degrees for Sumatra, Bali, and some other large islands of Southeast Asia) archaeologically acceptable data is conspicuously meager in quantity and generally poor in quality before *circa* 40,000 B.P., the Niah Cave excavations' baseline.
2. No fossil hominids are yet known. The few fossil animal teeth give rise to considerable uncertainty (as fully discussed in the text).
3. The fossil situation is complicated by swift and sweeping land changes; by the surprising persistence in Borneo of forms long extinct in Java and the occurrence of many, including *Manis palaeojavanica*, the giant pangolin, as nonfossil bone at Niah; and by a long established trade in fossils from the mainland (see Appendix).
4. Erosion by water has displaced tektites spatially to mask a time discrepancy of circa 700,000 years between their formation and their present deposition context, so that the tektite clue to possibly Early Paleolithic horizons is frustrated in Brunei.
5. The long continuity of a few stone artifact forms, including "choppers," persisting into the Neolithic, complicates typological identifications and time sequences.
6. Stone tools from open sites (Martapura, Sematan), initially regarded as Early Paleolithic, could be much later.
7. The possibility that early hominids did not adapt to Borneo jungle terrain is discussed and will be further considered, from the ecological point of view, elsewhere.
8. It would be ridiculous at this stage to conclude or suppose that Early Paleolithic activity did not reach north of Java.
9. More extensive, planned search and research are required, especially in Kalimantan, the largest of the four Borneo territories.

APPENDIX: THE CHINESE DRUGSTORES AND FOSSIL TRAFFIC

As mentioned in section 4.4, Ralph von Koenigswald (1958) has suggested that many fossil and other teeth reached the islands as charms and cures, coming from the mainland to local Chinese druggists. He specifically includes the Brunei *Stegolophodon* tooth (section 4.2), a view supported by Hooijer (1960: 354) and Oakley (personal communication 1973). In his recent and very valuable survey of Pleistocene faunas, Medway (1972) included this tooth as implicitly acceptable, overlooking their comments, as he now generously concedes, although he still favors the tooth's local validity (Medway, personal communication 1973).

Von Koenigswald's assessment was based on wide observation of Chinese drugstores in China and throughout Southeast Asia, plus a specific study of over twenty in three Sarawak towns, with the following broad results:

1. "Abundant" fossils from the Pliocene ("Pontian") *Hipparion* fauna of South China, including proboscideans (especially *Mastodon*), rhinos, antelope, and pigs.

2. Less fossilized teeth from the Kwangsi and Kwangtung caves, in small quantities, often gnawed by porcupine, of giant panda, tiger, tapir, proboscideans (*Stegodon, Elephas*), monkeys, and early hominids (*Gigantopithecus, Sinanthropus*, cf. *H. erectus*).

3. Molars from the Villafranchian fauna of the Jûste-Basin; only in Kuching, Sarawak's capital, and previously noted only from a few shops in Shanghai.

The great part of this drugstore material consists of single teeth, especially molars. Note that *Mastodon* (one), *Stegodon* (two), and *Elephas* (two) molars are all involved in the Borneo problems discussed in section 4.

This traffic between China and the islands goes back at least into the T'ang dynasty (Cheng 1969). After its advent in the fifteenth century, Islam became increasingly centralized through the Sultanates, especially at Brunei on the South China Sea. Animal products were important items of export including edible bird's nests (Niah is still the largest single source of supply to the continental Chinese palate), hornbill ivory (*hoting*), kingfishers' feathers for jewelery inlay, rhinoceros horn, deer's antlers, bezoar stones from monkeys and porcupines, and the scales of the smaller pangolin (*Manis javanica*) – all of which still continues in active export (Harrisson and Loh 1965; Harrisson 1968).

The goods were often brought by circuitous routes. One of these went overland across northern Thailand, in the fifteenth and sixteenth centuries, bringing great quantities of Chinese as well as Thai stonewares, among other material, down into the Gulf of Martaban in Burma (cf. *Stegolophodon*'s distribution in the Upper Irrawaddy which outflows there) – thus the name "Martabani wares" for one of the most valued kinds of jar held as status symbols in Borneo (Moore 1970). The trade then filtered south down the west side of the Malay peninsula and fanned out eastward past Sumatra.

REFERENCES

ALLEN, JIM
    1972   The first decade in New Guinea archaeology. *Antiquity* 44: 180–189.
ASHTON, PETER
    1972   "The quaternary geomorphological history of western Malesia," in
           The Quaternary era in Malesia. Edited by P. Ashton and M. Ashton,
           35–47. University of Hull, Department of Geography, Miscellaneous
           Series 13.
ASHTON, P., M. ASHTON, *editors*
    1972   *The Quaternary era in Malesia*. University of Hull, Department of
           Geography, Miscellaneous Series 13.
BROTHWELL, DON R.
    1960   Upper Pleistocene skull from Niah caves. *Sarawak Museum Journal*
           9: 323–349.
BRUNEI GOVERNMENT
    1968   *Brunei annual report for 1966*. Kuala Belait.

BUSK, GEORGE
1869 Discovery at Sarawak of the fossilised teeth of a rhinoceros. *Proceedings of the Zoological Society of London* 22: 409–416.

CHENG, TE K'UN
1969 *Archaeology in Sarawak*. Cambridge: Heffer.

DE VRIES, H., KENNETH B. OAKLEY
1959 The Piltdown jaw. *Nature* (London) 184: 224–226.

FOX, ROBERT
1970 *The Tabon Caves: archaeological explorations and excavations on Palawan Island, Philippines*. National Museum of the Philippines, Monograph 1. Quezon City: New Mercury Printing Press.

HAILE, N. S.
1968 The Quaternary history of north Sarawak. *Sarawak Museum Journal* 16: 277–281.

HARRISSON, BARBARA
1967 A classification of Stone Age burials at Niah. *Sarawak Museum Journal* 15: 126–200.

HARRISSON, TOM
1958a Carbon-dated palaeoliths from Borneo. *Nature* (London) 181: 70–71.
1958b The Caves of Niah: a history of prehistory. *Sarawak Museum Journal* 8: 549–595.
1959a New archaeological results from the Niah Caves. *Man* 59: 1–8.
1959b The Piltdown forgery: A. H. Everett and Niah. *Sarawak Museum Journal* 9: 147–156.
1968 "Birds and men in Borneo," in *The birds of Borneo*. By B. E. Smythies, 20–61. Edinburgh: Oliver and Boyd.
1970 The prehistory of Borneo. *Asian Perspectives* 13: 17–45.
1971 The missing Brunei Stone Age. *Brunei Museum Journal* 2: 81–8.
1972 Further radiocarbon dates from Kota Batu, Brunei. *Brunei Museum Journal* 24: 209–217.

HARRISSON, TOM, BARBARA HARRISSON
1971 *The prehistory of Sabah*. Kota Kinabalu: Sabah Society.

HARRISSON, TOM, D. A. HOOIJER, LORD MEDWAY
1961 An extinct giant pangolin from Niah Caves. *Nature* (London) 189: 166.

HARRISSON, TOM, CHEE YIN LOH
1965 To scale a pangolin. *Sarawak Museum Journal* 12: 413–415.

HARRISSON, TOM, LORD MEDWAY
1962a A first classification of prehistoric bone and tooth artifacts. *Sarawak Museum Journal* 19: 335–362. (Full version with raw data.)
1962b A first classification of prehistoric bone and tooth artifacts. *Asian Perspectives* 6: 219–229. (Shorter version.)

HARRISSON, TOM, J. L. REAVIS
1966 The Sarang Caves. *Sarawak Museum Journal* 14: 249–268.

HOOIJER, DIRK A.
1952 *Palaeoloxodon* cf. *namadicus* from Borneo. *Proceedings of the Koninklijke Nederlandse Akademie van Wetenschappen* (Amsterdam) series B55: 395–398.
1960 The giant extinct pangolin from Niah. *Sarawak Museum Journal* 9: 350–355.
1972a Prehistoric evidence for *Elephas maximus* in Borneo. *Nature* (London) 239: 228.

1972b *Stegodon trigonocephalus* from Flores and Timor. *Proceedings of the Koninklijke Nederlandse Akademie van Wetenschappen* (Amsterdam) series B75: 12–33.

1972c Pleistocene vertebrates from Celebes. *Zoologische Mededelingen* (Leiden) 46: 1–16.

HORNADAY, WILLIAM
1885 *Two years in the jungle.* New York: Doubleday.

KURTH, G., *editor*
1968 *Evolution und Hominisation.* Stuttgart: Gustav Fischer.

LYDEKKER, R.
1885 Description of a tooth of *Mastodon latidens* from Borneo. *Bulletin of the Zoological Society of London* 48: 477–479.

1886 *Catalogue of the fossil Mammalia in the British Museum (Natural History)*, volume three. London: British Museum.

MEDWAY, LORD
1965 Niah animal cave bone – VIII. Rhinoceros. *Sarawak Museum Journal* 12: 77–82.

1966 *The mammals of Borneo. Journal Malaysian Branch, Royal Asiatic Society* 36 (3). (Special monograph.)

1972 "The Quaternary mammals of Malesia," in *The Quaternary era in Malesia.* Edited by P. Ashton and M. Ashton, 63–83. University of Hull, Department of Geography, Miscellaneous Series 13.

MOORE, EINE
1970 A suggested classification of stonewares of Martabani type. *Sarawak Museum Journal* 18: 1–78.

MOVIUS, HALLAM L., JR.
1948 The Lower Palaeolithic cultures of southern and eastern Asia. *Transactions of the American Philosophical Society*, n.s. 38 (4): 329–420.

1958 Palaeolithic archaeology in southern and eastern Asia. *Journal of World History* 2: 257–282, 520–553.

MULLER, J.
1972 "Palynological evidence for change in Malesia," in *The Quaternary era in Malesia.* Edited by P. Ashton and M. Ashton, 6–34. University of Hull, Department of Geography, Miscellaneous Series 13.

MULVANEY, D. J.
1969 *The prehistory of Australia.* London: Thames and Hudson.

OSBORN, H. F.
1936 *The Proboscidea*, volume one. New York: Doubleday.

PETERSEN, R. M.
1969 Würm II climate at Niah Cave. *Sarawak Museum Journal* 17: 67–79.

PILBEAM, DAVID
1970 *The evolution of man.* London: Thames and Hudson.

SABELS, B.
1966 "Climatic variations in the tropical Pacific," in *Pleistocene and post-Pleistocene climatic variation.* Honolulu: University Press.

SHUTLER, R., C. KESS
1969 A lithic industry from New Britain. *Bulletin of the Institute of Ethnology* (Taiwan) 27: 129–140.

SMYTHIES, B. E.
1968 *The birds of Borneo.* Edinburgh: Oliver and Boyd.

SOLHEIM, W. G., II
1958 The present status of the Palaeolithic in Borneo. *Asian Perspectives* 2: 83–90.

1972   An earlier agricultural revolution. *Scientific American* 226 (4): 34–41.
TATE, R. B.
1970   Tektites in Brunei. *Brunei Museum Journal* 2: 253–259.
1971   Radiocarbon ages from Quaternary times. *Brunei Museum Journal* 3: 108–123.
VAN HEEKEREN, H.
1972   *The Stone Age of Indonesia* (second edition). Verhandelingen van het Koninklijk Instituut voor Taal-, Land- en Volkenkunde 61. The Hague: Martinus Nijhoff.
VON KEONIGSWALD, G. H. R.
1956   *Meeting prehistoric man.* London: Nelson.
1958   Fossils from Chinese drugstores in Borneo. *Sarawak Museum Journal* 8: 545–548.
1968   "Das absolute Alter des *Pithecanthropus erectus* Dubois," in *Evolution und hominisation.* Edited by G. Kurth, 195–203. Stuttgart: Gustav Fischer.
WALL, J. R. D.
1967   The Quaternary geomorphological history of Sarawak. *Sarawak Museum Journal* 15: 97–125.
WILFORD, G. E.
1961   *The geological and mineral resources of Brunei.* Kuching (British Borneo Geological Survey) Memoir 10.
ZAHRINGER, J.
1963   "K-Ar measurements of tektites," in *Radioactive dating.* Vienna: International Atomic Energy Agency.

The Philippine Paleolithic

ROBERT B. FOX

This paper will summarize briefly the current status of Paleolithic archaeology in the Philippines – the available data and the principal problems.[1] Special attention will be paid to the ongoing research of the National Museum in Cagayan Valley, northern Luzon, where since 1971 many new Paleolithic sites have been discovered which establish the coexistence of extinct Pleistocene fauna with flake and pebble (or cobble) tool industries. The recent excavations have revealed that flake industries were the basic and most widespread feature of Philippine Paleolithic technology. Flakes, as will be seen, form the major category of artifacts excavated in the probable Middle Paleolithic sites of Cagayan Valley, in the Upper Paleolithic cave sites of Palawan, and in relatively recent sites (post-Pleistocene) of hunter-gatherers which are now being found on a number of islands in the Philippines, including Luzon, Samar, Bohal, Mindanao, and Sulu. In 1971, a photograph was made of a flake scraper being used by a member of the Tasaday, a small group of Manobo-speaking food gatherers who still inhabit caves in the high mountains of South Cotabato Province, Mindanao, Philippines (Fox 1973: 58). Flake scrapers have had an incredible continuity in the Philippines, probably covering hundreds of thousands of years.

The archaeological data clearly establish that the Philippine Islands were closely linked with the development of early man and his cultures in Southeast Asia, despite the fact that the archipelago was

[1]   This paper was presented at the Conference on the Early Paleolithic of East Asia, Montreal, Canada, August 28–31, 1973, a pre-Congress conference of the IXth International Congress of Anthropological and Ethnological Sciences, Chicago, Illinois, August 28 to September 8, 1973. My attendance was made possible by a travel grant from the Ford Foundation.

marginal geographically and periodically isolated from the rest of Asia by sea barriers. One of the major problems related to the study of the Philippine Paleolithic is still the temporal definition of the periods of land connections, whether formed by eustatic changes or by up-lifting, which would have allowed early man and Pleistocene fauna to drift into the archipelago, as Beyer (1956) earlier discussed. Move-ments of man and mammals into the islands during the Pleistocene probably involved relatively limited numbers. The major movements of people into the Philippines did not occur until after the land connections had disappeared and when, beginning about 7,000 to 6,000 years ago, the great seafaring, Neolithic people began to settle along the coasts of the many islands. New archaeological data (Fox 1970) would further support the earlier view of Beyer and others that some of the Neolithic inhabitants of the Philippines were later to sail into the Pacific world.

Major emphasis in this paper will necessarily be placed on a descrip-tion of the types of tools utilized by early man and the assemblages of his artifacts. The descriptions of the flake tools will be highly general, however, for an exhaustive analysis, which is attempting to employ modern statistical methods and the use of a computer for correlating the many attributes of the tools, thereby achieving more objective data for future comparative studies, has still not been completed. These detailed data will be presented in future site reports.[2] The ongoing studies of the flake tools are employing an "edge analysis." This analysis was independently evolved but uses an approach which is practically identical to that of White (1969, 1972). Attempts to employ a striation analysis of the working edges of the chert tools which might demonstrate their basic functions, following Semenov (1964), have not been productive.

Synonymous with Philippine Paleolithic studies is the name Beyer – the late Professor Beyer of the University of the Philippines. He argued for many years that "Pleistocene man and large migrating mammals " were present in the Philippines (Beyer 1956: 16–17). Work-ing with him on too brief occasions were other great pioneers of the Asian Paleolithic, including von Koenigswald, van Stein Callenfels, and a few others. Beyer (1947, 1948) provided the first brief cultural chronology for the Philippine Paleolithic. Beyer's work, however, was based almost entirely upon analysis of artifacts from surface collections which were arranged typologically into time sequences following chronologies "established" for neighbouring areas of Asia

[2]   Papers read during the Seminar on Southeast Asian Prehistory and Archaeology, sponsored by the National Museum of the Philippines, Manila, June 26–July 3, 1972, and supported by The Ford Foundation; namely, Fox and Peralta (n.d.) and Lopez (n.d.).

and Europe. Hence the actual excavations by the staff of the National Museum are modifying both in detail and in general scope Beyer's earlier views.

Two distinct areas of the Philippines where excavations have been made by the Museum staff in Paleolithic sites are discussed here: (1) Palawan Island in the southwestern sector of the Philippines where three cave sites have been excavated which yielded stratigraphic sequences of Upper Paleolithic flake implements covering a period of about 50,000 years of the Late Pleistocene and early Post-Pleistocene period; and (2) Cagayan Valley in northern Luzon where many sites have been discovered and two partially excavated which yielded associations of extinct Pleistocene fauna with flake and pebble tool industries, some of these sites dating with certainty to the mid-Pleistocene or the late mid-Pleistocene. No attempts have been made as yet to employ the many new dating techniques which might establish the age of the Paleolithic assemblages in Cagayan Valley, but they would certainly date to some hundreds of thousands of years ago (see Figure 1).

PALAWAN ISLAND: UPPER PALEOLITHIC SITES

Tabon Cave

This great habitation site is one of many caves utilized by man and is found on Lipuun Point, a prominent limestone exposure. Lipuun Point is found near the town of Alfonso XIII (Quezon) located on the southwest coast of Palawan Island (Fox 1970). This long and narrow island stands as a natural bridge between Borneo and the northern Philippines, forming a corridor for movements of man into (and from) the archipelago. The cave was named after the *Megapode* or "tabon" bird which has used the cave's soft guano contents as a nesting place for countless millennia. The mouth of the cave is tucked into the face of a towering cliff, about 110 feet above the present sea level, and overlooks the South China Sea. The entrance to the cave is large, about sixteen meters in width and eight meters in height. The single, large chamber is shaped like the interior of a cathedral and is over forty-one meters in length. The cave is dry, free of dust and insects, and bathed by sunlight throughout the day. Tabon Cave provided a perfect setting for human habitation which, in addition to its location, explains why it was frequented by Paleolithic Man for about 40,000 years!

The entire cave except near the mouth is filled with a thick deposit of soft guano, droppings of birds, and bats, which in most areas of the cave reaches a depth of nearly six meters. Ancient floors

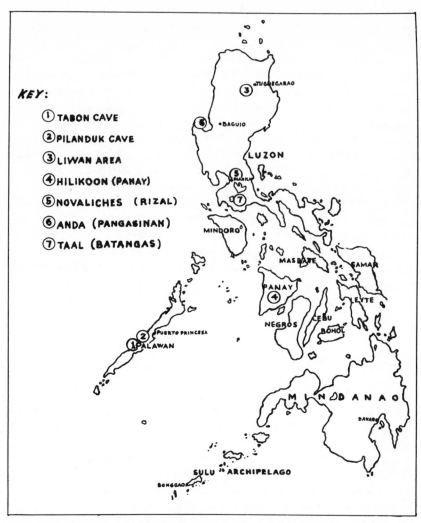

KEY:

① TABON CAVE
② PILANDUK CAVE
③ LIWAN AREA
④ HILIKOON (PANAY)
⑤ NOVALICHES (RIZAL)
⑥ ANDA (PANGASINAN)
⑦ TAAL (BATANGAS)

Figure 1.   Map of the Philippines showing location of Paleolithic sites discussed

distinguished by harder and darker deposits are found at various depths throughout the cave but the artifacts of man have been excavated only in the upper 160 centimeters. Test excavations have been dug in the main longitudinal trench to bed rock, nearly six meters in depth, but proved unhappily to be sterile below 160 centimeters. The ancient floors are associated with assemblages of flakes, tiny bones of birds, bats, and small mammals, and scattered charcoal and ash from cooking fires. The countless small bats in nearby caves, which elsewhere in Palawan are exploited for food by the indigenous people who still occupy caves seasonally, was certainly a major factor, as in the Great Cave at Niah (Harrisson 1964: 183), which attracted Paleolithic man to the Tabon Caves. Not a single marine shell was excavated in Tabon Cave even during the terminal periods of occupation of the cave about 9,000 years ago. The absence of shells cannot be attributed to deterioration and the pressure of the deposits. In nearby Guri Cave, a Tabonian flake industry which dates to 8,000 years ago has been found in a shell midden. Mr. Inocentes Paniza, Chief Geologist of the National Museum, and I believe that the absence of the remains of shellfish was due to the presence of a land shelf in the Palawan area, the sea coast being about thirty to thirty-five kilometers distant during most of the periods of occupation of Tabon Cave. It was too far for shellfish to have been brought back to the cave, although the Paleolithic inhabitants may well have made foraging trips to the coast in order to exploit shellfish and marine resources (Fox 1970: 37–38). The bones of larger animals, such as the wild pig, are notable by their scarcity; however, fragments of antlers of a deer which is now extinct in Palawan have been excavated in shallower levels. It must be emphasized that most of the occupied floors probably represent only relatively brief periods of "frequentation" which would be understandable in a tropical setting; a few, however, extend over a large area of the cave, notably during the period from about 22,000 to 24,000 years ago and later, when it is possible that the climate was wetter.

Fossilized bones of more than one individual have been excavated in Tabon Cave which have been tentatively dated to 22,000 to 24,000 years ago, but with the exception of isolated human teeth all were found in deposits which had been disturbed by the nesting activities of the *Megapode* bird. Small samples of human and animal fossils from a range of time levels in Tabon Cave have been given to Professor K. P. Oakley for fluorine testing and the results may clarify the age of "Tabon Man."

Five C^{14} determinations (see Table 1) have been obtained from the Institute of Geophysics, University of California at Los Angeles, for four distinct cultural levels; eight additional samples are still being processed, which will clarify their relationships with other floors exposed during the later excavations.[3] All charcoal samples for C^{14} determinations were recovered from undisturbed areas of Tabon Cave. The ages of two other levels in Tabon Cave have been estimated by a "depth-and-age" equation which, based upon the available C^{14} dates, would roughly suggest that it required more than 300 years to deposit one centimeter of guano and man's debris.

[3]   I wish to express my gratitude to Dr. W. F. Libby, Dr. G. J. Fergusson, and Dr. R. Berger, of the Institute of Geophysics, University of California at Los Angeles, for the series of C^{14} determinations from Tabon Cave.

Table 1. C^{14} determinations from Tabon Cave

Cultural or flake assemblage	Depth below present cave surface	C^{14} date or estimated age
I–A	Present surface to approximately 25 cm.	8500 to 9500 B.P. (estimated)
I–B	20 cm.	9250±250 B.P. (UCLA-284)
II	50 to 70 cm.	> 21,000 B.P. (UCLA-285)
III	97 cm.	> 22,000 B.P. (UCLA-288)
	99 to 109 cm.	23,000±1000 B.P. (UCLA-699)
IV	121 cm.	30,500±1100 B.P. (UCLA-958)
V	160 cm.	45,000 to 50,000 B.P. (estimated)

Sources: Fergusson and Libby 1963; Berger and Libby 1966.

THE TABONIAN FLAKE INDUSTRY. Thousands of waste flakes, cores, utilized flake tools, and retouched flake tools have been excavated in Tabon Cave which identify at least six distinct flake assemblages (see Table 1) and others will be undoubtedly established. The flakes were knapped entirely from chert, which is common in the nearby rivers. All deposits in Tabon Cave were screened, revealing hundreds of tiny chips of chert. These chips, the concentration of flakes in specific areas and levels of the cave, and the presence of hammerstones of quartz and chert denote workshops. Man not only lived in Tabon Cave but spent much of this time knapping suitable flake tools. River-worn nodules of chert or large chunks of chert are extremely rare in Tabon Cave which would suggest that preliminary knapping was accomplished at the sources of the chert, possibly as noted at the nearby rivers, in order to obtain smaller cores which were brought back to the cave for flaking.

The following notes on this direct percussion industry yielding generally amorphous forms of tools will be presented elsewhere. A few diagnostic observations, however, are pertinent at this time. First, there was no basic change in the method-of-manufacture of the tools or in the types of tools excavated from the first appearance of man in Tabon Cave until the final period of its occupation; a period covering, as indicated, about 40,000 years. The six flake assemblages which have been distinguished form one basic industry – a Tabonian Industry – which persisted through time despite some long gaps between the periods in which Tabon Cave was utilized by man. Much new comparative data from the Philippines and Borneo (Harrisson and Harrisson 1969–1970) would justify the description of an Upper Paleolithic Tabonian Flake tradition.

Secondly, in the category of tools, the great majority (over 90 percent as based upon an initial analysis) are utilized flakes. These flake tools – the "utilized tools" – may be readily distinguished from primary flakes by the many tiny use scars found along the working edges of the implements. Since reading Tindale (1965: 157–159), it will be necessary for me to reexamine all of the utilized tools to see if a "rolling pressure technique" may have been employed. A preliminary examination, however, shows that the scars were characteristically a product of use and not of a "rolling technique." A suitable flake which was utilized – to be distinguished from similar "primary" flakes that show no evidence of use – is generally thin and flat, about five centimeters in length, and has one or sometimes two sharp, low-angled edges. Observationally it would appear that the utilized flakes in the more recent assemblages of Tabon Cave tend to be smaller, but large and small utilized tools are found at all levels. The ongoing quantitative and comparative study will clarify such questions.

Thirdly, a small percentage (less than 10 percent) of the flake tools were retouched – "retouched tools" – in which one or more edges of a chunky flake were knapped with a hammerstone, thereby achieving an edge more suitable for scraping functions or simply to re-edge a dull tool. Characteristically, in the Tabonian Industry, there was little concern with the morphology of the tool but rather with the features of the working edges, explaining my use of an analytical procedure which focuses on the study of the edge(s) of the retouched tools. Edges of the retouched tools are typically convex with high angles (more) than 75 degrees) and step trimming. Unlike the flat, utilized flakes, the retouched tools tend to be thick or chunky, although thinner forms with irregular invasive retouching of low-angled edges are present. A few tools have retouched edges on more than one plane of the chunky whole implement (White 1972).

In the category of retouched tools, only one type of tool stands out – the *kuba* (from Tagalog) or "humpback" scraper. This is a relatively small dome-shaped scraper which has a flat base, high-angled edges, and step-trimming around most of the base (see Figure 2). This type of retouched tool is smaller but remarkably similar to the "horse-hoof" scrapers of Australia (Mulvaney 1961; McCarthy 1967) which are also found in the Philippines in earlier Paleolithic sites, probably of late Middle Pleistocene date. The *kuba* is the diagnostic tool of the Tabonian Industry and is now being found elsewhere in the Philippines. It appears that the retouched tools were primarily scrapers.

Finally, the assemblages of artifacts from Tabon Cave yielded a few unifacially flaked core tools made from river-worn basalt pebbles. In Palawan, similar pebble tools were also found in caves with later Neolithic and Metal Age assemblages, although their exact associations are still questionable. Their extreme rarity in Tabon Cave (a fraction of 1 percent) and other cave sites in Palawan with Upper

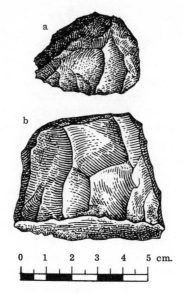

Figure 2.   Tabonian and Liwanian scrapers

Paleolithic Tabonian Industries emphasizes that pebble tools had limited use for these people – hunter-gatherers who we assume were exploiting a wide range of plant foods and who we know were hunting or trapping bats, birds, and smaller animals. Exploitation of the larger pig and deer was minimal until a later period (see Guri Cave below).

No bone tools were excavated in Tabon Cave and they are apparently very rare in other Upper Paleolithic sites in Palawan. The absence of bone tools may be attributed, in part, to the ready availability of workable chert, particularly notable when contrasted with the many bone tools which were found in the Niah excavations of nearby Borneo (Harrisson and Medway 1962).

It is now apparent that flake industries related to the Tabonian Industry formed the major lithic tradition in the Philippines during the Upper Paleolithic. It is also apparent that flake tools, as will be seen, comprise the dominant element of the artifacts recovered in the earlier Middle Paleolithic sites of Cagayan Valley.

Pilanduk Cave

Brief mention should be made of this cave, which is located about eleven kilometers by water north of Tabon Cave along the coast. It was discovered by Eric Casiño during an early period of explorations by the National Museum but was not excavated until 1969–1970 by

Jonathan Kress, now of Duke University. This large and open, shelter-like cave is found high on the northern exposure of a prominent limestone peak. The excavations revealed stratified sequences of flake artifacts which are probably identical to those of Tabon Cave and the range of C^{14} dates is consistent, the earliest determination being some 28,000 years ago (personal communication). The site report on Pilanduk Cave is now being prepared by Kress.

Guri Cave

This cave is found on the northern exposure of Lipuun Point only a relatively short distance from Tabon Cave. The Tabonian Industry was associated here, however, with some 20,000 shells of marine mollusks and land snails of which about 14,000 have been identified and enumerated by species in order to define the shell-gathering behavior of the Guri inhabitants. The cave was occupied seasonally, specifically during the wet period as a study of the land snails shows, beginning about 8,000 to 4,000 years ago as based upon three C^{14} determinations.[4] A few thousand bones of larger animals, the wild pig and the deer, were excavated in the middens of Guri Cave, whereas the bones of larger animals are strikingly rare in Tabon Cave, even in the assemblage which was dated to 9,000 years ago. This would suggest that improved methods of hunting and trapping appeared (or were developed) by Paleolithic Man during early post-Pleistocene times.

The later inhabitants of Guri Cave who continued to use a Tabonian Flake tradition apparently had actual contacts with Neolithic peoples who were also present in Palawan at least 5,000 years ago, as established by C^{14} determinations. Contacts are suggested by the excavation of one shell ornament in Guri Cave – the ground top of a cone shell which is perforated in the center – that is a typical ornament of the Early Neolithic sites. More effective hunting and trapping devices probably used by the Epipaleolithic inhabitants of Guri Cave – which is suggested, as noted, by the great quantities of the bones of pig and deer – may also have been borrowed from the Neolithic people. The fact that great numbers of marine shellfish were exploited by the people of Guri Cave would further indicate that the sea was now accessible for gathering shellfish, the coast being in

---

[4] I also wish to thank Dr. Pow-key Sohn and the Atomic Energy Research Institute (AERIK) of Korea for additional C^{14} determinations on Guri Cave; namely, AERIK-20 and 21 for outer and inner portions of shell, 8130 ± 180 B.P. and 7890 ± 90 B.P.; and AERIK-19 for charcoal, 4220 ± 140 B.P. which complements UCLA-698 for shell which had a C^{14} determination of 4070 ± 80 B.P.

approximately its present position some 8,000 years ago (but not before 9,000 years ago).

Except for one unifacially pointed tool, two fabricators, and five hammers, all of the tools from Guri Cave are flakes of chert. There is no change in tool types in the Guri middens and all are basically related to the Tabonian Industry, except for the appearance of a few blade-like implements which led me (Fox 1970) to speak of "blade tools." No prepared cores were obtained when further excavations were made, however, and it is doubtful if these blade-like tools are actually examples of a blade tradition. The present evidence would suggest that blade tools, such as those found in the Bato Caves (Fox and Evangelista 1957), were not associated with the Upper Paleolithic, or at least not with the Tabonian Flake tradition. Blades are associated with the small flake-and-blade industries (Fox 1970) of Duyong Cave during the post-Pleistocene period and appear to have been hafted (Mulvaney 1966) and used as composite tools. A fully developed blade technology is associated with the Neolithic, although small flake-and-blade industries are present by at least 7,000 years ago (or earlier) and were probably associated with a distinct tradition which reached the Philippines during a late phase of the Upper Paleolithic. The small "flake-and-blade industry" of Duyong Cave, Palawan, is not the classic "microliths" of South Asia which have retouched geometric forms (Fox 1970). In fact none of the tool industries which have been classified in South and East Asia as "Mesolithic," such as the "microliths" and the Hoabinhian types of tool assemblages, appear to be present in the Philippines. One continues to question strongly the usefulness of the confused concept of "Hoabinhian," at least as describing a widespread lithic tradition in Southeast Asia (Solheim 1970), until its presence is established in marginal areas of island Southeast Asia, such as the Philippines. I also see no need in the Philippines for the use of the construct Mesolithic; rather the Upper Paleolithic industries persisted among hunter-gatherers and coexisted with the distinct technologies of the early Neolithic swidden farmers. After the Paleolithic, the Philippines' archaeological record shows striking examples of distinct but coexisting lithic technologies; widespread technological developments did not occur in orderly "stages."

A preliminary analysis of the Tabonian Industry found in Guri Cave clearly establishes that retouched tools are now more common than utilized flakes. In the category of retouched tools, about two-thirds are high-angled scrapers of which the *kuba* type is the most common. A number of low-angled scrapers have beautifully knapped edges with long invasive flakes which cannot be seen in the earlier retouched tools from Tabon Cave. There were no large flake tools found in Guri Cave such as those excavated in Tabon Cave, but without detailed quantification the apparent reduction in the general size of the Guri flake tools is not certain. This is certain: the Tabonian Industry which was first recovered in Tabon Cave and dated about 50,000 years ago persisted in Guri Cave to only 4,000 years ago – a notable example of a Paleolithic tradition which persisted *in detail* for tens of thousands of years.

CAGAYAN VALLEY: MIDDLE PALEOLITHIC SITES

Excavations in Tabon Cave were suspended in 1970 in order to prepare a detailed site report on the excavations and to undertake explorations for earlier sites of Paleolithic man found elsewhere in the Philippines, including the sites in Cagayan Valley. The significance of the Cagayan sites was first realized by von Koenigswald (1958) after a brief visit there accompanied by Daniel Scheans, D. G. Kelley, and guided by Larry Wilson. Since 1971, working periodically, the staff of the National Museum has located sixty-four localities in Cagayan for which the Museum has accessioned materials – flakes and pebble (cobble) tools, and/or fossils of extinct Pleistocene mammals and tektites (see Table 2). Many more sites are known – the figure would probably exceed one hundred – but no additional collections are being made until detailed maps have been prepared for the sites. Also, in 1971 three large-scale excavations were begun which have revealed flake tools *in situ* in fossil-bearing deposits which are known as the "Awiden Mesa Formation" and correlated with the Middle Pleistocene or late Middle Pleistocene. During the past year, fieldwork has focused on preparing a field station, mapping by Inocentes Paniza, and base line geological studies by Silvio Lopez and Inocentes Paniza.[5] The following discussion is necessarily brief, as well as preliminary, and some statements are to be viewed as speculative but justifiable in this pioneer area of research. Credit for the archaeological data presented in this phase of the paper belongs equally to Jesús Peralta of the National Museum.

The Setting

The fossil and tool localities are found in low hills on the western flank of Cagayan Valley, northern Luzon (see Figure 1), within an area of

[5] Further data on Cagayan Valley may be found in a Progress Report (1971) prepared for President and Mrs. Ferdinand E. Marcos entitled "Ancient man and Pleistocene fauna in Cagayan Valley, northern Luzon, Philippines." This was prepared by me with the help of Jesús T. Peralta, Ned Ewart, Inocentes Paniza, Silvio Lopez, Israel Cabanilla, Reynaldo Flores, Yoji Aoyagi, and Manuel Ma. Santiago.

Kalinga–Apayao Province called Liwan by the local inhabitants. The Liwan area also embraces a few fossil localities which are found near the town of Solana in Cagayan Province. Rizal, in Kalinga–Apayao Province, is the small town which lies nearest the sites being excavated by the museum. This town, in turn, is about 37 kilometers by road west of Tuguegarao, a large marketing center and the capital of Cagayan Province. About 500 kilometers by road north of Manila, Tuguegarao may also be reached by daily flights of commercial aircraft.

The Liwan hills, once forested according to informants, are now open grasslands occupied by cattle and water buffalo ranches. The fossil and tool localities discussed in this paper are found largely within the Espinosa, Madrigal, and Wanawan Ranches. Extreme erosion in the hills has occurred as the result of past swiddening activities and the present practice of reburning the grasslands to obtain young grasses as pasture for the herds of cattle and water buffalo. Each year new fossil and tool localities are exposed by the heavy rains.

The Geology of the Liwan Area

As pointed out by Lopez (n.d.), the denuded Liwan hills are anticlines – the Cabalwan, Pangul, and Enrile – which trend in a north–south direction and border on both sides of a broad, flat syncline – the Liwan Plain. The "Ilagan Formation" of the anticlines is Pliocene in origin and composed of ". . . interbedded sandstone, mudstone, and a few lenses of conglomerate " (Lopez n.d.). The anticlines, however, were uplifted in Pleistocene times. On the lower slopes of the anticlines where the sites are found, the "Ilagan Formation" is overlaid by (1) the "Awiden Mesa Formation" of Middle Pleistocene date, (2) highly sculptured terraces and the "Old River Gravel Deposits" of the Upper(?) Pleistocene, and (3) geologically recent alluvium in the basins of present-day streams, such as the nearby Andarayan River.

Probably all of the sites discussed here, including those which yielded surface association of flake and pebble tools and Pleistocene fossils, are eroding from the Awiden Mesa Formation. This formation is composed of tuffaceous sediment which has a notable proportion of clay and some welded tuff (Lopez n.d.: 8). The excavations yielded flake artifacts *in situ* which were also found in the Awiden Mesa Formation. This formation is presently correlated by Philippine geologists with the vertebrate-bearing Middle Pleistocene "Guadalupe Formation " of the Central Plains of Luzon, including the Manila area.

Von Koenigswald (1956) would appear to correlate the deposits which contained tektites and molar fragments of a fossil rhinoceros found on the west side of the Pangul Anticline near Barrio Laya, Tabuk, in Kalinga-Apayao Province, with the "(Upper) Middle Pleistocene." A similar correlation – Middle Pleistocene to late Middle Pleistocene – may thus be attributed to the fossil-bearing deposits of the Awiden Mesa Formation in nearby Liwan. Tektites are also found in the Liwan area but their association is questionable due, in part, to the intense collecting of tektites which had been sponsored by people in Manila.

The major problems faced by the field team of the National Museum in Cagayan Valley are:

1.   To establish through large-scale excavations – the use of mechanical equipment is seriously being considered (Shutler 1967) – the details of the cultural and fossil assemblages of the many sites concentrated in the Liwan area, and their relative chronological positions.

2.   To correlate the broad geological features of the Pleistocene in Cagayan Valley with the Pleistocene of the Philippines and island Southeast Asia generally, the islands of Southeast Asia sharing specific historical problems.

3.   To reconstruct the environmental setting in which early man and Pleistocene fauna lived in Cagayan Valley.

The Philippines is without a type collection of Pleistocene fauna which could be used for reference. Only the genera are presently known.

It is certain that the fossil and tool sites in Cagayan Valley are of great antiquity, the geological evidence for the sites discussed suggesting that they are Middle Pleistocene or late Middle Pleistocene in date. Upper Paleolithic sites are also present, if the workshops found in the "Old River Gravel Deposits" are early Late (or Upper) Pleistocene.

Surface Collections

Prior to the selection of sites for excavation, extensive surface collections were made by the National Museum field team of fossils, man-made artifacts, and tektites on the Espiñosa, Madrigal, and Wanawan Ranches. Collections, as noted, were made from sixty-four sites and in one site – Espiñosa I – all surface artifacts were plotted on a contoured site map prior to an excavation. This excavation was suspended as no mammalian fossils were appearing. And surface collections in general have been suspended, as noted, until all of the sites have been carefully mapped. The sites where surface collections were made are concentrated in an area about one kilometer in width and probably ten kilometers in length. The great majority of the fossils and tools collected were eroding, as noted, from the Awiden

Table 2.   Surface associations of tools, fossils, and tektites from the Liwan sites

Surface associations	Percentages
Sites with fossils and pebble and flake tools	66
Sites with fossils, pebble and flake tools, and tektites	9
Sites with fossils only	15
Sites with flake tools only	13
Sites with pebble tools only	3
Sites with pebble and flake tools only	19
Sites with fossils and pebble tools only	0
Sites with fossils and flake tools only	21
Sites with fossils and tektites only	0
Sites with fossils, tektites, and pebble tools	0
Sites with fossils, tektites, and flake tools	4

Prepared by Jesús T. Peralta, National Museum.

Mesa Formation and, where excavations have been made, the materials are in deposits on this same formation. It cannot be stated that the man-made tools represent one assemblage of artifacts, but rather that they are closely related assemblages of flake and pebble tools which are associated with fossils and perhaps tektites (see Table 2). Thus the impression that one gains from reading von Koenigswald's brief article (1958) that only pebble tools are found with fossils in Cagayan Valley is not substantiated. Although also collecting on the Espiñosa Ranch where the museum field team is working, von Koenigswald (1958) does not mention and apparently did not collect the more common flake artifacts. A study of the surface artifacts from twenty-one Liwan sites yielding both pebble and flake tools show that about 93 percent (!) are flake artifacts. All were knapped from cryptocrystalline quartz – chert, jasper, and an opaline rock. It would appear that flake tools, including both retouched and utilized types, formed the dominant element of the tool tradition found in Cagayan Valley which I am describing as the Liwanian Flake Industry.

Von Koenigswald (1958) describes the pebble tool complex from Cagayan as Cabalwanian which remains useful, if in fact an assemblage of artifacts is recovered which includes only fossils with pebble (or cobble) tools. As indicated in Table 2, no site of this type was found during the survey. The flake tools do not appear to be heavily patinated, probably due to their recent exposure, although this attribute has not been carefully studied.

The Liwanian flake tools are an amorphous lot (see below for a preliminary analysis of the flakes from one excavation, Madrigal IV) but edge retouching is common. The flake tools are generally small, at least as compared with Mulvaney's restudy (1970: 186) of the Patjitanian Industry of Java. The tools have few diagnostic features – with one exception – which would distinguish them from other

Table 3. Types of Cabalwanian pebble (cobble) tools (twenty-one localities)

Letter designation (tentative type)	Type description	Text figure	Number	Percent
A	Unifacial pointed	Figure 3	16	25
B	Unifacial pointed and end-flaked	Figure 3	5	8
C	Unifacial pointed and dorsal-ridged	Figure 3	13	21
D	Unifacial pointed and ventral-humped	Figure 4	5	8
E	Unifacial and straight-edged	Figure 4	15	24
F	Unifacial and convex-edged	Figure 4	5	8
G (?)	Bifacial with alternate flaking		2	3
H	Hammerstones		2	3
		Totals	63	100

Paleolithic flake industries found in the Philippines (e.g. the Tabonian). The exception is the appearance of large, chunky, high-domed scrapers with flat bases – also with high-angled, step-trimmed edges around most of the circumference of the base – which are remarkably similar to the "horsehoof" scrapers (Figure 2b) widely distributed in Australia but which have not been reported from Southeast Asia (Mulvaney 1961, 1969; McCarthy 1967). Identical horsehoof-type scrapers associated with a flake industry and possibly with teeth of an elephant were recovered on the surface of a site at Hilikoon, Panay, by F. Landa Jocano and Inocentes Paniza (no pebble tools are represented in their initial collection from this site). Although there is a vast gap in time and the observation may have little meaning, the flake industries of the Philippine Paleolithic show striking similarities with those of modern Australia. Perhaps this is further evidence of the persistence of a great Paleolithic flake tradition in island Southeast Asia and Australia.

The Cabalwanian Pebble (Cobble) Tools

As pebble tools appear to be a diagnostic element of the Middle Paleolithic (and earlier) in Southeast Asia which apparently show relationships to Movius' classic description (1948) of the "chopper/chopping-tool" industries in South and East Asia, Jesús Peralta and I made a detailed study of pebble tools from twenty-one sites in Cagayan Valley (see Table 3 and Figures 3 and 4). Respecting precedence, we have retained von Koenigswald's description (1958) of these tools as Cabalwanian (Fox and Peralta n.d.). The corpus studied

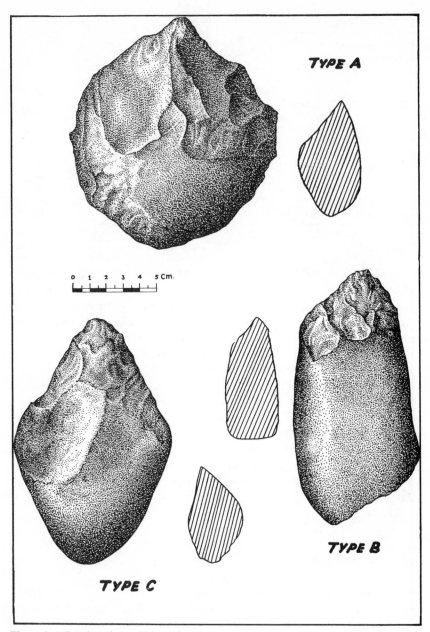

Figure 3.   Cabalwanian pebble tool types

was recovered from the surface of twenty-one distinct but nearby
localities and all eroding, as presently established, from the Awiden
Mesa Formation. Only a few tools are rolled. They are made from
weathered igneous pebbles (about 62 percent) or silicious river-worn

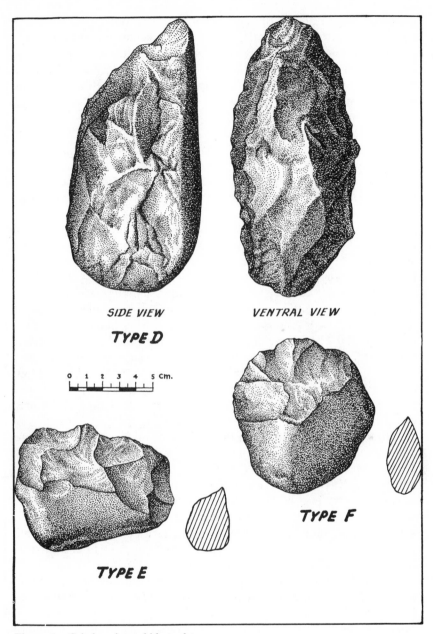

Figure 4. Cabalwanian pebble tool types

pebbles. Patination is present on the tools made of the silicious rock but attempts to describe the degree of patination were set aside until an acceptable standard could be found.

It must be stressed that there is nothing "primitive" about the method of manufacture of the pebble (cobble) tools, nothing which would suggest that the flake tools were a more advanced technology than the pebble tools. Secondary retouching with step trimming is found on the pebble tools, as well as on the flake artifacts. We were impressed again and again by the sophisticated percussion technique used in knapping the pebbles. Form, for example, was achieved by a minimal number of carefully directed and controlled blows, quickly apparent to anyone who has attempted to duplicate these tools. The natural form of the pebble was analyzed by early man before flaking the tool in which, for example, the ridge of the pebble was utilized as an axis of the point, as in Type C (Table 3). Unlike the flake tools, the morphology of the pebble (cobble) tools must be considered during the analysis.

These tools in general are large and we would like to call them all "cobble" tools, as suggested by Ned Ewart, a volunteer worker during one phase of the excavations. This follows the geological criteria (Dunbar and Rodgers 1957) of a "pebble" as being 4 to 64 millimeters in length and a "cobble" as being 64 to 256 millimeters in length. Following these criteria, only one tool from Cagayan can be described as a "pebble" and a number of the tools are truly massive, reaching one-and-a-half kilos in weight, hardly even the popular conception of a "pebble." If Paleolithic industries are recovered which are "pebble" in size, then it would be desirable to distinguish "pebble" tools from the "cobble" tools. At present we are retaining the term "pebble" tool because it is widely established in the published literature, regardless of the size of the tool.

Utilizing an approach which emphasizes the method of manufacture of pebble tools rather than imputed functions, eight (?) tentative types of the pebble tools have been established (see Table 3) – established for more effective comparison with other Asian industries. The Cabalwanian Industry is characterized by at least four general features: (1) all of the diagnostic tool types are unifacially flaked, except two relatively small bifacial implements with alternate flaking which have appeared in only one locality and may represent a distinct industry; (2) tools are formed with a minimal number of flakes, as noted; (3) edges may be retouched, including step trimming; and (4) the butts of the tools are formed by the natural cortex of the river-worn stone, although a few instances of "grip flaking" have been observed apparently done in order to facilitate holding the tool. It is highly probable, following Mulvaney's analysis (1966), that the tools were "nonhafted." A more detailed description of the types of pebble tools which belong to the Cabalwanian industry, as presently distinguished, follows (unfortunately none of the pebble tools collected by Wilson or von Koenigswald are available for comparison although some identical types are illustrated by von Koenigswald 1958).

A. UNIFACIAL POINTED TOOLS (Figure 3). This tool would appear to be roughly similar to Movius' description (1948) of the "proto-handaxe" found in South and East Asia and Sieveking's "large points-pick" of the Tampanian Industry (1958). It is made by unifacially flaking the converging sides of a river pebble, usually elongated, to a point. The few flake scars on the converging sides are approximately opposite to each other, yielding a well-formed and symmetrical tool.

It is probable that the tool had a "chopping" or "picking" function in which the weight of the tool was concentrated (and directed) on the point. Few of these tools (and others) have scars which were a result of use, suggesting that they may have been employed for working softer materials.

B. UNIFACIAL POINTED AND END-FLAKED TOOLS (Figure 3). An identical type of tool from the Tampanian Industry has been described by Sieveking (1958) as a "pebble pick." Its overall form is similar to the unifacial pointed tool (Type A) but it is distinct in that the converging sides of the tool are formed by the natural cortex of the elongated cobble. The unifacial flaking is confined to the point of the tool. Thus there is relatively little flaking on even the ventral surface of the tool – about 20 percent on all but one of the tools examined – and none on the dorsal surface.

C. UNIFACIAL POINTED AND DORSAL-RIDGED TOOLS (Figure 3). This class of tool, although similar in form to Types A and B, differs markedly in that Paleolithic man used a natural ridge on the dorsal surface of the pebble to form the axis of the point of the tool. (The "dorsal surface" is described as the surface with cortex, usually 100 percent.) The manner in which the dorsal ridge of the pebble is often employed (21 percent of the corpus) is highly suggestive, as noted, that early man carefully preselected the pebbles for flaking. Similar types of tools but with varied "functional" descriptions appear elsewhere in studies of the Paleolithic in Southeast Asia.

D. UNIFACIAL POINTED AND VENTRAL-HUMPED TOOLS (Figure 4). This distinctive type of tool has a marked hump on the ventral or flaked surface. The hump is formed by extensive flaking along both sides, including secondary retouching and step-trimming which yields high-angled edges. The entire ventral surface is usually flaked, and it is the only pebble tool which does not have a smooth butt formed by the natural cortex of the pebble. A similar type of tool is recorded in the Patjitanian Industry and again described by Movius (1948: Figure 14–4) as a "proto-handaxe."

It is presumed that these four types of tools (described above) had generally similar chopping functions, but Type D may have been used as a large, two-handed scraper. This type of tool is truly large, three out of four examples in the corpus being over a kilo in weight. A study of the cross-section of this tool type reveals that the body is narrow and deep. This, coupled with the fact that the ventral hump was deliberately flaked, would suggesst that a heavy and narrow tool was sought for deeper penetration if it was used for "chopping" or "picking."

E. UNIFACIAL AND STRAIGHT-EDGED TOOLS (Figure 4). These relatively common (see Table 2) unifacially flaked pebbles are described by Movius (1948) as "choppers" or "massive scrapers." In terms of the method of manufacture, four features of this distinctive tool stand out and would suggest that they were, in fact, large scrapers: (1) a relatively straight edge knapped at right angles to the axis of the cobble; (2) a high-angled edge with step trimming; (3) a short, wide, and thick body; and (4) a smooth butt formed by the natural cortex of the pebble.

F. UNIFACIAL AND CONVEX-EDGED TOOLS (Figure 4). This tool is similar in form to Type E in that the edge is at right angles to the axis of the pebble. The working edge, however, is more convex and the *angle of the working edge tends to be low*. The form of the edge and the examination of the use scars along the edges would suggest that this type of tool was primarily used for "chopping," not "scraping." (The illustrations, unfortunately, do not show the marked differences which exist between Types E and F.)

Additional collections may reveal unifacial tools with concave edges. One possible implement of this type was recovered – a round, flat pebble with a concave edge formed by the removal of a single, large flake. The concave edge of the scar appears to have been utilized. Confined to a single example, this probable concave scraper has not been established as a tentative type of the Cabalwanian Industry.

G. BIFACIAL TOOLS WITH ALTERNATE FLAKING. We have also hesitated to include two bifacial tools in this preliminary study of the Cabalwanian pebble tools – a characteristic unifacial industry. They are made on relatively small pebbles with alternate flaking from both surfaces which gives the edge a serrated appearance. Only one of the bifaces shows use. Whether or not this type of tool is to be included with the Cabalwanian pebble tools will have to be determined when a larger collection is available for study. There is no reason, however, that limited bifacial flaking could not be associated with the Cabalwanian Industry, although it is characteristically unifacial.

H. HAMMERSTONES. A number of flat, ovoid implements have been handled in Cagayan which show some evidences of use around the edges and two are represented in the collection studied.

In summary, the Cabalwanian pebble tools would appear to be a diagnostic part of artifactual assemblages (see Table 2) which also include flake tools. At least there is no question (see below) that flake tools are found in the Awiden Mesa Formation of Middle Pleistocene or late Middle Pleistocene date. The flake and pebble industries are closely related in the techniques of knapping employed; both show sophisticated primary and secondary flaking, including retouching and step trimming. It is highly questionable that unifacial pebble tools represent a distinct and older industry, as evidenced by the available archaeological record in the Philippines, but rather that the *pebble tools had specialized functions*. In the Palawan excavations, pebble tools formed only a fraction of 1 percent of the artifacts excavated; in the Cagayan Valley surface collections, large pebble tools also formed only about 7 percent of the artifacts recovered. The pebble tools recovered in Cagayan Valley form, nevertheless, a diagnostic element of the total number of artifacts. The Upper Paleolithic inhabitants of Tabon Cave exploited bats, birds, and small mammals; the Paleolithic men of Cagayan Valley exploited large and extinct Pleistocene mammals, including *Elephas* and *Stegodon*, and possibly *Rhinoceros* and *Bubalus* as well as others. Is there a direct correlation between the pebble tools used by early man in Cagayan Valley and the larger species of animals which he hunted or trapped and butchered?

The Excavations

Three large-scale excavations were initiated in Cagayan Valley, two of which are described briefly here – Espiñosa Ranch Locality 4, and Madrigal Ranch Locality 12. The excavations in one site – Espiñosa Locality 1 – were suspended due to the rarity of materials, as noted, particularly of fossils which might be associated with the artifacts. The excavations were undertaken in order to establish an *in situ* correlation between the fossils and tools. The three sites are found on the denuded crowns and slopes of rolling hills separated by gulleys. The sites of Espiñosa Locality 1 and Madrigal Locality 12 are adjacent to each other (these two sites might be treated by others as one locality) and Espiñosa 4 lies about 400 meters to the north. Surface artifacts were numerous, as well as the exposure of proboscis fossils in Madrigal Locality 12 and Espiñosa Locality 4. The sedimentary deposits of the three sites, as established by Silvio Lopez, are in Awiden Mesa

Formation of probable Middle Pleistocene or late Middle Pleistocene date. Details of the excavations are being presented elsewhere[6] and the excavations will be continued in 1974 after the rainy season.

ESPIÑOSA RANCH LOCALITY 4. This site lies on a small but relatively steep hill. The bones of an elephant and one pebble tool had been exposed – about a year before the excavations were begun in 1971 – at the base of the hill but above a small gulley. A trench four meters wide and forty-four meters in length was partly excavated from the gulley up the slope of the hill to the crown. Later, this trench was extended through the gulley and up the slope of another small hill to the west. This extension of the trench proved to be sterile. Ten meters up the slope from the elephant bones, two flake scrapers were excavated at eighty-three centimeters in depth from the surface in an undisturbed layer of silt of the Awiden Mesa Formation. Both tools have bulbs of percussion, one having been utilized and the other retouched.

A detailed study of the trench profile by Silvio Lopez, micro-paleontologist and geologist of the museum, and others, indicates that the fossils are in a slightly lower mudstone strata. Except for the surface association of the fossils and one pebble tool, no other tools were found *in situ* with the fossils. Excavations of the trench have not been completed and disconformities appear to exist due to micro-faulting and an appreciable erosion. We can only state with certainty that flake tools of man and fossils have been recovered in the Awiden Mesa Formation – recovered *in situ* in closely related sedimentary deposits.

In Locality 1 of the Espiñosa Ranch, man-made waste flakes were also recovered by Yoji Aoyagi, a student of archaeology from Japan who was working with the National Museum, at 183 centimeters below the surface in the Awiden Mesa Formation. The detailed stratigraphic relationship between the deposits of the two sites – Espiñosa Locality 1 and Espiñosa Locality 4 has not as yet been worked out.

MADRIGAL RANCH LOCALITY 12. This is located on the crown and slopes of a low, denuded hill which is bisected by a road that connects the Madrigal and Espiñosa Ranches. The excavations in the site which are discussed here are found on the southern slope of the site formed by a newly eroded gulley which reaches down to the Andarayan River about 200 meters away. Sections of this slope had developed minor slumps from which were eroding fossils of a proboscis, probably *Elephas* sp., and flake and pebble artifacts. As Jesús Peralta notes, the disposition of the fossils and flakes, coupled with the fact that the

[6] Cf. fn. 2, p. 60.

materials are not rolled, would suggest a very recent exposure of the materials; this view was also held by the local residents.

A study of the profiles from the excavations in the shallow deposits on the slope – complicated by erosion and redeposition of soils – indicate, nevertheless, that flake artifacts and fossils are found in the same matrix – a light brown, clay-like deposit – which is underlain by a layer of sterile sand. The deepest flake artifact was excavated only twenty-three centimeters below the surface. Higher up the slope but in the same light brown, clay-like soil, Jesús Peralta uncovered a large fossilized tusk measuring some one-and-a-half meters in length, the base of the tusk being about thirty-five centimeters in depth. The artifactual materials and fossils down the slope are found largely in a thin, humus surface layer – five to fifteen centimeters from the surface – which, as based on mineralogical observations, is a redeposition of the deeper, light brown, clayey soil. And the fossil fragments are generally those from the large tusk which is *in situ* up the slope, only two to three meters away. Thus the excavations in Madrigal Ranch Locality 12 establish an association of flake artifacts – retouched as well as utilized – with the fossil tusk of a proboscis. Continuation of the excavations at Locality 12 will likely reveal an association of pebble tools, for these are represented in the surface collections from the site, about 15 percent of the total number of tools, including the familiar types described above.

Peralta's analysis of the flake artifacts from surface collections made throughout the site is highly significant in terms of the thesis that flake industries are old and widespread in the Philippine Paleolithic. About 41 percent of the total number of tools are those which can be described as "retouched." Notable again is one example of a small "horsehoof" scraper with a high-angled edge and with about 80 percent of the circumference of the base showing retouched scars. Low-angled flakes are recorded which surprisingly show retouching on the ventral surface (bulb of percussion side). The flakes are generally small, varying in length from 2.1 to 8 centimeters with a greater number in the smaller categories.

SUMMARY

The excavations in Tabon Cave have established that man was present in the Philippines during the Upper Paleolithic (Fox 1970) and the more recent excavations in Cagayan Valley provide clear evidence that he was here during the Middle Paleolithic, living among and hunting extinct Pleistocene mammals such as the elephant. Geologically speaking, early man would appear to have been living in the Philippines

during the Middle Pleistocene or at least by the late Middle Pleistocene. The limited paleontological evidence would suggest that he was
also contemporaneous with pygmy forms of the proboscises, such as
Elephas beyeri (von Koenigswald 1956) of Pangasinan, which locally
evolved as a result of insular conditions established by dramatic
geological changes during the Pleistocene. Geological and environmental changes were probably the major factor leading to the extinction of the distinctive Pleistocene fauna in the Philippines, but I would
also like to suggest that the hunting activities of man may also have
played a significant part. Some of the localities in Cagayan Valley
appear to be "kill sites" (see Table 2) where Pleistocene mammals
had concentrated on low hills paralleling a wet plain and been
butchered by man. One bifacial core tool made of the ivory of a
proboscis (!) was recovered in the Liwan hills. This tool, however,
is not fully fossilized. It is possible that some of the extinct fauna
which appeared in the Philippines by at least Middle Pleistocene times
survived to a relatively recent date.

The marginal position of the Philippines would further argue that
the biomass of Pleistocene mammals was relatively limited; at least
localities producing fossils continue to be extremely limited in number.
The fossil sites are found largely in northern Luzon – Cagayan Valley
and Bolinao, Pangasinan – and central Luzon. Von Koenigswald
(1956) in fact favors a northern movement of the typical Middle
Pleistocene mammals into the Philippines, based on paleozoological
evidences, from mainland Asia by way of Taiwan. This has suggestive
relationships to the large number of fossil sites which are appearing
in northern Luzon. In Pleistocene times Cagayan Valley would have
formed a *cul-de-sac* for these larger mammals, subsequent movements
to the south being by way of the Ilokos coast which might explain the
fossil localities in Pangasinan at Bolinao and new sites which have
been reported from the Iloko Provinces. But there are also two other
probable routes for the migrations of larger mammals into the
Philippines from the south, as von Koenigswald and others (Lopez
n.d.) have pointed out. Only more complete paleozoological and
geological evidence from the Philippines and Asia generally will
clarify the major problem of land connections and Pleistocene
faunal migrations, including those of early man.

No fossils of early man have been recovered in Cagayan Valley
but it is only a matter of time. His tools have been found in large
numbers. Assuming that the Awiden Mesa Formation is correlated
with at least the late Middle Pleistocene of Java, then it is likely that
a precursor of *Homo sapiens* would have been present.

It would appear to be firmly established that flake artifacts were the
dominant tradition in the Philippines during both the Middle and Upper

Paleolithic, pebble tools having some specialized functions during the earlier period. One finds it difficult to imagine man living in a tropical environment without a flake tradition, for it is flake tools which would have enabled him to exploit great numbers of useful and edible plants, as do hunter-gatherers today. This assumes that there has been no great change in the characteristic flora, which geological evidence indicates, and that cryptocrystalline quartz of various forms was available where he lived.

Even casual comparisons would suggest widespread relationships between the Upper Paleolithic Tabonian Industry of Palawan and the Cagayan Valley, and Paleolithic tool industries found elsewhere in Asia, as Movius' classic study (1948) has done for South and East Asia, including Indonesia. This, however, has not been the purpose of this paper; the purpose was rather to introduce briefly a discussion of the Paleolithic tool assemblages recently recovered in the Philippines, their archaeological contexts, and to speculate on the significance of the types of these tools for early man's adaptation to two distinct ecological niches. One final impression gained from an examination of Paleolithic industries in the Philippines is that if *Homo erectus* was present, he passed his tools on to his successors, *Homo sapiens* and *Homo sapiens sapiens*. There seems to be little correlation between the evolution of man in Asia and distinct types of Paleolithic tools. At least *Homo* was "wise" in toolmaking when he first appeared in the Philippines.

REFERENCES

BERGER, RAINER, W. F. LIBBY
  1966   UCLA radiocarbon dates V. *Radiocarbon* 8.
BEYER, H. OTLEY
  1947   Outline review of Philippine archaeology by islands and provinces. *Philippine Journal of Science* 77 (3–4). Manila.
  1948   *Philippine and East Asian archaeology and its relation to the origin of the Pacific Islands population.* National Research Council of the Philippines Bulletin 29 (December). Quezon City.
  1956   *New finds of fossil mammals from Pleistocene strata of the Philippines,* (Advance) reprint, National Research Council of the Philippines Bulletin 41. Quezon City.
DUNBAR, C. O., JOHN RODGERS
  1957   *Principles of stratigraphy.* London, New York: John Wiley and Sons.
FERGUSSON, G. J., W. F. LIBBY
  1963   UCLA radiocarbon dates III. *Radiocarbon* 3.
FOX, ROBERT B.
  1970   *The Tabon Caves: archaeological explorations and excavations on Palawan Island, Philippines.* National Museum of the Philippines, Monograph 1. Quezon City: New Mercury Printing Press.

1973   "The Tasaday: Stone Age tribe of Mindanao," in *1973 Britannica Yearbook of Science and the Future*. [Fox is the sole author of this article.]

FOX, ROBERT B., ALFREDO EVANGELISTA

1957   The Bato Caves, Sorsogon Province, Philippines: a preliminary report on a stone tool-jar burial culture. *University of Manila Journal of East Asiatic Studies* 6 (1). Manila.

FOX, ROBERT B., JESÚS T. PERALTA

n.d.   "Preliminary report on the Paleolithic archaeology of Cagayan Valley, Philippines, and the Cabalwanian Industry." Mineographed. Manila: National Museum.

HARRISSON, TOM

1964   100,000 years of Stone Age culture in Borneo. *Journal of the Royal Society of Arts* (February).

HARRISSON, TOM, BARBARA HARRISSON

1969–1970   The prehistory of Sabah. *Sabah Society Journal* 4. Hong Kong: Cathay Press.

HARRISSON, TOM, LORD MEDWAY

1962   A first classification of prehistoric bone and tooth artifacts (based on materials from Niah Great Cave). *Sarawak Museum Journal* 19: 335–362.

LOPEZ, SILVIO

n.d.   "Contributions to the Pleistocene geology of Cagayan Valley, Philippines: I. Geology and paleontology of the Liwan Plain." Mimeograph. Manila: National Museum.

MCCARTHY, F. D.

1967   *Australian aboriginal stone implements, including bone, shell and teeth implements*. Sydney: The Australian Museum.

MOVIUS, H. L., JR.

1948   The Lower Paleolithic cultures of southern and eastern Asia. *Transactions of the American Philosophical Society*, n.s. 38 (4): 329–420.

MULVANEY, D. J.

1961   The Stone Age of Australia. *Proceedings of the Prehistoric Society* 27: 56–107.

1966   The prehistory of the Australian aborigine. *Scientific American* 214 (3): 84–93.

1969   *The prehistory of Australia*. London: Thames and Hudson.

1970   The Patjitanian industry: some observations. *Mankind* 7 (3): 184–187.

SEMENOV, S. A.

1964   *Prehistoric technology: an experimental study of the oldest tools and artifacts from traces of manufacture and wear*. Translated and with a preface by M. W. Thompson. Bath, England: Adams and Dart.

SHUTLER, RICHARD, JR., et al.

1967   *Pleistocene studies in southern Nevada*. Nevada State Museum Anthropological Papers 13.

SIEVEKING, A.

1958   The Paleolithic industry of the Kota Tampan, Perak, northwestern Malaya. *Asian Perspectives* 2 (2): 91–102.

SOLHEIM, WILHELM G., II

1970   *Reworking Southeast Asian prehistory*. Social Science Research Institutes Reprint 34. University of Hawaii. [From *Paideuma*, Band XV, 1969.]

TINDALE, NORMAN B.
   1965   Stone implement making among the Nakako, Ngadadjara and Pit-
          jandjara of the Great Western Desert. *Record of the South Australian
          Museum* 15 (1): 131–164. Adelaide: Government Printer.
VON KOENIGSWALD, G. H. R.
   1956   *Fossil mammals from the Philippines. Special Reprint, National
          Research Council of the Philippines.* Quezon City. [With revisions
          in 1955.]
   1958   Preliminary report on a newly-discovered Stone Age culture from
          northern Luzon, Philippine Islands. *Asian Perspectives* 2 (2): 69–70.
WHITE, J. PETER
   1969   Typologies for some prehistoric flake stone artifacts of the Australian
          New Guinea Highlands. *Archaeology and Physical Anthropology in
          Oceania* 4 (1): 18–46.
   1972   *Ol Tumbuna: Archaeological Excavations in the Eastern Central
          Highlands, Papua, New Guinea.* Terra Australis 2. Department of
          Prehistory, Research School of Pacific Studies, The Australian
          National University.

PART TWO

Continental Southern Asia

Some Problems of the Paleolithic of South and Southeast Asia

P. I. BORISKOVSKY

The Paleolithic of South and Southeast Asia has been studied to varying degrees. There are many blank spots in this field, and in a number of countries which have yielded many Paleolithic sites certain types of Paleolithic remains, such as caves and sites with an undisturbed cultural layer, are lacking. At the same time, some very good progress has been made in Paleolithic investigations in South and Southeast Asia over the last twenty-five years. This is due, to a considerable extent, to the emergence of national research schools in a number of countries which have freed themselves from colonial oppression. In this connection mention should be made primarily of India which has scores of competent Paleolithic researchers. The time is long past when writers about the Paleolithic period in India had to refer only to the summarizing works on India's archaeology, by Piggott, Wheeler and other English researchers. At present, the fundamental works in this field are those by Indian prehistorians (Sankalia 1974; Misra and Mate 1965; and many others). The latter, specifically, have revised critically a number of key propositions established some thirty-five years ago by De Terra and Paterson by their major works in the Punjab (De Terra and Paterson 1939; Subbarao 1958; Joshi 1965). The emergence of the national school of archaeology in what was formerly the Democratic Republic of Vietnam was also an event of great importance. Among its achievements is, first of all, the discovery of a prolific Lower Paleolithic site on Mount Do and caves with bone remains of fossil men.

The development of Paleolithic studies in various countries is a complex and, not infrequently, contradictory process. Thus in France, excavations at individual Paleolithic cave sites were conducted way back in the twenties and thirties of the last century. But the decisive stage came in the middle of the nineteenth century with the discovery of alluvial Lower Paleolithic assemblages in the Somme basin (Abbeville). There was a similar process in the Indochinese peninsula in the twentieth century. Numerous excavations made in the caves in Indochina by Mansuy, Colani, and others failed to discover any distinct archaeological relics older than the Mesolithic or the Hoabinhian (Boriskovsky 1966: 38–40; 1968–1969). And it was only a shift of attention to alluvial sites that helped discover the Lower Paleolithic in the south of Vietnam and in Cambodia (Boriskovsky 1971; Saurin 1969a, 1969b; Carbonnel 1969).

Now we are in a new stage of investigation, and the most important task both for the Indochinese peninsula and for the vast territories of South and Southeast Asia, from Pakistan to Vietnam and Indonesia, is to look for settlements and caves with an undisturbed Paleolithic cultural layer, containing *in situ* bones of fossil animals, remnants of dwellings, hearths and occupation sites, as well as specimens fit for assigning absolute age by the C^{14} technique. Such remains are extremely rare there. But the probability that they may be discovered is very high. Very significant in this respect was the discovery of an Acheulian occupation site at Chirki near Nevasa (Maharashtra) in 1967, the first site of this type ever found in the territory of India (Corvinus 1968, 1968–1969). It is also significant that the first radiocarbon dates are beginning to appear for the Stone and Bronze Ages of Indochina. In addition to C^{14} dates for Cambodia's Neolithic (Carbonnel and Delibrias 1968; Mourer 1970), several C^{14} dates for Neolithic and Bronze Age relics in Vietnam were established by the laboratory of the Leningrad Branch of the Archaeology Institute, the Academy of Sciences of the USSR, in 1971.[1]

In agreements with V. P. Alekseev (1964) and M. F. Nesturkh (1964), we believe that the territories of India and Pakistan probably lay within the bounds of the cradle of mankind. This is indicated by the following facts: (1) Numerous remains of Upper Tertiary anthropoids, specifically the Pliocenic *Ramapithecus* and the Pliocenic *Gigantopithecus*, have been discovered in the Siwalik. (2) In the same area, the remains of numerous big mammals of the Upper Tertiary period and the Lower and Middle Pleistocene have been discovered, and there have been similar finds in the Middle Pleistocene deposits of the Narmada basin and apparently the Godavari basin. These finds indicate that there were favorable conditions for the life and development of our ancestors at the end of the Tertiary and the beginning of the Quaternary periods. Some of the animals were, perhaps, hunted by men. (3) Numerous stone tools of the early stages

[1]   These C^{14} dates were prepared for publication by the Institute of Archeology, in what was formerly the Democratic Republic of Vietnam.

of the Lower Paleolithic have been found in the Siwalik Hills and further south in India. (4) A variety of landscapes, both mountainous and steppe, existed in the Siwalik Hills and to the south of them at the end of the Tertiary period and the beginning of the Quaternary period. This variety was a factor that contributed to the development of ancestral primates into prehistoric men.

We believe that the absence of the discovery of bone remains of Paleolithic man in the territory of Pakistan and India is a temporary thing and that such remains will be found there in due course. As to Southeast Asia, indications of its being part of the cradle of mankind are still more convincing. Remains of Paleolithic man of different times have been found in Java, Kalimantan (Niah), and in the east of the Indochinese peninsula. In comparison with Africa, only K/Ar dates which prove the antiquity of the human race are now missing there. We agree with researchers who believe that primates developed into prehistoric men in the process of their active adaptation to various and changing environmental conditions. It may be assumed that the cradle of mankind was rather vast and included large areas in Africa, southern Europe, southwestern, southern, and southeastern Asia. It is significant that new discoveries of bone remains of our ancestors and exactly dated Lower Paleolithic sites make us push back again and again the boundaries of what we believe was the original cradle of mankind.

At present the following stages have been outlined with a fair degree of certainty in the development of the Paleolithic culture in the territory of India and Pakistan (Boriskovsky 1971).

1. The first stage is the ancient period corresponding to the pre-Chellean or the Oldowan culture, represented by the Mahadevian finds on the Narmada River (Khatri 1963), and the pre-Soanian of the Punjab dating back approximately to the Mindel time. Also in this stage are, perhaps, the recent finds of flake tools in the area of Srinagar dated by Sankalia to the Lower Pleistocene, the first Inter-glacial period, i.e. the pre-Mindel time (Sankalia 1971).

2. The stage corresponding to the Lower Acheulian (Abbeville, Chelles) and the Middle and Upper Acheulian is characterized by numerous stone artifacts found in different parts of Pakistan and India and dated to the Chellean–Acheulian, the Madras culture, and the early Sohanian.

3. The Middle Paleolithic of India (including the Late Soanian of Pakistan) corresponds to the Mousterian of the Middle East but is not "the Mousterian of India and Pakistan." Some of the finds of the Ratnapur culture in Ceylon apparently belong to this stage. Only an insignificant portion of these artifacts persists into the Upper Paleolithic.

4.   The Upper Paleolithic is represented so far by only a few sites, particularly the assemblages near Renigunta (Andhra Pradesh) (Murty 1968).

The earliest, Oldowan, stage is little known. There are few pre-Soanian stone artifacts and they do not differ greatly from those of the Early Soanian which replace them, except for their context. More distinctive are Mahadevian tools made from big quartzite pebbles fifteen to twenty-five centimeters across. There are no typical hand-axes among them. They include crude pebble tools, resembling the Oldowan and bearing few traces of strokes, as well as crude choppers associated with them. Both have a zigzag working edge. Chopping tools occur from time to time. Cores are primitive and are close to pebble tools and choppers with few signs of chipping. Striking platforms are not trimmed. Flake tools correspond to cores; they are massive and have large, high-angle, plain striking platforms. There is a very ancient complex recalling the Oldowan culture. This is the beginning of the Lower Paleolithic of South Asia. Mahadevian complexes are sometimes overlapped by the later stone tool complexes belonging to the Lower, Middle, and Upper Acheulian.

The second stage is represented, first of all, by the Early Soanian of the Punjab which is characterized by a wide distribution of choppers and chopping tools made from river pebbles. But now it may be considered firmly established that handaxes and cleavers also occurred in the Early Soanian (Graziosi 1964). In some places they predominated, but at most of the Early Soanian sites they were comparatively rare while choppers and chopping tools were prevalent. The dominance of the latter and the small role of handaxes and cleavers are typical of the Lower Paleolithic of the Punjab and make it different from the Lower Paleolithic of many other countries. Thus the Early Soanian of the Punjab is not identical with the Lower Paleolithic of South India (Madras culture), nor does it differ sharply from the latter. The Lower Paleolithic assemblages found in the suburbs of Madras (Attirampakam, Wadamadurai, etc.) yield, apart from handaxes and cleavers which are the dominant types there, a profusion of choppers and chopping tools which are in no way different from Soanian artifacts of the same type. Like the Early Soanian, the Madras culture is characterized by a great number of primitive non-Levalloisian flake tools, the role of which is often underestimated in the Lower Paleolithic of India. By and large, it would be wrong to speak of the Lower Paleolithic culture of the Soanian as the one lacking handaxes and cleavers, or of the Lower Paleolithic Madras culture as the one having only handaxes and cleavers and no choppers or chopping tools. The discoveries made in recent years in Vietnam (Mount Do) and the Mongolian People's Republic (see Okladnikov, this volume) show that Lower Paleolithic handaxes are widely distributed in various parts of Asia. In Kazakhstan where a number of Lower Paleolithic sites have been studied (Alpysbaev 1961), choppers and chopping tools reminiscent of the Early Soanian are found in quantity in south Kazakhstan while handaxes are rare and not typical. But in central Kazakhstan, in the area of Balkhash Lake, distinctive Lower Paleolithic handaxes occur in considerable numbers.

Generally, the concept concerning the existence of two vastly different cultures or culture provinces in the Lower Paleolithic – (1) handaxe culture and then the Levallois technique, and (2) the chopper/chopping-tool culture and pebble-tool culture in general – which persisted up to the Upper Paleolithic, or even to the Neolithic, is a rather schematic one. The above-indicated facts about the Lower Paleolithic in different parts of Asia do not fit into this scheme. Lower Paleolithic assemblages of the same age in different parts of Asia, specifically those in India and Pakistan, are not homogeneous. But this is an unstable, amorphous variety.

The third stage, the Middle Paleolithic of India (Nevasian culture) differs greatly from the Mousterian culture which is distributed in the territory of Soviet Central Asia, Afghanistan, Iran, and other countries lying to the west and northwest of Pakistan and India. There is a case for contraposition. Typological differences between them are much sharper than those between the Early Soanian or the Madras culture and the Lower Paleolithic assemblages of neighboring areas contemporary with them. Here are some traits of the Middle Paleolithic of India.

We consider it inadvisable to refer to it as the Middle Stone Age and, generally, we consider it wrong to apply the Stone Age chronology of southern Africa to India. We believe that such an extension of terminology separates the Paleolithic of India from that of Central Asia, the Middle East, Europe, and North Africa and renders difficult comparison between the Paleolithic of India and the Paleolithic of these countries. At the same time it should be stressed that the Middle Paleolithic of India and Pakistan is not "the Mousterian culture of India and Pakistan." A large number of the flake tools of the Middle Paleolithic of India have plain, unfaceted, high-angle striking platforms. Typical Mousterian and Levalloisian flake tools are also found; small slabs, splinters, and flat pebbles were also widely used, along with flakes, for tool manufacture. Core forms vary widely including discoical as well as Levalloisian and tortoise ones. The tools of this period lack definite form and typical features, and they do not occur in distinctive series of repetitious objects. Aterian points mentioned in some of the works of the Stone Age in India are also absent. The only artifacts present are triangular pointed flakes with small irregular retouching that does not shape the tool edge and the associated borers. These pointed flakes exhibit different striking platforms – large unfaceted high-angle or faceted, right-angle types, striking platforms which lack definite form, etc. Scrapers seem to have a greater affinity with the Mousterian type. The assemblages also include pièces écaillées as well as small bifaces, choppers, and chopping tools. Cleavers are absent. Thus, stone tool complexes of the Middle Paleolithic of India differ considerably from the earlier tools of India and Pakistan. At a number of sites, Middle Paleolithic assemblages occur in distinctive stratigraphic conditions which show them to be younger than the Early Soanian and Madras culture and older than Mesolithic microliths.

Like the Aterian of North Africa and the specific Middle Stone Age cultures of South Africa, the Middle Paleolithic of India and Pakistan represents an original Paleolithic culture. With the present level of our knowledge we can single out in the Middle Paleolithic of India and Pakistan only one local group of assemblages differing considerably from others which are contemporary with it. It is the Late Soanian of the Punjab. It combines two elements which are sometimes opposed to each other: first, a considerable number of large pebble choppers and chopping tools and, second, a considerable number of typical Levalloisian flake tools and cores. Choppers and chopping tools indicate that the Late Soanian evolved from the Early Soanian of the same area. Such genetic links with preceding sites cannot be traced for the Middle Paleolithic in other parts of India, nor can we trace connections between the Middle Paleolithic of India and the Mousterian culture of any definite areas.

Unlike India's Middle Paleolithic, its Upper Paleolithic, discovered in recent years, exhibits an unmistakable affinity with the Upper Paleolithic of the Middle East. The Zarzi, Shanidar, and Palegawra caves in Iraq demonstrate a particularly close analogy with the Renigunta. No such close analogies are shown by the Kara Kamar of Afghanistan. This is, perhaps, because the corresponding horizons of the Zarzi, Shanidar, and Palegawra sites belong, just as the Renigunta, to the very end of the Upper Paleolithic, whereas the Kara Kamar III industry is much older. It should also be taken into account that the Kara Kamar III industry is represented by very few tools and it is hard to compare it with such much more prolific complexes as the Zarzi and Renigunta. The Samarkand Upper Paleolithic site with its original and numerous stone artifacts exhibits no affinity with the Renigunta.

The temporal placement of the Renigunta in the Upper Paleolithic compels a revision of a number of less distinctive Indian assemblages found earlier in the districts of Kurnool and Guntur (Andhra Pradesh), in the area of Aurangabad and in the vicinity of Nevasa and Bombay (Maharashtra) as well as Singhbhum (in the south of Bihar state). All or some of them apparently can be referred to the Upper Paleolithic.

There is no reason now to class Pakistan and India with territories where choppers, chopping tools, handaxes, and the Mousterian and Levalloisian techniques of flaking and working stone persisted throughout the Paleolithic up to the Mesolithic Age. The Upper Paleolithic of India, intervening between the Middle Paleolithic of India and Mesolithic microliths and based on prismatic cores and narrow elongated parallel-facet blades, has been established rather firmly. But what about Indochina? The Late Anyathian of Burma, dated to the Upper Pleistocene, closely resembles the Lower Paleolithic Early Anyathian of Burma. The Upper Paleolithic stone tools from Niah cave (Kalimantan) also bear a close resemblance to the Lower Paleolithic of Southeast Asia. Is this similarity enough to claim that the extreme southeastern frontier of distribution of Upper Paleolithic technique with its prismatic cores, elongated blades, burins as well as blades and points with blunted backs, runs somewhere between India and Burma? Can it be claimed that in Southeast Asia the Hoabinhian Mesolithic culture was evolved directly from complexes recalling Lower Paleolithic ones but dated to the Upper Paleolithic? We think that there is still too little material for final conclusions on these questions. Indeed, the impression is that a far more complex intermingling of cultures took place. In India, the Hoabinhian Mesolithic culture with its large chipped pebble tools is absent while the Mesolithic is characterized by microliths which exhibit traits of genetic relation to the local Upper Paleolithic of Renigunta type. The Hoabinhian was not known in Burma until quite recently when a cave site was excavated in the territory of the Shan state, which yielded large chipped stone tools that may be compared with the Hoabinhian and Bacsonian of central and eastern Indochina (U Aung Thaw 1973). Geometric microliths are also unknown in Burma where the Late Anyathian is overlain by the Neolithic which contains, apart from pottery and ground stone implements, also hand adzes and scrapers of fossil wood reminiscent of the Late Anyathian, as well as small oval scrapers, burins, elongated blade tools, and prismatic cores (Movius 1943) which exhibit some traits in common with the Upper Paleolithic and microliths of India. On the territory of central and eastern Indochina, microliths are totally absent while many Hoabinhian caves and sites with large pebble tools have been discovered. Elongated parallel-facet microblades occur only in the Hoabinhian assemblage of Sai-Yok rock-shelter in Thailand (van Heekeren and Knuth 1967). Elongated blades and cores from which they were flaked are found also in the Upper Neolithic of Nhommalat grotto in Laos and the Bau Tro shell heap in Vietnam (Saurin 1952). But typical microliths made from such blades are absent there. On the other hand, geometric microliths and the closely associated pigmy stone tools are widely distributed in Ceylon as well as in the islands of the Malayan Archipelago, specifically in Sulawesi (Toalian culture) (van Heekeren 1957; Allchin 1966). Their distribution there was probably linked with movements by sea and diffusion of cultural elements from island to island. In the mainland countries of Indochina, just as in the south of China, the functions of microliths could be fulfilled, to a considerable extent, by bamboo splinters and spokes. Thus, there emerges a rather complex picture involving processes of intermingling of various cultures.

REFERENCES

ALEKSEEV, V. P.
1964   "Antropologicheskij sostav naselenija Drevnei Indii [The anthropological composition of the population of ancient India]," in *Indija v drevnosti*. Moscow: Nauka.
ALLCHIN, B.
1966   *The stone-tipped arrow: Late Stone Age hunters of the tropical Old World*. New York: Barnes and Noble.
ALPYSBAEV, KH. A.
1961   Otkrytie pamjatnikov drevnego i pozdnego paleolita v Juzhnom Kazakhstane [The discovery of Old and Late Paleolithic monuments in Southern Kazakhstan]. *Sovetskaja Arkheologija* 1: 28–138.
BORISKOVSKY, P. I.
1966   *Pervobytnoe proshloe V'etnama* [The primitive past of Vietnam]. Leningrad: Nauka.
1968–1969   Vietnam in primeval times (part II). *Soviet Anthropology and Archaeology* 7 (3): 10–11.
1971   *Drevnij kamennyi vek Juzhnoj i Jugo-Vostochnoj Azii* [The ancient Stone Age of South and Southeast Asia]. Leningrad: Nauka.
CARBONNEL, J. P.
1969   Quaternaire de la péninsule Indochinoise. *Etudes françaises sur le Quaternaire. Présentées à l'occasion du VIIIe Congrès International de l'INQUA*. Paris.
CARBONNEL, J. P., G. DELIBRIAS
1968   Premières datations absolues de trois gisements néolithiques cambodgiens. *Comptes rendus de l'Académie des Sciences*, serie D, 267: 1432–1434. Paris.
CORVINUS, GUDRUN K.
1968   An Acheulian occupation floor at Chirki-on-Pravara. *Current Anthropology* 9 (2–3): 216–218.
1968–1969   Stratigraphy and geological background of an Acheulian site at Chirki-on-Pravara. *Anthropos* 63/64: 921–940.
DE TERRA, H., T. T. PATERSON
1939   *Studies on the Ice Age in India and associated human cultures*. Carnegie Institution Publication 493: 313–323. Washington, D.C.

GRAZIOSI, P.
 1964 *Prehistoric research in North-Western Punjab*. Leiden: Brill.
JOSHI, R. V.
 1965 Acheulian succession in Central India. *Asian Perspectives* 8 (1): 150–163.
KHATRI, A. P.
 1963 Mahadevian: an Oldowan pebble culture in India. *Asian Perspectives* 6: 186–197.
MISRA, V. N., M. S. MATE, *editors*
 1965 *Indian prehistory: 1964*. Poona: Deccan College Postgraduate and Research Institute.
MOURER, R., C. MOURER
 1970 The prehistoric industry of Laang Spean. *Archaeology and Physical Anthropology in Oceania* 5 (2): 128–145.
MOVIUS, H. L.
 1943 The Stone Age of Burma: researches on Early Man in Burma. *Transactions of the American Philosophical Society*, n.s. 32 (1): 341–393.
MURTY, M. L. K.
 1968 Blade and burin industries near Renigunta. *Proceedings of the Prehistoric Society* 34: 83–99.
NESTURKH, M. F.
 1964 "Problema pervonachal'noj prarodiny chelovechstva [The problem of the original homeland of mankind]," in *U istokov chelovechestva*. Moscow: University of Moscow.
SANKALIA, H. D.
 1971 New evidence for early man in Kashmir. *Current Anthropology* 12 (4–5): 558–562.
 1974 *Prehistory and protohistory of India and Pakistan*. Poona: Deccan College Postgraduate and Research Institute.
SAURIN, E.
 1952 Station néolithique avec outillage en silex à Nhommalat (Cammon, Laos). *Bulletin de l'Ecole Française d'Extrême-Orient*. Paris–Hanoi.
 1969a Regional reports. Cambodia, Laos, Vietnam. *Asian Perspectives* 9: 32–35.
 1969b Le paléolithique du Cambodge Oriental. *Asian Perspectives* 9: 96–110.
SUBBARAO, B.
 1958 *The personality of India*. Baroda: Maharaja Sayajirao University.
U AUNG THAW
 1973 The Neolithic culture of the Padah-lin caves. *Asian Perspectives* 14: 123–133.
VAN HEEKEREN, H. R.
 1957 *The Stone Age of Indonesia*. Verhandelingen van het Koninklijk Instituut voor Taal-, Land-, en Volkenkunde 21. The Hague: Martinus Nijhoff.
VAN HEEKEREN, H. R., EIGIL KNUTH
 1967 "Archaeological excavations in Thailand, I: Sai-Yok," in *Stone Age settlements in the Kanchanaburi province*. Copenhagen: Munksgaard.

The Early Paleolithic
in India and Pakistan

H. D. SANKALIA

Despite the fact that considerable work in the various phases of the Stone Age has been done in India and Pakistan since 1939 (particularly since 1947) and has been published in readily available forms (e.g. Sankalia 1963), it appears, from the writings on world prehistory by leading Western archaeologists (cf. Clark 1962; Bordes 1968; Cole and Higgs 1968), that little of this work is known outside these countries. In recent years, however, this oversight or neglect has been to a great extent remedied by scholars like Allchin and Allchin (1968), Boriskovsky (1971), Clark (1969), and Fairservis (1971). In this paper, we have the opportunity to present an up-to-date account of Paleolithic studies in India and Pakistan, with special reference to the Early Paleolithic.

Publication of the work of De Terra and Paterson in the Punjab (now in Pakistan) and Kashmir in 1939 gave real impetus to the revival of Paleolithic studies in India. The University of Calcutta, the Archaeological Survey of India, and Deccan College initiated study, based on earlier work in Orissa (Bose and Sen 1948), and North Gujarat (Sankalia 1942, 1943a, 1946a, 1946b). Deccan College then took up investigation in the Godavari Valley, Maharashtra (Sankalia 1943b), while continuing its work in Gujarat. Zeuner (1950) tried to relate both of these investigations to climatic phases. R. V. Joshi (1955), while a student at Deccan College, then examined the Malaprabha and Ghataprabha basins in Karnataka. This was followed by the work of Banerjee (1957), which for the first time recognized the Middle Paleolithic character of the industries in Karnataka (these had been found earlier by Sankalia [1956b] at Nevasa in the Pravara Valley in Maharashtra).

Khatri (1957, 1958b), as a student at Deccan College, surveyed the

Shivna and other rivers of western Madhya Pradesh, using clues supplied by Wakankar (1956). Other districts of this large state were carefully investigated by two other students of Deccan College, R. Singh (1965) and Ahmad (1966). Since then, sporadic discoveries have been made.

Northern Orissa was explored by Mohapatra (1962), while Misra (1961, 1962a, 1962c, 1964, 1965; Misra and Nagar 1963) explored eastern and western Rajasthan; the initial discovery at Nathdwara was made by Sankalia (1956a).

Later Murty (1966), Rao (1966), K. T. Reddy (1968), and V. R. Reddy (1968) surveyed the Chittoor, Nalgonda, Cuddappa, and Anantpur districts respectively of Andhra Pradesh. The district of Kurnool was intensively examined by Isaac (1960), where the pioneering work has been done by Burkitt and Cammiade (1930). Paddayya (1968a) confined his attention to the Shorapur Doab in the district of Gulbarga, Karnataka State, and is currently excavating a camp-*cum*-factory site near Hungsi in the same district.

In Maharashtra and Karnataka, Pappu (1974) took up the survey of the Upper Krishna, and Rajaguru (1970) began a systematic geochronological survey of the Mula-Mutha with the initial discoveries at Poona having been made by Sankalia (1966).

Lele (1972) has tried to tackle the question of the presence of early man in Saurashtra, raised by Sankalia's discovery at Rojdi (1965), by studying the sea levels in relation to the Bhadar Stone Age sequence.

The University of Calcutta's Department of Anthropology has completely explored the district of Singhbhum, Bihar (Ghosh 1970), extending its survey into other districts in that state and into the adjoining districts of West Bengal (Ghosh 1961b). There a promising and rich site has been discovered at Susunia by the Directorate of Archaeology of West Bengal (Dasgupta et al. 1973). It has also discovered other sites in the districts of Bankura, Burdwan, Midnapore, and Purulia (Dasgupta et al. 1968, 1971).

The Department of Archaeology of the University of Allahabad has devoted its attention since about 1960 to the districts of Allahabad, Banda, and Mirzapur in Uttar Pradesh. In these areas, very rich, but as yet only briefly reported, discoveries have been made in the valleys of the Belan and the Ganga (G. R. Sharma et al. 1971, 1973). Deposits from the former area have also yielded numerous animal fossils which are said to be Middle Pleistocene in character. The river deposits on the Belan have been chemically and petrologically analyzed by Mujumdar and Rajaguru (1970).

The University of Benaras, Varanasi, surveyed a small area in Banda District in Uttar Pradesh and reported the existence of pebble tools only (Pant 1964).

Traces of early man and his successors have been found further eastwards near Rajgir and Bhimbandh in Bihar (R. G. P. Singh 1959). These areas are islands in the vast alluvial plains of the Ganga and its tributaries. Assam (now split up into the states of Kamarupa, Meghalaya, and Arunachal), which was hitherto supposed to be out-of-bounds for early man and his successors until the advent of food production (Neolithic) has, because of the efforts of the teachers and students of the University of Gauhati (Goswamy and Sharma 1968), yielded tools of the Early, Middle, and Upper Paleolithic.

In the tiny state of Manipur, three caves have been found near Khang Khui village, eleven kilometers southeast of Ukhrul town. These have yielded a unique type of chopper, a handaxe, and artifacts of a later period (O. K. Singh 1971).

Mehta and his colleagues of the University of Baroda have discovered tools of the Early, Middle, and Late Paleolithic periods in a small stream site at Champaner, District Panchmahal (Mehta et al. 1971).

In the south, the University of Mysore explored Kibbanhalli and other sites, and the earlier work of Foote was reexamined (Seshadri 1956).

While working for the Archaeological Survey of India, Krishnaswami (1947) summarized the work done up to that time. Later he, Soundara Rajan, and other officers explored for the first time parts of south Uttar Pradesh (Krishnaswami and Soundara Rajan 1951), Bihar, and West Bengal (Krishnaswami et al. 1960). Lal (1956) reported on the discovery of stone tools in the Kangra Valley (in what is now Himachal Pradesh), and the region was later examined by a joint expedition of the Archaeological and Geological Survey and Deccan College in 1958 (Lal et al. 1958). Further investigations into the same area were conducted by Mohapatra (1966) and R. V. Joshi (1968). Since then, sporadic discoveries have been made by R. K. Pant (1971, 1973) and other officers of the Archaeological Survey. Recently (1974), a joint expedition of Deccan College and the Geological Survey of India discovered tools in the Saketi area in the Markanda Valley, Himachal Pradesh (R. V. Joshi, personal communication).

Systematic studies of the rivers of Damoh and other districts of Madhya Pradesh were conducted by R. V. Joshi (1961). Soundara Rajan (1958) and his colleagues began a similar study of the Krishna river at Nagarjunakonda, Guntur District, Andhra Pradesh. He also published a detailed study of the industry at Giddalur in District Kurnool (Soundara Rajan 1952). Both these studies were later followed up by a critical appraisal of the pebble, core, and flake cultures of the Indian subcontinent (Soundara Rajan 1961).

Several other officers of the Survey have occasionally reported the existence of stone tools in the districts of Arunachal Pradesh (formerly part of Assam), Andhra Pradesh, Madhya Pradesh, Maharashtra, Gujarat, Karnataka (formerly Mysore) and Tamil Nadu (formerly Madras). These have been listed with the references to this paper, but attention may be drawn in particular to the works of Bopardikar (1970, 1972, 1973a, 1973b), Chitale (1968, 1971, 1973), and Sali (1965, 1967, 1970, 1973a, 1973b).

While many of these discoveries were made during the process of exploring new areas, those made in Gujarat by Deccan College and the Archaeological Survey of India in 1941 were initiated with a more specific aim in mind: that of resolving the question of the hiatus between the Paleolithic and Neolithic posed by Robert Bruce Foote in the last century (Sankalia 1942, 1946b). Similarly, the Council of Scientific and Industrial Research sponsored M. R. Sahni's plan to try to find the relics of early man himself. Under this scheme A. P. Khatri and later Gudrun Corvinus explored the Narbada and Pravara-Godavari rivers respectively. Though Khatri made large collections of Early Stone Age tools and animal fossils from the Narbada and its tributaries, publishing several articles on these finds, man himself continues to elude us (Khatri 1961, 1962, 1963, 1966a, 1966b, 1966c).

Corvinus, following clues from earlier work at Nevasa (Sankalia 1956b; Sankalia et al. 1960), was entrusted with a survey of the Pravara from its source and discovered a rich site on the Chirki Nala, near Nevasa itself. This was dug under the Council of Scientific and Industrial Research scheme mentioned above, first by Corvinus (1970) and later by Ansari and Pappu (1973a). But except for a rich hoard of mint-fresh tools – handaxes, cleavers, and a few other implements – no trace of early man was found. Similar results were found at the excavations under this scheme near Betamcharla, District Kurnool, Andhra Pradesh, conducted by Murty – though these gave evidence for the first time of bone tools and animal fossils of the Upper Paleolithic period in India (Murty 1974).

In 1964–1965 the University of California at Berkeley, under the late Professor T. D. McCown, explored the Narbada intensively between Hoshanghabad and Narsinghpur in Madhya Pradesh with a similar aim, i.e. that of discovering the campsite of early man. During this survey the question was also raised whether the deposits on the Narbada were all alluvial, or if some were not also colluvial, and if the latter were true, what were the sources. Unfortunately, I have seen no report, even a preliminary one, on this excellent fieldwork (probably because the project was abandoned after the sudden death of McCown).

All this work, part of which was well planned, and the rest of which was sporadic, has not only helped fill up the Paleolithic map of India and Pakistan, but has brought to light the existence of three other Stone Age cultures, i.e. the Middle Paleolithic, Upper Paleolithic, and Mesolithic (Sankalia 1963, 1964a, 1970a, 1972, 1974, 1975). Whereas in 1939 we knew only of the Stone Age sites on the Indus, Haro, and the Soan Valleys (all now in Pakistan), a few on the Narbada, and some on the southeast coast of India (De Terra and Paterson 1939), now there is virtually no area in India where Early Paleolithic tools have not been found, although the absence of the true handaxe on the western coast from Bombay in the north to Kanyakumari in the south is notable. This might be due to the fact, as is discussed elsewhere while dealing with the Middle Paleolithic, that the entire west coast belongs geologically to the late Quaternary or the Upper Pleistocene period, a fact implied in persistent Indian tradition but only now being proved geologically and archaeologically. Thus we have found no Early Paleolithic tools at Thana, Kolaba Ratnagiri, Goa, Manglore and Kerala, the whole of Kutch and all the four corners of Saurashtra, or at the small peninsulas on the west coast (which were supposed to be under the sea during the Pleistocene). Western Maharashtra was regarded as too thickly forested and lacking suitable raw material for Early Paleolithic tools, but even Arunachal and Meghalaya (both of which are still heavily forested and receive extremely heavy rain for more than six months a year) and the Kashmir Valley proper (at a height of 7,000 feet) have yielded such tools (Sankalia 1974).

This wide distribution of the Early Paleolithic assemblages (see Figure 1) has raised many problems. First, it removes many preconceived notions that certain regions were not congenial for early man's habitation, either because they were too heavily forested and rain-fed or snow-covered; or because they were under the sea; or because they did not possess suitable raw material. Second, almost everywhere two types of tools are found: pebble tools (chopping tools or choppers) and handaxes and cleavers. The most common material for these tools is quartzite, but wherever this was not available, dyke basalt and even ordinary basalt as well as sandstone, limestone, and quartz, were used. The following are the modes of occurrence for these tools (see Plates 1–8):

1. Extra-peninsular India
   a. Kashmir in glacio-fluvial deposits.
   b. Western Punjab (Pakistan) and Eastern Punjab and Himachal Pradesh, Arunachala and Meghalaya in river valleys, usually the middle and upper reaches (the terraces), but not in the plains.
2. Peninsular India
   a. Middle and upper reaches of rivers and streams.

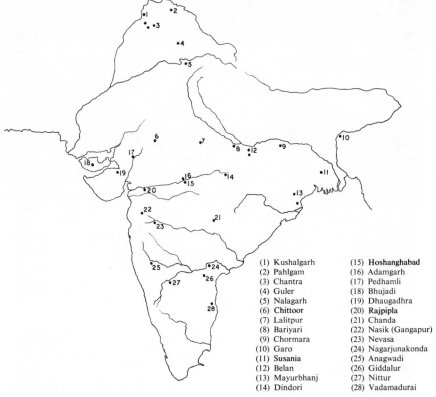

(1) Kushalgarh	(15) **Hoshanghabad**
(2) Pahlgam	(16) Adamgarh
(3) Chantra	(17) Pedhamli
(4) Guler	(18) Bhujadi
(5) Nalagarh	(19) Dhaugadhra
(6) **Chittoor**	(20) **Rajpipla**
(7) Lalitpur	(21) Chanda
(8) Bariyari	(22) Nasik (Gangapur)
(9) Chormara	(23) Nevasa
(10) Garo	(24) Nagarjunakonda
(11) Susania	(25) Anagwadi
(12) Belan	(26) Giddalur
(13) Mayurbhanj	(27) Nittur
(14) Dindori	(28) Vadamadurai

Figure 1.   Distribution of important Early Paleolithic (Early Stone Age) sites in the Indian subcontinent

   b. Foothills with streams.
   c. Caves and rockshelters: Madhya Pradesh, Uttar Pradesh, Manipur, Ratnagiri (Maharashtra).

At Pahlgam in Kashmir (Sankalia 1969c, 1971), as well as at six or seven other sites in the Punjab (Pakistan), pebble tools and large flakes have been found in the Boulder Conglomerate (Paterson and Drummond 1962). At Pahlgam a handaxe was also found at the point at which the Boulder Conglomerate converges with brownish silt (Sankalia 1971; R. V. Joshi et al. 1974), whereas elsewhere pebble tools and flakes were found in gravels or on open terraces assigned to the Third Glacial deposits. Advanced or Acheulian handaxes and cleavers occur in deposits of the Third Interglacial both in Eastern and in Western Punjab (Pakistan) (Paterson and Drummond 1962).

In peninsular India, pebble tools and pebble-butted handaxes generally occur in coarse gravel at some places assignable to the earliest phase of its formation (De Terra and Paterson 1939; Sankalia

Plate 1.   Early Paleolithic choppers and chopping tools from various parts of India

Plate 2.   Early Paleolithic handaxe types from various parts of India: 1–7 and 12–14, pebble-butted; 8–11, with finer workmanship; 15–17, ovates

Plate 3.   Early Paleolithic handaxe types from various parts of India: 1–13, pointed

Plate 4. Early Paleolithic cleaver types from various parts of India: 1–5, straight-edged; 6–11, convex-edged; 12–15, miniature

Plate 5.   Early Paleolithic cleaver types from various parts of India: 1–7, oblique-edged; 8–10, hollow-edged; 11–13, rectangular

Plate 6. Middle Paleolithic tool types from various parts of India: 1–5, scrapers; 6–8, points; 9–11, borers; 12, Levallois core; 13–15, Levallois flakes

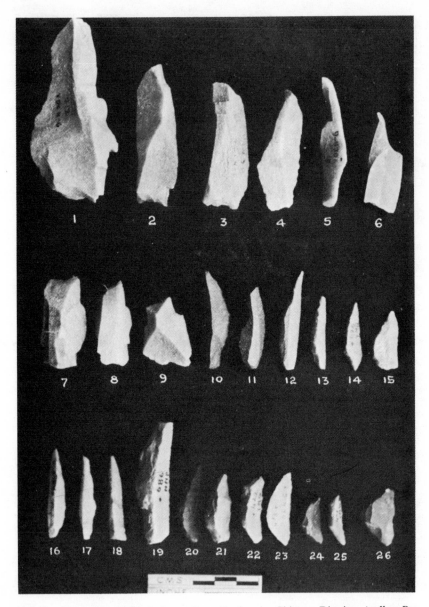

Plate 7.   Upper Paleolithic industry from Renigunta, Chittoor District, Andhra Pradesh: 1–9, burins; 10–18, backed points; 19–21, backed blades; 22–24, crescents; 25–26, triangles

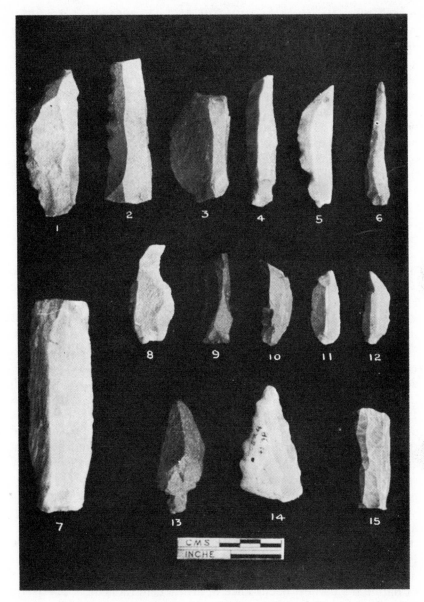

Plate 8. Upper Paleolithic industry from Renigunta, Chittoor District, Andhra Pradesh: 1–3, scrapers; 4–12, simple blades; 13, point; 14, bifacial point; 15, fluted core

1946b, 1952; Krishnaswami 1947; R. V. Joshi 1955; Banerjee 1957; Ansari 1970; Armand 1974), whereas Acheulian handaxes and cleavers are normally found in finer gravel close to the overlying silt (Sankalia 1946b; Krishnaswami 1947; R. V. Joshi 1966a; Murty 1966; Misra 1961; Ghosh 1970; Banerjee 1967; G. R. Sharma 1973). On the basis of this stratigraphical evidence an earlier Abbevillian and later Acheulian phase in the Early Paleolithic might be postulated in peninsular as well as in extra-peninsular India, although some scholars have attempted explanations depicting a more phasewise development in the Acheulian (Ghosh 1971). However, it is quite premature to say that in India there existed a pure Oldowan or pebble-tool phase (Khatri 1963). On the contrary, excavations in the Narbada gravels by Supekar (1968) at Mahadeo Piparia, near Narsinghpur, and Armand (1974) near Navdatoli have shown conclusively that there is no justification for this view, although large percentages of the tools found at both sites were pebbles. Assemblages must be large enough to support a view; they must not consist of only ten or twenty tools. Statistics have value only when the number is fairly large and the assemblages from the excavated sites are comparable.

Something similar to the situation described above is also true of the tools found in the secondary laterite in Orissa (Bose and Sen 1948; Ghosh 1970), Gudiyam cave (Banerjee 1967), and Poondi (Banerjee et al. 1973), Adamgarh (R. V. Joshi 1965) and Bhimbetka (Misra 1975) and open-air factory sites like Lalitpur (R. Singh 1965), Anagwadi (Pappu 1974), Gangapur (R. V. Joshi 1966a), Chirki-Nevasa (Corvinus 1970), and Hungsi (Paddayya, personal communication). Banerjee's excavations (Banerjee et al. 1973) at Poondi and Neyveli have shown that even in the south, around Madras, the handaxe culture is associated with the secondary laterite. Not even its beginnings or early phase can be placed during the formation of the primary laterite, as has been suggested by earlier scholars (Krishnaswami 1947).

The Narbada gravels and, to some extent, the gravels of the Godavari and the Pravara, as well as gravels of a few other rivers like the Belan in Uttar Pradesh might broadly be dated to the Middle Pleistocene period because of the presence of such fossil fauna as *Bos namadicus* and *Elephas antiquus*. At present, we have no other means of dating the earliest occurrence of artifacts in India more precisely. If this dating is accepted, the highly advanced Acheulian handaxes and cleavers would belong to a late phase of the Middle Pleistocene or to an early phase of the Upper Pleistocene, a dating also suggested by glacial studies in Western Punjab (Pakistan) (Paterson and Drummond 1962) and sea-level fluctuations reflected on the Narbada (Wainwright 1964). In any case, this conclusion is true of such rich factory-site assemblages as those of Chirki-Nevasa and Gangapur, where tool types have begun to appear which characterize the Middle Paleolithic. And if we accept a few C^{14} dates for this period from Maharashtra, we place the closing phase of the Early Paleolithic roughly at 50,000 B.P., whereas the earlier phase might extend to circa 100,000 years B.P. or earlier, and the earliest Boulder Conglomerate deposit in Kashmir and the foothills of the Punjab and Himachal Pradesh might be dated at least at 500,000 years B.P. Thus we would make sufficient provision for the Second Interglacial, Third Glacial, and Interglacial periods, or the corresponding cone formations in the Kangra Valley (R. V. Joshi et al. 1970b) in extra-peninsular India.

PROBLEMS RAISED

From this brief description, it should be apparent that the last twenty-five years have raised a number of new problems beyond the question of dating the assemblages:

1. Concerning peninsular India, what has caused such extensive aggradation in the river valleys? These reach almost up to the foothills or to the sources of the rivers. Are the causes climatic, tectonic, or due to rise and fall in sea levels? Were there barriers in the river basins which enclosed small lakes, as for instance at Maheshwar on the Narbada, and Gangapur on the Godavari?

2. Are the two or three erosional phases due to a drop in sea levels, or are they caused by pluvial conditions, or both?

3. With regard to the extra-peninsular region, i.e. West Punjab (Pakistan) and Himachal Pradesh, where pebble tools continue to occur in terrace deposits, should these tools – known generally as choppers and chopping tools – still be regarded as constituting a separate culture? Or should they be considered a part of the general Handaxe Culture?

Similarly the whole problem of the four glacial and three interglacial periods needs to be reexamined. After the discovery at Pahlgam and preliminary study of the moraines and glacio-fluvial deposits in this region, the evidence for four periods of glaciation has been questioned. It is only the tool-bearing glacio-fluvial deposit of Pahlgam which suggests the lowering of the glacial line during the Middle Pleistocene. Moreover, there is only one morainic deposit (R. V. Joshi et al. 1974), whereas in the Kangra Valley the terraces are tectonic and not alluvial (R. V. Joshi et al. 1970b).

With regard to the deposits in peninsular India, is it possible to postulate pluvial and dry phases or merely drier and more humid phases within the Pleistocene? Along the same lines, the discovery of pebble tools and handaxes at the same spot, though in different strata, at Pahlgam in Kashmir, and the discovery of pebble tools at several sites in peninsular India should now make us reconsider the extent to which it is advisable to continue toying with the idea of two separate and distinct cultures: the Soan (chopper/chopping) and the Handaxe. To what degree is it correct to regard the bearers of these cultures as passive vegetarians and warlike nonvegetarians respectively (Paterson and Drummond 1962)? In this connection, the functional study of handaxes and cleavers has shown that while the former might be useful for digging, etc., the latter are useless for felling trees, and all inferences of this nature based on the abundance of cleavers in a collection are, therefore, premature (Zeuner 1963; Sankalia 1964b, 1970b).

As far as the development or evolution of handaxes and cleavers is concerned, broadly speaking two phases may be discerned all over India and Pakistan at present. In the later phases, the tools are largely made of flakes (for instance, Chirki-Nevasa; Gangapur, where the tools are generally made from dyke basalt; Khyad; Mensgi [R. V. Joshi 1955]; Chittoor [Misra 1961]; and Rajpipla [Sankalia 1946b]). These flakes have been removed by proto-Levallois and Levallois techniques (Jayaswal 1973). However, some changes or differences in this broad development are bound to be discerned when larger collections from an excavated site are studied or the collections from several sites in a region are treated statistically (Misra 1967b).

While these details should certainly engage our attention, at the moment what is more intriguing is the broad inference, resulting from his distribution throughout India, that early man was not bothered either by very heavy rain and forests (Meghalaya, south Gujarat) or extreme cold (Kashmir); moreover, aridity or semiaridity, judging from present climatic conditions, would not have caused him any trouble at all! Such an inference can be tested if we succeed in getting pollen samples from various zones and subzones and gain a more precise knowledge about the past climatic conditions. At many places it has been noticed recently that the tools are not only fresh, but also not even patinated. The collections made by Chakrabarti on the Kalubjar, District Bhavnagar, by Corvinus and Pappu at Chirki-Nevasa, and by Misra and Wakankar at Bhimbetka, for instance, would lead us to infer that no major climatic changes have occurred! For such knowledge, the few ill distributed and haphazardly collected fossil fauna are not at all adequate. We have had no fossils from the deposits which have yielded artifacts in Western Punjab (Pakistan), East Punjab, Himachal Pradesh, and Kashmir. This is also the case in South India, Gujarat, Kutch, Saurashtra, and much of Maharashtra. Even in Madhya Pradesh, only a portion of the Narbada between Hoshanghabad and Narsinghpur has yielded fairly rich material.

Unfortunately this material was not well collected in the past so that the exact stratigraphical position of a given sample is questionable. The available information on fossil fauna, therefore, is not sufficient to permit a division of the Indian subcontinent into climatic zones in the Middle and Upper Pleistocene times.

The problem of the origin of the Early Paleolithic culture is still to be considered. While the pebble tools might be left out of consideration – as they do not show completely specialized types – among the handaxes and cleavers each tool could easily be replaced by one from either the Olduvai Gorge collection or from South Africa. If we were to make a comparison based on the emergence of the cleaver types in Africa, it would seem that the Indian industries appeared comparatively late. While the Indian handaxes compare well with the Acheulian in Europe, the cleavers can only be compared with those from Africa. Hence if foreign origin or contact is to be sought, it could only be in or with Africa, where the great antiquity of pebble tools is indisputable (Clark 1969) – but the question is whether the handaxes and cleavers are also very old, dating from, say, 500,000 years B.P. If so, one might postulate a slow diffusion to India from Africa. With the discovery of the Early Paleolithic tools of an advanced type from Kutch and Saurashtra, this is very likely, although so long as Arabia remains unknown, the exact route or direction this diffusion took cannot be indicated. If this was not the case, an independent but slightly later development of the Early Paleolithic culture in India must be envisioned.

Excellent stratigraphical evidence for dating both the Lower and Middle Paleolithic, and for the likely derivation from East Africa and/or West Asia has been found by Shri A. R. Marathe from Umrethi, about 17 kilometers upstream from the Patan, on the Hiran River in Saurashtra. As further examination of the adjacent areas by Dr. S. N. Rajaguru and Marathe showed (see Figure 2), the section would be an early fluvialite deposit capped by about twenty-two meters' deposit of miliolite limestone of marine origin. Over this lies another fluvialite deposit containing tools like points, borers, and scrapers of chert overlain by a three-meter-thick miliolite deposit. Not only do these miliolite deposits provide evidence of two marine transgressions, but when the latter deposit is dated by a C^{14} determination to circa 20,000 B.P., the former could be quite old, dating from 100,000 years B.P. at least. The site is situated in the only surviving lion sanctuary in Asia, and in terms of its situation in relation to East Africa, it is quite possible that there exists in Saurashtra one of the best proofs of early man's migration from Africa when the sea level was low (Rajaguru and Marathe, personal communication).

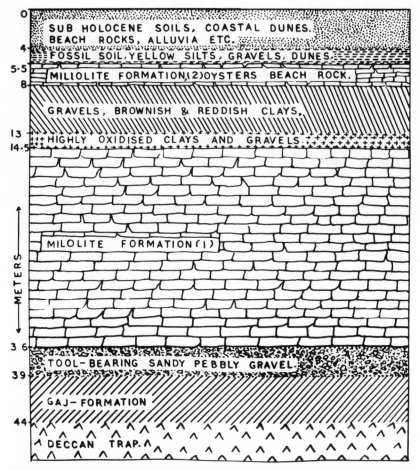

Figure 2.   Schematic section of the quaternary formations in the Hiran Valley

THE SEARCH FOR CAMPSITES

Once the discoveries were made in different parts of India, the question
of evolution naturally engaged the attention of scholars. However, as
in Africa, we are now interested in knowing more about the life of
early man – hence the search for his campsites. These would naturally
be likely to be away from the present riverbanks. Since the Narbada
once abounded with rich animal life between Hoshanghabad and
Narsinghpur, T. D. McCown tried to locate such a campsite there
during 1965. Although the results of this have not been published, I
was associated with this project and was able to learn that prolific
collections were made in the Peera Nala, off Narsinghpur. One of
the important conclusions reached in this work was that the Narbada

had shifted its bed during the Middle Pleistocene and that its gravels were partly formed by colluvial action from the Vindhyan quartzites.

A few years ago, R. Singh (1965) discovered two sites at Lalitpur in Madhya Pradesh. These were undoubtedly factory sites although no further evidence of man's habitation could be obtained.

Another occupation site in Madhya Pradesh was the rockshelter at Adamgarh, where an excavation has uncovered a good sequence of cultures (Joshi 1965).

It appears from the rich collections and my personal observation at Chittoor, at Nagari (eastern Rajasthan), at Sisunia in West Bengal, at Anagwadi, Khyad, and Mensgi (Karnataka), and at numerous sites in Andhra and Tamil Nadu that these were all open factory sites, where a man sat, fashioning tools as needed from the readily available raw material. Excellent evidence of this was found at Gudiyam, District Chingleput, Tamil Nadu, where the entire cave is formed in the conglomerate (Banerjee 1967). However, of all the likely campsites located so far, the site at Chirki-Nevasa has the best claims to being regarded as a factory-*cum*-habitation site. For there, in a very limited area (fifteen by fifteen meters), more than 2,000 tools were found in mint condition (Corvinus 1970). Unfortunately, as the site is on a rock surface close to the river, the debris which one would expect from such a workshop has been washed away. Repeated efforts have failed to trace any contrivance for erecting a windbreak. However, the remains of fossil wood and elephant bones are reason to hope that this and similar sites may be patiently and tenaciously uncovered.

Camp-*cum*-factory sites are presently being excavated by Misra and Wakankar in the rockshelter known as Bhimbetka, near Bhopal in Madhya Pradesh. Clues obtained in 1973 (when this paper was first being written) were followed up with some success in 1974. However, a larger, horizontal excavation appeared to be necessary, and this was being attempted in 1975. It is to be expected, therefore, that very soon Early Paleolithic settlements will be discovered in Madhya Pradesh. Similar searches, in eastern Madhya Pradesh, southwestern Uttar Pradesh, in the present districts of Allahabad and Mirzapur, and elsewhere, should also prove rewarding. For example, a colleague, K. Paddayya, has located a camp-*cum*-factory site near Hunsgi, District Gulbarga in Karnataka. There, within an area of four by five meters, no less than 300 tools, mostly cleavers, have been found. However, just as today there are primitive or preliterate people in India with very few possessions and few recognizable structures, it would be great good luck to come upon any identifiable house remains of early man. But a painstaking and concerted attempt has to be made in different parts of India and Pakistan.

The question will have also to be explored of why these people gave up making large tools and took to forming smaller ones in a different material. Here, if nowhere else, we shall have some justification for postulating the arrival of new influences, biological, cultural, or both (Sankalia 1973, 1974). For at a rockshelter like Adamgarh or Bhimbetka, both in Madhya Pradesh, there is little evidence of any marked climatic change.

REFERENCES*

AGRAWAL, D. P., R. K. AVASIA, S. GUZDER
  1973 "A multidisciplinary approach to the Quaternary problems in Maharashtra," in *Radiocarbon and Indian archaeology*. Edited by D. P. Agrawal and A. Ghosh, 3–17. Bombay: Tata Institute of Fundamental Research.

AHMAD, N.
  1966 "The Stone Age cultures of the Upper Son valley." Unpublished Ph.D. dissertation, Poona University.
  1967 Two Early Stone Age sites on the river Son in District Bilaspur, Madhya Pradesh. *Puratattva* 1: 87–89.
  1969 Stratigraphy, probable climatic phases and dating of Early Stone Age culture of the Upper Son valley. *Puratattva* 2: 41–45.

AIYAPPAN, A., F. P. MANLEY
  1942 The Manley collection of Stone Age tools with topographical and other notes. *Memoirs of the Archaeological Survey of India* 68. New Delhi.

ALLCHIN, B.
  1963 The Indian Stone Age sequence. *Journal of the Royal Anthropological Institute of Great Britain and Ireland* 93 (2): 210–234.

ALLCHIN, B., F. R. ALLCHIN
  1968 *The birth of Indian civilization*. Harmondsworth: Penguin.

ALLCHIN, B., K. T. M. HEGDE
  1971 Exploration in District Broach. *Indian Archaeology: A Review* 1968–69: 8.

ALLCHIN, F. R., et al.
  1968 Explorations in Districts Baroda, Broach and Surat. *Indian Archaeology: A Review* 1967–68: 9–12.

ANSARI, Z. D.
  1970 Pebble tools from Nittur (Mysore State). *Indian Antiquary* 4 (1–4): 1–7.

ANSARI, Z. D., R. S. PAPPU
  1973a Excavation at Chirki, Nevasa. *Indian Archaeology: A Review* 1968–69: 17.
  1973b Stone Age in Kutch, Gujarat. *Bulletin of the Deccan College Research Institute* 32: 149–167.

ARMAND, J.
  1974 Excavations near Navdatoli, District West Nemiar. *Indian Archaeology: A Review* 1970–71: 20–22.

* This list of references includes those which are specifically mentioned in the text, as well as many others which are likely to be useful to the reader. For his assistance in the preparation of this list, I would like to thank Dr. V. N. Misra.

BANERJEE, K. D.
  1957 "Middle Palaeolithic Industries of the Deccan." Unpublished Ph.D.
        dissertation, Poona University.
  1967 Excavations at Gudiyam, District Chingleput. *Indian Archaeology:
        A Review* 1962–63: 12; 1963–64: 33.
BANERJEE, K. D., *et al.*
  1971 Exploration in Districts Chittoor and Nellor and excavation at Bat-
        talavallam. *Indian Archaeology: A Review* 1968–69: 1.
  1973 Excavation at Poondi, and Neyveli, District Chingleput. *Indian
        Archaeology: A Review* 1965–66: 24–25.
BOPARDIKAR, B. P.
  1970 Early Stone Age site at Manegaon on the Purna river, Jalgaon
        District, Maharashtra State. *Indian Antiquary* 4 (1–4): 8–12.
  1972 "Prehistoric investigations – Daphabhum scientific survey expedi-
        tion, NEFA," in *Archaeological congress and seminar papers*. Edited
        by S. B. Deo, 1–8. Nagpur: Nagpur University.
  1973a Excavations in District Lohit. *Indian Archaeology: A Review* 1969–70:
        30.
  1973b Explorations in Districts Akola, Amaroti and Jalgaon. *Indian Arch-
        aeology: A Review* 1965–66: 27.
BORISKOVSKY, P. I.
  1971 *The ancient Stone Age of South and Southeast Asia* [in Russian].
        Leningrad: Nauka.
BORDES, F.
  1968 *Old Stone Age.* London: World University Library.
BOSE, N. K.
  1941 Age of boulder conglomerate at Kuliana, Mayurbhanj. *Anthropo-
        logical papers* n.s. 6. Calcutta: Calcutta University.
BOSE, N. K., D. SEN
  1948 *Excavations in Mayurbhanj.* Calcutta: Calcutta University.
BROWN, J. C.
  1917 *Catalogue of prehistoric antiquities in the Indian Museum, Calcutta.*
        Simla: Government Central Press.
BURKITT, M. C., L. A. CAMMIADE
  1930 Fresh light on the Stone Age in south-east India. *Antiquity* 4: 327–339.
BURKITT, M. C., L. A. CAMMIADE, F. J. RICHARDS
  1932 Climatic changes in south-east India during Palaeolithic times. *Geo-
        logical Magazine* 69.
CHITALE, D. B.
  1968 Exploration in District Surat. *Indian Archaeology: A Review* 1967–68:
        19.
  1971 Exploration in Districts Bulsar and Surat. *Indian Archaeology: A
        Review* 1968–69: 8.
  1973 Exploration in Goa, Daman and Diu. *Indian Archaeology: A Review*
        1965–66: 80.
CLARK, J. G. D.
  1962 *World prehistory – an outline.* Cambridge: Cambridge University
        Press.
  1969 *World Prehistory – a new outline.* Cambridge: Cambridge University
        Press.
COLE, J., E. HIGGS
  1968 *The archaeology of Early Man.* London: Faber and Faber.

CORVINUS, G.
1970   The Acheulian workshop at Chirki on the Pravara river, Maharashtra. *Indian Antiquary* 4 (1–4): 13–22.

DANI, A. H.
1960   *Prehistory and protohistory of eastern India.* Calcutta: Firma K. L. Mukhopadhyay.
1964   Sanghao Cave excavations. *Ancient Pakistan* 1: 1–50.

DASGUPTA, H. C.
1931   Bibliography of prehistoric Indian antiquities. *Journal of the Asiatic Society of Bengal* 17: 1–96.

DASGUPTA, P. C.
1973   Explorations in District Bankura. *Indian Archaeology: A Review* 1965–66: 55.

DASGUPTA, P. C., *et al.*
1968   Exploration in District Purulia. *Indian Archaeology: A Review* 1967–68: 49–50, Plate XXIV.
1971   Exploration in Districts Bankura, Burdwan, Midnapore, Purulia and 24-Pargana. *Indian Archaeology: A Review* 1968–69: 41.
1973   Explorations in Districts Bankura and 24-Pargana. *Indian Archaeology: A Review* 1965–66: 59.

DE TERRA, H.
1937a Cenozoic cycles in Asia and their bearing on Asian prehistory. *Transactions of the American Philosophical Society* 77: 289–308.
1937b "The Siwaliks of India and early man," in *Early Man.* Edited by G. G. MacCurdy, 257–268. London: J. B. Lippincott.

DE TERRA, H., T. T. PATERSON
1939   *Studies on the Ice Age in India and associated human cultures.* Carnegie Institution Publication 493: 313–323. Washington, D.C.

FAIRSERVIS, W. A., JR.
1971   *The roots of ancient India.* London: George Allen and Unwin.

GHOSH, A. K.
1961a Prehistoric studies in ancient India. *Science and Culture* 27: 369–375.
1961b Discovery of prehistoric stone implements from north-west Midnapore, West Bengal. *Science and Culture* 28: 338–339.
1966a "Implementiferous laterite in eastern India," in *Studies in prehistory: Robert Bruce Foote memorial volume.* Edited by D. Sen and A. K. Ghosh, 149–162. Calcutta: Firma K. L. Mukhopadhyay.
1966b "Stone Age cultures of West Bengal." Unpublished P.R.S. thesis, Calcutta University.
1967   Laterite and associated artifact-bearing strata in eastern India. *Proceedings of VIIth INQUA Congress* 9: 146–155.
1970   The Palaeolithic cultures of Singhbhum. *Transactions of the American Philosophical Society* n.s. 60 (1): 1–68.
1971   Ordering of Lower Palaeolithic traditions in South and South-east Asia. *Archaeology and Physical Anthropology in Oceania* 6 (2): 87–101.

GHOSH, A. K., *et al.*
1971a Exploration in Districts Bankura, Birbhum and Midnapore. *Indian Archaeology: A Review* 1968–69: 42.
1971b Exploration in District Mayurbhanj, Orissa. *Indian Archaeology: A Review* 1968–69: 25.
1973   Exploration in District Purulia. *Indian Archaeology: A Review* 1965–66: 58.

GORDON, D. H.
1958 *The prehistoric background of Indian culture.* Bombay: Bhulabhai Memorial Institute.

GOSWAMY, M. C., T. C. SHARMA
1968 Exploration in District Garo Hills. *Indian Archaeology: A Review* 1967–68: 7.

GUPTA, K. P.
1971 Exploration in District Broach. *Indian Archaeology: A Review* 1968–69: 7, Plate IX.

ISAAC, N.
1960 "The Stone Age cultures of Kurnool." Unpublished Ph.D. dissertation, Poona University.

JAYASWAL, V.
1973 "A study of prepared core technique in Palaeolithic cultures of India." Unpublished Ph.D. dissertation, Banaras Hindu University.

JOSHI, J. P.
1973 Early Stone Age site, Pindara, District Jamnagar. *Indian Archaeology: A Review* 1965–66: 80.

JOSHI, J. P., et al.
1968 Exploration in District Kutch. *Indian Archaeology: A Review* 1967–68: 13, Plate VIIIA.

JOSHI, R. V.
1952 High level gravels on the Mahi river. *Journal of the M.S. University of Baroda* 1: 69–72.

1955 *Pleistocene studies in the Malaprabha basin.* Poona and Dharwar: Deccan College and Karnatak University.

1956 Morphological analysis of Malaprabha basin (N. Mysore State), *Bombay Geographical Magazine* 1: 33–39.

1958 Narmada Pleistocene deposits at Maheshwar. *Journal of the Palaeontological Society of India* 3: 201–204.

1961 Stone Age industries of the Damoh area, Madhya Pradesh. *Ancient India* 17: 5–36.

1965 Acheulian succession in Central India. *Asian Perspectives* 8 (1). 150–163.

1966a Animal fossils and Early Stone Age tools from Gangapur on the Godavari river. *Current Science* 35 (13): 344.

1966b Mohagaon Kalan: Middle and Late Stone Age factory site in Central India. *Journal of the M.S. University of Baroda* 15 (1): 49–55.

1966c "Middle Stone Age in India," in *Atti del VI Congresso Internazionale della Science Prehistoriche Protohistoriche.*

1968 Early Stone Age discoveries in the Banganga–Beas region. *Cultural Forum* 9: 96–99.

1969 "Environment and evolution of Stone Age cultures in India, with special reference to the Middle Stone Age cultures," in *The origin of* Homo sapiens. Edited by François Bordes, 96–99. Paris: UNESCO.

JOSHI, R. V., W. CHMILEWSKI, S. ROZISKI
1968 Exploration in Districts Kangra and Mandi. *Indian Archaeology: A Review* 1967–68: 22–23.

1970a Significance of cleavers in Indian Acheulian industries. *Achaeocivilization* n.s., 7–8: 39–46.

1970b The characteristics of the Pleistocene climatic events in the Indian subcontinent – a land of monsoon climate. *Indian Antiquary* (Third series) 4 (1–4): 53–63.

1971a "A note on the Stone Age sites around Pauni, Bhandara District, Maharashtra State," in *Archaeological congress and seminar papers.* Edited by S. B. Deo, 43–46. Nagpur: Nagpur University.

1971b "Stone Age cultures of Konkan (Coastal Maharashtra)," in *Archaeological congress and seminar papers.* Edited by S. B. Deo, 47–51. Nagpur: Nagpur University.

1971c Fossils and Middle Stone Age tools from Nandur–Madhmeshwar on the Godavari river (Nasik District), Maharashtra State. *Current Science* 40 (1): 13–14.

1973a "Pleistocene problems in India," in *Radiocarbon and Indian archaeology.* Edited by D. P. Agrawal and A. Ghosh, 54–58. Bombay: Tata Institute of Fundamental Research.

1973b Exploration and excavation in District Dhulia. *Indian Archaeology: A Review* 1965–66: 29–32.

1973c Quaternary studies in sub-Himalayas. *Bulletin of the Deccan College Research Institute* 33 (1–4): 101–116.

1974 Prehistoric exploration in Katmandu Valley, Nepal. *Ancient India* 22: 75–82.

JOSHI, R. V., *et al.*
1974 Quaternary glaciation and palaeolithic sites in the Liddar valley (Jammu-Kashmir). *World Archaeology* 5 (3): 369–379.

KHARE, M. D.
1973 Early Stone Age tools at and near Bhopal. *Indian Archaeology: A Review* 1965–66: 80.

KHATRI, A. P.
1957 Palaeolithic industries of the river Shivna. *Bulletin of the Deccan College Research Institute* 17: 159–172.

1958a Stone Age tools of the Gambhiri basin. *Journal of the University of Bombay* 26 (4): 35–49.

1958b "Stone Age cultures of Malwa." Unpublished Ph.D. dissertation, Poona University.

1961 Stone Age and Pleistocene chronology of the Narmada Valley (Central India). *Anthropos* 56: 519–530.

1962 Origin and development of Series II culture of India. *Proceedings of the Prehistoric Society* 28: 191–208.

1963 Mahadevian: an Oldowan pebble culture in India. *Asian Perspectives* 6: 186–197.

1964a Recent exploration for the remains of Early Man. *Asian Perspectives* 7: 160–182.

1966a "Origin and evolution of handaxe culture in the Narmada valley (Central India)," in *Studies in prehistory: Robert Bruce Foote memorial volume.* Edited by D. Sen and A. K. Ghosh, 96–121. Calcutta: Firma K. L. Mukhopadhyay.

1966b Prehistoric cultures of Malwa (Central India). *Anthropos* 58: 485–506.

1966c The Pleistocene mammalian fossils of the Narmada river valley and their horizons. *Asian Perspectives* 9: 113–133.

KRISHNASWAMI, V. D.
1947 Stone Age in India. *Ancient India* 3: 11–57.

KRISHNASWAMI, V. D., K. V. SOUNDARA RAJAN
1951 The lithic-tool industries of the Singrauli basin, District Mirzapur. *Ancient India* 7: 40–65.

KRISHNASWAMI, V. D., *et al.*
1960 Explorations in Districts Bankura and Purulia. *Indian Archaeology: A Review* 1959–60: 48.

KUMAR, KRISHNA
  1973   Exploration in District Chatarpur and District Aurangabad and Jalgaon. *Indian Archaeology: A Review* 1965–66: 21 and 30.
LAL, B. B.
  1956   Palaeoliths from the Beas and Banganga valleys. *Ancient India* 12: 58–92.
LAL, B. B., *et al.*
  1958   Exploration in the Banganga valley, District Kangra. *Indian Archaeology: A Review* 1957–58: 43.
LELE, V. S.
  1972   "Late Quaternary studies in the Bhadar valley, Saurashtra." Unpublished Ph.D. dissertation, Poona University.
McCOWN, T. D., *et al.*
  1965   "Explorations in Hoshanghabad and Narsinghpur Districts, Madhya Pradesh." Unpublished report.
MEHTA, R. N., *et al.*
  1971   "Exploration in District Panchmahal Gujavat." Unpublished report.
MISRA, V. N.
  1961   "The Stone Age cultures of Rajputana." Unpublished Ph.D. dissertation, Poona University.
  1962a Palaeolithic industry of the Banas, eastern Rajputana. *Journal of the Asiatic Society of Bombay* 34–35: 138–160.
  1962b Problems of terminology in Indian prehistory. *Eastern Anthropologist* 15 (2): 112–124.
  1962c Palaeolithic culture of western Rajputana. *Bulletin of the Deccan College Research Institute* 21: 85–156.
  1964   Palaeoliths from District Udaipur, Rajasthan. *Journal of the Asiatic Society of Bombay* 36–37: 55–59.
  1965   Govindgarh, a Palaeolithic site in western Rajasthan. *Journal of the Asiatic Society of Bombay* 38: 205–208.
  1966   "Stone Age research in Rajasthan – a review," in *Studies in prehistory: Robert Bruce Foote memorial volume.* Edited by D. Sen and A. K. Ghosh, 122–130. Calcutta: Firma K. L. Mukhopadhyay.
  1967a "Prehistory and protohistory," in *Review of Indological research in the last seventy-five years.* Edited by P. J. Chinmulgund and V. V. Mirashi, 351–425. Poona: Bhartiya Charitra Kosh Mandal.
  1967b *Pre- and proto-history of the Berach Basin, south Rajasthan.* Poona: Deccan College.
  1968   "Middle Stone Age in Rajasthan," in *La préhistoire: problèmes et tendances.* Edited by F. Bordes and D. de Sonneville-Bordes, 295–302. Paris: CNRS.
  1972   "Evolution of Palaeolithic cultures in India," in *The origin of Homo sapiens.* Edited by François Bordes, 116–120. Paris: UNESCO.
MISRA, V. N., M. NAGAR
  1963   Two Stone Age sites on the river Chambal, Rajasthan. *Bulletin of the Deccan College Research Institute* 22: 156–169.
  1973   "Twenty-five years of Indian prehistory," in *Man and society.* Edited by K. S. Mathur and S. C. Varma, 1–54. Lucknow: Ethonographic and Folk Culture Society.
  1975   "The Late Acheulian industry of rock shelter IIIF-23 at Bhimbetka, central India: further analysis of the material." *Puratattva, Bulletin of the Archaeological Society of India.* New Delhi.
MOHAPATRA, G. C.
  1962   *Stone Age cultures of Orissa.* Poona: Deccan College.

1966   Preliminary report on the exploration and excavation of Stone Age sites in eastern Punjab. *Bulletin of the Deccan College Research Institute* 25: 221–230.

MOVIUS, H. L., JR.
1943   The Stone Age of Burma: researches on Early Man in Burma. *Transactions of the American Philosophical Society*, n.s. 32 (1): 341–393.
1948   The Lower Palaeolithic cultures of southern and eastern Asia. *Transactions of the American Philosophical Society*, n.s. 38 (4): 329–420.
1953   "Old World Prehistory: Palaeolithic," in *Anthropology today: an encyclopedic inventory*. Edited by A. L. Kroeber, 163–192. Chicago: University of Chicago Press.
1957   Pebble tool terminology in India and Pakistan. *Man in India* 3 (2): 149–156.

MUJUMDAR, G. G., S. N. RAJAGURU
1970   Investigation of the Pleistocene sediments of the Belan valley. *Indian Antiquary* 4 (1–4): 96–105.

MUJUMDAR, G. G., S. N. RAJAGURU, R. S. PAPPU
1970   Recent Godavari flood and its relevance to pre-historic archaeology. *Bulletin of the Deccan College Research Institute* 29: 118–134.

MURTY, M. L. K.
1966   "Stone Age cultures of Chittoor." Unpublished Ph.D. dissertation, Poona University.
1968   Blade and burin industries near Renigunta on the southeast coast of India. *Proceedings of the Prehistoric Society* 34: 83–101.
1970   Blade and burin and Late Stone Age industries around Renigunta, Chittoor District. *Indian Antiquary* 4 (1–4): 106–127.
1974   A Late Pleistocene cave site in southern India. *Proceedings of the American Philosophical Society* 118 (2): 196–230.

NARASIMHAYYA, B.
1973   Exploration in District Dharampuri and District North Arcot. *Indian Archaeology: A Review* 1965–66: 24.

NARAYAN, B., et al.
1968   Exploration in Districts Gaya and Patna. *Indian Archaeology: A Review* 1967–68: 8.

NAUTIYAL, K. P.
1971   Early and Middle Stone Age Tools in Qwalior, Madhya Pradesh. *Indian Archaeology: A Review* 1968–69: 11.

PADDAYYA, K.
1968a   "Pre- and proto-historic investigations in Shorapur Doab." Unpublished Ph.D. dissertation, Poona University.
1968b   Exploration in District Gulbarga. *Indian Archaeology: A Review* 1967–68: 36–37.
1969   Hagaragundgi: a fossiliferous Middle Stone Age site on the Bhima river. *Journal of the Asiatic Society of Bengal* 11: 12–14.
1970   The blade tool industry of Shorapur Doab. *Indian Antiquary* 4 (1–4): 165–190.
1971a   High level gravels and related Palaeolithic sites in Shorapur Doab. *Quartar* 22: 95–110.
1971b   Explorations in Districts Bijapur and Gulbarga, and explorations in District Mahbubnagar. *Indian Archaeology: A Review* 1968–69: 2, 21.

PANT, P. C.
1964 Some pebble tool industries of Banda. *Bharati, Bulletin of the College of Indology, Varanasi* 7: 4–42.
PANT, R. K.
1971 Explorations in Districts Kaithal, Jammu and Kashmir. *Indian Archaeology: A Review* 1968–69: 9.
1973 Exploration in District Kathua. *Indian Archaeology: A Review* 1965–66: 19.
PAPPU, R. S.
1971a Pleistocene geomorphology of the Upper Krishna basin. *Indian Antiquary* 4: (1–4): 191–204.
1971b Some unusual tool types from Anagawadi, District Bijapur. *Puratattva* 4: 58–62.
1974 *Pleistocene studies in the Upper Krishna basin.* Poona: Deccan College.
PAPPU, R. S., G. CORVINUS
1971 Excavation at Chirki Nala, near Nevasa. *Indian Archaeology: A Review* 1968–69: 13–14.
PAPPU, R. S., *et al.*
1968 Excavation at Chirki Nala, near Nevasa. *Indian Archaeology: A Review* 1967–68: 31.
PATERSON, T. T.
1945 Core, culture and complex in the Old World. *Proceedings of the Prehistoric Society* 11: 1–19.
PATERSON, T. T., H. J. H. DRUMMOND
1962 *Soan, the Palaeolithic of Pakistan.* Karachi: Department of Archaeology, Government of Pakistan.
RAJAGURU, S. N.
1968 "Pleistocene period in southcentral Maharashtra," in *La préhistoire: problèmes et tendances.* Edited by F. Bordes and D. de Sonneville-Bordes, 349–357. Paris: CNRS.
1969 On the Late Pleistocene of the Deccan, India. *Quaternaria* 11: 241–253.
1970 "Studies in the Late Pleistocene of the Mula-Mutha Valley." Unpublished Ph.D. dissertation, Poona University.
1972 "Environment and chronology of Early Man in western Maharashtra," in *The origin of Homo sapiens.* Edited by François Bordes, 101–107. Paris: UNESCO.
1973 "Late Pleistocene climatic changes in western India," in *Radiocarbon and Indian archaeology.* Edited by D. P. Agrawal and A. Ghosh, 80–87. Bombay: Tata Institute of Fundamental Research.
1974 Explorations in District Ratnagiri: Stone Age sites near Malwan. *Indian Archaeology: A Review* 1970–71: 26–27.
RAJAGURU, S. N., G. CORVINUS
1968 Exploration in Districts Nasik, Poona and Satara. *Indian Archaeology: A Review* 1967–68: 34–35.
RAJAGURU, S. N., K. T. M. HEGDE
1972 "The Pleistocene stratigraphy in India," in *Archaeological congress and seminar papers.* Edited by S. B. Deo, 69–80. Nagpur: Nagpur University.
RAJAGURU, S. N., R. S. PAPPU
1971 Environments as reflected in the alluvial deposits of Chirki-Nevasa, District Ahmednagar. *Journal of Poona University* 40: 115–121.

RAO, S. N.
    1966   "Stone Age cultures of Nalgonda." Unpublished Ph.D. dissertation,
           Poona University.
REDDY, K. T.
    1968   "Prehistoric cultures of the Cuddarah district, Andhra Pradesh."
           Unpublished Ph.D. dissertation, Saugor University.
REDDY, V. R.
    1968   "Pre- and proto-history of south-western Andhra Pradesh." Unpub-
           lished Ph.D. dissertation, Poona University.
SALI, S. A.
    1965   The collection of Stone Age lithic tools from Pitalkhora. *Marathwada
           University Journal* 5 (2): 18–22.
    1967   Quaternary stratigraphy in the Kan basin at Bhadne and Yesar:
           results of recent preliminary explorations. *Journal of the Asiatic
           Society of Bombay* 39–40: 157–167.
    1970   Some geomorphic and tectonic observations in the central Tapti
           basin in Dhulia District. *Indian Antiquary* 4 (1–4): 205–215.
    1973a "Direct evidence of Late Pleistocene tectonic movement in the
           central Tapti basin in Maharashtra," in *Radiocarbon and Indian
           archaeology*. Edited by D. P. Agrawal and A. Ghosh, 96–105.
           Bombay: Tata Institute of Fundamental Research.
    1973b Some aspects of the Pleistocene stratigraphy of peninsular India.
           Bulletin of the Deccan College Research Institute 31–32: 70–80.
SANKALIA, H. D.
    1942   In search of Early Man along the Sabarmati. *Journal of the Gujarat
           Research Society* 4: 75–80.
    1943a Pre- and proto-history of Gujarat," in *The glory that was Gurjar-
           desha*. Edited by K. M. Munshi, 12–40. Bombay.
    1943b Studies in prehistory of the Deccan (Maharashtra): a survey of the
           Godavari and the Kadva near Niphad. *Bulletin of the Deccan College
           Research Institute* 4 (3): 186–203.
    1944   The second Gujarat prehistoric expedition. *New Indian Antiquary*
           7: 1–5.
    1945   Studies in prehistory of the Deccan (Maharashtra): a further survey
           of the Godavari (March 1944). *Bulletin of the Deccan College Re-
           search Institute* 6 (3): 131–137.
    1946a A Palaeolithic handadze from the Sabarmati valley. *Journal of the
           University of Bombay* 4: 8–10.
    1946b *Investigations into prehistoric archaeology of Gujarat*. Baroda:
           Baroda State.
    1952   *The Godavari palaeolithic industry*. Poona: Deccan College.
    1956a Nathdwara, a Palaeolithic site in Rajputana. *Journal of the Palae-
           ontological Society of India* 1: 99–100.
    1956b Animal fossils and Palaeolithic industries from the Pravara basin at
           Nevasa, District Ahmednagar. *Ancient India* 12: 35–52.
    1963   *Prehistory and protohistory in India and Pakistan*. Bombay: Bombay
           University Press.
    1964a Middle Stone Age culture in India and Pakistan. *Science* 146 (3642):
           365–375.
    1964b *Stone Age tools: their techniques, names and probable functions*.
           Poona: Deccan College.
    1965   "Early Stone Age in Saurashtra, Gujarat," in *Mescelánea en home-
           naje al Abate Henri Breuil*. Edited by E. Ripoll Perelló, vol. 2, pp.

327–346. Barcelona: Diputación Provincial de Barcelona, Instituto de Prehistoria y Argueología.

1966   "Early Stone Age in Poona," in *Studies in prehistory: Robert Bruce Foote memorial volume.* Edited by D. Sen and A. K. Ghosh, 77–89. Calcutta: Firma K. L. Mukhopadhyay.

1969a   Problems in Indian archaeology and methods and techniques adopted to tackle them. *World Archaeology* 1 (1): 29–39.

1969b   Prehistoric man and primitives in south Gujarat and Konkan. *Journal of the Anthropological Society of Bombay* 12: 34–38.

1969c   Early man in Ice Age Kashmir. *Science Today* (December): 16–26.

1970a   "The Middle Palaeolithic cultures of India, central and western Asia and Europe," in *Central Asia.* Edited by A. Guha, 25–53.

1970b   The human and functional approach in archaeology. *Proceedings of the 157th Indian Sciences Congress,* vol. 2, pp. 181–194.

1971   New evidence for Early Man in Kashmir. *Current Anthropology* 12 (4–5): 558–562.

1972   "The Middle Palaeolithic cultures of India, central and western Asia and Europe," in *The origin of Homo sapiens.* Edited by François Bordes, 109–113. Paris: UNESCO.

1973   Prehistoric colonisation in India. *World Archaeology* 5 (1): 86–91.

1974   *Prehistory and protohistory of India and Pakistan.* Poona: Deccan College Postgraduate and Research Institute.

1975   *Prehistory in India.* Delhi: Munshiram Manoharlal.

SANKALIA, H. D., A. P. KHATRI
1957   The Stone Age cultures of Malwa. *Journal of the Palaeontological Society of India* 2: 183–189.

SANKALIA, H. D., B. SUBBARAO, R. V. JOSHI
1951   Studies in prehistory of the Karnatak. *Bulletin of the Deccan College Research Institute* 11: 56–82.

SANKALIA, H. D., *et al.*
1958   *Excavations at Mahashwar and Navdatoli.* Poona and Baroda: Deccan College and M.S. University.

1960   *From history to prehistory at Nevasa (1954–56).* Poona: Deccan College.

1968   Exploration in District Kutch. *Indian Archaeology: A Review* 1967–68: 18.

1969   Explorations in Districts Hoshanghabad, Jabalpur, Mandla and Narsinghpur. *Indian Archaeology: A Review* 1964–65: 13–16.

1971   Exploration in District Pune. *Indian Archaeology: A Review* 1968–69: 13–14.

SASTRI, T. V. G.
1968   Exploration in District Mahbubnagar. *Indian Archaeology: A Review* 1967–68: 5.

SEN, D.
1953   Prehistoric researches in India. *Man in India* 33 (3): 185–194.

1954   Lower Palaeolithic culture complex and chronology in India. *Man in India* 34 (2): 121–150.

1957a   Correlation of pluvial and glacial cycles in India. *Proceedings of the Indian Science Congress* IV: 93–94.

1957b   The Soanian and the pebble tool complex in India. *Man in India* 37 (2): 157–159.

SEN, D., *et al.*
1956   A new Palaeolithic site in Mayurbhanj. *Man in India* 36 (4): 233–246.

SESHADRI, M.
  1956   *The stone using cultures of prehistoric and protohistoric Mysore.*
         London: Institute of Archaeology.
SHARAN, B. K.
  1971   Exploration in District Ranchi. *Indian Archaeology: A Review*
         1968–69: 5.
SHARMA, G. R.
  1973   "Stone Age in the Vindhyas and the Ganga valley," in *Radiocarbon
         and Indian archaeology.* Edited by D. P. Agrawal and A. Ghosh,
         106–110. Bombay: Tata Institute of Fundamental Research.
SHARMA, G. R., *et al.*
  1971   Explorations in Districts Allahabad, Azamgarh, Banda, Mirzapur,
         Pratapgarh and Sultanpur. *Indian Archaeology: A Review* 1968–69:
         33–38.
  1973   Exploration in District Shahdol. *Indian Archaeology: A Review*
         1965–66: 22–23.
SHARMA, T. C., H. C. SHARMA
  1968   A report on the investigations into the prehistoric archaeology of Garo
         Hills. *Journal of the University of Gauhati* 15–17: 73–74.
  1971   On the discovery of Stone Age sites in central Garo Hills. *Journal
         of the Assam Research Society* 14 (1): 18–26.
  1973   Exploration in District Garo Hills. *Indian Archaeology: A Review*
         1969–70: 2.
SINGH, H. N., S. N. JAISWAL
  1968   Exploration in District Nellore and Chingleput. *Indian Archaeology:
         A Review* 1967–68: 5–6, 25.
SINGH, O. K.
  1971   Excavations at Khangkhui, Mahipur. *Indian Archaeology: A Review*
         1968–69: 20.
SINGH, R.
  1965   "The Palaeolithic industries of northern Bundelkhand." Unpub-
         lished Ph.D. dissertation, Poona University.
SINGH, R. G. P.
  1959   Palaeoliths from Bhimbandh. *Journal of the Bihar Research Society*
         45: 195–203.
SOUNDARA RAJAN, K. V.
  1952   Stone Age industries near Giddalur, District Kurnool. *Ancient India*
         8: 64–92.
  1958   Studies in the Stone Age of Nagarjunakonda. *Ancient India* 14:
         49–113.
  1961   Quaternary pebble, core and flake cultures of the Indian sub-
         continent: an appraisal of data. *Ancient India* 17: 68–85.
SUBBARAO, B.
  1952   Archaeological explorations in the Mahi valley. *Journal of the M.S.
         University of Baroda* 1: 33–69.
  1958   *The personality of India.* Baroda: Maharaja Sayajirao University.
SUPEKAR, S. G.
  1968   "Pleistocene stratigraphy and prehistoric archaeology of the central
         Narmada basin." Unpublished Ph.D. dissertation, Poona
         University.
  1969   Excavations at Mahadeo-Piparia. *Indian Archaeology: A Review*
         1964–65: 16.

TIWARI, V. K.
    1971   Early and Middle Stone Age tools, District Jabalpur. *Indian Archae-
            ology: A Review* 1968–69: 65.
TIWARI, V. K., V. S. WAKANKAR
    1974   Explorations in Districts Indore, Ratlam, and West Nimar. *Indian
            Archaeology: A Review* 1970–71: 19.
TRIVEDI, C. B.
    1971   Early Stone Age tools, Malthone, District Sagar, and District
            Vidisha. *Indian Archaeology: A Review* 1968–69: 66–67, 81.
TODD, K. R. V.
    1939   Palaeolithic industries of Bombay. *Journal of the Royal Anthropolo-
            gical Institute of Great Britain and Ireland* 69: 257–272.
WAINWRIGHT, G. J.
    1964   *The Pleistocene deposits of the Lower Narmada river, and an Early
            Stone Age industry from the river Chambal.* Baroda: M.S.
            University.
WAKANKAR, V. S.
    1956   Palaeolithic sites in the Madhya Bharat. *Indian Archaeology: A
            Review* 1955–56: 68.
    1971a   Explorations in District Raisen. *Indian Archaeology: A Review*
            1968–69: 12.
    1971b   Stone tools at Jawad, District Mandasor. *Indian Archaeology: A
            Review* 1968–69: 68.
    1974a   Explorations in District Ratlam: Acheulian tools near Sailana, Dis-
            trict Ratlam. *Indian Archaeology: A Review* 1970–71: 19.
    1974b   Pebble tools near Burwaha and Mortakka, District West Nimar.
            Indian Archaeology: A Review 1970–71: 19.
ZEUNER, F. E.
    1950   *Stone Age and Pleistocene chronology in Gujarat.* Poona: Deccan
            College.
    1951   *Prehistory in India.* Poona: Deccan College.
    1963   *Environment of Early Man with special reference to tropical regions.*
            Baroda: M.S. University.

Pleistocene Faunal and Cultural Stations in South China

JEAN S. AIGNER

The last and still most comprehensive English summary of geological, faunal, floristic, human paleontological, and archaeological data from Pleistocene China is Teilhard de Chardin's 1941 work. More recent summaries for China appear mainly as short articles and book chapters weighted heavily with archaeological data. Aside from Teilhard and Leroy's faunal lists (1942) and a chapter in the recent Chinese monograph *Ti Ssu Chi Ti-chih Wen-t'i* (Academia Sinica 1964), the faunal histories for Pleistocene China are poorly reported. While revisions in nomenclature are also long overdue, attempts have begun but only on a site basis.

The main objective of this paper is to synthesize the available information on the archaeologic and paleontologic localities of Pleistocene South China and make the data more readily available to western archaeologists. A relative sequence of faunal collecting stations is attempted in order to provide a tentative framework for dating archaeological remains with associated faunas. Such attempts are more successful for North China where climatic alterations during the Pleistocene were more marked and affected the local vegetational, and as a consequence faunal, histories and distributions (Aigner 1969, 1972b).

Archaeological sites and surface collecting stations are listed in a regional and provincial sequence with some attempt to maintain natural regions when these cross-cut the provincial boundaries. Annotations cite locational, geological, faunal, human paleontological, and cultural data whenever these are available.

This paper is a revised version of my 1969 doctoral dissertation which includes post-1949 faunal, floristic, human biological, and archaeological data but is not widely available as a publication.

Artifactual remains recovered since 1949 differ from most better known Hoabinhian material and occur principally in the form of stone flakes and a few formalized tools that do not lend themselves easily to standard western typological analysis. The nearly total lack of coherent archaeological assemblages and the plethora of random collections made from secondary depositional stations are major shortcomings in the South Chinese data.

Since materials described in the literature are usually selected items, and since they lack archaeologic congruity, no attempt is made here to formulate a new descriptive typology or terminology. Descriptive categories which appear in the literature tend to be general and largely nonfunctional and have been for the most part retained.[1]

In passing, some of the archaeological remains from adjacent regions are alluded to but, owing to the fact that data from South China are anthropologically so unsatisfactory and the area is so superficially known, any interregional comparisons are premature at best. The evidence for *in situ* hominid evolution in South China may also be considered; here the data are richer.

SOUTH CHINA PLEISTOCENE ZOOGEOGRAPHIC REGIONS

South China Faunal Province

The area south of the Yangtze between 100° and 122° E longitude and 20° and 32° N latitude comprises South China. This includes the provinces of Yunnan, Kweichou, Kwangsi, Kwangtung, and Fukien in the far south, and Szechuan (including old Sikang), Hupeh, Kiangsi, Chekiang, Kiangsu, and Anhui south of the Yangtze and the Tsinling. The area is divided by P'ei (1957b) into two faunal regions, the South China Faunal Province covering South China generally but excluding the lower Yangtze regions and the Huaiho, which together comprise the Huai River Faunal Province.

The Pleistocene geology of this area is poorly known. Faunal remains of Quaternary age and most of the archaeological remains come from limestone caves and fissures. Other faunal assemblages are compilations of surface collections, museum pieces, and drugstore specimens (bones and teeth were commonly quarried for sale as medicines). Some of these faunas are detailed in Appendix 3.

Matthew and Granger (1923) early noted the basic faunal characteristics of the South Chinese *Stegodon-Ailuropoda* assemblages and

---

[1]   The reader is referred to Aigner 1972a for details of the cultural and hominid remains which are listed in this paper.

also the similarities with fossil assemblages from the Mogok caves of Burma and with the Tam Nang and Lang Son collections from Indochina. The authors referred to these Chinese collections from Yenchingkuo, Szechuan, as "Upper Pliocene." In the early 1930's the collection was redated to the "Lower Pleistocene" in keeping with revised Quaternary terminologies (Teilhard de Chardin 1935). Teilhard equated the fauna from Yenchingkuo with the better known materials from the Kwangsi Cave "yellow deposits." Not until 1940 did Colbert suggest that all these remains, including Yenchingkuo, Makai (or Yuanmou) of Yunnan, and the "yellow deposit" materials, were of Middle Pleistocene age.

On the basis of this rather conservative South China Pleistocene fauna several attempts at temporal subdivisions have been made, most notably by P'ei (1957b), Chou (1957), and Kahlke (1961). According to P'ei the characteristic elements of the fauna are *Pongo*, *Gigantopithecus*, *Ailuropoda*, *Megatapirus*, *Rhinoceros sinensis*, *Stegodon orientalis*, and several others. *Arctonyx*, *Hystrix*, *Rhizomys*, *Paguma*, *Rusa*, and *Muntiacus* are considered by him as also characteristically southern forms, while extinct *Crocuta crocuta*, *Palaeoloxodon namadicus*, and *Pseudaxis grayi*, and living *Panthera* (*Felis*) *tigris*, *Cuon*, *Bubalus*, *Sus*, *Ursus*, and a number of rodents are shared with the north.

But the faunal lists from South Chinese sites (Appendix 3) show that both *Pongo* and *Gigantopithecus* are spatially and temporally restricted. Furthermore, it is clear that during the Pleistocene *Hystrix* enjoyed a much wider distribution than today. *Pseudaxis grayi* is not present in any southern assemblage as P'ei claimed, though a more recent form, *P. hortulorum*, and *Pseudaxis* sp. are recorded (rarely) in Yunnan and Kwangtung. Recent evidence from North China suggests that *Stegodon* is a form which ranged there (at Lantian and K'oho) well into the Middle Pleistocene (during interglacials) and cannot be considered strictly a southern form (Aigner 1969, 1972b).

P'ei made three temporal divisions of the *Stegodon-Ailuropoda* fauna, recognizing a Lower Pleistocene[2] assemblage containing Pliocene relicts such as *Chalicotherium* and mastodon (Liuch'eng fauna) and a Middle Pleistocene fauna including *S. orientalis*, *Megatapirus augustus*, and *Rhinoceros* which are recorded at nearly all of the known faunal stations. His third division is a very late Upper Pleistocene complex represented at the site of Tzeyang by *Homo sapiens* and mammoth and characterized by the absence (presumably through extinction) of *Stegodon*, *Rhinoceros*, *Megatapirus* and *Gigantopithecus*. In more recent works, P'ei (1965) continues his reference

[2] Chinese Villafranchian.

of the Liuch'eng *Gigantopithecus* fauna to the Lower Pleistocene, but considers the remains from the "yellow deposits" as Middle Pleistocene.

In 1961 Kahlke attempted to subdivide the Pleistocene fauna from the south and recognized three main faunal horizons (excluding the Tzeyang remains). He deviates from earlier Chinese views in assigning the Liuch'eng fauna to the early Middle Pleistocene.[3] Kahlke believes it is indeed an early association of the *Stegodon-Ailuropoda*, but explains the archaic features of the faunas as a result of forms persisting in a zone which served as a refugium for Pontian forms. His basis for dating the assemblage to the Middle Pleistocene, perhaps the "Günz,"[4] is the advanced nature of the rest of the fauna (Appendix 3).

Kahlke's second faunal horizon contains the last Villafranchian remnants such as *Hyaena brevirostris sinensis* and its age is considered to be mid-Middle Pleistocene (= Holstein). Finally there is his faunal data of the middle Upper Pleistocene[5] which takes those with the "yellow deposits" as type localities. Several faunas dated by Kahlke are listed in Appendix 2 though his datings are not always retained. His datings are summarized in Table 1.

Faunal Localities (Table 2)

The mammalian remains which appear significant for relative dating are listed in Appendix 2. Among these, *Hyaena* evidently is found in the mid-Middle Pleistocene but *Crocuta* later. *Gigantopithecus* may be a form confined to the Lower Pleistocene, while *Ursus thibetanus* is found in the mid-Middle Pleistocene and later. *Ursus etruscus* is the ancestral form. In addition the stegodonts, elephants, mastodonts, and the tapirs are also important since species tend to be temporally confined. *Equus yunnanensis* is early Middle Pleistocene and older and therefore is important in dating as well.

Sites which are clearly early are uncommon. The controversy over dating sites such as Liuch'eng and Tahsin with *Gigantopithecus* remains is easily resolved if one considers the likelihood that the fauna covers a very long time interval, including Villafranchian forms as well as typically Middle Pleistocene forms. Kahlke found this to be the case for Yenchingkuo as well. The earliest faunal locality appears to be

[3]   Post-Villafranchian in both the European and the Chinese sense.
[4]   Presumably post-Tiglian: probably early Mosbachium in Müller-Beck's terminology.
[5]   Evidently Early Würm equivalent; also note that some Chinese schema place the Riss-equivalent, considered a pluvial phase, in the Chinese Upper Pleistocene (see Chang 1968; Aigner 1969, 1972b).

Table 1.　Relative sequence of South China faunas proposed by Kahlke (1961)

Age (European equivalent)	Faunal locality (Figure 1)
Mid-Upper Pleistocene	Mapa (19),[a] Ch'angyang (29)[a]
Middle Pleistocene (Holstein and later)	Hoshantung (3), Koloshan (25), late Yenchingkuo (27), Chihchin (7), Hsingan (15), Chilinshan (21), Liuhsia (33), Tanyang (34)
Early Middle Pleistocene = Cromer? = Günz?	early Yenchingkuo (27), Tahsin (8) Makai (2), Liuch'eng (11)

[a]　I have suggested an earlier dating based upon the faunal remains and the morphology of the hominid fossils scaled against morphologically relevant forms more securely dated from Europe and North China (see Table 2).

Table 2.　Relative sequence of South China faunas

Age (European equivalent)	Locality (Figure 1 and text)
Upper Pleistocene = Würm and Eem	Yangchangkiang(1), late Tzeyang (23), Laipin (9), Hoshangpo (26), Northern Kwangtung (20), Hsingan (15)
Late Middle Pleistocene = Riss Complex and Advance Stage	Mapa (19), early Tzeyang (23), Liuhsia (33), Tanyang (34), Hsiaotsaowan (35), Koloshan (25), Chilinshan (21), Ch'angyang (29), Hsingan? (15), Northern Kwangtung? (20), Yungshan (31), Hoshantung (3), Ch'ienhsi = Chihchin (7), Lingyen (12), Chihchiang (28), Yangchiachung (22), Tsaotienfen (32), Kaoyao, Loting, Fengk'ai (17), Shaochin (18)
Mid-Middle Pleistocene = Holstein	Yungshan? (31), Fengmenshan (11), Tungshen (14), Hsiaoyen (13)
Early Middle Pleistocene = Mindel and Mosbachium	Tahsin (8), Yuanmou = Makai (2), Yenchingkuo (27), Liuch'eng? (10)
Lower Pleistocene = Chinese Villafranchian = Tiglian and pre-Tiglian	Liuch'eng (10), Chaot'ung (5)

Chaot'ung in northeast Yunnan Province (Figure 1, locality 5) with archaic forms such as *Zygolophodon*, the very primitive *Stegodon chaotungensis*, *Tapirus*, and *Equus yunnanensis*. The latter may indicate a mid-Villafranchian dating, while the other remains favor an earlier age. Liuch'eng (Figure 1.10) with *Gigantopithecus* appears to be more archaic than Tahsin (Figure 1.8). Liuch'eng contains such archaic forms as *Hyaena brevirostris licenti*, *Mastodon*, and *Chalicotherium* along with such (possible) Middle Pleistocene forms as *Stegodon praeorientalis*, *Tapirus*, and *Equus yunnanensis*. Tahsin, on

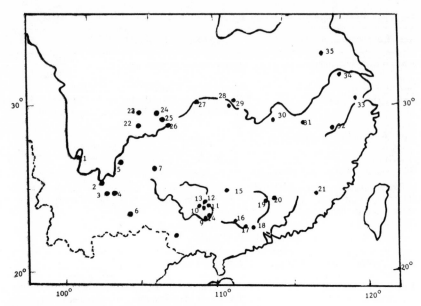

Figure 1.   Distribution of the *Stegodon-Ailuropoda* fauna

Key: Pleistocene Faunal Localities
Yunnan
1.   Yangchangkiang, Lichiang Basin, Lichiang District[a]
2.   Makai = Yuanmou, Makai Valley, Ch'u-Hsiung-Yi Region
3.   Hoshantung, near Fumin and K'unming, K'un-ming Municipality
4.   Tatsaike, Fumin
5.   Chaot'ung, Chao-t'ung District
6.   Heichinlungts'un, Ch'iupei, Wen-shan Chuang-Miao Region
Kweichou
7.   Chihchin, Pi-chieh District
Kwangsi
8.   Tahsin, Niushuishan, Nan-ning District
9.   Chilinshan, Laipin, Liu-chou District
10.   Liuch-eng, Hsinhsuehchungts'un, Liu-chou District
11.   Fengmenshan, Liuch'eng, Liu-chou District
12.   Lingyen, Liuchiang = Liukiang, Liu-chou District
13.   Hsiaoyen, Liuchiang, Liu-chou District
14.   Tungshen, Laipin, Liu-chou District
15.   Hsingan Cave E, Kuei-lin District
16.   Wuchou Cave, Wu-chou Municipality
Kwangtung
17.   Kauoyao, Loting and Fengk'ai Caves, Chao-ch'ing District
18.   Shaochin, Chao-ch'ing District
19.   Mapa, Ch'uchiang, Shao-kuan District
20.   Northern Kwangtung localities, Shao-kuan District, etc.
Fukien
21.   Chilinshan, Lungyen, Lung-yen District
Szechuan
22.   Yangchiachung near Taanchai, Tzeliuching (approximately the Tsu-kung Municipality)

[a]   *Communist China Administrative Atlas*, Central Intelligence Agency, March 1969.

23. Tzeyang, Nei-chiang District
24. Tungnan on the Ai-kiang, southern Mien-yang District
25. Koloshan near Chungking, Ch'ung-ch'ing Municipality
26. Hoshangpo Cave, Pahsien, Ch'ung-ch'ing Municipality
27. Yenchingkuo near Wanhsien, Wan-hsien District
Hupeh
28. Chihchiang = Chihkiang Cave, I-ch'ang District
29. Lungtung near Hsiachungchiawan, Ch'angyang, I-ch'ang District
30. Tats'un, T'ungshan, Hsien-ning District
Kiangsi
31. Yungshan Cave near Lop'ing, Shang-jao District
Chekiang
32. Tsaotienfen Cave near Chiangshan = Kiangshan, Chin-hua District
33. Liuhsia Cave near Hangchow, Hang-chou Municipality
Kiangsu
34. Tanyang Cave, Chen-chiang District
Anhui
35. Hsiatsaowan, Ssuhsien, Ssu-hsien District

the other hand, contains several clearly Middle Pleistocene forms (*Ursus thibetanus* and probably *Megatapirus*) associated with a typically earlier type (*Cuon majori*). An early Middle Pleistocene age is likely for Tahsin, while in Liuch'eng evidently at least a portion of the fauna is older as P'ei suggested.

The early Middle Pleistocene dating of Yuanmou or Makai (Figure 1.2) is apparently based on the presence in the collection of *Equus yunnanensis* and the absence of typically later forms. Yenchingkuo (Figure 1.27) contains archaic forms such as Chalicotheriidae indet. and *Nestortherium* in addition to *Megatapirus*, a typically Middle Pleistocene form. The five sites discussed above contain archaic forms absent at other sites and are evidently slightly earlier than the typical cave faunas from the south.

Hsiaoyen (Kwangsi) Cave (Figure 1.13) reportedly contains *Stegodon praeorientalis* and *S. orientalis* (P'ei 1965). The latter suggests a mid-Middle Pleistocene age while the presence of both forms suggests mixing or contemporaneity of both species[6] in the Middle Pleistocene. Other localities with typical Middle Pleistocene faunas are Fengmenshan (Figure 1.11) with *Hyaena brevirostris sinensis, Stegodon orientalis*, and *Megatapirus*, Tungshen (Figure 1.14) with *Ursus thibetanus, Stegodon orientalis, Megatapirus*, etc., remains from the "yellow deposits" in western Kwangtung (at Kaoyao, Loting, Fengk'ai; Figure 1.17), Shaochin (Figure 1.18), and Yangchiachung (Figure 1.22).

A mixed assemblage containing early and late Middle Pleistocene forms is found at Chihchiang (Figure 1.28) with *Equus yunnanensis* and *Crocuta* (unless the horse is a very late holdover in Hupeh), while a possible mid-Middle Pleistocene fauna is found at Tsaotienfen in

[6] Or simply the range of variation within a single species.

Chekiang Province (Figure 1.32). None of the above is associated with cultural remains.

Somewhat later, dating probably to Holstein and post-Holstein times, are a number of sites; only one (Yungshan) has associated cultural remains. Hoshantung in Yunnan (Figure 1.3) with *Ursus thibetanus*, *Crocuta*, *Stegodon*, *Palaeoloxodon*, *Megatapirus*, and *Rhinoceros* is most characteristic. *Crocuta* provides the post-Holstein date for the locality. Chihchin faunas from Kweichou (Figure 1.7) seem more clearly mid-Middle Pleistocene in age, probably dating to the Holstein. Similar faunas are found at Lingyen in Kwangsi (Figure 1.12) and Koloshan in Szechuan (Figure 1.25). The presence in the fauna of *Crocuta* suggests a post-Holstein age for Hsingan in Kwangsi (Figure 1.15), the northern Kwangtung collections (Figure 1.20), Liu-hsia in Chekiang (Figure 1.33), Hsiatsaowan in Anhui (Figure 1.35), and Chilinshan in Fukien (Figure 1.21).

Part of the Tzeyang fauna from Szechuan (Figure 1.23), the Tanyang remains from Kiangsu (Figure 1.34), and the Yungshan Cave fauna from Kiangsi (Figure 1.31) are all probably mid- to late Middle Pleistocene in age. The last site reportedly has associated artifacts though these are not well described (Huang and Chi 1963a).

Faunal localities which evidently are Upper Pleistocene in age are usually dated geologically. Among these are Hoshangpo in Szechuan (Figure 1.24) with forms such as *Stegodon orientalis*, *Megatapirus*, and *Rhinoceros* (Chou 1957), and Yangchangkiang in Yunnan where *Homo sapiens* and *Rhinoceros* were found together (Li 1961).

Other localities such as Ch'angyang in I-Ch'ang (Hupeh, Figure 1.29), Chilinshan in Laipin (Figure 1.9), Mapa in Kwangtung (Figure 1.19), and later Tzeyang in Szechuan (Figure 1.23) contain hominid remains which provide the basis for their relative dating. Other localities contain too few diagnostic forms for dating.

Huai River Faunal Province

Based on mammalian remains from Changshan in Shuyang, northern Kiangsu, Hsiatsaowan in Szehung and Chitsuai in Wuho, northern Anhui, and Hsintsai in southeastern Honan, P'ei (1957b) hypothesized a Huaiho or Huai River Faunal Province. The faunas upon which he bases his definitions were collected by construction workers from sandy and marly deposits near rivers. The faunal province is charac-terized by the presence of *Trogontherium*, *Palaeoloxodon namadi-cus*, and *Megaloceros*, also found in North China, and *Elaphurus davidianus*, *Coelodonta antiquitatis*, *Stegodon* sp., *Rusa*, and prob-ably *Cuon*. The last three are reportedly shared with the typical southern fauna. P'ei believes the Huaiho region served as a connection between South and North China and considers that it was a distinct faunistic province during the Quaternary, not merely a transitional area.

The mammalian forms which he cites as diagnostic do not in my opinion constitute a temporal assemblage. *Trogontherium* is not found after the Holstein but other forms, including *Stegodon, Rusa, Megaloceros* (species not defined by P'ei), and *Coelodonta*, last well into the Upper Pleistocene. *Cuon* and *Stegodon* are not typically southern forms; *Cuon* is well known in North China and *Stegodon* is not uncommon in Middle Pleistocene assemblages from the southern part of North China. Evidently the only form confined to the region is *Elaphurus davidianus*. Considering the poor geological control of collecting stations and the clearly mixed fauna the definition of a distinct Huai River Faunal Province is questionable.

Evidently the Tsinling Mountains provided an effective barrier to faunal movements from north to south, at least by the Middle Pleistocene (Aigner 1969). Li (1962) reports "pure" southern assemblages on the upper Han River in southern Shensi, with Middle Pleistocene remains including *Crocuta, Ursus thibetanus, Stegodon orientalis* or *S. praeorientalis, Rhinoceros sinensis, Equus yunnanensis, Rusa, Muntiacus*, and others. Hsieh (1960) reports similar forms from several localities, including some on the Han River and others near the Chialing and near the Tan, all found in southern Shensi on the south side of the Tsinling. No typically northern forms are found.

Just north of the Tsinling in southern Shansi, the early Middle Pleistocene site, Lantian 63506,[7] contains more than 30 percent southern forms, the greatest concentration of southern forms found in the north. *Stegodon* is reported at K'oho in the Sanmen region, but in an otherwise typical northern assemblage. The route by which southern forms entered into the northern province is not clear, but the absence of intervening localities between the Huaiho region and Lantian seems to preclude that route. It is possible that prior to the Villafranchian/Middle Pleistocene Tsinling uplift there was freer movement and exchange between the two faunal provinces in this area. However, until Villafranchian localities are found on both sides of the Tsinling this cannot be proved. The Lantian Villafranchian assemblages with *Myospalax, Ochotona, Hyaena brevirostris licenti, Proboscidipparion, Equus sanmeniensis, Leptobos, Megaloceros, Bison priscus = B. palaeosinensis, Euctenoceros*, and *Gazella* are for the most part "typically" northern. Evidently the exchange was primarily unidirectional, south to north, and confined to warm periods prior to uplift.

[7]　See Aigner 1969 and 1972b.

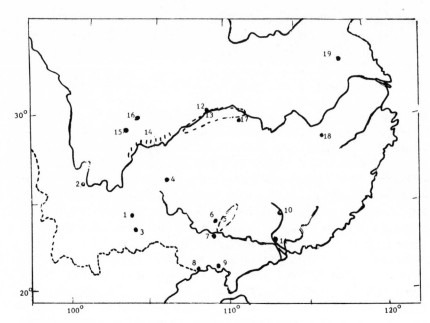

Figure 2.   Pleistocene localities with cultural and hominid remains

Key: Pleistocene hominid fossils and cultural remains from South China

Yunnan

1. Pap'an sites near Panch'iao, Lunan, Ch'ü-ching District 103° 20′ E×24° 40′ N
2. Locality 6003 near Lichiang, Li-chiang District 100° 20′ E×26° 45′ N
3. Ch'iupei rockshelter, Heichinglung, Wen-shan Chuang-Miao Region 104° 15′ E
    ×24° 5′ N

Kweichou

4. Ch'ienhsi, Pi-chieh District 106° 5′ E×27° 5′ N

Kwangsi

5. Caves between Laipin, Liu-chou District, and Hsingan, Kuei-lin District
    109°–110° 30′ E×23° 50′–25° 30′ N
6. Liukiang = Liuchiang, Liu-chou District 109° 20′ E×24° 20′ N
7. Laipin (Chilinshan), Liu-chou District 109° 20′ E×23° 40′ N
8. Yapushan and Malangchi, Tunghsing, Ch'in-chou District 108° E×21° 30′ N
9. Lingshan, eastern Ch'in-chou District 109° 25′ E×22° 25′ N

Kwangtung

10. Mapa, Ch'u-chiang, Shao-kuan District 113° 30′ E×24° 50′ N
11. Hsich'iaoshan, Nanhai, Fo-shan District 113° 10′ E×23° 5′ N

Szechuan

12. Yenchingkuo, Wanhsien, Wan-hsien District 108° 20′ E×30° 50′ N
13. Between Ich'ang, I-ch'ang District (111° 20′ E×30° 30′ N) and Chungking,
    Ch'ung-ch'ing Municipality (106° 30′ E×29° 25′ N)
14. Stations from Ch'ung-ch'ing, Wen-chiang west, on terraces of the Yangtze, Min,
    and Yalun
15. Fulin = Hanyüan, Ya-an District 102° 40′ E×29° 20′ N
16. Tzeyang, Nei-chiang District 104° 40′ E×30° 10′ N

Hupeh

17. Lungtung Cave near Hsiachungchiawan, southwest of Ch'angyang, I-chang
    District 111° E×30° 10′ N

Kiangsi
18. Yungshan Cave north of Lop'ing near the juncture of the Shang-jao District and Ching-te-chen Municipality boundaries 117° 10′ E×29° 20′ N
Anhui
19. Hsiaotsaowan, probably Ssu-hsien District

A SURVEY OF PLEISTOCENE LOCALITIES WITH CULTURAL AND HOMINID REMAINS (Figure 2 and Table 3)

It will be noted that among the cultural stations listed below there are several whose attribution to the Pleistocene is questionable. For the rest, some are clearly Pleistocene in age but whether Middle Pleistocene or early, middle, or late Upper Pleistocene is not always certain. In addition to the generally unsatisfactory nature of the associated fauna or of the geologic context, the anthropological information conveyed by the cultural materials themselves is disappointingly meager.

There is a positive note, however, in the success during the last few years of the Institute of Vertebrate Palaeontology and Palaeoanthropology (Peking) in locating flake assemblages in apparently good pre-Würm geologic and faunal contexts where heretofore there were none. Further reconnaissance and problem-oriented prehistoric studies in South China should in this decade produce exciting new materials and elicit tentative hypotheses concerning hominid and cultural evolution and variation for subsequent testing.

Yunnan

LOCALITY 1 (Figure 2). Collections on terraces of the Pap'an near Panch'iao Commune, Lunan, Ch'u-ching, were made by P'ei and Chou (1961) and by Li and Huang (1961, 1962). The former located three collecting stations, two on high terraces of the Pap'an, considered Upper Pleistocene in age. Locality 6102 produced nine flakes and Locality 6101 "flakes and a few tools." Four additional stations from the forty- to fifty-meter upper terrace and the thirty-meter second terrace were studied by Li and Huang. The total sample from all localities including some believed Recent is about ninety flakes, cores and retouched flakes of chert and chalcedony. No pottery was associated with the remains.

LOCALITY 2. Lichianghsien Locality 6003 near Lichiang produced a segment of *Pseudaxis* antler drilled through which was associated with

Table 3. Relative sequence of the South Chinese hominid localities and cultural stations

Period	Subperiod	Age equivalent	Flake assemblages	Hoabinhian-like materials and contexts/pebble industries	"Artifacts"	Hominids
UPPER PLEISTOCENE	Late	"Terminal" Würm	Nanhai (11), Fulin (15), Lichianghsien (2)	Hsienjentung and others (5), Yapushan, Malangchi (8), ᵇHoabinhian	Lingshan (9), Ch'iupei (3)	Lingshan (9), Hsiaotsaowan (19), Lichianghsien (2)
		"Maximum" Würm	Pap'an (1)		Tzeyang awl (16), Wanhsien (12?), Edgar's (14?)	ᵃUpper Cave, Tzeyang (16), Laipin (7)
		"Pre-maximum" Würm	ᵃHsiaonanhai			Liuchiang (6), ᵇNiah
	Middle	circa 40,000 B.P.	ᵇPalawan, ᵇNiah, ᵃOrdos			
	Early	"Early" Würm	ᵇTingts'un	ᵇPatjitanian?	Edgar's (13?)	Mapa (10)
		Eem-Chingshui Erosion = Itu Loam				
MIDDLE PLEISTOCENE	Late	Riss II / Riss I/II	Yungshan (18?), Ch'ienhsi = Chihchin (4)		Wanhsien antler (12?)	Ch'angyang (17)
		Riss I	ᵃChoukoutien 15			
	Middle	Holstein Advance	ᵃChoukoutien 1	ᵇAnyathian		ᵃChoukoutien 1
		Holstein	Yungshan (18)			
			ᵃChoukoutien 1			ᵃChoukoutien 1
	Early	Mindel / "Mid" Mosbachium	ᵃLantian 63706			ᵇTrinil H. erectus, ᵇDjetis H. erectus, ᵃLantian 63706

ᵃ North China.   ᵇ Southeast Asia.

the remains of *Pseudaxis*, *Bubalus*, and fragmental femora of *Homo sapiens* at an elevation of 2,800 meters (Li 1961).

LOCALITY 3. Ch'iupei, a rockshelter in the Wen-shan Chuang-Miao Region, produced a pebble chopper, perhaps of Hoabinhian type and possibly from the terminal Pleistocene (Pien and Chia 1938; Aigner 1969).

LOCALITY 4. Ch'ienhsi = Chihchin Cave Locality 64063, 170 kilometers northwest of Kweiyang in Pi-chieh District, produced stone artifacts associated *in situ* with the remains of *Rhinoceros sinensis*, *Megatapirus augustus*, *Stegodon orientalis*, Cervidae, carnivores, *Ailuropoda fovealis*, *Hystrix*, *Macaca*, Bovidae, *Sus*, and an hyena. A middle or late Middle Pleistocene age has been suggested (Aigner 1969). The artifacts consist of about 100 chert flakes, several of which are retouched (P'ei et al. 1965).

Kwangsi

LOCALITY 5. Cave sites in Kwangsi are difficult to date owing to the former local excavations for "dragon bones." Formerly believed entirely Recent (P'ei 1935a, 1935b), restudy of a few sites which preserve some cultural materials has been possible (Chia and Chiu 1960).

Interestingly, five cave localities which were reexamined produced cultural materials from the "gray deposits" overlying fossiliferous "yellow deposits" including Hoabinhian-like pebble tools. There were no associated ceramics and no edge-ground artifacts. A late Pleistocene age for these remains can no longer be considered unreasonable (Aigner 1969; see Solheim 1967, 1969).

LOCALITY 6. Tungtienyen (cave), Liuchiang, Liu-chou District, produced a human skull and some postcranial materials (= Liuchiang Man). The hominid skull and a nearby skull of *Ailuropoda* with adhering "reddish deposits" are to be considered geologically more recent than fossils from the typical hard "yellow deposits." Among the latter are *Rhinoceros sinensis*, *Stegodon orientalis*, *Megatapirus*, *Sus*, and *Ursus* of the *Stegodon-Ailuropoda* Complex (Woo 1959). Considered morphologically more primitive than Upper Cave, and possessing patent Mongoloid characteristics (Woo 1959; Coon 1963; Thoma 1964), an age of 25,000 to 40,000 years B.P. has been suggested (Aigner 1969).

LOCALITY 7. A cave near Holung, Chilinshan, Laipin in Liu-chou District also produced a hominid skull fragment, a maxilla with a few teeth *in situ*, and an isolated upper molar ("Laipin Man") (Chia and Woo 1959). Sealed beneath the topmost of several "stalagmitic crusts" in upper yellowish-gray breccia, the human remains were associated with a split pebble, two flakes, teeth of *Cervus* and *Sus*, a large number of molluskan shells, diffuse ash, and burnt bone. A Hoabinhian-like context is suggested. Measurements on the hominid remains fall within the range for modern *H. sapiens* and primitive Mongoloid morphological traits are clearly present (Chia and Woo 1959; Coon 1963; Thoma 1964). The correspondence in southern China between "Negroid" morphological type and a Hoabinhian lithic technology suggested by Chang (1968) is clearly not tenable. Similar to but more advanced than Liuchiang, described immediately above, a late or terminal Upper Pleistocene age is reasonable (Aigner 1969).

LOCALITY 8. Yapushan near Hsichiao and Malangchi near Malangchi village in Tunghsing, Ch'in-chou District near the Vietnamese border, have produced cave materials similar to those Hoabinhian-like remains described above from between Liu-chou and Kuei-lin district: pebble "axes" and choppers, a few potsherds, and remains of *Rusa* and "two forms of *Bubalus*" below levels with shell, ceramics, and polished stone (Anonymous 1960a, 1960b).

LOCALITY 9. In several caves in Lingshan, eastern Ch'in-chou District, Ku's survey (1962) revealed primarily lithic remains with ceramics; he also reports a level of compacted brownish gravel below in three sites, each of which produced a limited collection of human and mammalian remains. Tungshenyen, Putiyen, and Hungk'utung sites with hominid fragments and bones of *Rhinoceros sinensis*, *Sus scrofa*, *Tapirus*, Cervicornia and bovids may be dated to the latest Upper Pleistocene (Aigner 1969).

Kwangtung

LOCALITY 10. From Mapa, Ch'uchiang, Shao-kuan District in northern Kwangtung, a broken human skull ("Mapa") associated with an apparently Middle Pleistocene fauna is reported (Woo 1958; Anonymous 1959a, 1959b). Found in a cave some twenty-five meters above the present ground surface and more than thirty-seven meters from the modern entrance to that fissure, the primitive hominid and remains of an hyena, *Ursus*, *Ailuropoda*, *Panthera tigris*, mustelid, and *Palaeoloxodon namadicus* have been taken as evidence of a later Middle

Pleistocene age by the Chinese and by me (Aigner 1969) or Würm-equivalent age by Kahlke (1961). Woo and Peng (1959) report that the human remains belong to a morphological grade roughly equivalent to that of European Neanderthals (thus accounting for Kahlke's conservative dating). Coon (1963) notes premodern morphological features and Mongoloid characteristics and he stresses that this is not a Neanderthal *sensu stricto*. It is more primitive than Liuchiang. I have suggested a latest Middle Pleistocene to early Upper Pleistocene age (ca. 100,000 B.P.) as fully possible based upon the associated fauna and the hominid morphology (Aigner 1969).

LOCALITY 11. Nanhai in Fo-shan District has produced surface stations on the slopes of the volcanic hill (Hsich'iaoshan) seventy kilometers southwest of Canton (Mo 1959; Peng and Wang 1959). Two of the fourteen stations were tested but only surface Locality 2 with forty-six pointed flakes, small pebbles and sixteen utilized flakes described as "scrapers," and other artifacts, lacked shard associations. No great antiquity is indicated.

Szechuan

LOCALITY 12. Scattered remains, including a retouched flake from an Upper Pleistocene terrace near Wanhsien and a possibly utilized antler from a Middle Pleistocene faunal collection studied by Hooijer from Yenchingkuo in Wanhsien District, were collected in the 1930's (Teilhard de Chardin 1941; Teilhard de Chardin and Young 1935; Hooijer 1951).

LOCALITY 13. Between Ich'ang in I-ch'ang District, western Hupeh, and Chung-king (Ch'ung-ch'ing Municipality), central Szechuan, Edgar collected five artifacts from the basal conglomerate of the Itu Loam. The Itu Loam gravel may be equivalent in age to basal gravels of the Chingshui Erosion in North China (= Eem-equivalent) (Graham 1935; Teilhard de Chardin 1935, 1941).

LOCALITY 14. Between Ch'ung-ch'ing, Wen-chiang, and far western Szechuan on terraces of the Yangtze, Min, and Yalun, Edgar (1933–1934) reported collecting a large series of "paleoliths." The age of the materials could be Pleistocene but the primary or secondary nature of the depositions is open to question (Bowles 1933; Edgar 1933–1934; Graham 1935; Teilhard de Chardin 1941).

LOCALITY 15. From Fulin = Hanyüan, Ya-an District, nuclei, flakes, and several worked flakes are reported in association with Pleistocene mammals (*Ursus* cf. *thibetanus*), shells of *Lancerolaria*, and diffuse ash, in sandy loams of possible Upper Pleistocene age (Yang 1961). Some 162 artifacts including 3 nuclei, 14 worked flakes, and 149 nonutilized flakes were recovered from a one-meter-square test at 2.1 to 2.2 meters below the surface.

LOCALITY 16. A fossil human skull and a bone awl were found near Huanshanchi bridge, 0.5 kilometers west of Tzeyang and eighty kilometers southeast of Chengtu in Nei-chiang District. Fluorine and specific gravity tests run on mammalian remains recovered from various strata suggest that the human remains and awl come from sandy loams 1 to 1.5 meters below the surface and are associated with *Equus*, *Muntiacus reevesi*, *Moschus*, *Mammuthus primigenius*, and evidently also *Panthera tigris*, and hyena, *Sus*, *Hystrix*, and *Rhizomys* (P'ei 1952; Chia 1954; Chiu 1955; Movius 1955; P'ei and Woo 1957). The skull is more primitive than Upper Cave, according to P'ei and Woo (1957; also see Coon 1963; Ch'in 1962), but is clearly modern *H. sapiens*. I have suggested an age on the order of 25,000 to 35,000 years ago (Aigner 1969).

Hupeh

LOCALITY 17. From Lungtung (cave) near Hsiachungchiawan, some forty-five kilometers southwest of Ch'angyang, I-Chang District, a fragment of human maxilla (Ch'angyang) and remains of *Cuon antiquus*, *Crocuta crocuta ultima*, *Stegodon orientalis*, *Megatapirus augustus*, *Rhinoceros sinensis*, and others were found in fine, dark yellow, sandy clay (Chia 1957). The fauna suggests a Middle Pleistocene age (Aigner 1969) but an Upper Pleistocene age has also been suggested (Kahlke 1961), perhaps based upon the report that the hominid remains are "near" *H. sapiens*. Coon (1963), noting several Mongoloid features as does Chia, sees the remains as morphologically and metrically resembling *H. erectus* from Choukoutien I (Holstein-equivalent in age), although more modern. A later Middle Pleistocene age seems reasonable to me.

Kiangsi

LOCALITY 18. A collection of mammals from Yungshan Cave, thirty-six kilometers north of Lop'ing (near the border of Shang-jao District and Ching-te-chen Municipality) in northeastern Kiangsi is said to have associated some altered flakes (Huang and Chi 1963a). Materials come from yellow deposits beneath a breccia composed of angular limestone fragments, shale, and quartzite. The associated fauna is typical of the yellow deposits reported from the Kwangtung and Kwangsi caves and assigned to the Middle Pleistocene: *Hystrix*, *Rattus rattus*, *Stegodon*, *Rhinoceros*, *Rusa*, Bovidae cf. *Bubalus*, and Ovinae.

Anhui

LOCALITY 19. A hominid femur from Hsiaotsaowan in Ssu-hsien District was reported from a Middle Pleistocene faunal collection but subsequent fluorine tests invalidated the association (Woo and Chia 1955; Chiu 1955). An Upper Pleistocene age for the hominid is possible and a Middle Pleistocene age may be ruled out.

OVERVIEW

Only brief summary remarks concerning the cultural and hominid remains are provided here since their significance is treated elsewhere (Aigner 1969, 1972a; Aigner and Laughlin 1973). Specifically, flake artifacts which are either (or both) geographically and temporally distinct from Hoabinhian-like remains and contexts are now known from South China (Table 3). Geologically and faunistically at least some are assignable to the Middle Pleistocene and later.

Utilized stone flake industries have been found *in situ* in datable cave contexts in several regions of Southeast Asia – western Palawan in the Philippines and Niah in Sarawak (Solheim 1969). Associated with modern-type *Homo sapiens*, with or without chopping tools and choppers, absolute dates of about 30,000-plus years have been obtained. Solheim suggests that utilized flake industries were derived from pebble industries in Southeast Asia by at least 50,000 years ago. Furthermore, they may be the only remains of that time we shall find in Borneo and the Philippines. Yungshan (Figure 2, Locality 18) and Ch'ienhsi = Chihchin (Locality 4) with two or three times that antiquity in South China may be part of the same general phenomenon.

Hoabinhian lithic materials should reflect technological descendants of the original pebble tool industries of southern Asia. And while the cultural association with shellfish, ceramics, edge grinding of some tools, and evidently cultivation as well may be largely a terminal Pleistocene and Holocene development, Hoabinhian lithic technology should be found in increasingly earlier geologic contexts as new archaeological finds produce stages in the development of that lithic technocomplex.

Although most if not all of the known Hoabinhian-like collections from caves between Laipin and Hsingan in Kwangsi are associated with edge-ground tools and ceramics, and have until recently been considered post-Pleistocene in age, it is now the opinion of Southeast Asian scholars that pottery and edge grinding in Southeast Asia both may be pre-Holocene; a similar argument is made for gardening (Solheim 1967, 1969; Gorman 1969). Upper Pleistocene dates associated with ceramics in southern Japan which almost certainly were introduced from the mainland fully support this hypothesis (Kotani 1969). Furthermore, the earliest ceramics from Hsienjentung, Kiangsi, considered early Holocene by Huang and Chi (1963b) (but which presumably could be earlier – Aigner 1969), suggest that terminal Pleistocene Hoabinhian-like materials and adaptive strategies should be expected in South China as well.

Finally, of enormous theoretical import is the morphological-temporal series of hominid fossils from China all of which display (1) Mongoloid characteristics and (2) progressively more modern morphology (Table 3). Weidenreich's early recognition of Mongoloid characteristics in Chinese fossil hominids of considerable antiquity led him to suggest that China's *H. erectus* may have evolved directly into modern Mongoloid *H. sapiens* in China, an hypothesis seriously considered by Coon (1963) and others as well. The South China human fossil remains which temporally and morphologically provide a series linking the Kungwangling Lantian cranium and later "Sinanthropus," and the remains from Upper Cave, provide strong support to this view (Aigner 1969; Aigner and Laughlin 1973).

APPENDIX 1: FAUNAL LISTS

Locations

The faunal localities annotated below refer to Appendices 2 and 3 below. The numerical identification also refers to Figure 1.

Yunnan

1. Bank of the Yangchangkiang in the Lichiang Basin; fauna and possible associated artifacts from latest Pleistocene (Li 1961).
2. Makai or Yuanmou fauna collected at several stations in the "red beds" of the Makai Valley; Lower or early Middle Pleistocene (Pien 1940; Colbert 1940, 1943; P'ei 1961).
3. Hoshangtung, a cave southwest of Fumin and northwest of K'unming, near the Putu; possibly Holstein (Pien and Chia 1938; Young 1932).

4. Cave near Tatsaike, Fumin, northeast of K'unming; forms diagnostic for dating are lacking (Young and Mi 1941).
5. Chaot'ung collections from deposits roughly equivalent or earlier than Liuch'eng *Gigantopithecus*; Lower Pleistocene (Chou and Chai 1962).
6. Heichinlungts'un rockshelter fauna from Ch'iupei; too few forms for dating (Pien and Chia 1938).

Kweichou

7. Chihchin District cave faunas; possibly Holstein (Hsu, Li, and Hsieh 1957).

Kwangsi

8. Tahsin *Gigantopithecus* Cave of Niushuishan,[1] possibly Cromerian-equivalent (P'ei 1957c, 1960a, 1960b, 1965; P'ei and Woo 1956).
9. Chilinshan hominid from Laipin; no other fauna; Upper Pleistocene (P'ei 1956, 1957c; Chia and Wu 1959).
10. Liuch'eng *Gigantopithecus*[2] cave of Hsinhsuehchungts'un; Lower or early Middle Pleistocene (Chou 1957; P'ei 1957a, 1957b, 1957c, 1965; Li 1960; Kahlke 1961).
11. Fengmenshan Cave fauna from Liuch'eng; Middle Pleistocene (P'ei 1965).
12. Lingyen Cave fauna from Liukiang; Middle Pleistocene? (P'ei 1965).
13. Hsiaoyen Cave fauna from Liukiang; early Middle Pleistocene? (P'ei 1965).
14. Tungshen Cave fauna from Laipin; Middle Pleistocene? (P'ei 1965).
15. Hsingan fauna from Cave E, north of Kweilin; post-Holstein (P'ei 1935b; Kahlke 1961).
16. Cave fauna from near Wuchou; too few forms for dating (Young 1932).

Kwangtung

17. Fauna from yellow deposits in three karst-cave regions of the west (Kauoyao, Loting, Fengk'ai); Middle Pleistocene (Huang 1963).
18. Fauna from Shaochin; possibly Middle Pleistocene (Ch'ang 1959).
19. Mapa fauna and hominid; late Middle Pleistocene? (Woo 1958; Anonymous 1959a; Woo and Peng 1959; Kahlke 1961).

[1] Even though the Tahsin cave was known in 1961 and reported, in 1965 it was still known only preliminarily. The cave is located ninety meters above ground level as is the Liuch'eng cave. P'ei (1965) believes that the ninety-meter caves began filling by the Lower Pleistocene while the lower caves at thirty to fifty meters did not begin to fill until later. Still some of the Tahsin fauna appears to be Middle Pleistocene in age (*Megatapirus*). Either *Gigantopithecus* lasts into the mid-Middle Pleistocene, *Megatapirus* developed earlier than formerly believed, or the fauna covers a long time period (or is mixed).
[2] Recently in the popular magazine *China Reconstructs* (1963), J. K. Woo summarized his view (set forth in *Mandibles and dentition of* Gigantopithecus) that *Gigantopithecus* is a prehominid form (typologically) which became extinct at the end of the Lower Pleistocene. On the basis of the dentition with relatively small canines, very small incisors, and well-developed post-canine teeth, Wu suggests that *Gigantopithecus* was strictly a vegetarian and an unlikely inhabitant of the caves in which its remains were found; P'ei had earlier suggested that *Gigantopithecus* inhabited the caves and was at least partly carnivorous (1957a).

20. Collections from northern part of the province; late Middle Pleistocene or later? (Liu 1962).

Fukien

21. Chilinshan fauna from Lungyen; post-Holstein (Mi 1943; Kahlke 1961).

Szechuan

22. Yanchiachung rockshelter near Ta-an-chai, Tzeliuching; limited fauna from Holstein-equivalent? (Mi 1943).
23. Tzeyang redeposited faunas from near Huanshanchi bridge, Chengtu-Chungking railroad; early fauna late Middle Pleistocene?, hominid fauna late Upper Pleistocene (P'ei and Woo 1957).
24. Tungnan site of redeposited fauna in fluvial or lacustrine deposits of the Ai-kiang; Upper Pleistocene (Chou 1957).
25. Koloshan fauna from a cave near Chungking; probably post-Holstein (Young and Liu 1950; Kahlke 1961).
26. Cave fauna near Hoshangpo, Pahsien, Chungking; probably later Pleistocene (Young and Mi 1941).
27. Yenchingkuo fissures, southwest of Wanhsien; Kahlke distinguishes an early Cromerian-equivalent and a later Holstein-and-later component (Matthew and Granger 1923; Young 1936, 1939; Kurten 1956; Colbert and Hooijer 1953; P'ei 1957b; Kahlke 1961).

Hupeh

28. Fauna from a cave in Chihkiang with *Crocuta* and *Equus yunnanensis*; Middle Pleistocene (Chiu, Ch'ang, and Tung 1961).
29. Fauna from Lungtung Cave near Hsiachungchiawan and known as Ch'angyang; a primitive hominid is associated; late Middle Pleistocene? or later (Chia 1957; Kahlke 1961).
30. Fauna from a cave near Tats'un, T'ungshanhsien; undated (Huang and Han 1959; P'ei and Li 1958).

Kiangsi

31. Fauna from Yungshan Cave, north of Lop'ing; associated artifacts; late Middle Pleistocene? (Huang and Chi 1963a).

Chekiang

32. Fauna from a cave near Tsaotienfen, near Kiangshan; Middle Pleistocene? (P'ei 1957c).
33. Cave fauna near Liuhsia; post-Holstein equivalent (P'ei 1957b; P'ei and Chiu 1957).

Kiangsu

34. Cave fauna near Tanyang; Holstein or later (P'ei 1940).

Anhui

35. Compiled fauna, Hsiatsaowan, Ssuhung (= Ssuhsien?): Middle Pleisto-
    cene? (P'ei 1957b).

APPENDIX 2. SOUTH CHINA FORMS IMPORTANT FOR DATING PURPOSES

Location numbers (Figure 1)

Form	1	2	3	4	5	6	7	8	9	10	11	12	13	14	15	16	17	18	19	20	21	22	23a	23b	24	25	26	27	28	29	30	31	32	33	34	35
Homo sp.	×																																			
Homo sapiens lMP-																	×											×								
Gigantopithecus sp. LP-?								×	×													×														
Trogontherium sinensis -mMP																																				×
Ursus thibetanus MP			×			×	×	×						×	×										×	×	×	×	×							
Hyaena brevirostris licenti = LP									×																											
H. brevirostris sinensis -mMP										×																										
Hyaena sp. -mMP													×				×											×								
Crocuta crocuta mMP-			×											×		×										×			×			×	×			
Cuon majori -LP									×																									×		
Zygolophodon sp. -LP					×											×					×															
Stegolophodon sp. -?					×											×					×															
Stegodon chaotungensis -LP											×	×	×	×	×																					
Stegodon praeorientalis -eMP?										×	×	×	×	×																						
Stegodon orientalis -lMP?						×	×			×	×	×	×	×	×									×			×	×				×	×			
Palaeoloxodon sp. -eUP?			×														×							×			×	×				×	×			
Mammuthus sp. UP-																						×														
Mastodon sp. -LP?									×	×																										
Chalicotherium sp. -LP?																											×									
Nestortherium sp. -LP?																				×	×															
Megatapirus sp. MP						×			×	×							×										×				×			×		
Tapirus sp. ?								×					×			×		×	×																	
Rhinoceros sp. ? -present	×		×		×								×			×		×								×					×	×	×	×	×	×
Equus yunnanensis L -eMP	×	×	×	×					×																×				×			×	×	×	×	×
Pseudaxis hortulorum lMP-																													×		×					

Key: e, m, l = early, middle, late;
 L, M, U = Lower, Middle, Upper.
 P = Pleistocene: -LP, up to the Lower Pleistocene; UP-, from the Upper Pleistocene on.

APPENDIX 3. SOUTH CHINA PLEISTOCENE FAUNAS (For footnotes see p. 155)

Location numbers (Figure 1)

Form	1	2	3	4	5	6	7	8	9	10	11	12	13	14	15	16	17	18	19	20	21	22	23a	23b	24	25	26	27	28	29	30	31	32	33	34	35
Homo sp.	×																																			
Homo sapiens																		×									×									
Gigantopithecus sp.			×					×	×																											
Pongo pygmaeus Hooijer			×						×	×			×																							
Pongo sp.				×				×		×				×																						
Hylobates sp.								×																												
H. (Bunopithecus) sericus Matthew and Granger								×																			×									
Macaca sp.					×	×		×		×															×	×										×
Szechuanopithecus yangtzensis Young and Liu																										×										
Simia sp.																				×																
Primates indet.													×			×				×																
Erinaceus koloshanensis Young and Liu												×													×											
Anourosorex kui Young and Liu																									×											
Nectogale sp.																									×											
Scaptochirus moschatus Milne-Edwards																	×								×											
Myotis sp.																									×											
Hesperopternus sp.																	×																			
Soricidae indet.							×																													
Citellus sp.																									×											
Petaurista cf. *brachyodus* (Young)								×																	×											
Brachyrhizomys ultimus Young and Liu															×										×											
Rhizomys sinensis Gray[1]																×													×	×						
R. provestitus Young and Liu																									×				×	×						
R. szechuanensis Young and Liu																									×											
Rhizomys sp.																															?	?				
Ellobius sp.																									×											

Appendix 3. South China Pleistocene faunas (continued)

Form	Location numbers (Figure 1)																																				
	1	2	3	4	5	6	7	8	9	10	11	12	13	14	15	16	17	18	19	20	21	22	23a	23b	24	25	26	27	28	29	30	31	32	33	34	35
Trogontherium sinensis Young																															×					
Sylvaenys sylvaticus (L)																									×											
Rattus cf. *edwardsi* (Thomas)																									×											
R. rattus (L)							×																		×						×					
Muridae indet.							×																		×					×						
Microtinae indet.							×																		×											
Hystrix subcristata Swinhoe[2]			×						×							×	×								×		×					×				
H. kiangsensis Wang										×	×																						×			
Hystrix sp.					×		×																			×										
Lepus sp.																		×	×																	
Canidae indet.			×	×		×								×		×				×					×											
Canis sp.												×	×					×																		
Cuon sp.									×																			×								
C. antiquus[3] Matthew and Granger																	×								×											
C. simplicidens Young and Liu																																				
C. majori dCamp = *C. dubius* Teilhard								×																												
C. alpinus = *C. javanicus* Desman													×																							
Ursidae indet.						×																														
Ursus thibetanus = *U. angustidens*			×				×	×						×		×	×		×						×		×		×			×				
Ursus sp.									×	×		×		×	×		×	×	×						×									×		
Ailuropoda melanoleuca			×					×	×		×	×		×			×	×	×						×		×		×			×				
Ailuropoda sp.												×							×						×		×	×								
Ailurus fulgens Thomas			×						×		×									×																
Mustelidae indet.																						×														
Mustela (Putorius) siberica (Pallas)																									×		×									
Martes sinensis Young and Liu																									×		×									
Charronia flavigula																									×		×									

Appendix 3. South China Pleistocene faunas (continued)

Form																																			
	Location numbers (Figure 1)																																		
	1	2	3	4	5	6	7	8	9	10	11	12	13	14	15	16	17	18	19	20	21	22	23a	23b	24	25	26	27	28	29	30	31	32	33	34	35

Form	1	2	3	4	5	6	7	8	9	10	11	12	13	14	15	16	17	18	19	20	21	22	23a	23b	24	25	26	27	28	29	30	31	32	33	34	35
Parameles simplicidens Young and Liu																																				
Meles sp.																													×							
Arctonyx collaris Cuvier[4]								×		×																										×
Arctonyx sp.			×																				?	?				×								×
Paguma larvata (Smith)[5]								×		×																		×								
Viverra zibetha									×																		×									
Hyaena brevirostris licenti							×			×																	×									
H. brevirostris sinensis[6]																																				
Hyaena sp.														×					×				?	?												
Crocuta crocuta ultima (Matsumoto)			×											×			×		×	×	×						×	×	×		×	×				×
Panthera tigris (L)[7]			×					×						×					×	×	×		?	?	×	×	×	×	×							×
P. pardus (L)[8]			×			×																														
Felis cf. *lynx* (L) = *Lynx*			×			×																														
F. cf. *chinensis* Gray					×																															
Felis sp.								×	×				×																							
Felidae indet.						×											×											×								
Zygolophodon sp.				×	×																															
Stegolophodon hueiheensis Chou																													×							
Stegodon chaotungensis Chou					×																															
S. praeorientalis Young							×		×		×	×			×		×			×																
S. orientalis Owen[9]										×	×	×			×			×	×	×			×				×		×		×					
Stegodon sp.	×	×						×		×	×												×		×		×						×			
Palaeoloxodon namadicus[10] Falconer and Cautley			×																×																	
Palaeoloxodon sp.												×																					×	×	×	×
?*P.* sp. (cf. *hysudricus*) or *Archidiskodon*				×																																
Chalicotheriidae indet.						×																														

Appendix 3. South China Pleistocene faunas (continued)

Form	Location numbers (Figure 1)																																			
	1	2	3	4	5	6	7	8	9	10	11	12	13	14	15	16	17	18	19	20	21	22	23a	23b	24	25	26	27	28	29	30	31	32	33	34	35
Nestortherium sinensis (Owen)	×	×	×																																	
Megatapirus augustus Matthew and Granger[11]			×																								×									
Megatapirus sp.							×	?			×			×			×								×	×	×	×					×		×	
Tapirus sinensis Owen[12]					×									×					×																	
Tapirus sp.								?					×					×																		
Tapiridae indet.																×																				
Rhinocerotidae indet.																										×										
Rhinoceros sinensis Owen[13]							×	×		×			×	×	×			×					×		×	×	×		×		×	×				
Rhinoceros sp.																												×								
Equus yunnanensis Colbert[14]					×					×													×			×			×	×	×	×	×	×		×
Equus sp.			×	×			×											×		×		×			×				×			×				
Suidae indet.				×				×																												
Sus scrofa[15]				×				×		×	×																			×						
Sus sp.[16]		×	×	×	×		×	×		×	×		×				×	×							×	×	×	×	×	×	×	×			×	
Cervidae indet.										×	×		×	×	×			×		×	×	?	?			×		×	×		×					×
Cervus sp.[17]					×	×											×		×		×								×	×	×	×	×	×		×
C. (*Rusa*) *unicolor* (Kerr)							×					×			×	×							×	×		×						×				
C. (*Rusa*) sp.[18]																								×						×						
C. (*Sika*) sp.																																				
Pseudaxis hortulorum Swinhoe																				×																
Pseudaxis sp.	×																																			
C. (*Elaphurus*) sp.																							×													
Moschus moschiferus																											×									
?*Moschus* sp.																												×								
?*Hydropotes* sp.																							×													
Elaphodus cephalophus																																				
Muntiacus muntiak Hoojier[19]																											×		×							
M. *szechuanensis* (Young and Liu)[20]																							×													

Appendix 3.   South China Pleistocene faunas (continued)

Form	\multicolumn{35}{c}{Location numbers (Figure 1)}

Form	1	2	3	4	5	6	7	8	9	10	11	12	13	14	15	16	17	18	19	20	21	22	23a	23b	24	25	26	27	28	29	30	31	32	33	34	35
M. cf. reevesi (Ogilby)																																				×
Muntiacus sp.[21]		×	×	×	×		×									×									×			×								
Naemorhedus goral (Hard)			×																							×		×								
Ovinae indet.[22]																																	×			
Ovis sp.																		×							×											
Ovicapricornae indet.					×																							×								
Capricornis sumatrensis							×																													
?Capricornis sp.																											×	×								
Bubalus bubalus (L)																												×								
B. cf. brevicornis																											×	×								
Young = B. bubalus?																									×											
Bubalus sp.	×						×																		×											
Bos sp.																			×																	
Bos (Bibos) sp.		×																																		
Bibos gaurus																											×									
Bovidae indet.[23]	×	×	×	×	×		×	×	×	×	×	×	×	×		×	×			×	×		?	?	×		×	×	×	×		×		×		×

[1] R. sinensis troglodytes Matthew and Granger at Locality 27.
[2] H. cf. subcristata at Localities 10, 17, 20, 27, 28, 23, 34.
[3] C. antiquus antiquus Matthew and Granger at Locality 27.
[4] A. collaris cf. rostratus Matthew and Granger at Localities 7, 34, 27; A. collaris rostratus at Locality 8; A. collaris collaris Cuv. at Locality 27.
[5] P? larvata at Locality 10.
[6] H. brevirostris licenti = H. licenti; H. b. sinensis = H. sinensis.
[7] P. cf. tigris at Localities 3, 7, 25.
[8] P. cf. pardus at Locality 3.
[9] S. cf. orientalis at Localities 7, 33.
[10] P. cf. namadicus at Localities 3, 34.
[11] H. cf. augustus at Locality 3.
[12] T. cf. sinensis at Locality 21.
[13] R. cf. sinensis at Localities 7, 18.
[14] E. cf. yunnanensis at Locality 5.
[15] S. cf. scrofa at Localities 7, 18, 24.
[16] Two species at Locality 10.
[17] Two species at Locality 2.
[18] Two species of Rusa at Localities 3, 7.
[19] M. muntiak margae at Locality 27.
[20] M. szechuanensis and M. ? szechuanensis at Locality 25.
[21] Two species at Locality 32.
[22] Two forms at Locality 3.
[23] Two forms at Locality 29.

REFERENCES

ACADEMIA SINICA, INSTITUTE OF GEOLOGY
1964   *Ti Ssu Chi Ti-chih Wen-t'i* [Quaternary China]. Peking: Science Press.

AIGNER, JEAN S.
1969   "The archaeology of Pleistocene China." Unpublished Ph.D. dissertation, University of Wisconsin, Madison.
1972a   Pleistocene archaeological remains from South China. *Asian Perspectives* 16 (1): 16–38.
1972b   Relative dating of Pleistocene faunal and cultural complexes in North China. *Arctic Anthropology* 9 (2): 36–79.

AIGNER, JEAN S., WILLIAM S. LAUGHLIN
1973   The dating of Lantian Man and the significance for analyzing trends in human evolution. *American Journal of Physical Anthropology* 39 (1): 97–110.

ANONYMOUS
1959a   Preliminary report on the excavation of human and mammalian fossils at Mapa, Kwangtung. *Vertebrata Palasiatica* 3 (2): 104.
1959b   Skull of Middle Pleistocene age discovered in Kwangtung. *Wen-wu* 1: 47. (In Chinese.)
1960a   The Palaeolithic of Tungshing, Kwangtung. *Vertebrata Palasiatica* 4 (1): 38.
1960b   Many Neolithic sites found in Kwangtung. *Vertebrata Palasiatica* 4 (2): 112.

BOWLES, GORDON T.
1933   A preliminary report of archaeological investigations on the Sino-Tibetan border of Szechwan. *Bulletin of the Geological Society of China* 13: 119–141.

CHANG, KWANG-CHIH
1968   *The archaeology of ancient China* (revised edition). New Haven: Yale University Press.

CH'ANG, YU-P'ING
1959   Pleistocene mammals from Shaochin, Kwangtung. *Paléontologie et Paléoanthropologie* 1 (3): 141–143. (In Chinese.)

CHIA, LAN-PO
1954   New anthropological discovery. *China Reconstructs* 6 (4): 36. Peking.
1957   Notes on the human remains from Ch'angyang, Hupei. *Vertebrata Palasiatica* 1 (3): 247–257. (In Chinese.)

CHIA, LAN-PO, CHUNG-LANG CHIU
1960   On the age of the chipped stone artifacts in Kwangsi caves. *Vertebrata Palasiatica* 4 (1): 39.

CHIA, LAN-PO, JU-KANG WOO
1959   Fossil human skull base of late palaeolithic stage from Chilinshan, Leipin District, Kwangsi, China. *Vertebrata Palasiatica* 3 (1): 37–40.

CH'IN, HSUEH-SHENG
1962   On the age and sex of the Tzeyang Skull. *Vertebrata Palasiatica* 6 (1): 111–115. (In Chinese.)

CHIU, CHUNG-LANG
1955   On fluorine dating of Chinese hominids. *Acta Palaeontologica Sinica* 3 (4): 323–329. (In Chinese.)

CHIU, CHUNG-LANG, YU-P'ING CH'ANG, YUNG-SHENG TUNG
  1961   Pleistocene mammalian fossils from Chinkiang District, western Hupei. *Vertebrata Palasiatica* 5 (2): 155–159. (In Chinese.)

CHOU, MIN-CHEN
  1957   Mammalian faunas and correlation of Tertiary and Early Pleistocene of South China. *Scientia* 13: 394–400.

CHOU, MIN-CHEN, JEN-CHIEH CHAI
  1962   Early Pleistocene mammals of Chaotung, Yunnan, with notes on some Chinese stegodonts. *Vertebrata Palasiatica* 6 (2): 138–144. (In Chinese.)

COLBERT, EDWIN H.
  1940   Pleistocene mammals from the Makai Valley of northern Yunnan, China. *American Museum Novitiates*: 1099.
  1943   Pleistocene vertebrates collected in Burma by the American Southeast Asiatic Expedition. *Transactions of the American Philosophical Society*, n.s. 32 (3): 395–429.

COLBERT, EDWIN H., DIRK A. HOOIJER
  1953   Pleistocene mammals from the limestone fissures of Szechuan, China. *Bulletin of the American Museum of Natural History* 102 (1).

COON, CARLETON S.
  1963   *Origin of races.* New York: Alfred Knopf.

EDGAR, J. H.
  1933–1934   Prehistoric remains in the Hsikang or eastern Tibet. *Journal of the West China Border Research Society* 6: 56–61.

GORMAN, CHESTER F.
  1969   Hoabinhian: a pebble-tool complex with early plant associations in Southeast Asia. *Science* 163: 671–673.

GRAHAM, D. C.
  1935   Implements of prehistoric man in the West China Union University Museum of Archaeology. *Journal of the West China Border Reseach Society* 7: 47–56.

HOOIJER, DIRK A.
  1951   On the supposed evidence of early man in the Middle Pleistocene of southwest China. *Southwestern Journal of Anthropology* 7 (1): 77–81.

HSIEH, HSIANG-HSU
  1960   Some new localities of Pleistocene mammals in Shensi. *Vertebrata Palasiatica* 4 (1): 44–45. (In Chinese.)

HSU, Y. H., Y. C. LI, H. H. HSIEH
  1957   Mammalian fossils from the Pleistocene cave deposits of Chi-chin, northwestern Kweichou. *Acta Palaeontologica Sinica* 5 (2): 343–350. (In Chinese.)

HUANG, WAN-PO
  1963   Notes on the cave and cave deposits in Kaoyao, Loting, and Fengkai districts of Kwangtung. *Vertebrata Palasiatica* 7 (1): 79–83. (In Chinese.)

HUANG, WAN-PO, TI-FEN HAN
  1959   On the formation and mammalian fossils of Tatits'un, Tungshenhsien in Hupei Province. *Paléontologie et Paléoanthropologie* 1 (1): 43–45.

HUANG, WAN-PO, HUNG-CH'IANG CHI
  1963a   Discovery of *Ailuropoda-Stegodon* fauna from the Loping district,

northeastern Kiangsi. *Vertebrata Palasiatica* 7 (2): 182–189. (In Chinese.)

1963b Note on the Holocene Hsien-jen-tung deposit of Wannian, Kiangsi. *Vertebrata Palasiatica* 7 (3): 263–277. (In Chinese.)

KAHLKE, HANS-DIETRICH

1961 On the complex of *Stegodon-Ailuropoda* fauna of southern China and the chronological position of *Gigantopithecus blacki* von Koenigswald. *Vertebrata Palasiatica* 5 (2): 83–108. (In Chinese.)

KOTANI, YOSHINOBU

1969 Upper Pleistocene and Holocene environmental conditions in Japan. *Arctic Anthropology* 5 (2): 133–156.

KU, WANG-MIN

1962 Report on the investigations of Lingshan caves, Kwangtung. *Vertebrata Palasiatica* 6 (2): 193–201. (In Chinese.)

KURTEN, BJORN

1956 The status and affinities of *Hyaena sinensis* Matsumoto. *American Museum Novitiates* 1764: 1–48.

LI, YEN-HSIEN, WEI-WEN HUANG

1961 Palaeoliths from I-liang, Yunnan. *K'ao-ku* 12: 641–642. (In Chinese.)

1962 Report on palaeoliths discovered in I-liang, Yunnan. *Vertebrata Palasiatica* 6 (2): 182–192. (In Chinese.)

LI, YIU-HENG

1960 Preservation of the fossils in the Gigantopithecus cave, Liu-ch'eng, Kwangsi. *Vertebrata Palasiatica* 4 (1): 40.

1961 A Pleistocene mammalian locality in the Likiang Basin, Yunnan. *Vertebrata Palasiatica* 5 (2): 143–149. (In Chinese.)

1962 Reconnaissance of some mammalian fossil localities in the region of the upper Han river. *Vertebrata Palasiatica* 6 (3): 280–290. (In Chinese.)

LIU, CHANG-CHI

1962 Quaternary mammalian localities of northern Kwangtung. *Vertebrata Palasiatica* 6 (2): 202–207. (In Chinese.)

MATTHEW, W. D., W. GRANGER

1923 New fossil mammals from the Pliocene of Sze-chuan. *Bulletin of the American Museum of Natural History* 48: 563–598.

MI, T. H.

1943 New finds of late Cenozoic vertebrates. *Bulletin of the Geological Society of China* 23 (3/4): 155–167.

MO, CHIH

1959 Stone artifacts found at Hsi-chiao-shan in Han-hai, Kwangtung. *K'ao-ku hsueh-pao* 4: 1–15. (In Chinese.)

MOVIUS, HALLAM L., JR.

1955 Recent research on early man in China. *American Anthropologist* 57: 334–337.

P'EI, WEN-CHUNG

1935a On a mesolithic (?) industry of the caves of Kwangsi. *Bulletin of the Geological Society of China* 14 (3): 413–425.

1935b Fossil mammals from the Kwangsi caves. *Bulletin of the Geological Society of China* 14 (3): 393–412.

1940 Note on a collection of mammalian fossils from Tanyang in Kiangsu Province. *Bulletin of the Geological Society of China* 19: 379–392.

1952 Report on the excavation of Tzeyang man remains and associated faunal remains from the Huang-shan-ch'i in Szechuan. *K'o-hsueh-tung-pao* 3 (10): 7–13. (In Chinese.)

1956 New material on man's origin. *China Reconstructs* 8: 9.

1957a New links between ape and man. *China Reconstructs* 6 (6): 2–5.

1957b The zoographical divisions of Quaternary mammalian fauna in China. *Vertebrata Palasiatica* 1 (1): 9–24.

1957c Discovery of *Gigantopithecus* mandibles and other material in Liuch'eng district of central Kwangsi in South China. *Vertebrata Palasiatica* 1: 65–71.

1960a The living environments of the Chinese primitive men. *Vertebrata Palasiatica* 4 (1): 40–44.

1960b The living environments of Chinese primitive men. *Paléontologie et Paléoanthropologie* 2 (1): 9–21. (In Chinese.)

1961 Fossil mammals of the Early Pleistocene age from Yuanmo (Makai) of Yunnan. *Vertebrata Palasiatica* 5 (1): 16–32. (In Chinese.)

1965 *Excavation of Liuch'eng* Gigantopithecus *caves and explorations in other Kwangsi caves.* Institute of Vertebrate Palaeontology and Palaeoanthropology, Memoir 7. Peking.

P'EI, WEN-CHUNG, CHUNG-LANG CHIU

1957 On a collection of mammalian fossils from Liuhsia, Hangchow, Chekiang, China. *Vertebrata Palasiatica* 1 (1): 42–46.

P'EI, WEN-CHUNG, MIN-CHEN CHOU

1961 Discovery of palaeoliths in I-liang, Yunnan. *Vertebrata Palasiatica* 5 (2): 139–142. (In Chinese.)

P'EI, WEN-CHUNG, YIU-HENG LI

1958 Discovery of a third mandible of *Gigantopithecus* in Liuch'eng, Kwangsi, South China. *Vertebrata Palasiatica* 2 (4): 193–200.

P'EI, WEN-CHUNG, JU-KANG WOO

1956 New materials of *Gigantopithecus* teeth from South China. *Acta Palaeontologica Sinica* 4 (4): 477–490. (In Chinese.)

1957 *Tzeyang Man.* Institute of Vertebrate Palaeontology and Palaeoanthropology, Memoir 1. Peking.

P'EI, WEN-CHUNG, *et al.*

1965 Discovery of remains from Kuan-yin-tung, in Chienshi, Kweichou. *Vertebrata Palasiatica* 9 (3): 270–279. (In Chinese.)

PENG, JU-TSE, WEI WANG

1959 Ancient stone artifacts from Hsi-chiao-shan. *Wen-wu* 5: 75. (In Chinese.)

PIEN, M. N.

1940 Preliminary observations on the Cenozoic geology of Yunnan. *Bulletin of the Geological Society of China* 20: 179–204.

PIEN, M. N., LAN-PO CHIA

1938 Cave and rock-shelter deposits in Yunnan. *Bulletin of the Geological Society of China* 18: 325–348.

SOLHEIM, WILHELM G., III

1967 "Prehistoric pottery of Southeast Asia." Symposium: Early Chinese Art and Its Possible Influence in the Pacific Basin, Paper 16, Columbia University, August 23.

1969 Reworking Southeast Asian prehistory. *Paideuma* 15: 125–139.

TEILHARD DE CHARDIN, P.

1935 Notes on continental geology. *Bulletin of the Geological Society of China* 16: 195–200.

1941   *Early man in China*. Institut de Géo-Biologie, Publication 7. Peking.
TEILHARD DE CHARDIN, P., PIERRE LEROY
    1942   *Chinese fossil mammals*. Institute de Géo-Biologie, Publication 8. Peking.
TIELHARD DE CHARDIN, P., C. C. YOUNG
    1935   The Cenozoic sequence in the Yangtze Valley. *Bulletin of the Geological Society of China* 14: 171–178.
THOMA, A.
    1964   Die Entstehung der Mongoliden. *Homo* 15 (1): 1–22.
WOO, JU-KANG
    1958   Fossil human skull probably of Protoanthropic stage found in Ch'u-chiang, Kwangtung. *Vertebrata Palasiatica* 2 (4): 296.
    1959   Human fossils found in Liukiang, Kwangsi, China. *Vertebrata Palasiatica* 3 (3): 109–118.
WOO, JU-KANG, LAN-PO CHIA
    1955   Fossil human femur fragment of Hsiao-tsao-wan. *Acta Palaeontologica Sinica* 3: 67–68.
WOO, JU-KANG, JU-TSE PENG
    1959   Fossil human skull of early Palaeoanthropic stage found at Mapa, Shaoquan, Kwangtung Province. *Vertebrata Palasiatica* 3 (4): 176–182.
YANG, LING
    1961   Discovery of palaeoliths from Fulengchen, Hanyuan, Szechuan. *Vertebrata Palasiatica* 5 (4): 353–359. (In Chinese.)
YOUNG, C. C.
    1932   On some fossil mammals from Yunnan. *Bulletin of the Geological Society of China* 11: 383–394.
    1936   New finds of fossil Bubalus in China. *Bulletin of the Geological Society of China* 15 (4): 505–518.
    1939   New fossils from Wan-hsien, Szechuan. *Bulletin of the Geological Society of China* 19: 317–331.
YOUNG, C. C., P. T. LIU
    1950   On the mammalian fauna of Koloshan near Chungking, Szechuan. *Bulletin of the Geological Society of China* 30: 43–90.
YOUNG, C. C., T. H. MI
    1941   Notes on some newly discovered late Cenozoic mammals from southwestern and northwestern China. *Bulletin of the Geological Society of China* 21 (1): 97–106.

PART THREE

Northeast Asia

Important Archaeological Remains from North China

JEAN S. AIGNER

Between 1921 and 1937 the Geological Survey of China undertook extensive field study of Pleistocene stratigraphy and paleontology. The most important basic work was done in the north where fossil remains were abundant in the deposits and permitted correlation of strata over distance. In the course of their reconnaissances, field geologists and paleontologists made important archaeological discoveries in the Choukoutien fissures and in the Ordos region. Up to 1937, when the fieldwork was halted by the Japanese military invasion, considerable work was done at Choukoutien archaeological localities and some data were collected from western and northeastern China as well.

Since the resumption of work in 1949, the active agency has been the Institute of Vertebrate Palaeontology and Palaeoanthropology (IVPP), formerly the Laboratory of Vertebrate Palaeontology and the Institute of Vertebrate Palaeontology. Literally hundreds of potential "paleolithic" stations have been discovered, principally along major waterways such as the Huangho and Fenho, but also in the Ordos, on the border of the Hopei Plain, and in the foothills and karst regions of South China. The new work has considerably expanded our information on the archaeology of Pleistocene China, formerly limited to major sites at Choukoutien and those in the Ordos.

The last and still most comprehensive summary of data on the Pleistocene period of China up to 1949 is Teilhard de Chardin's 1941 work. Movius' 1944 and 1948 papers provide a broad picture of east Asian archaeology and an attempt to correlate Pleistocene depositional units. But Movius' fourfold scheme of glacials and pluvials/interglacials and interpluvials, synchronous with the old Himalayan sequence, is no longer tenable (Aigner 1969, 1972a). The more recent summaries for China appear mainly as short articles and as book chapters heavily weighted with archaeological data and largely dependent upon dating schemes which should be abandoned.

Aside from Teilhard de Chardin and Leroy's faunal lists (1942) and a chapter in the recent Chinese monograph *Ti Ssu Chi Ti-chih Wen-ti* [Quaternary China] (Academia Sinica 1964), detailed reports on the faunal history of the Pleistocene are few (see Aigner 1969, 1972a; P'ei 1957). While revisions in nomenclature are also long overdue, attempts have begun but unfortunately only on a site basis. Among the few studies to provide in depth data on the geology, paleontology, and archaeology of a single locale is the Academia Sinica publication *Cenozoid of Lantian* (1966). It does not constitute a successfully integrated study, however, but consists rather of individual papers dealing with various aspects of the geology, etc. of the area.

Some recent summaries of important archaeological finds are available. Chang (1963) lists Pleistocene and Recent archaeological sites. His geological summary is taken from early sources and is only partly satisfactory. Details of remains from specific sites may be found in Cheng (1959) but the quality of scholarship is uneven. Cheng is prone to paraphrase uncritically from reports and incorporates some factual errors. *Hsin chung-kou ti k'ao-ku shou-huo* [Archaeology in New China] (Academia Sinica 1962) deals with the archaeological materials rather than with the details of geology and paleontology in China (most of the information in Cheng's 1966 supplementary volume is a direct translation from this source). Individual sites have recently been summarized by Aigner (1973; Aigner and Laughlin 1973).

The most up-to-date information on Pleistocene remains in China which is *readily* available in English is Chang's revised *Archaeology of ancient China* (1968) (Aigner 1969 is available only on microfilm). He expands his earlier coverage for the Pleistocene and includes useful information on the current views expressed in *Quaternary China* (1964) and *Cenozoic of Lantian* (1966). Still, Chang details only the outstanding early sites, making little attempt to evaluate relative dating of remains, and he omits faunal histories completely. This is a critical omission since faunal histories provide the best evidence for relatively dating Pleistocene cultural and hominid remains (Aigner 1969, 1972a, 1973, and my other contribution to this volume). Furthermore, the *theoretical* implications of the cultural remains and hominid materials from Pleistocene China are largely ignored.

Chinese paleobotanical study is not regularly employed in the interests of archaeological investigation and techniques of absolute dating are surprisingly rarely utilized although the facilities and technology exist. Finally, information on the hominid remains from China is scattered in the literature and poorly treated in the archaeological texts cited above. Coon's review (1963) is still the most complete; it is updated in Aigner (1969).

The main objective of this brief paper is to list what appear to be important archaeological sites from North China and provide references. I have dealt with these materials in some depth elsewhere, including a general compendium of geological, climatic, floral, and faunal data, cultural and hominid remains (1969), South Chinese archaeological materials (1972b), North Chinese Pleistocene faunas and a relative sequence of faunal and archaeological stations (1972a), South Chinese Pleistocene faunas and cultural materials in the other article I contributed to this volume, and details of several important sites including Hsiao-nan-hai (1973) and Lantian (Aigner and Laughlin 1973). The reader is referred to these works for additional information.

A major premise of mine is that the North Chinese Pleistocene cultural and hominid remains, despite their not always satisfactory context and detail, are enormously significant (1) for reconstructing the pattern of hominid biocultural development in eastern Asia and (2) for our understanding of hominid evolution, specifically for refuting the replacement theory for the emergence and spread of modern *Homo sapiens* most recently reiterated by Birdsell (1972). A full elaboration of these points is currently in progress in a paper of mine (Aigner 1976).

For present purposes I shall list archaeological sites in North China by geographic region and summarize each in terms of Pleistocene materials of passing and potential interest. For those few sites where both the geological and cultural contexts are controlled, and where some human adaptational information may be elicited, longer summaries are provided. References to geological and faunal reports may be found in bibliographies of my other papers; the sites considered specifically here are referenced as completely as necessary but a full bibliography may be found in Aigner 1969 and 1976.

ARCHAEOLOGICAL MATERIALS

Localities on the Edge of the Hopei Plain

SHANTUNG PROVINCE. A brief report (Tai and Pai 1966) locates quartz implements and fossil mammalian remains in ashy layers of a cave for which no location is provided. Poor illustrations diminish the ability to evaluate the small collection of "scrapers," flakes and "nuclei," and *Equus przewalskyi* (or *E. hemionus*) and *Sus* cf. *lydekkeri* which suggest an Upper Pleistocene date.

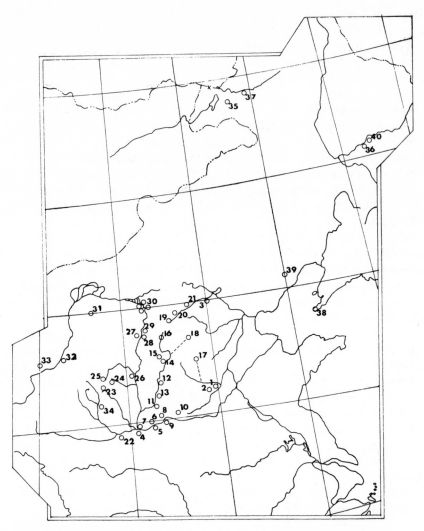

Figure 1.   Archaeological sites in North China

1.   Hsiao-nan-hai
2.   Pei-lou-ting-shan, Anyang
3.   Choukoutien localities
4.   T'ung-kuan area, Shensi
5.   Ch'ang-chia-wan, Honan
6.   P'ing-lu area, Shansi
7.   Jui-ch'eng area, Shansi
8.   Yuan-ch'u, Shansi
9.   Mien-ch'ih, Honan
10.   Ku-lung, Shansi
11.   Lower Fenho sites
12.   Huo-hsien sites
13.   Tingts'un
14.   Middle Fenho sites

15.   Chiao-ch'eng-hsien sites
16.   Upper Fenho sites
17.   Upper Changho sites
18.   Shou-yang and P'ing-ting areas
19.   Upper Sankanho sites
20.   Shuo-hsien sites
21.   Ta-t'ung and Tso-yun sites
22.   Lantian localities
23.   Sjara-osso-gol
24.   Yu-ho-pao
25.   Southern Ordos region
26.   Wu-pao
27.   Hala-tza
28.   Yung-hsing-pao
29.   Hu-shan

HONAN PROVINCE. The important cave site Hsiao-nan-hai was located in 1960 some thirty kilometers southwest of Anyang in northern Honan on the edge of the Hopei Plain (An 1965; P. S. Chou 1965; Aigner 1969, 1972a, 1973) (Figure 1.1). The cave is 257 meters above sea level and 177 meters above and 500 meters from the Hsuan River. The materials collected come from a ten-square-meter test pit and from materials at the mouth of the cave which had been excavated by workmen and thrown out as backdirt.

Site stratigraphy clearly shows five layers of aeolian deposits with associated cultural and mammalian remains in at least three or four (Table 1). Identifiable faunal remains are not numerous (*Struthio* 180 pieces, *Equus* 40, *Coelodonta* 20, others 6 or less). Of the 18 species, *Crocuta*, *Equus*, *Coelodonta*, and *Gazella* are extinct; *Myospalax*, *Canis*, *Coelodonta*, *Struthio*, *Meles*, *Crocuta*, *Equus*, and *Gazella* are present in the pooled Ordos faunal collections of as recent as mid-Würm times; *Canis*, *Struthio*, *Meles*, *Crocuta*, *Equus*, *Gazella*, *Panthera*, *Capreolus*, and *Ursus* are present at Choukoutien Upper Cave of perhaps pre-Würm-Maximum times (Aigner 1969, 1972a). Thus Hsiao-nan-hai may fall in the range 20,000–50,000 B.P.

In terms of ecological/habitat preference, *Pongo* (so far the northernmost report of the form) suggests forest; *Sus* and *Panthera* range widely; *Cervus* (*Pseudaxis*), if the hypodontic form of Upper Pleistocene times, *Equus*, *Coelodonta*, *Gazella*, and perhaps *Canis* prefer open land as does *Struthio*.

In addition to the open landscape which the fauna suggest for the plain below the cave, they also indicate human preference for very young and evidently similarly more easily hunted very old individuals. Often the bones are fragmented and burned and it is suggested these forms were hunted by the human inhabitants of the cave (rather than by cave hyenas which are present in the lowest cave level).

The artifacts, most of which are concentrated in level 4, are of considerable interest (Figure 2). Cores and perhaps several "choppers" show considerable variation but form a graded series. Most are blocky in form but a small proportion are more regular in form with unprepared platforms. A few are small with scars indicating the removal of small, directed, or blade-like flakes.

Most of the flakes are unutilized and unworked. The vast majority are apparently irregular in form (quantification is not provided in the

Table 1. A. Stratigraphy of Hsiao-nan-hai

1. Aeolian deposits with sublevels
   A (0.07–0.25 meters): sterile;
   B (0.15–0.95 meters): yellowish-brown matrix with ten artifacts and mammalian remains;
   C (0.30–0.80 meters): dark yellow deposit with three artifacts and mammalian remains.
2. A thin (0.20–0.65 meters) zone of white-mottled yellowish-brown loess from which 469 artifacts and mammalian fossils were removed.
3. A thin (0.10–0.60 meters) layer of grayish yellow loess with numerous artifacts (425) and a diverse fauna.
4. Yellowish-brown loess (0.30–2.0 meters) containing 6,080 (86 percent) artifacts and numerous faunal remains.
5. The lowest level, formed on bedrock, consisting of 0.25–0.90 meters of yellowish loess with grayish gravels; 90 artifacts and some mammal bones were recovered.

B. Fauna from Hsiao-nan-hai

| | | | | Level | | | |
Faunal form	1A	1B	1C	2	3	4	5
Struthio anderssoni Lowe						×	
Erinaceus sp.			×				
Pongo sp.					×	×	
Myospalax fontanieri (Milne-Edwards)		×				×	
Rattus sp.		×					
Ursus cf. *arctos*[a]							×
Meles leucurus Hodgeson		×		×			
Crocuta crocuta ultima (Matsumoto)		×		×	×	×	
Canis cf. *lupus* L				×			
Panthera pardus (L)		×					
Equus hemionus Pallas		×			×	×	×
Coelodonta antiquitatis (Blumenbach)		×			×	×	
Sus sp.					×	×	
Capreolus cf. *manchuricus* Lydekker		×					
Cervus (*Pseudaxis*) sp.		×	×	×	×	×	
Bubalus sp.		×			×	×	
Gazella przewalskyi Buchner		×		×		×	
Capricornis sp.					×	×	

C. Hsiao-nan-hai lithic remains

Level	"Chunks"	Nuclei	Flakes	Pointed tools	"Scrapers"	Choppers	Nuclei	Flakes	Pointed tools	"Scrapers"	Flakes	"Scrapers"	Flakes	"Scrapers"	Flakes	Total	Percent
1B	2	1	6	0	1	0	0	0	0	0	0	0	0	0	0	10	0.14
1C	0	1	1	0	0	0	0	0	0	1	0	0	0	0	0	3	0.04
2	14	6	433	1	9	0	0	1	0	1	2	2	0	0	0	469	6.62
3	10	28	357	2	13	0	0	13	0	1	1	0	0	0	0	425	6.00
4	32	346	4972	6	48	4	15	634	8	9	1	3	1	1	0	6080	85.89
5	6	0	75	0	6	0	0	2	0	1	0	0	0	0	1	91	1.28
Total	64	382	5844	9	77	4	15	650	8	13	4	5	1	1	1	7078	99.97

Grand total	6,360 Chert				686 Quartz				9 Flint	2 Chalcedony	1 Limestone

[a] *Ursus* was identified as *U.* cf. *spelaeus* (see Appendix 4, Aigner 1969).

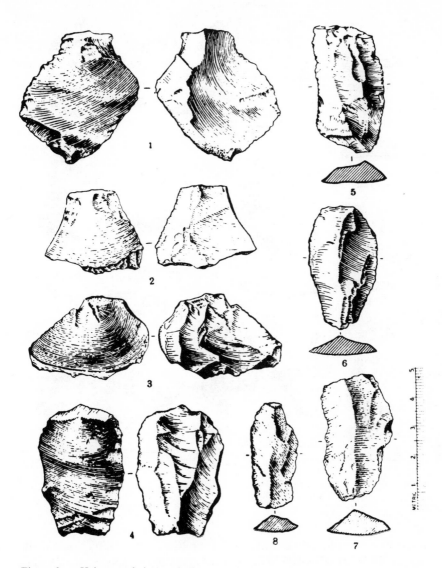

Figure 2a.   Hsiao-nan-hai (An 1965)

original report) while long, directed flakes and rare regular flakes are also pictured. There are only seventeen pointed flake tools in the collection. These are unifacially retouched and show little alteration in shape by retouch. Some ninety-six flakes with retouch are referred to as "scrapers" and the disposition and extent of retouch on these varies. Again, regularized or formalized shape categories seem not to

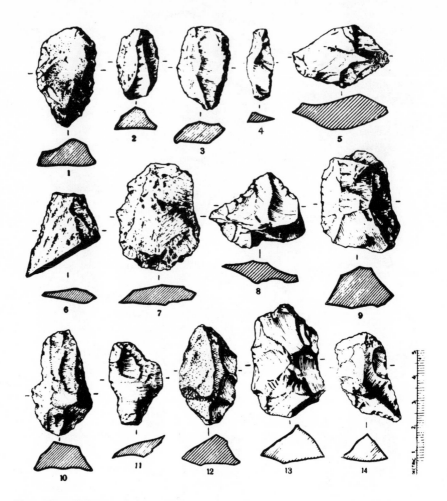

Figure 2b.   Hsiao-nan-hai (An 1965)

have been produced, an interesting continuity in technological behavior with most Hopei Plain and other North Chinese assemblages
and collections.

The "scrapers" tend to be medium to small and made on irregular
flake blanks for the most part. Blanks tend to be longer than broad,
with angles between 90° and 120° but most near 110°. The angle on
short, narrow flakes is nearer 100°.

The only piece of worked bone was recovered in backdirt
materials but is probably associated with the lithic remains. This is a
small bead, 2.5×1.1×0.6 centimeters.

We can make several tentative hypotheses about the Hsiao-nan-hai

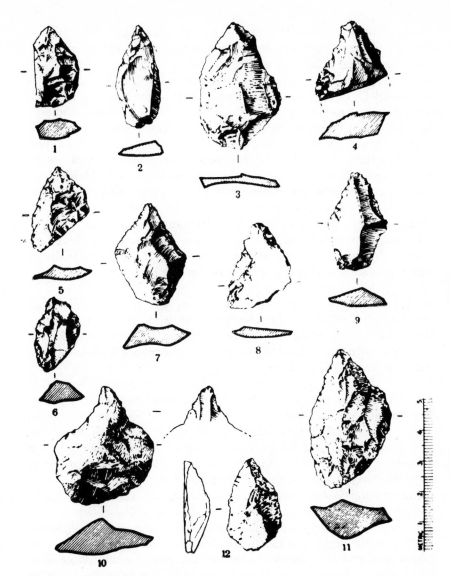

Figure 2c.   Hsiao-nan-hai (An 1965)

cave site and its occupation. The age is Upper Pleistocene and the
presence of ash and burnt bone indicate occupation for warmth and
meal preparation in addition to tool manufacture. We may extend this
to mean that the site served as a seasonal hunting station or camp.
Few of the tools at the site appear to be broken.

Technologically the assemblage shows little typological variety
largely because natural blank shapes are not altered and in this sense

Hsiao-nan-hai more closely resembles the much older Choukoutien localities than it does those related to the so-called Tingts'un complex which are more nearly contemporaneous.

Hsiao-nan-hai is an important site because it represents the only *in situ* locality of substance from Upper Pleistocene times. The dating and stratigraphic history of the Ordos localities are unclear and controversial, and Tingts'un remains are water-transported, a compilation from several collecting stations. The Hsiao-nan-hai remains will provide materials for a good and thorough technological analysis owing to the large sample size. The faunal preservation is fair and the forms indicate consistently a dating to a cool phase of the Upper Pleistocene, probably pre-Maximum as well. The site itself appears to be fairly extensive and is clearly rich, with 7,000 artifacts from a small test cut. Stratigraphy is good and the site location on the edge of the Hopei Plain should make possible an interesting study of the local conditions which prevailed during occupation of the site by humans.

HOPEI PROVINCE. Three major sites are known from early work in Hopei: Choukoutien 1, Choukoutien 15, and Choukoutien Upper Cave. All are located on the edge of the Hopei Plain and are limestone cave sites with fair to good archaeological context and with associated faunal remains (Figure 1.3).

1. Choukoutien Locality 1. The Choukoutien region is the type area for the mid-Middle Pleistocene "Choukoutien Formation" – clefts and caves filled with brecciated clayish and sandy fossiliferous deposits and dating to a long period of aggradation in which the "red materials" still remaining on the mountains above washed down to form the conspicuous mantle of "red clay" and loose breccias along the lower slopes above the level of the Lower Gravels. The archaeological site of Choukoutien 1 belongs to this same Pleistocene phase. For a detailed description of the geological studies and stratigraphic analysis of the region and locality the reader is referred to Aigner 1969, which also contains an extensive bibliography. Geomorphological, lithological, in-depth faunal analyses, and recent pollen studies confirm that Locality 1 was occupied by humans during an interglacial, the Chinese equivalent of the Holstein of Europe (Aigner 1969 and references; Kahlke and Chou 1961; Hsu 1965; Sun 1965; Kahlke 1963; Aigner 1972a: also see Teilhard de Chardin 1941; Movius 1944, 1948) (Figure 3 and Table 2).

Human remains from Choukoutien Locality 1 are abundant and the material is well published in English (see especially Weidenreich 1943 for descriptions and bibliography and Aigner 1969 for references to

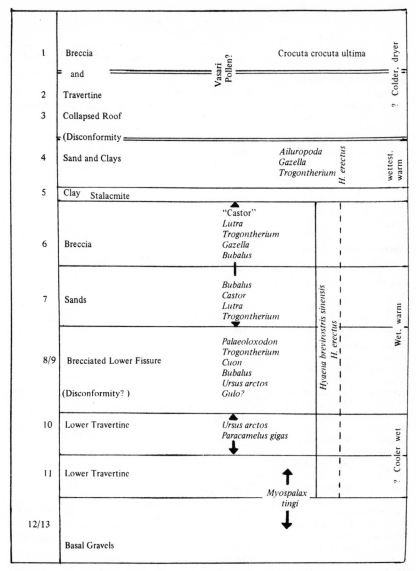

Figure 3.   Geomorphological division of the cave deposits, Locality 1 (Aigner 1969)

new materials). More than 45 individuals are represented by 15 fragments or portions of calvaria, 12 mandible fragments, more than 150 teeth, 6 facial fragments and postcranial material including 7 femoral and 3 humeral fragments, 1 tibia, 1 clavicle fragment, and 1 os lunatum.

Table 2.   Locality 1 fauna

Faunal form	Individuals (elements)	Layer												
		1	2	3	4	5	6	7	8	9	10	11	12	13
Homo erectus pekinensis (Black)	40+(100's)	×	×	×	×	×	×	?	×	×	×	?	?	?
Macaca robustus Young	9+(9+)	o	o	o	o	o	o	o	o	o	o			
Scaptochirus primitivus Zdansky	46(340+)				×	×						o	o	
Neomys sinensis Zdansky	1(1)				=									
N. bohlini Young	5(5)				×						o	o		
Crocidura sp.	20(36+)				×									
Erinaceus olgai Young: very like living *E. amurensis*	26(62+)													
Sorex sp.	?													
Rhinolophus pleistocaenicus Young	21(39+)													
Myotis sp.	48(90+)													
?*Hesperoptenus giganteus* Young	4(6+)													
?*Pipistrellus* sp. (above bats from non-brecciated layers)	2(4)													
Ia io	8(14)								=					
Minopterus schreibergii	25(49)								=					
Citellus cf. *mongolicus* (Milne-Edwards) *Spermophilus*	6(8)													
Tamias wimani Young	5(9)													
Petaurista brachyodus (Young) = *Pteromys*	1(1)													
Marmota bobak (Radde) = *Arctomys robustus* Milne-Edwards = *M. complicidens* (Young)	3(6+)							×	=	=	=			
Marmota sp.	?(30)								o	o				
Chalicomys anderssoni Schlosser = *Castor* sp.	1(4)						×							
Trogontherium cuvieri Fischer	1(4+)					×	×	×	o	o				
Cricetinus varians Zdansky	350(635+)				×	×								
Cricetulus cf. *griseus* Milne-Edwards	365(648+)				=	=					o	o	?	?
C. cf. *obscurus* Milne-Edwards	70(100)				=	=								
Mus sylvaticus (L) = *Apodemus*	200(386+)				?						o	o		
M. musculus bieni Young	13(25)				?						o	o	?	?
Micromys cf. *minutus* Pallas	12(18)				?									
Rattus rattus (L) = *Epimys*	108(198)				×	×								

Notations used:

×   Presence in original faunal reports is noted.
o   Presence noted by Kahlke and Chou from Peking specimens.
=   Presence in original reports according to Aigner: lower cave equivalent to Layer 10; lower fissure = Layers 8–9.
?   Presence likely though reports leave some doubt.
(blank) Presence not noted in reports but absence not necessarily indicated.
*   High concentration of bones of this species at this level.

Table 2. Locality 1 fauna (continued)

Faunal form	Individuals (elements)	Layer 1	2	3	4	5	6	7	8	9	10	11	12	13
Gerbillus roborowskii Buchner	265(687+)				×						O	O		
Clethrionomys rufocanus (Sundvell) = *Evotomys*	2(2)													
?Eothenomys sp.	1(1)													
Alticola sp.	1(1)													
Pitymys simplicidens Young	1(2)													
Microtus brandtioides Young	696(1370)	=	=	=	×*	×*	=	=	=	=	=			
M. epiratticeps Young	262(500+)	?	?	?	×	×	?	?	?	?	×	?		
Phaiomys sp.	1(1)													
Myospalax wongi (Young) = *Siphneus*	1(2+)													
Myospalax sp.	1(2+)													
M. tingi = *M. epitingi*?	?												=	=
Hystrix cf. *subcristata* Swinhoe	2(3+)									O	O			
Lepus cf. *wongi* Young (throughout)	5(11+)	?	?	?	?	?	?	?	?	?	?	?		
Lepus sp. A	2(3)													
Lepus sp. B	3(4)													
Ochotona koslowi Buchner	70(191+)				×					O	O	O		
Ochotona sp. A					=					=	=			
Ochotona sp. B					=						=			
Canis lupus L	10+(10+)					×				O	×			
C. lupus variabilis P'ei	100+(250+)	O	O	×	×	×	×	×	×*	×*	O	O	?	?
C. cyonides P'ei	10+(12+)								×	×				
Nyctereutes sinensis (Schlosser)	100+(?)				×	×	×	×	×	×	O			
Cuon sp. (*C.* cf. *alpinus, C. antiquus* in P'ei 1934b and Kurten 1961)	2(4+)									O	O	=		
Vulpes cf. *vulpes* (L) = *V.* cf. *vulgaris*	10+(16)	O	O	=		=	=		×	×	?			
V. cf. *corsac* (L)	100+(135+)								×	×	×			
Canidae indet.	?								×	×	?			
Ursus thibetanus kokeni Matthew and Granger = *U. angustidens* Zdansky	10+(27+)	×	×	×	×*	×*	×*		×*	×*	=			
Ursus arctos L. (= *U. spelaeus* according to Kurten 1961)	11+(40+)	O	O	O	O	O	O		×	×	×	O	?	?
?Ailuropoda sp. = *Ailuropus*	1(1)					×								
Meles cf. *leucurus* Hodgeson	10+(36+)	O	O	×		×	=		×	×	=			
Lutra melina P'ei	2(4)							×						
Gulo sp. (*G. gulo* in Kurten 1961)	1(2)								?	?				
Mustela cf. *siberica* Pallas	10+(18+)					×				=	=	=		
Mustela sp.?										×	O			
Hyaena brevirostris sinensis (Owen) = *H. sinensis, H. zdanskyi, Crocuta crocuta sinensis*	2000+				×	×	×	×	×*	×*	O	?	?	

Table 2.   Locality 1 fauna   (continued)

Faunal form	Individuals (elements)	Layer 1	2	3	4	5	6	7	8	9	10	11	12	13
Crocuta crocuta ultima (Matsumoto) = *H. ultima*	1+(1+)	○	○	×										
Meganthereon inexpectatus (Teilhard) = *Machairodus inexpectatus*	2(5)					?			?	?	?	?		
Homotherium ultimus (Teilhard) = *Machairodus?*						?			?	?	?	?		
Panthera (*Tigris*) *tigris* (L) = *Felis* cf. *tigris*	3(7)	○	○			×	×	×	×	×	=			
P. (*Tigris*) *tigris youngi* = *Felis youngi*	1+(?)								=	=				
P. (*Panthera*) cf. *pardus* (L) = *F.* cf. *pardus*	10+(14+)					×			×	×	×	○		
Felis (*Lynx*) *teilhardi* P'ei	10+(?)					×			×	×	×	○		
Felis sp. A	1(2+)					×			×	×				
Felis sp. B	1(1)							×						
Felis microtis Milne-Edwards	10+(11)					×			×	×	=			
Acinonyx sp. = *Cynailurus* sp.	1(1)					×								
Palaeoloxodon cf. *namadicus* (Falconer and Cautley)	?					○			○	○				
Dicerorhinus cf. *kirchbergensis* (Jager) = *D. mercki* = *Rhinoceros mercki*	1000's	○	○	○	○		○	○	○	○	○	○	?	?
Coelodonta sp. (reported also as *C. antiquitatis* Blumenbach)	?								○	○				
Equus cf. *sanmeniensis* (reported recently also as *Equus* sp.)	?	○	○	○	○		○	○	○	○	○	○	?	?
Sus lydekkeri Zdansky	200+	=	=	=	=	=	=	×	=	=	×	○	?	?
Camelus (*Paracamelus*) *gigas* Schlosser	1(2)											=		
Camelidae indet.	1(2)													
?*Hydropotes* sp.	3(7+)											=		
Moschus moschiferus pekinensis Young (brachyodont, found throughout)	30(140+)	=	=	=	×	×	×	=	=	=	?			
Capreolus sp.	1(5)													
Pseudaxis grayi Zdansky (somewhat hypsodontic)	1000 +	○	○	×		×	×	×	×	×	×	○	?	?
Megaloceros pachyosteus (Young) = *Megaceros, Euryceros, Sinomegaceros flabellatus* [lowest levels] and *pachyosteus* [upper levels]	2000 +	×	×	×	×	×	×	×	×	×	×	○	=	=
Cervus sp.	?	○	○	○										
Gazella sp.	1(4)					×	×							
Spirocerus peii Young	3(4+)				=				○	○	?	?		
S. cf. *wongi* Teilhard	?													
Ovis cf. *ammon* L.	?					=	×	×	○	○				

Table 2. Locality 1 fauna (continued)

Faunal form	Individuals (elements)	Layer 1	2	3	4	5	6	7	8	9	10	11	12	13
Ovis sp.	2(5+)				O				=	=	=			
Ovibovinae indet.	1(2)													
Bubalus teilhardi Young	80+							×	O	O				
Bison sp.	2(?)					×								
?*Naemorhedus* sp. (or *Namorhaedus* sp.)	?													
Bovidae indet.	?										O	O		

Other remains:
Gastropods (need taxonomic
  revision): probably from
  layers 1–3
Planorbis chihliensis Ping 1
  (fluviatile)
Eulota (*Cathaica*) *pyrrhozona*
  (Philippi) = *Helix* (terrestrial)
E. schensiensis (Hilber) 1
E. choukoutiensis (Ping) 3
Pupa micra Ping 2
Succinea hopeiensis Ping 5
  (= *S. debilis*)
S. tenuis Ping 3
Opeas lata Ping 2
O. fragilis Ping 3

Amphibia
Bufo bufo cf. *asiaticus* L	65(300):	limb bones common
B. raddei Strauch	48(200)	
Rana cf. *nigromaculata* Hallowell	?	
R. cf. *asiatica* Bedriaga	?	

Reptilia
Lacertidae indet.	5(10):	similar to living *Eremias argus*?
Ophidia indet.	?:	similar to living *Elaphe schrenkii* and *E. dione*?
Chelonia sp.	?	
Geoclemys reevesii Gray	?	

Other forms:
Myriapods
Julis cf. *terrestrus* (millipede)	9
Julis peii	9

Aves:

Asio sp.	Owl	Possibly present (locality unclear)
Dryobates sp.	Pied woodpecker	*Coturnix* sp. Quail
Galerida sp.	Lark	*Phasianus* sp. Pheasant
Alauda sp.	Lark	*Perdix barbata* Daurian partridge
Hirundo sp.	Swallow	*Crossoptilon mantchuricum* Manchurian
Dicrurus sp.	Swallow	snow pheasant
Motacilla sp.	Wagtail	*Purcrasia xanthospila* Mongolian
Six finch species		pucras

Table 2.   Locality 1 fauna   (continued)

Emberiza sp.	Buntings	*Symaticus reevesii* Reeves' pheasant
		Ostrich
Passer sp.	Tree sparrow	
Pringilla sp.	Brambling	*Gypaetus* sp. Bearded vulture
Carpodaxis sp.	Rose finch	*Aquila* sp. Sea eagle
Coccothraustes sp.	Hawfinch	

Sources:	*Material described:*
Chao and Tai 1961	New materials
Chia and Liu 1950	Myriapods
Kahlke 1963	General summary of all mammals
Kahlke and Chou 1961	General summary of all mammals
Kowalski and Li 1963	Insectivora, Chiroptera
Kurten 1968	Some mammalian remains discussed
P'ei 1934b	Carnivora
P'ei 1939a	Some Artiodactyla
Pien 1934	Amphibia, Reptilia
Ping 1929, 1931	Gastropods
Shaw 1935	Aves
Teilhard de Chardin and Leroy 1942	Some Carnivora revisions
Teilhard de Chardin and Leroy 1945	Some Carnivora revisions
Young 1932	Artiodactyla
Young 1934	Primates, Insectivora, Chiroptera, Rodentia, Lagomorpha
Zdansky 1928	Proboscidea

In Weidenreich's massive study (1943) of the materials pertaining to *Homo erectus* ("Sinanthropus") he identified more than 30 individuals by age and sex. He determined 20 adolescents or adults and 12 juveniles, each group with half male and half female. Since his works are available in English and have been widely incorporated into a number of books (most notably Coon 1963), details of the dentition, measurements, skull, etc. are not given here. Structural characteristics of the skull (cranial capacity averages 1075 with a range from 850 to 1300 including one juvenile; reinforcement system; etc.) and comparisons with relevant Pleistocene specimens (*H. erectus* from Java, *H. sapiens* [Solo] from Java, *H. sapiens* [Classic Neanderthal] from Europe) are found in Weidenreich (1943). In that same publication he also hypothesized that Sinanthropus was ancestral to modern Mongoloids basing his judgment upon features which they share in common, notably in the dental complex, and on the mandible and calvarium. Virtually all subsequent Pleistocene hominid remains from China support his hypotheses (Coon 1963; Thoma 1964; Aigner and Laughlin 1973).

Stratigraphically it is important to understand that at least 75 percent of the individuals represented at Choukoutien Locality 1 derive from levels 8 to 10 of the deposits; these include the skull fragments prominently and many of the isolated teeth as well. The remaining materials are principally from level 4 where again a heavy concentration of hominid activity is represented by hearths and food remains in equivalent levels. The statement that Sinanthropus shows virtually no "evolution" through the deep deposits is misleading unless one remembers that teeth (notoriously conservative, evolutionarily speaking) and not calvaria are meant. The concentration of materials in levels 8 to 10 makes this collection the only one earlier than the Upper Pleistocene which may be considered a "population" in a meaningful sense. It may be studied in terms of population variation and considered a geographic or "racial" variant of *H. erectus*, again *meaningfully*.

Artifactual materials from Choukoutien are concentrated in several parts of the deposit, in layers equivalent to those which produced most of the hominid remains and from which the ash from hearths is reported. Thus, layers 8 to 10 and layer 4 showed three main concentrations of cultural materials; isolated artifacts only were found in the remaining mass of brecciated Choukoutien sediments. The published reports concerned with these materials deal with 2,000 artifacts collected in the early 1930's from lower layers; unpublished remains from layer 4 were collected from backdirt (removed in 1928) after it was ascertained that quartzite flakes and cobbles were attributable to hominids (Teilhard de Chardin and P'ei 1932; Movius 1944, 1948; Chia 1960; Ch'ang 1962).

A restudy of the Choukoutien collections reportedly has been made by scientists from the Institute of Vertebrate Palaeontology and Palaeoanthropology but it is not available. Early studies of the materials differ in the classificatory systems employed, understandable considering the general lack of comparable materials and previous analyses in the area and the nature of the technology represented. Quantification of groupings is lacking and recent restudies indicate some controversy over the intrasite correlations of levels (Ch'ang 1962). However, the argument for regrouping seems to be purely typological, ignoring the stratigraphic and faunistic data which are used by other workers.

Illustrations of some Choukoutien tools are provided (Figure 4). Most remains are flakes and these are irregular and although variable in size tend to be large (one is 21.2 × 14.5 centimeters). Perhaps 85–90 percent of the specimens recognized as altered by retouch are flake tools. Quartz flakes with a single, unifacially percussed edge which may be concave, convex, straight, or oblique account for fully 82 percent of the *tools*. Naturally pointed flakes with retouch are present

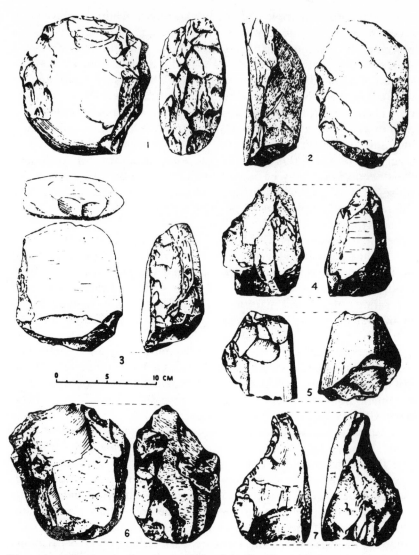

Figure 4a.   Choukoutien Locality 1 (Teilhard de Chardin and P'ei 1932)

but uncommon (67 examples in nearly 6,000). So-called chopper tools, presumably made on cobbles but primarily on flakes, are not particularly common. They show little shape alteration by retouch and small use scars. Stone hammers to produce flakes, and anvils and their hammers said to have been used in the production of bi-polar flakes are also recognized. Several unique categories have recently been described by Ch'ang (1962) as stone awls (15), discs (10), engraving tools, and stone spheres. Hopefully a definitive and extensively illus-

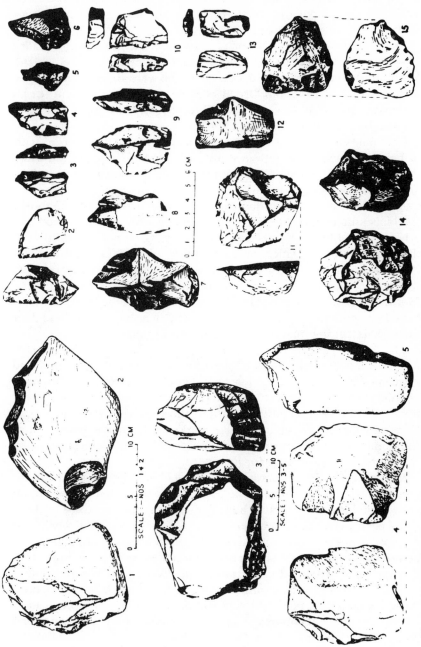

Figure 4b. Choukoutien Locality 1 (Teilhard de Chardin and P'ei 1932)

trated study of these important Choukoutien materials will soon be available. Until then we must rely upon the less than satisfactory analyses currently available.

The problem of the use of bone for artifacts and as tools at Locality 1 has long been the focus of discussion among Chinese archaeologists. Materials deliberately incised, cut, or broken were almost immediately recognized (P'ei 1932) but Breuil became an early proponent for an extensive bone industry (1939). More recently the topic has been revived by P'ei (1960) and Chia (1959b).

Chia notes that many archaeologists are convinced that a large series of bone fragments and antlers show traces of human alteration while the opponents claim such fragmentation could result from rock falls and animal activity; they add that even if remains were broken by hominids it was to extract marrow and not to make/use bone tools.

Chia's studies indicate that some remains are water-polished and others broken by rock falls and carnivores. However, in addition to these and the bones which were split by *H. erectus* for marrow, there is a collection not so easily explained away. Most *Pseudaxis* antlers were chopped from their frontals by humans. And even though the *Megaloceros* antlers were naturally shed, these and those of *Pseudaxis* have been cut into sections, some retaining their base and others their tines. This cutting may only be attributed to hominids.

There is a pattern to the alteration of antlers. On *Megaloceros* normally 12–20 centimeters of the base was left with the upper end showing clear traces of having been chopped. Antlers of *Pseudaxis* characteristically preserve a greater length. Sometimes they show traces of chopping at both ends and the removal of the first tine. Generally there are deep transverse marks on the tines similar to those found on the antler bases of *Megaloceros* which Chia interprets as the result of use, presumably for hammering.

In addition to the antlers which were deliberately altered and used, there are sharpened bones in the collection which Chia argues do not arise from hominids splitting bone for marrow. Rather, some of these show clear evidence of sharpening and Chia suggests they were used in piercing or cutting activities. Chia hypothesizes that both the numerous cut tines and sharpened limb bones in the collection were digging implements and important in the food quest. We may antici-pate that a definitive, quantified, and well-illustrated monograph on these Choukoutien bone artifacts will provide important information on *H. erectus'* technological abilities, manipulative behavior, and procurement and manufacturing activities.

Although the materials from Choukoutien were not collected in a way directly amenable to anthropological manipulation, we can elicit some useful stratigraphic and associational information and tender some tentative hypotheses concerning hominid occupation and adaptation (Aigner 1969). I have suggested that most of the individuals in the site derive from a relatively short time interval, perhaps 10,000 years, and I have argued that these were cave occupants (and not victims). Thus we know at least that old people of both sexes (two females and one male more than fifty years old), adults in their prime, adolescents, and children of all ages occupied the cave.

Breuil's study of the antler remains in the deposits (1939) suggests that hominids were hunting and utilizing Choukoutien at least from September to March or April. That is, this was a winter occupation site and the scene of a good deal of activity, not an ephemeral camp of hunters. The position of the cave on the side of a ravine that descends from the Hsishan to the plain was a favorable one for scanning and eventually capturing animals migrating to the lowlands. The stream below the cave was a source of fresh water (and perhaps of the amphibians represented in the faunal collections as well).

During the Holstein-equivalent occupation of the cave, at least part of the alluvial plain (however much was formed at that time) was drowned by higher sea levels (+20 meters is hypothesized for the Holstein). Thus the cave may have been nearer the coast which was potentially available for seasonal utilization. However, no remains of ocean fish or marine invertebrates have been reported in the cave deposits. The Hsishan themselves were an alternate seasonal habitat area which could also have been part of the exploitational area of the Choukoutien inhabitants.

Rather less speculative is the evidence for extensive exploitation in the area. The lenses of ash are extensive and numerous hearths are indicated for each of the more than 100 separate lenses in layer 4 alone. Earlier in the Holstein, especially in layers 8 to 10, was another period of heavy and repeated hominid use of the locality.

Homo erectus manufactured large choppers and cleavers as well as rather complexly finished flake tools of smaller size around the hearths in the cave. Materials for manufacture were present near the cave – quartz in veins to the south and sandstone in large deposits to the north. Rarer materials such as chert and quartz crystal had to be selectively sought in areas several kilometers southwest of the cave. In general the quartz was poor quality and probably precluded fine secondary work; however, the few tools made of quartz crystal are technically superior and indicate the actual level of refinement and manipulation attained.

That *H. erectus* was a skillful hunter is attested by extensive remains of young rhinos and the large megacerine deer. *Celtis* berries and possibly other fruits and nuts were collected from shrubs and trees nearby. *Celtis* and *Cercus*, which provide wood for fires, today grow along the stream below the cave and the pollen from the locality indicates the presence of oak, hazel, and other edible vegetable materials.

Small animals including rodents and amphibians are well represented in the faunal collections; these and tubers, nuts, and berries were readily available to those members of the group not actively engaged in hunting large mammals and it is unlikely that they were not perceived as resources by *H. erectus*.

The large game forms which are best represented are *Megaloceros*, a large forest deer (2,000+ individuals); *Dicerorhinus kirchbergensis*, also a woodland form (1,000+ individuals); the small deer of grasslands or semi-open terrain, *Pseudaxis* (1,000+ individuals); and probably the open grazing horse (*Equus sanmeniensis* is probably well represented). Seventy-five percent of all individuals for whom a habitat preference may be determined are woodland and forest forms.

Hunting techniques employed by *H. erectus* at this site are not reflected in the lithic remains. Few if any flake implements would have been suitable thrusting points and none of the worked bone suggests use in hunting (except perhaps for the possible clubs/hammers). A few perforators have been identified and several stone spheres which may have been missiles. Perhaps hunting equipment had a large investment in perishables such as wood spears (as indicated at Torralba in Spain), clubs, falls, and snares, as well as in behavioral/ethological information. It is clear that sophisticated information on the habits of a diverse range of small and also rather formidable large mammals was necessary for their capture in significant numbers. Some cooperation between hunters would have enhanced hunting success in the case of forms like rhinos, megacerine deer, water buffalo, and horse with the major investiture of time in scanning and stalking. We must attribute considerable skill and intellectual development to *H. erectus* at this time in order to account for the hunting success and ability to support such probable underproducers as the aged and very young.

2.   Choukoutien Locality 15. Locality 15 was not systematically excavated until 1934–1937 and has not been excavated subsequently. The definitive report is P'ei (1938), but much of the faunal material was not prepared for study at that time. The locality is a fissure of collapsed cave seventy meters south of Locality 1. Internal subdivisions of the deposit were not made although middle layers contained ash, *Celtis* seeds, burnt bones, and stone tools; tools were collected from elsewhere in the deposit as well.

The fauna is meager (Aigner 1969, 1972a) but datable to a cool Pleistocene phase more recent than Choukoutien 1 and earlier than the last glacial. Hence a late Middle Pleistocene age, the Riss Complex-

Table 3.   Comparison of lithic remains

	Locality 15	Locality 1
a. Material used		
Vein quartz	abundantly used; from river pebbles or its native place	abundantly used, chiefly mined from its native place
Crystal quartz	rarely used; obtained as above	rarely used; obtained as above
Flint	rare	very rare
Chert	common	rare
Chalcedony	rare	rare
Jasper	not present	rare
Quartzite	often used, collected as cobbles only	same as Locality 15
Sandstones	abundantly used, collected as cobbles only	same as Locality 15
Volcanic rocks	as above	as above
b. Techniques used		
Freehand flaking	stone and wooden hammer	same
Bipolar flaking	dubious examples	very common
Freehand chipping	common	common
Flat chipping	rare	very rare
Vertical retouch	very rare	not present
c. "Types" of implements		
"Scrapers"	abundant	abundant
Pointed tools	abundant	abundant
"Discoid tools"	abundant	abundant
Small tools (flakes)	common	rare
Pebble choppers	common	common
Small tools (pebbles)	common	rare

equivalent, is indicated. Bone is poorly represented and fragmentary, with *Pseudaxis* most common and *Sus*, *Felis*, *Canis*, and the rest of the mammals and birds represented by a few pieces each. *Dipus*, ostrich, *Gerbillus*, *Ochotona*, and hypsodontic *Pseudaxis* account for 90 percent of the individuals showing a clear habitat preference. Only *Cervus elaphus* and *Moschus* may be taken to indicate nearby forest (and there is some question about the presence of the latter). The many species of passerine birds and the paucity of bats and large birds in the faunal collection may indicate that Locality 15 was an open-air site rather than a true cave; in this case the concentration of materials in the middle zone is perhaps derived.

The lithic remains from Locality 15 are described in quite different terms by P'ei (1938) and Movius (1948) (Table 3 gives P'ei's comparison of Localities 1 and 15). One can see that at Locality 15 chert is more common and that quartz nodules are used in preference to mined quartz. The bipolar technique seems not to be recognized at Locality 15.

Table 4.   The cultural levels at Choukoutien Upper Cave

In the entrance and upper room:
Level 1:   30 centimeters thick, with a few human bones, a perforated tooth, and two flint artifacts.
Level 2:   Subdivided into several thin beds, a few human bones, 28 perforated teeth (badger and fox canines) found together.
Level 3:   A thick (to 60 centimeters) black zone with few artifacts but clear traces of human occupation (the stalagmitic floor and limestone are burnt).

In the lower room:
Level 4 and Level 5:
              Thick levels with only a few isolated human teeth, many perforated teeth, bone pendants and a chert flake. Near the top, three human skulls and post-cranial materials were recovered. More than 5 meters thick (upper 5 meters = 1.4).

In the lower recess:
              Below the lower room. Bones of various animals were common but no human or cultural remains were found.

Evidently in the kinds of implements present, and in the absence of shape retouch and established morphological types, the two localities share a common behavioral approach to stone tools. A major difference at Locality 15 is in the more refined flaking and production of more regular flakes (Figure 5). From the figures provided for this collection, there appears to be an interesting and continuous trend represented by the assemblages at Choukoutien 1, Choukoutien 15, and Hsiao-nan-hai.

3. Choukoutien Upper Cave. The Upper Cave locality was discovered in 1930 when workers stripped off soil from the limestone hill in order to trace the southern limit of the Locality 1 sediments. Systematic excavations were undertaken in 1933–1934 and the site entirely removed. It proved rich in human fossils – four skulls, a considerable amount of postcranial material and fragmental cranial material. A good faunal sample and some cultural materials were collected as well.

The cave was determined to be a true dissolution cavity which was filled by deposits and capped by soil and several interior areas are recognized (P'ei 1939b, 1940) (Table 4). A few human bones and artifacts were removed from levels 1 and 2 in the entrance and the upper room while level 3 showed clear traces of human occupation (a few artifacts and burning). In the lower room, level 4 contained a few isolated human teeth, many perforated teeth, and bone pendants, the latter ornaments associated with burials represented by three human skulls and postcranial materials. In the lower recess below the lower room bones of various animals were found but no human or cultural remains (Table 5).

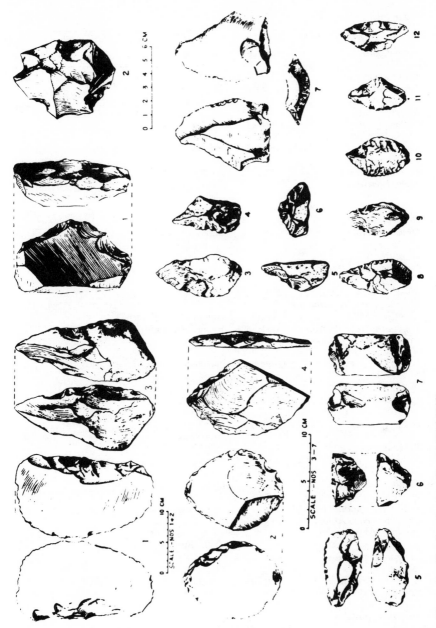

Figure 5. Choukoutien Locality 15 (P'ei 1938)

Table 5.   Upper Cave fauna

Faunal form	Individuals (Material)	Remarks	EN	UR	lr	Lr
Scaptochirus sp.	3(13)	similar to Loc. 3 form	×	×	×	×
Erinaceus sp.	80(300+)	large; similar to Loc. 3	×	×	×	×
Rhinolophus sp.	3(5)					
Myotis sp. A	19(40+)	smaller than following	×	×	×	×
Myotis sp. B	16(30+)					
Chiroptera indet.	2(3)	very small mandibles				
Canis lupus L.	several	similar to living form		×	×	
C. (Nyctereutes) procyonoides Gray	3(7)	modern, at Loc. 1		×		×
Vulpes corsac L.	5(10+)	smaller than Loc. 1, modern	×	×	×	×
V. vulgaris L.	common		×	×	×	×
Cuon alpinus Pallas	rare	at Locs. 1, 4, 13		×		
Ursus thibetanus	1(2)	derived from Loc. 1 below?				
U. arctos	4(4+)	ident. as *U. spelaeus*		×	×	×
Meles leucurus Hodgeson	30	some intrusive, unfossilized	×	×	×	×
Mustela cf. *altaica* Pallas	2(2)	similar to living form		×		
M. (Putorius) eversmanni Hollister	5(12)	similar to living form	×	×	×	×
Paguma larvata (Smith)	1(1)	living form south of area				
Crocuta crocuta ultima (Matsumoto)		skeletons		×		×
Panthera tigris (L)	common	especially young; cave dweller?	×	×	×	×
P. pardus (L)	5+(?)	smaller than Loc. 1 form	×	×	×	×
Felis (Lynx) lynx L.	3(6+)	= *F. teilhardi* of 1934 report	×	×	×	×
F. cf. *microtis* Milne-Edwards	4(16)	specific ident. in question?	×	×	×	×
F. (Lynx) sp.	3(9)	small form				
F. catus L.	4(7+)	some examples introduced?				
Acinonyx cf. *jubatus* (L)	1(1+)	large; not entirely modern		×		
?Sciurus sp.	17(33+)		×	×	×	×
Petaurista sulcatus Howell	5(?)	larger than living	×	×	×	×
Cricetinus (Cricetulus) varians Zdansky	30+(59+)	related to living *C. nestor* Thomas of Manchuria	×	×	×	×
Cricetulus obscurus Milne-Edwards	179(359)	very small	×	×	×	×
Apodemus sylvaticus L	79(167+)	= *Mus sylvaticus*				
Rattus rattus (L)	9(18)	= *Epimys*				
Gerbillus sp.	1(1)					
Microtus epiratticeps Young	100+(250+)		×	×	×	×

Key: ×   Presence in original faunal report is noted.
      EN Entrance.
      UR Upper room.
      lr   Lower room.
      Lr   Lower room.

Table 5. Upper Cave fauna (continued)

Faunal form	Individuals (Material)	Remarks	EN	UR	lr	Lr
Alticola cf. *stracheyi* Thomas	1(1)					
Myospalax armandi (Milne-Edwards)	100+(500+)		×	×	×	×
Hystrix sp.	1(2)	1934 reports form in all levels				
Lepus europaeus Pallas	thousands of individuals		×	×	×	×
Ochotona daurica Pallas	hundreds of individuals		×	×	×	×
Rhinoceros	1(1)	derives from Loc. 1 below				
Equus hemionus Pallas	2(?)	smaller than Sjara-osso-gol		×		
Sus sp.	5(?)					
Capreolus manchuricus Noack	18(60)	similar to living	×	×	×	×
Cervus elaphus	many	large, hypsodontic, many young are present	×	×	×	×
Pseudaxis hortulorum Swinhoe	50+(130+)	skeletons mainly of young	×	×	×	×
Gazella przewalskyi Buchner		"scant material"	×	×	×	×
Ovis sp.	1(1)					
Bos sp.	1	partial skeleton of a large but young individual		×	×	
Palaeoloxodon sp.	1(1)	evidently contemporaneous				
Homo sapiens	8(?)			×	×	

Pisces
Cyprinidae indet.   1(1)   *?Ctenopharyngodon idellus*

Reptilia
Natricidae indet.   1(?)   genus of local Coronellinae?
Serpentes indet.   1(1)

Amphibia
Bufo bufo asiaticus
  Steindachner   13(70)   similar to living form in the area today
B. raddei Strauch   34(180)   similar to living form of area
Rana sp.   17(75+)   many forms in area today

Aves
Struthio anderssoni   1(2)   only form clearly from the Upper Cave; the following may also be present; locality unclear:

Gypaetus sp.
Aquila sp.
Coturnix sp.   common
Phasianus sp.
Perdix barbata   uncommon
Crossoptilon mant-
  churicum   uncommon
Purcrasia xanthospila   uncommon

Table 5.   Upper Cave fauna   (continued)

Faunal form	Individuals (Material)	Remarks	EN	UR	lr	Lr
Symaticus reevesii	uncommon					
Columbus sp.	very common					
Corvus sp.						
Coloeus sp.						
Pica pica sericea						
Pyrrhocorax sp.						
Pterorhinus sp.						

Sources: Data on birds from Shaw 1935; other remains described by P'ei 1934a and revised and expanded in P'ei 1940.

Prior to use by humans, the cave was either a natural trap or a carnivore lair. During its sporadic use by humans principally for burial or occasional ephemeral camping, carnivores used the cave – tiger, hyena, and bear successively. The mammalian but not ostrich remains are abundant and attributable to carnivore activities in the cave. For dating purposes *Pseudaxis*, *Struthio*, *Erinaceus*, *Capreolus*, *Equus hemionus*, and *Gazella przewalskyi* suggest a cool, dry climatic episode and open habitats. *Crocuta crocuta ultima*, *Struthio*, and *Palaeoloxodon* are locally extinct and suggest an Upper Pleistocene age for the remains. Not so "cool" as the Hsiao-nan-hai fauna and with fewer extinct forms, I have suggested a pre-Würm Maximum age is possible. The fully modern hominid maintains generalized Mongoloid characteristics and morphologically would fit such an age; 25,000–30,000 years might be the maximum indicated (Aigner 1969, 1972a).

Tools are rare with only five pieces of flint and chert located. However, a number of river cobbles and pebbles occur and three show definite traces of use. Quartz flakes and tools number about 18. But of more interest are the several bone tools (a needle or awl 8.2 centimeters long, 3 centimeters diameter, has a scratched eye, a Wapiti (*Cervus elaphus*) antler shows polish, longitudinal grooves, and zig-zag lines on the shaft, several other bone chips and polished bones are also present) and the numerous "ornaments." No less than 125 perforated teeth were recovered and at least 25 were colored with ochre. Most appeared in concentrations in levels 2 and 4. Three perforated marine shells from layer 4 are *Arca*, a form presently common along the coast only 200 kilometers southeast of the cave. These and *Lamprotula* and oolitic hematite at the site also suggest trade or ranging over considerable areas.

Nine fish vertebrae and one perforated bone (colored red) also come from level 4. Fragments of "mother of pearl" are fairly common in the deposits and are also to be attributed to humans.

In interpreting the nature of cave occupation several points bear stressing. Three zones in the cave are distinguished but only the eastern, uppermost was occupied by hominids, possibly at two different periods. Two tool-containing ash layers are restricted to the eastern area. In the western upper zone all the human bones were concentrated. P'ei views this as a burial area which was later disturbed and his argument is presented with convincing data.

The number of individuals present is now judged to be 8 (Weidenreich 1939a, 1939b; Wu 1961a, 1961b) and the racial affiliation is judged proto-Mongoloid by recent workers (Thoma 1964). Two males, one old and one younger, three females, two middle-aged and one near twenty, a youth of undetermined sex, a child of about five and an infant or foetus are represented.

There are other localities near Choukoutien 1 which produced traces of human activity (Aigner 1969) but these do not enhance our understanding of human occupation in the Pleistocene on the edge of the Hopei Plain. With regard to this area, it is tempting to establish a sequence of hominid and technocomplex continuity from Choukoutien 1 (or Locality 13 which produced one tool) to Locality 15 to Hsiao-nan-hai and Upper Cave. There is clearly a tendency in the technocomplex present to improved flaking and retouch techniques yet a retention of a pattern for little or no shaping of flake tool blanks. Improvements in cores and blanks and the development of a superior bone industry are chronicled from the earlier localities to Hsiao-nan-hai, yet innovations such as extensive shape retouch and heavy investment in bifaciality are absent. For these technological reasons, there is congruence in the sequence.

The sites are cave habitations located over several hundred thousand years and several climatic episodes. The skill and ability attained by *H. erectus* living in the harsh North China area some 300,000 years ago is undeniable. A case for *in situ* hominid evolution was made by Weidenreich as well as Coon despite the lack of hominid fossils between Choukoutien 1 and Upper Cave. This was possible because traits considered continuous with modern Mongoloid groups are found in both, are conservative, and are not the characteristics represented on fossils with a similar grade of organization found outside China. (The South Chinese materials now known [Aigner 1969 and my other contribution in this volume; Coon 1963; Aigner and Laughlin 1973] fully support this contention of evolution of Chinese geographic variants of *H. erectus* into fully modern Mongoloid variants of *H. sapiens*.)

Table 6.   K'oho localities

6051	1.5 km. south of K'oho village, Juich'eng, southwestern Shansi
6052	3.5 km. north northwest of K'oho village
6054	0.75 km. east of K'oho village; the principal locality
6055	4 km. north of K'oho village
6056	4.2 km. north of K'oho village
6057	2 km. north of K'oho village
6058	4.5 km. north of K'oho village
6059	0.5 km. west of 6054, 0.25 km. east of K'oho village
6061	north of 6051, 1.3 km. south of K'oho village
6062	9 km. southeast of K'oho village
6065	3 km. southeast of K'oho village

Localities on the Middle Huangho, Fenho, and Sankanho of Shensi, Honan, Shansi Provinces (Figure 1.4–10)

A number of localities along the Huangho in the area of Sanmen Gorge on the Fenho and Sankanho produced a few flakes from levels deep in the "reddish clay" out of eroding cuts and cliff faces. The exact stratigraphic derivation of the materials for the most part cannot be determined with accuracy and only rough dating to the mid-Middle Pleistocene (Holstein equivalent) and later (at least to the Eem equivalent) is possible in most cases.

SANMEN GORGE AREA OF THE MIDDLE HUANGHO

K'oho. The principal location of interest in the Sanmen Gorge area of the Middle Huangho is K'oho in Shansi (Chia, Wang, and Wang 1961a, 1961b, 1962, 1964; Aigner 1969, 1972a) (Figure 1.7). Actually eleven localities are included in the pooled faunal and cultural samples which compose K'oho (Tables 6 and 7). Most of the cultural and fossil remains, however, do derive from the single collecting station Locality 6054. Stratigraphically it is concluded that K'oho materials come from very deep in the Middle Pleistocene layers in the region; at least the transported materials are now associated with these geologic strata. The authors suggest that the relative age is equivalent to the lowest layers at Choukoutien 1 but I have indicated elsewhere that the fauna and presumably, for the context cannot be sure, the artifacts are roughly equivalent to the middle layers at Choukoutien (Aigner 1969, 1972a).

The faunistic argument is based upon the presence at K'oho of *Stegodon chiai*, originally wrongly attributed in initial reports to the Pliocene *S. zdanskyi*, and the presence of *Megaloceros flabellatus*. It is now clear that *Stegodon* is not necessarily early and the presence of both forms of megacerine deer indicates a later Holstein equivalent age than the base of Choukoutien 1. Once again, the geologic and

Table 7. K'oho fauna

Lamprotula antiqua (Odhner)	from locations 6054, 6052, 6051
Rodentia indet.	incisor fragment from location 6054
Coelodonta sp.	one broken right M_3 from location 6054
Equus sp.	a few isolated teeth and several foot bones from locations 6054 and 6056
Sus sp.	one mandibular canine from 6051
Megaloceros pachyosteus (Young)	the pachyosted form is known from one maxillary fragment and several mandibles from locations 6054 and 6051; the older "flabellatus" form is represented by one mandible fragment
Pseudaxis sp.	fragmentary antlers and limb bones from 6054 could be *P. grayi* Zdansky
Cervidae indet.	fragmentary antlers from 6054
Bubalus sp.	isolated teeth and limb bones from 6054 and 6056
Bison sp.	a broken skull and mandible from 6054
Stegodon chiai (*S. zdanskyi* of original reports)	a nearly complete M_3 from 6054 of large size
Stegodon cf. *orientalis* Owen	a broken M_2 from 6054 (could be same as above, an advanced *Stegodon*)
Palaeoloxodon cf. *namadicus* Falconer and Cautley	one M_3 from 6054

cultural contexts are not firm and the association of the transported fossils and artifacts must be presumed.

Most of the 138 flakes, tools, and stone "nuclei" come from Localities 6054 and 6055 and are made out of local quartzite. The presence of 53 nuclei in the collection is suspicious – possibly the transported nature of the materials has resulted in a concentration of heavy stone artifacts (much the same is true of the original Patjitan collections; materials *in situ* and attributable to Patjitan show a small flake component which was not recognized and proportionately far more flakes than pebbles, etc. [G. Bartstra, personal communication, 1973]). If these are indeed cores then a marked contrast with Choukoutien 1 is indicated, for at the latter site there were few cores which were not completely reduced.

Nuclei are said to have large flake platforms with the angle in excess of 110° (platform and plane of fracture). It is claimed that the anvil technique, the hammerstone technique, and a method of dropping a boulder on another to knock off large flakes were employed, but confirmation of such techniques is nearly impossible (F. Bordes, personal communication 1973). The 66 flakes in the collection are large with conspicuous bulbs of percussion.

Nineteen artifacts are considered true implements (Table 8, Figure 6). The authors identify chopping tools, flakes with retouch, several pointed tools, and several flaked spherical stones. The pointed tools have received the greatest attention since it is claimed morphologically they are ancestral to forms later present in the Tingts'un localities. The so-called heavy triangular point is roughly flaked (and the point

Table 8.   K'oho tool types[a]

---

1. *Chopping tools*: seven including three on flakes and four on nuclei and pebbles. Two unifacially worked specimens are present. One on a nucleus is alternately flaked while a pebble-chopper reportedly has some bifacial working on its upper edge.
2. *Retouched flakes or "scrapers"*: are rare in the collection. Only seven are recognized; two with end retouch are shown. Flakes with use marks, considered functionally equivalent to "scrapers" are common.
3. *Heavy triangular point*: one example is present and recalls those discussed with Tingts'un artifacts. It is more roughly flaked with the end broken near the point.
4. *Small thick point*: one example is identified; it is thick and flaked on the dorsal face.
5. *Flaked spherical stones*: three are identified as bolas though functionally they could be either missile stones or hammerstones; these are similar to tools from Tingts'un and are also reported as "hammerstones" from Choukoutien Locality 15.

---

[a]   Figures in Aigner 1969.

broken) and the smaller, thick point has flaking on the dorsal face. Flaked spherical stones (variously called bolas, missile stones, hammerstones) are also present in Tingts'un but several are now recognized at Choukoutien Locality 1 as well (see above).

Other Localities. Worthy of mention is the locality referred to as Hsihoutu or Locality 6053 near K'oho. Locality 6053 contains a Lower Pleistocene fauna (Villafranchian), including *Proboscidipparion, Equus sanmeniensis, Cervus boulei, C. bifurcatus, Elasmotherium, Rhinoceros, Bos, Palaeoloxodon*, or *Archidiskodon* (referred to as *Elephas* as well in reports), carp, ostrich, and wild pig (Chia, Wang, and Wang 1962; Chia and Wang 1962). It is claimed that artifacts are found in the same gravels. These consist of "giant" flakes, small "scrapers," "nuclei," and irregularly "chipped flakes."

The reputed artifacts have not been published. Their derivation from sandy gravels makes them automatically suspicious, particularly considering the great age which is indicated. Based upon his knowledge of the *context* and the morphological characteristics of the stone specimens, Kahlke doubts they are altered by human agency (Hansjürgen Müller-Beck, personal communication 1966).

Elsewhere in the Sanmen Gorge region, of Honan and Shensi as well as Shansi, numerous collecting stations with materials probably equivalent to the Holstein Advance Stage, the Riss Complex, Eem, and the Würm of Europe are reported in the 1961 monograph by Chia, Wang, and Chiu (see also Aigner 1969).

LOWER FENHO (Figure 1.11–13)

Hsi-kou. There are several promising collecting stations from the Lower Fenho although the geological context of most of these appears to be that of secondary deposition. For example, from Hsi-kou (Figure

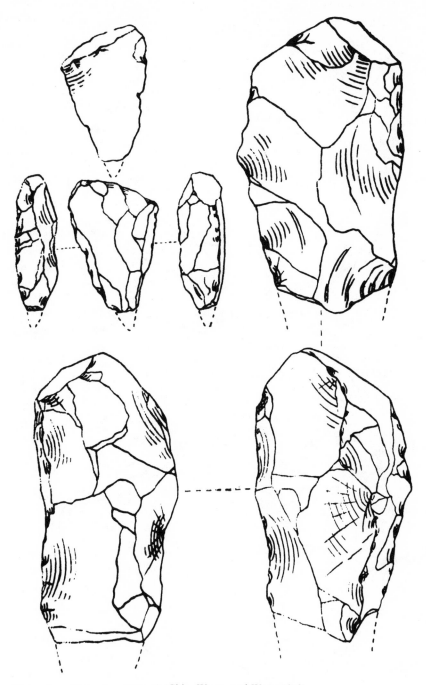

Figure 6a. K'oho (see Plate 1) (Chia, Wang, and Wang 1962)

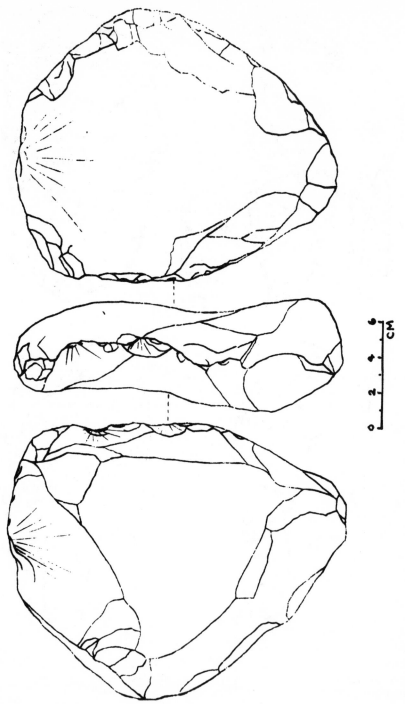

Figure 6b.   K'oho (see Plate 1) (Chia, Wang, and Wang 1962)

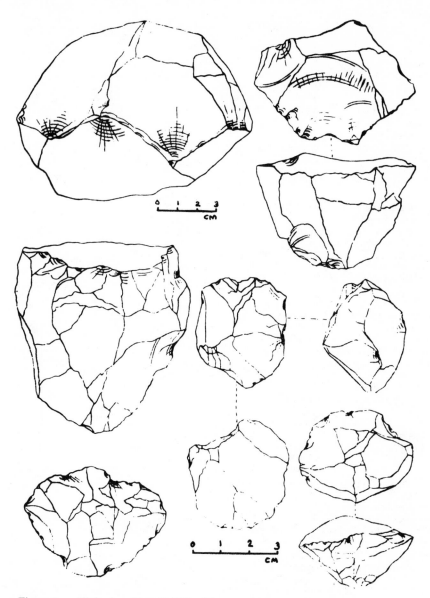

Figure 6c.   K'oho (see Plate 1) (Chia, Wang, and Wang 1962)

1.11) in Houma, some twelve kilometers southeast of Tingts'un in Shansi Province, artifacts and fossils were found in a sandy layer containing concretion bands (Chia 1959a). The fauna includes *Lamprotula antiqua* and *L. chiai* in addition to *Nodularia douglasiae* and mammals such as hyena, rhino, *Cervus* sp., *Gazella* sp., and *Bos*

Table 9.   Tingts'un faunal remains

Faunal form		Locality													
		54	90	91	92	93	94	95	96	97	98	99	100	101	102
Homo sp.	1 (3 teeth)												×		
Talpidae indet.	1(1)												×		
Canis sp.	1(1)								×						
Nyctereutes cf. *procyonoides* Gray	1(1)						×								
Vulpes sp.	1 (2 teeth)												×		
Ursus sp.	(3)								×	×			×		
Meles sp.	1(1)								×						
?Castor sp.	1(1)												×		
Muridae indet.	1(1)												×		
Myospalax fontanieri (Milne-Edwards)	1(1)												×		
Ochotona sp.	1(1)												×		
Coelodonta antiquitatis Blumen.	many teeth	×							×		×	×	×		×
Dicerorhinus kirchbergensis	(3)	×													
Equus hemionus Pallas	many teeth			×					×		×	×	×		
E. przewalskyi Poliakoff	(20 teeth)			×					×		×	×	×		
Sus sp.	(isol. teeth)		×								×	×			
Cervus elaphus	1 (antler frag)										×				
Pseudaxis cf. *grayi* Zdansky	(teeth, antler fragments)		×						×		×	×			
Megaloceros sp.	(7)								×		×		×		
M. cf. *ordosianus*	(20+antler fragments, 5 other bones)								×				×		×
?Moschus sp.	locality unknown														
Gazella sp.	(2 horn cores, 2 teeth)								×		×		× .		
Spirocerus sp.	(1 tooth)										×				
Bubalus sp.	(3 bones, teeth)								×		×		×		×
Bos primigenius Bojanus (all may be surface or in different context from other remains)	(skull + ?)								×		×		×		×
Palaeoloxodon spp.	(taxonomy confused; see text)	×							×	×					
Original identifications															
P. cf. *tokunagai* (Falconer and Cautley)			−												
Elephas cf. *indicus* L.			−								−				
E. cf. *namadicus* (Falconer and Cautley)											−	−			
Elephantidae indet. (not *in situ*) Chinese text does not identify this as *Mammuthus primigenius* as does the English translation															

Table 10. Artifacts by provenance

	Provenance unknown	90	91	92	93	94	95	96	97	98	99	100	102
Simple chopping tools		3ᵃ					1			4	2		
Complex chopping tools	4							1	4	1			1
"*Coup de poing*"	1ᵇ												
Missile stones	1ᶜ								1				
Simple flake tools													
Oval	6	1		1				1		1			
Irregular	1	2							1				
Small irregular	1	1						3	1	2	1		
Pointed tools													
Large, thick, triangular (6)													
and flat (5)	3	2						1	3	2			
Small pointed tools									2	2			1
Scrapers (many more present													
than described)		3								1		1	
Total (2005)	439	244	0	0	1	7	25	90	318	529	219	171	176

ᵃ Or 98 or both?
ᵇ Surface.
ᶜ Probably many others.

primigenius. Chia follows convention in suggesting a preloessic age (based upon the equation of the stratum with the Basal Gravels) but an early Würm equivalent age is as likely.

The 1972 artifacts are principally quartzite (72 percent) with some use of sandstone, vein quartz, quartz, and limestone. Most of these are waste flakes with large platform remnants and flake angles between 91° and 129° and averaging 118°. The majority are from unprepared core platforms and tend to be broad, thick, and irregular. Nuclei are reported as are three "core choppers," one spherical stone "missile," one small pointed tool, and several "scrapers."

Tingts'un. The best known of the Fenho sites is Tingts'un, actually 13 localities with artifacts, fauna, or both (Tables 9 and 10; Figure 7). The final site report (P'ei et al. 1958) opts for a loessic date while Movius (1956) provides an Eem-equivalent age. Materials are derived by transport but evidently have not been moved very far. They are found in strata reputedly above Basal Gravels. Since the faunal remains clearly indicate an interglacial/interstadial phase we cannot definitely date the pooled sample of fauna beyond indicating an Eem or early Würm interstadial age as most likely. The Chinese use of the term Loessic as a chronologic period is misleading since by convention this is associated with the last glacial (or in China, pluvial) which is not subdivided microclimatically.

If we accept the correlation of most of the localities as contemporaneous and pool the faunal and artifactual collections from *in situ* (some of the widely illustrated handaxe-like tools are surface finds,

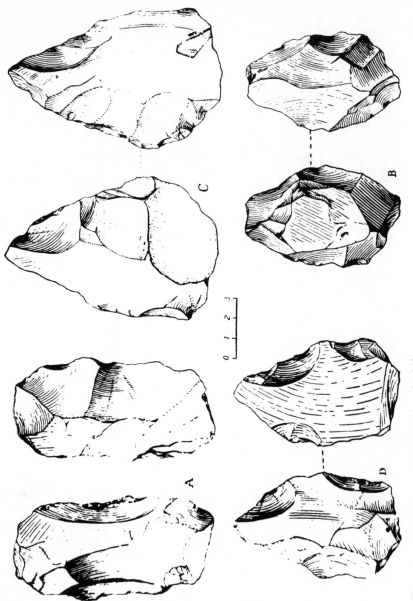

Figure 7a.   Tingts'un (see Plate 2) (P'ei et al. 1958)

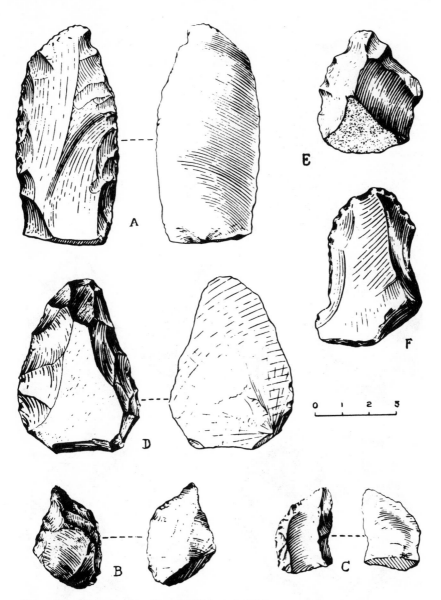

Figure 7b.   Tingts'un (see Plate 2) (P'ei et al. 1958)

as are some of the faunal remains which are discussed in the P'ei et al. monograph *as such* in the Chinese text, but not so in the English summary) the following information is available: an extensive faunal series, more than 2,000 artifacts, and some hominid material. Major defects in the data include small sample size for mammalian fauna, lack of quantification of artifacts and publication of but a small series

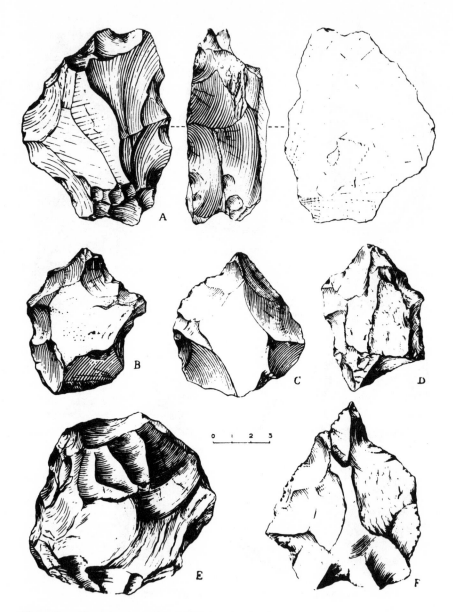

Figure 7c. Tingts'un (see Plate 2) (P'ei et al. 1958)

including a disproportionately large number without provenance, and absence of the pollen data which reportedly were collected for study.

The hominid remains consist of three teeth recovered from gravels at Locality 100, all belonging to the same twelve- to thirteen-year-old individual. Certain primitive features are retained, and a morphological age between *H. erectus* and fully modern human, but perhaps closer to the latter, is indicated.

The mammalian fauna lists twenty-eight species but there appear to be some questionable identifications and stratigraphic attributions (Aigner 1969). The sika, *Pseudaxis* cf. *grayi*, is actually closer to *P. hortulorum*, the extremely hypsodontic form. The identification of elephant remains is confused (later, K. C. Chang referred them all to *Palaeoloxodon*); *Mammuthus primigenius* is from unknown provenance and in the original faunal analysis was not definitely identified (P'ei uses *M. primigenius* as evidence of a Loessic age) and there is reason to question the *in situ* recovery of *Bos primigenius* also used in the dating (Aigner 1969).

The shell remains come from levels in the same stratigraphic unit as the derived mammalian and lithic remains, but below them and apparently *in situ*. The authors conclude from their study of the more than 1,000 unionids, mostly *Lamprotula*, that a reasonable dating is to the early Upper Pleistocene. Several forms indicate more quiet stream conditions and wetter conditions than now prevail at Tingts'un. The same is indicated by the fish fauna which come both from the shell and mammal zones. All the fauna and the geology are consistent with the interglacial/interstadial, Upper Pleistocene age suggested by Movius (1956) and reiterated by me (1969).

The artifacts include 1,566 from *in situ*, primarily from Localities 90, 96–100, and 102. Some 439 are either surface finds or of unknown provenance (including most of the best made and most often illustrated tools referred to as "Tingts'un"). Nearly 95 percent of the artifacts are hornfel and show little evidence of rolling or wear, strengthening the position that the fossils and artifacts are probably contemporaneous.

The tools were grouped into classes on the basis of blank, then subdivided into functional categories and finally into morphological groupings: 24 tools on pebbles, 17 *in situ* including 10 "simple chopping tools" with a single or simple cutting edge, 11 "complex chopping tools" with two cutting edges, a well-made complex chopping tool from the surface referred to as a "*coup de poing*," a number of missile stones some of which may have been hammerstones (actually enlarging the 24 cited in the text by some unknown number).

Thirty-two flake tools are described. These are divided into "simple" and "complex" categories. "Simple flake tools" include one 17-centimeter-long example. The 24 "complex flake tools" are grouped into "oval" examples (11), large nonregular ones, and smaller, thick, and irregular flakes with some evidence of use or retouch. In addition to the 32, there are "pointed tools" – some are large and thick (11) and others have flatter profiles and sections (6); some are small pointed tools (4 subgroups).

I was not very convinced by the typology of pointed tools in the Tingts'un monograph and suggested that other groupings of artifacts were more useful. For example, among the large pointed tools those with pick-like points and those with rather large, broad points may be distinguished (Aigner 1969). At the same time others classified as pointed seem to be almost incidentally pointed; the use was along the margins and grouping with the so-called scrapers seems more natural. The category of small pointed tools with its four subgroupings seems artificial. Few show use at the point and most are retouched and utilized along the margins; the last perhaps should be considered with the category of "scrapers," relatively small, thin flakes with edge retouch or use.

Unused flakes and nuclei are plentiful in the pooled sample. On 708 flakes the angle measurements ranged from 80–148° with most 110–130°. Again, based upon the angle and size of the bulb of percussion the authors claim to distinguish the anvil technique as the primary method of flake production. No evidence of the bipolar technique is present. The hammerstone technique is reportedly present but not common (such technological identifications are difficult or impossible according to F. Bordes, personal communication 1973). Nuclei are said to make up nearly 10 percent of the collection. Among these there are large (12+ centimeters) multifacetted nuclei, most of which lack platform preparation. A smaller number of medium and small nuclei is also present. Angles formed by the platform and sides range from 90° down to 60°.

The most recent Chinese summary of Tingts'un is by P'ei (1965). While Breuil interpreted many of the Tingts'un chopping tools as bifaces similar to the late Acheulian, P'ei views the collection in terms of a typology and technological history not dependent upon Europe as a source – his views on the independence of Tingts'un "phylogenetically" from extra-China contacts are shared by Aigner (1969) and Bordes (personal communication 1973). P'ei also states that there are no equivalents for Mousteroid points and other typological categories of the French Middle Paleolithic. Furthermore, the remains are dissimilar to *any* of the Ordos materials, showing affinities presumably of a phylogenetic nature in certain tools (large trihedral pointed tools, missile stones) to the earlier site(s) called K'oho.

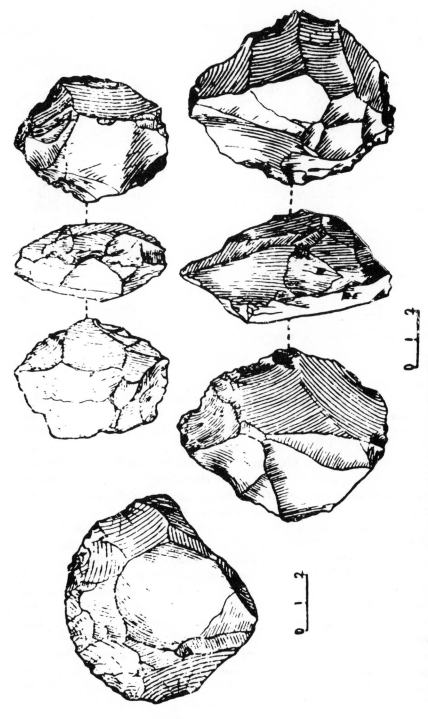

Figure 8a. Chiao-ch'eng (see also Plate 3) (Chia, Wang, and Chiu 1961)

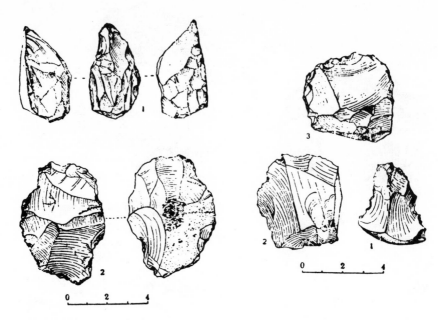

Figure 8b.   Shou-yang and P'ing-ting (see also Plate 3) (Chia, Wang, and Chiu 1961)

MIDDLE AND UPPER FENHO AND SANKANHO (Figure 1.14–21). Further north in Shansi Province, reconnaissance has located a number of collecting stations for artifacts. More than 1,000 are reported from mainly surface localities in Chiaoch'eng on the Middle Fenho (Chia and Wang 1957; Chia, Wang, and Chiu 1961). Most are hornfel flakes with striking angles of 110 to 130° and the anvil technique is identified as most common (as at Tingts'un). Only about 2 percent of the artifacts have retouch and the authors describe these as "pebble choppers," "core retouched flakes," ("scrapers") and drill-like pointed flakes. Evidently many of the remains are early Upper Pleistocene, if one can accept the geological associations (Figure 8a, b).

Collecting stations along the Upper Fenho and its tributaries provide tools but not in good association. Fengch'engshan near Chingloch'eng on the Fenho produced 300 artifacts, including 2 tools believed roughly equivalent in age and technology to Tingts'un (P'ei 1958). Artifacts have also been gathered on the Upper Changho (Kuo 1959) and on the Sankanho (Chia, Wang, and Chiu 1960; P'ei 1958). Only Houko-tafeng is worth mentioning for its *in situ* materials. These derive from gravels and are transported and are equated typologically with Choukoutien 15; comparisons to Tingts'un and Sjara-osso-gol are not included. Typologically the authors suggest a late reddish clay (Riss?) or Basal Gravel (Eem?) age for the materials.

SUMMARY OF THE MIDDLE HUANGHO, FENHO, AND SAN-KANHO MATERIALS (see Aigner 1969 for an exhaustive bibliography). Archaeological remains from the middle Huangho, the Fenho, Changho, and Sankanho, with the exception of a few sites such as Tingts'un and K'oho, are not easily dated even relatively. For the most part the remains are collected from off the surface and lack any kind of faunal association. For a few sites, however, remains are reported from *in situ* and though the precise context (washed out or strated, excavated, etc.) is not clear, relative age can at least be suggested.

Fortunately sites such as K'oho and Tingts'un provide points in the sequence. Probably nothing dates earlier than K'oho, except for Hsihoutu for which the age is fairly sure (Villafranchian), but the presence of human artifacts is questionable. A number of localities in Yuan-ch'u, Shansi, are reported in low levels of the reddish clay (Kuan-kou, Tung-ling, Chung-pei-ling, Chai-hou-ko-t'a, Hsi-yuan-ko-t'a, Ping-t'ao, Pa-chiao-yao, Hsiao-ch'ao-ts'un, Shen-chia-chuang, Hsing-ma-nan-yao, Chao-chia-po, Hsu-chia-miao, and Ho-hsi-po) as are Wo-lung-p'u and Chang-chia-wan of T'ung-kuan in Shensi, and Hou-chia-po, Shen-hsien in Honan. The artifacts reportedly found *in situ* at these locales are characterized as simple typologically and not unlike the remains from Choukoutien 1 (the tools are made on flakes). However, remains are too limited to preclude similarity with well-represented local assemblages such as K'oho.

In general the blanks are large with a large platform remnant and angle in excess of 100°. A natural pebble surface is invariably the platform. Flakes were produced by the hammerstone technique (striking flakes directly from a nucleus) and by the anvil technique (working the nucleus on a stone anvil).

Among the forms recognized are unifacial choppers similar to Choukoutien 1 (but not necessarily dissimilar to K'oho) worked using both techniques. In general there are no examples which duplicate the thick, large, pointed tools from K'oho and appear in an evolved form at Tingts'un and related contemporary and later localities. Age is presumably Middle Pleistocene but no finer determination or affiliation is possible.

Among the sites reported to yield artifacts from levels high in the reddish clays is Tingts'un. Apparently contemporaneous are Hou-yen-ling and Lu-tzu-mo from Fan-chia-chuang, Chiao-ch'eng-hsien, Shansi, Fengch'engshan in Ching-lo, Shansi, Li-ts'un-hsi-kou, and Nan-liang, both in Houma, Shansi, and Ch'ang-chia-wan in Honan. The sites share related tool forms foreshadowed at K'oho. Among these are the large, thick, trihedral pointed tool, the missile stone, and rather better worked (by alternate flaking) choppers. The actual forms are present at Fengch'engshan in particular, but the other locales are said to share similar techniques of flake production (the anvil technique) and "other" characteristics. Some authors equate Choukoutien 15 and Nan-hai-yu with the above temporally, but this seems unlikely insofar as Choukoutien 15 and Tingts'un are surely not contemporary.

Equation with Tingts'un or last interglacial times is almost purely typological. The "sites" in Fan-chia-chuang consist of materials found in the exposed tubercle band earlier than the Basal Gravels; age is determined on the basis of typology.

The geological situation for Tingts'un suggests that these uppermost reddish clays are in fact post-Middle-Pleistocene deposits associated with the Chingshui erosion period and equivalent to the last interglacial or slightly later. The geological evidence indicates the remains must be younger than those from sites reported from deep in the reddish clay. The latter, as suggested above, could date from the mid-Middle to the late Middle Pleistocene.

From deposits equated with the Basal Gravel of the loess there are only two localities: Houkotafeng in Shuo-hsien, Shansi, and Yang-chuang in Ning-wu, Shansi. Also perhaps equivalent in age are several localities in Yin-chia-chuang, Shansi, and Ta-liang-ting in P'ing-ting-hsien, Honan. Sjara-osso-gol in the Ordos is considered contemporary and Shuitungkou just slightly later. The remains from Houkotafeng are medium to small in comparison with earlier remains. Many "scrapers" are reported on which secondary retouch is refined; perhaps a wooden striker was employed. Chi-li-po-ts'un in P'ing-lu may be added to the list but remains there are also too few to provide meaningful comparisons.

In the loess deposits, artifacts are reported at Ma-po-shan in Ta-t'ung and at Houkotafeng in Shuo-hsien. Again the remains are too limited to permit comparisons. The bulk of the collections made in the Middle Huangho, Fenho, and Sankanho are surface collections. Age is unknown but, considering the Pleistocene depositional history of the areas, probably not earlier than the Upper Pleistocene.

There is an interesting regional distribution of sites with the oldest found furthest south (K'oho and Yuan-ch'u sites), those of intermediate age (i.e. Tingts'un and related localities) just north, and late remains and especially surface finds further north.

The extent to which a Tingts'un "complex" is spread is unclear due largely to the poor nature of the localities. It contrasts with sites to the east largely in possessing several shaped-tool categories; however, there are not particular technological differences which are notable. The possibility of a semi-distinctive variation in lithic technology is interesting but in itself provides and suggests no information on major cultural-sociological differences between this region and the Hopei Plain. Continuities between K'oho and Tingts'un seem to preclude outside influences from the north.

The Lantian Localities of the Wei in Southern Shensi

Reconnaissances in the 1960's in the vicinity of Sian in southern Shensi produced several localities with faunal and cultural remains and two with Middle Pleistocene hominid fossils. These are the well-known Lantian localities. Lantian Locality 63708 (Figure 1.22) is dated to Upper Pleistocene strata and so far has produced a small collection of unworked flakes (reportedly produced by the hammerstone technique) and nuclei. Some 30 artifacts including a unifacial "chopper," 4 pointed flake tools, and 25 worked flakes identified as "scrapers" are described (Tai and Chi 1964).

CHENCHIAWO LOCALITY 63709. Chenchiawo has produced a mid-Middle-Pleistocene fauna including the mandible of *H. erectus* (M. C. Chou 1964; Y. P. Ch'ang et al. 1964; Woo 1964a, 1964b, 1964c; Aigner 1969, 1972a; Aigner and Laughlin 1973). The mandible was removed from an eroding cut from deep in the "reddish clays" above the Basal Gravels. Most of the teeth are retained. Morphologically the mandible is close to *H. erectus* from Choukoutien 1 though somewhat smaller; the congenital absence of M_3 is noteworthy. The faunal collection including the hominid is close to that for the middle zones at Choukoutien 1 (Aigner 1969, 1972a).

KUNGWANGLING LOCALITY 63706. The second *H. erectus* locality at Lantian produced the earliest known *Homo* in China and the oldest verified stone tools from eastern Asia. Although the faunal and geological contexts are good and a Mosbachium equivalent age (up to some 700,000 years using conventional geological-extrapolative dating) is indicated, the archaeologic context is not primary. Materials are evidently derived from upslope and the, geologically speaking, contemporaneous tools as well. Mammalian remains come from near the concretionary basal part of the "reddish clays" overlying a series of sandy gravels themselves underlain disconformably by Pliocene clays with *Hipparion* and *Chilotherium*.

The middle of five buried soils contained the hominid skull cap and mammalian fossils (level 6) and the stone artifacts (just above in levels 7–8). Important for assigning geologic and relative age to the calvarium are the primitive *Ursus thibetanus*, *Nestortherium*, a new *Megaloceros* sp., the very common *Leptobos*, and the morphologically primitive *H. erectus*. Notably, southern faunal elements (Aigner 1972b) are common among the fauna – *Ailuropoda*, *Stegodon*, *Nestortherium*, *Tapirus*, *Elaphodus* and *Rusa*. Sixty percent of the species (only *Leptobos* is well represented in terms of numbers of individuals) are also known from Choukoutien 1 and 13 but 42 percent are also known in the older Nihowan fauna. Only 37 percent of the species are extant compared to 50 percent at Choukoutien 1.

A study of the pollen remains (Academia Sinica 1966) and the paleoecological preferences of the fauna were crucial in suggesting an interglacial age for the site, and a pre-Holstein equivalent is certain (Aigner and Laughlin 1973). There is a dominance of forest and woodland forms among the animal species represented and the pollen indicates open woodland with *Pinus*, *Carpinus*, *Celtis*, *Ulmus*, *Quercus*, and *Betula* presumably present on the hillsides above.

Among the artifacts collected there are several which appear to be worked (Tai 1966). These include a small flake, a large one, and four "nuclei." The hominid remains are of considerable importance for they bear upon the origin of *H. sapiens* and of Mongoloids in eastern Asia. Morphologically the calvarium is as primitive as Djetis from Java and clearly more primitive than *H. erectus* from Choukoutien 1 as one would expect (775 cubic centimeters compared to 1,075 average; a more extreme reinforcement system; greater skull thickness – see Aigner and Laughlin 1973 for a discussion of the significance of this Lantian fossil for discerning trends in human evolution). Unlike the Djetis material, Lantian displays traits later found on Chinese fossil hominids which are also characteristic of modern Mongoloid populations (Aigner and Laughlin 1973), again maintaining the trend required if Weidenreich is correct that regional populations of *H. erectus* evolved *in situ* into regionally distinctive populations of *H. sapiens*.

Interior China (West of the Huangho and North of the Wei)
Including the Steppe and Desert Areas of Interior China

Western China including the Ordos, Ningsia, Kansu, Tsinghai, and Tibet can be dealt with together at this time because of the near absence of verified Pleistocene archaeological materials. The far west is poorly known faunistically and archaeologically. The Ordos region, often included in the North China Faunal Province, seems removed from it on the basis of the present environment, including vegetation and fauna, and past archaeological remains (P'ei 1957; Aigner 1969, 1972a). The Ordos ought not to be taken as the type locality for Upper Pleistocene North China.

ORDOS REGION. The stratigraphy for the Ordos is still imperfectly known despite a long history of study (Barbour 1935; Teilhard 1941; P'ei and Li 1964). As a consequence of the most recent work in the area the datings assigned to archaeological materials collected during the 1920's are to be questioned. P'ei and Li would not make a definite statement concerning the relative age of sites in the Ordos, in Sjara-osso-gol or Shuitungkou regions of interior China.

Sjara-osso-gol. The bulk of the Ordos faunal remains were recovered from sites on the Sjara-osso-gol (Figure 1.23) but the stratigraphy of the sites in the area is not well established. Remains rest on "ancient soils" covered by "ancient dunes" but it is possible that the fauna (Table 11) and tools are not geologically associated (Aigner 1969). Tools are rare in the collection and represent a pooled sample consisting mainly of nondescript and minimally retouched flakes. The purported microlithic elements of the collection and the affinities with the European Upper Paleolithic claimed by Breuil (Boule, Breuil, Licent, and Teilhard 1928) are specifically denied in a recent restudy by P'ei (1965). Several recent reconnaissances of the Ordos and Sjara-osso-gol areas produced small but not informative artifactual collections (Aigner 1969) (Figure 9).

Chingshuaiho. Chingshuaiho in Inner Mongolia (Figure 1.30) has produced some interesting surface materials which are considered typologically "Paleolithic" by S. S. Ch'ang (1959, 1960) and probably so by P'ei (1965). There are "workshops" with detritus confined within a small area and ephemeral "camps" with a few tools but no hearth remains according to Ch'ang. Among the highly selective examples which he illustrates, Ch'ang includes unifacially retouched pointed tools, "scraping" tools, and several "heavy boring tools" made on cortex flakes and pebbles roughly flaked unifacially to a point. A few "chopping tools" made on large pebbles and missiles or hammers showing heavy crushing are also identified (Figure 10a, b, c).

The strongest evidence for a Pleistocene age is the absence of consistent association with "Neolithic" and "microlithic" tools, the location of the materials on hills and terraces which are littered with sand and clay concretions normally associated with Pleistocene deposits, and their patination (sand blasting) and encrustation while the occasional typologically later materials are in pristine condition.

Shuitungkou. Shuitungkou materials provide the type collection of the Ordos "culture" and most of these were collected in the early 1920's (Boule, Breuil, Licent, and Teilhard 1928 summarizes the work). A zone of loess over gravels produced most of the cultural materials

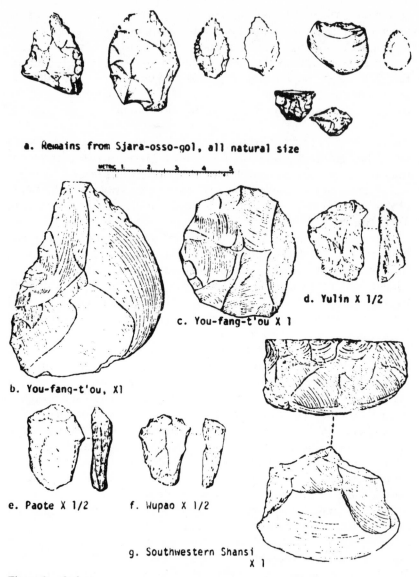

a. Remains from Sjara-osso-gol, all natural size

METRIC 1   2   3   4   5

c. You-fang-t'ou X 1

d. Yulin X 1/2

b. You-fang-t'ou, X1

e. Paote X 1/2   f. Wupao X 1/2

g. Southwestern Shansi
X 1

Figure 9.   Ordos

described although isolated loessic and surface finds are also included
(Figure 1.32). The collecting areas known as Shuitungkou are not
clearly defined (see the original monograph and Aigner 1969). Breuil's
study of the lithic materials heavily utilizes his European typological
system which P'ei correctly notes (1965) is unsuitable for this collection. Furthermore, the affinities claimed to the "evolved Mous-

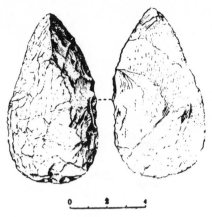

Figure 10a. Chingshuaiho (Ch'ang 1960)

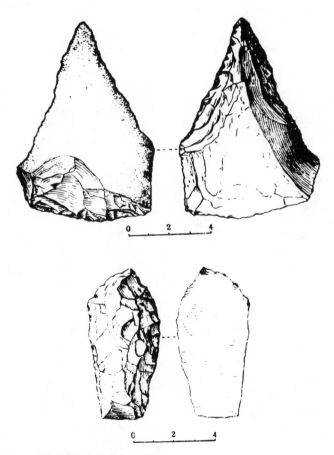

Figure 10b. Chingshuaiho (Ch'ang 1960)

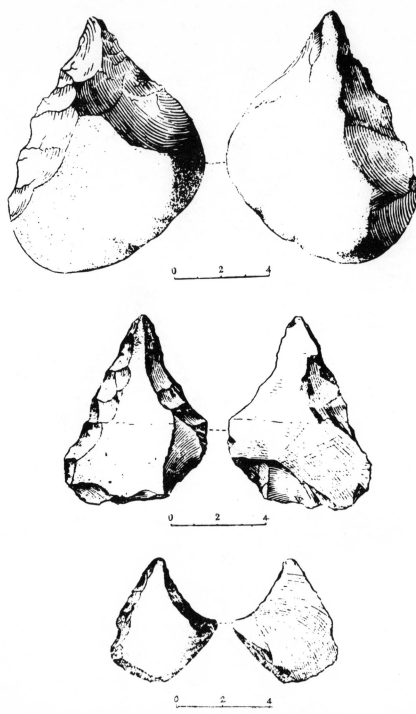

Figure 10c.   Chingshuaiho (Ch'ang 1960)

Table 11.   Sjara-osso-gol fauna

Faunal form	Material
Palaeoloxodon cf. *namadicus*	1 tooth
Coelodonta antiquitatis	3 skeletons, 12 skulls
Equus hemionus	1 skeleton, skull, and other bones
E. cf. *przewalskyi*	cervicals, phalanges
Sus scrofa	a mandible
Camelus knoblocki	maxilla, mandible, and bones of 6
Cervus elaphus	antler pieces, mandibles
C. mongoliae	antler fragment
Megaloceros ordosianus	antler fragments
Gazella przewalskyi	300 horns, facial bones
G. subguttorosa?	?
Spirocerus kiakhtensis	3 horns, a mandible
Ovis ammon	many frontals with horns (surface finds)
Bubalus wansjocki	skull with facial and other bones
Bos primigenius	horn, isolated teeth, and other bones
Canis lupus	mandibles
Crocuta crocuta ultima	fragments of a skull and other bones
Meles taxus	a tooth
Erinaceus sp.	mandibular fragment
Scaptochirus moschatus	mandibular fragment
Chiroptera indet.	radius
Lepus sp.	maxillary fragment
Ochotona sp.	common maxillae and mandibles
Citellus mongolicus	skull fragments
Dipus sowerbyi	maxilla and foot bones
Alactaga cf. *annulata*	teeth
Gerbillus meridianus	most common gerbil: tooth rows
Myospalax fontanieri	"rare"
Eothenomys sp.	2 tooth rows
Alticola cf. *crecitulus*	3 mandibles
Microtus cf. *ratticeps*	3 mandibles
Microtus sp.	2 mandibles
Cricetulus sp.	2 mandibles
Buteo cf. *ferox*	1 humerus
Vulture monachus	3 coracoids, forchet fragment, fragments of humerus, and tibia
Perdix cf. *perdix*	cubitus, tarsal-metatarsal
Coturnix sp.	humerus, tarsal-metatarsal
Syrrhaptes paradoxus	tibia, tarsal-metatarsal
Podiceps auritus	tibia
Anas boschas	fragments of humerus, tibiae
Struthio sp.	?

terian" and early Aurignacian are today unsupportable (Bordes, personal communication 1973; P'ei 1965; Aigner 1969). P'ei notes that there are no Mousterian types, no burins, and no microliths (Figure 11). Furthermore, he asserts that the reputed blades are in fact directed flakes. In addition to the large number of flakes and retouched flakes, the original collections include "nuclei" which are variable in form and preparation, several crude pebble tools, and a tendency for unifacial and marginal retouch of most tools.

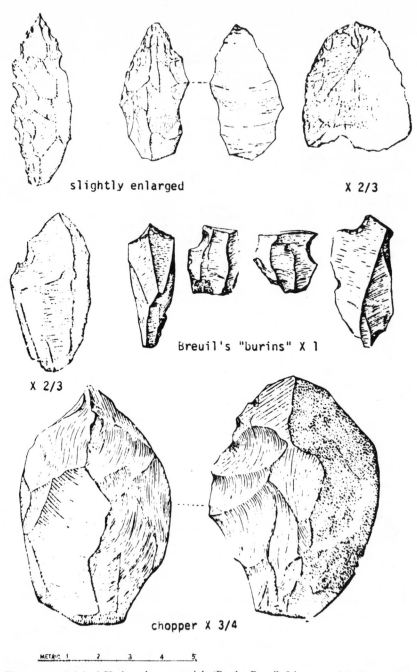

slightly enlarged   X 2/3

Breuil's "burins" X 1

X 2/3

chopper X 3/4

Figure 11.   Original Shuitungkou materials (Boule, Breuil, Licent, and Teilhard 1928)

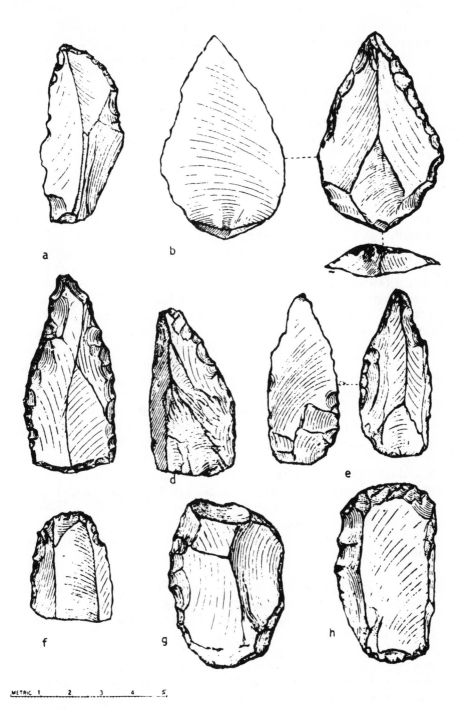

Figure 12. New Shuitungkou materials (Chia, Kai, and Li 1964)

P'ei revisited the Shuitungkou region to reevaluate the local stratigraphy of the original collecting localities. He believes the tools come
from the basal layer of lacustrine deposits formed by the Huangho.
They are not associated directly with the Shuitungkou as originally
believed. Therefore, while a dating within the Upper Pleistocene is
still valid, finer placement in that period is not possible (there were
few associable faunal remains). It now appears that what was once
considered the Upper Pleistocene "standard" for North Chinese
cultural remains are now to be seen as temporally mixed collections
or from uncertain stratigraphy.

Other revisits to the area produced additional materials (Chia, Kai,
and Li 1964; Wang 1962). Chia, Kai, and Li excavated some 2,000
artifacts from the ten-meter terrace on the left bank of the Pienkou,
a small tributary of the Shuitungkou (Figure 12). Unfortunately there
are no associated faunal remains and the terrace is evidently not
datable. Cultural materials are of interest typologically even though
only a few are modified. Most of the remains consist of flakes which
are longer than broad and evidently struck from cores with prepared
platforms. Seven, unifacially retouched, pointed flake tools are in the
collection. On these, retouch is mainly dorsal and marginal, and little
shape alteration of the original blank is indicated (Aigner 1969). Seven
"scraping" tools and three "chopper-chopping" tools (not true
bifaces) are described, the latter held to show relationships with
Tingts'un (certainly a tenuous connection).

In my opinion the significant features of the new Shuitungkou
materials are the presence of regular flakes struck from cores with
prepared striking platforms, the absence of a so-called microlithic
component, and the tendency for the retouch to be both marginal and
unifacial. The assemblage is not large enough to permit more
meaningful comparison and the absence of faunal associations and
unclear geological situation render it impossible to accurately date the
remains. In 1969 I suggested that a middle Würm equivalent age was
possible if the tenuous connections among the fauna and Sjara-osso-
gollithic materials are vaguely accurate.

KANSU AND SINKIANG. No very likely Pleistocene-aged cultural
materials are known from either area although there are now several
fossil collections from Kansu which date to the Upper Pleistocene
(Aigner 1969 for references).

TIBET-TSINGHAI. In Tibet finds of artifacts are rare, scattered, and
generally dated only typologically as "Paleolithic" or "Neolithic."
Chiu (1958) describes some of the materials from northeastern Tibet
and Tsinghai (Chinghai), all from elevations between 3,500 and 4,300
meters.

MATERIALS FROM ADJACENT REGIONS

Siberia and Mongolia. Generally there is nothing older than 20,000 B.P. reported in Siberia, though there are hints of earlier occupation in the form of (possible) crude tools in old but undatable geological contexts. Among these are finds from Ulalinka Creek near Gorno-Altaisk in the Altai region, Filimoshki on the Zeya River in the middle Amur basin, and one flake-blade with a faceted platform from deposits ascribed to the Tazov (Riss?) near Rubtsousk in the Altai foothills. Later, but probably prior to the last glaciation, are finds of artifacts with a mammoth in a cave in the Vladivostok region (Chard 1969).

Mongolia presumably was settled in the early Würm by populations with Mousteroid industries of western affinity who came from Soviet Central Asia. To date there is no evidence of them in Siberia. Later, Mongolia is characterized by industries with heavy tools made from split pebbles. In China there are no northern collections with a heavy investment in pebble tools. The Mongolian tradition has a strong survival of Mousteroid elements and forms one major component of the Siberian Paleolithic and hence points to Mongolia as the primary source of the latter according to Chard (1969). The second major influence seen in Siberia comes from Aurignacoid big game hunters of the Eurasian steppe to the west. These influences are best seen at Mal'ta near Irkutsk (14,700 years ago). Afontova Gora II on the Yenesei (21,000 years ago), and in the far east at Ushki Lake in central Kamchatka (14,000 years ago).

Central Asia. In Central Asia the earliest human artifacts consist of scattered crude pebble tools in the mountainous regions of the east and southeast (Chard 1969). However, virtually all of the materials are surface finds and late survivals in the area make typological dating questionable. The initial alignment of the remains is with East Asia and the Soan of Punjab since in the area only a trace of the Acheulian handaxe tradition of the Mediterranean-African sphere is seen in the extreme southwest of Soviet Central Asia.

Mousteroid sites in Soviet Central Asia, in addition to the famous Teshik-Tash, are located in or near the mountainous regions. Remains consist of workshops and open sites on the one hand and cave sites on the other. Chard suggests the remains may be accounted for either by an extensive occupation of the region or a persistent technical-cultural tradition. In addition, faunal dating of the materials is difficult since nearly all of the forms are modern inhabitants of the region. Perhaps this suggests that the area was environmentally similar to the present.

Technically Upper Paleolithic remains are absent in the region save for perhaps Samarkand where Upper Pleistocene (?) lithic remains recall the Siberian Paleolithic with a strong Mousteroid component. However, this may be another case of later survival. Clear evidence of Near Eastern influences, small tools and prismatic cores, penetrating the region are not seen until the end of the Pleistocene or even the early Holocene.

Most relevant for our interpretation of the Chinese Tsinghai-Tibet remains is the high mountain occupation of the eastern Pamirs in very early postglacial times. Here open sites are often found on glacial remains and dates between 10,000 and 13,500 B.P. have been obtained. A date on the only *in situ* remains, Osh-khona, is 9530 (Chard 1969). There is evidence that juniper and birch were used as fuel but stands of these trees are now about 100 kilometers distant from the site. A milder climate may have prevailed at the time. It has also been suggested that the remains are those of summer camps used by hunters attracted by game in alpine pastures. The lithic technology includes a Siberian Paleolithic component with pebble cores and heavy pebble tools along with microcores, blades, and small arrowpoints.

Ranov suggests that the remains are those of similarly adapted people who occupied the western margin of the inner Asian high mountains. He indicates that these cultures are technologically conservative. We may expect them to turn up in Tibet and Chinese Central Asia.

Northeastern China. Little of the archaeological evidence from Manchuria and northeast Inner Mongolia indicates the presence of pre-Recent cultural remains in the northeast, although tools are found in secondary association with Upper Pleistocene faunas. Without good geologic controls and primary deposits, faunal associations in all cases (see Aigner 1969 for a summary and references) provide dubious data for the lithic materials in the "black earths" of the northeast. Only the Chien-p'ing hominid humerus and the Panlachengtze steppe rhinoceros are candidates for Pleistocene cultural associations in Manchuria (M. C. Chou and Hsien 1958; Jernakov and Ponosov 1958).

GENERAL SUMMARY REMARKS

South China

Unfortunately the number of *in situ* archaeological remains from which we can extract cultural information is small. From China south of the Yangtze the several collections of flakes have poor faunal associations and generally lack evidence of human activities such as butchering, cooking, etc. (Aigner 1969, 1972b, and my other contribution to this volume). I have already indicated that the lithic remains which are clearly pre-Recent in age are strictly flake assemblages and lack a pebble and heavy tool component. Typologically and technologically there is no evidence that the remains from the southwestern upland regions are similar to either the Burmese or Javanese cultural remains or the later Hoabinhian (Bacsonian) industries. There are however remains in the karst areas in the maritime provinces of China which probably are part of the Hoabinhian, and southern affiliations or influences are indicated.

The hominid remains from the south, beginning with Ch'ang-yang, show that during the European period of "classic Neanderthals" and earlier, South Chinese hominids were not extreme in form and were actually intermediate between *Homo erectus* and *H. sapiens*. There is a continuity in traits which indicates *in situ* evolution of these South Asian Mongoloids.

North China

In northern China, the lithic and hominid remains are best treated by subregion. On the western edge of the Hopei Plain there is evidence of human occupation beginning at least during the mid-Middle Pleistocene at Choukoutien 1. The hominid form present does constitute a coherent sample which is significantly distinct from African, European, and Javanese members of *H. erectus*. Traits identifiable on the remains suggest evolutionary continuity through the Upper Cave proto-Mongoloids to modern East Asian Mongoloids.

Of particular interest, we have fair information that beginning no later than the Holstein-equivalent humans were making use of an extensive and formidable suite of forest and grassland mammals for food and raw materials. A high level of intellectual sophistication and technological competence must be attributed to *H. erectus* in order to account for success in the region.

Unfortunately lithic remains are poor indicators of the economic, intellectual, and social complexity attained. In general, the East Asian assemblages are crude and nondiagnostic but obviously satisfactory nonetheless. Techniques employed in flake manufacture are maintained over time with improvements clear from Choukoutien 1 through Choukoutien 15 to Hsiao-nan-hai and the Upper Cave. The last two both indicate that bone-working was advanced and Upper Cave provides the richest information on personal adornment and burial practices.

The lower Fenho region, particularly K'oho and Tingts'un, is a distinct technological subregion on the basis of flake production and heavy tool typology. The remains do not permit interpretation of hunting preferences since they are mainly redeposited camp remains, and not *in situ* occupation materials. There is technological continuity from the Holstein into at least the Eem and the lower Fenho–middle Huangho region probably is distinguishable on the basis of its widespread Tingts'un tool complex. Details of exploitation and pattern of occupation are not available.

. In view of the apparent distinctiveness of lithic types in the lower Fenho area, it is peculiar that Lantian lacks both the diagnostic tool types and heavy dependence on the alleged anvil technique for flake production. The only barrier between the regions is the Huangho though it is possible that the Fenho and Lantian areas were markedly different in vegetative cover and therefore in available food resources. The Lantian region reveals the earliest evidence of hominid occupation in China, as early as in Java. Obviously movement into the zone was restricted either to a route along the eastern coastal margin or from the southwest. The former route may have been less favorable since the zone was not particularly rich in large populations of mammalian forms. The hilly regions of southwestern China, which were major routes of movement during the Neolithic and historic periods, seem more likely as channels of movement from the south.

In the extreme western highland areas of Tsinghai and Tibet, the typologically old lithic remains may in fact be related to Ranov's mountain culture of summer hunters who followed herds into alpine meadow regions. Certainly the Chinese remains in these areas are above the limits easily inhabited by humans today and even during the most favorable times were available only seasonally.

The remains in the now desolate portions of the Ordos suggest that during the occupation of the area in the middle and later parts of the last glacial, a favorable steppe environment prevailed and game such as *Gazella* was relatively abundant. Typologically the Chingshuaiho remains of the northern Ordos in China are advanced but unfortunately they lack faunal and other associations.

In Manchuria the presence of Pleistocene cultural remains is in some doubt. Most of the lithic collections appear to be redeposited and are advanced in the sense that they appear with pottery in other contexts. From this region and Mongolia come the best evidences of typological similarity with extra-Chinese areas (aside from Hoabinhian-like remains in the far south). The so-called boat-shaped, tongue-shaped, or wedge-shaped cores and microblades and blades are distributed across steppe areas of north Asia into the Japanese islands. Whether or not economic similarities are also shared between these areas is unknown but these are clearly more relevant to culture history and contexts than lithic similarities. Hominid remains are entirely lacking, even in poor Pleistocene contexts.

Isolation of North China

Of considerable interest is the conservative nature of Chinese Pleistocene stone tool technology and the absence of outside cultural influences as indicated by lithic similarities. At the same time the relatively good record of hominid evolution, from early periods in the north and from later in the south, also strongly points to *in situ* developments from the early Middle Pleistocene to at least latest Pleistocene times.

It is probably significant that mountain systems and deserts form considerable barriers to free movement both west and north of North China. In the northwest the access is along the high mountains while the less well known southern region is blocked by high mountains on the west but is continuous with tropical Southeast Asia. The areas of contact, mountains and tropics, are the poorest in resources for hunting peoples and one can expect that no major movements or innovations were likely along these routes.

The lowland cave remains are generally part of the larger Southeast Asian area and in China at least are associated with shellfish collecting as well as hunting, and later with ceramics and presumably cultivation of at least some plants. The hominid remains from the south indicate *in situ* physical development. Nothing in the meager lithic assemblages indicates migrations of physically different people into the region.

In North China the common technological base and continuity of the entire area is strongly suggested even though separate local manifestations appear in the lower Fenho, Hopei Plain, Ordos, and Lantian. Very likely, lithic differences are partly related to historical divergence but also to economic differences and requirements. Basic is the gradual refinement of technique within a typologically simple lithic assemblage, from at least the mid-Middle Pleistocene. The K'oho-Tingts'un line has some distinctive large pointed tools; the Choukoutien-Hsiao-nan-hai line shows clearly increased technological competence in the form of refined blank manufacture but not in the development of a distinctive suite of tool types as are found in European remains of the same age. There are not enough remains from Lantian to characterize it but the reported heavy investment in the anvil technique seen in the lower Fenho is not present and in this respect the early remains recall Choukoutien 1.

The Ordos remains are Upper Pleistocene and show refinement within the same general northern tradition. By the time of Chingshuaiho, pointed tools are shaped by retouch but are mainly unifacial. Earlier most of the retouch is marginal.

There is no Pleistocene collection from China which reflects the absorption to any degree of European or Eurasian technological developments during any period of the Pleistocene. Hominid remains are highly indicative as well of internal evolution without outside migrations after the initial Lower or Early Middle Pleistocene input from the south. Together the cultural and hominid evidence imply long-term and effective isolation from outside influences.

Deficiencies in the Data

Unfortunately, truly meaningful data on cultural improvements in hunting practices, group age, sex structure and size, and other important facets of Pleistocene Chinese hominid occupation and behavior cannot be reconstructed from the lithic technology. Hints about the level of sophistication are present in the faunal diversity and hearth remains in the Choukoutien localities and in the Upper Cave burials. But the lack of good sites and the relative recency of problem-oriented archaeology for Pleistocene sites are largely responsible for the absence of useful cultural information.

In brief, the record of hominid occupation in China begins with the isolated Lantian skull cap from Cromer-equivalent times and becomes better with the cave remains in the Choukoutien region. But the record from the later Middle Pleistocene is poor, represented by scattered surface finds and the scanty Choukoutien 15 occupation. The Upper Pleistocene is poorly represented by Tingts'un since the remains have been redeposited and only Hsiao-nan-hai records an actual habitation site. The nearly total absence of data from the latest Pleistocene, except for the limited and uninterpretable information from the south, obscures the dynamic changes which obviously were underway.

REFERENCES

ACADEMIA SINICA, INSTITUTE OF ARCHAEOLOGY
  1962 *Hsin chung-kou ti k'ao-ku shou-huo* [Archaeology in New China].
         Peking: Wenwu Press.
ACADEMIA SINICA, INSTITUTE OF GEOLOGY
  1964 *Ti Ssu Chi Ti-chih Wen-t'i* [Quaternary China]. Peking: Science
         Press.
ACADEMIA SINICA, INSTITUTE FOR VERTEBRATE PALAEONTOLOGY AND
PALAEOANTHROPOLOGY
  1966 *The Cenozoic of Lantian.* Peking. (In Chinese.)
AIGNER, JEAN S.
  1969 "The archaeology of Pleistocene China." Unpublished Ph.D. dis-
         sertation, University of Wisconsin, Madison.
  1972a Relative dating of Pleistocene faunal and cultural complexes in North
         China. *Arctic Anthropology* 9 (2): 36–79.

1972b Pleistocene archaeological remains from South China. *Asian Perspectives* 16 (1): 16–38.
1973 Hsiao-nan-hai, an important Hopei Plain camp site. *Anthropologie* 10 (2–3): 39–50.
1976 "North Chinese Pleistocene cultural and hominid remains: a consideration of their significance to reconstructing the pattern of hominid bio-cultural development in eastern Asia." In *Le Paléolithique inférieur et moyen en Inde, en Asie centrale, en Chine et dans le Sud-Est asiatique*. Edited by A. Ghosh. UISPP colloquium 7: 65–90. Nice.

AIGNER, JEAN S., WILLIAM S. LAUGHLIN
1973 The dating of Lantian Man and the significance for analyzing trends in human evolution. *American Journal of Physical Anthropology* 39 (1): 97–110.

AN, CHIH-MIN
1965 Trial excavations of the Palaeolithic cave of Hsiao-nan-hai, Anyang. Honan. *K'ao-ku hsueh-pao* 1: 1–28. (In Chinese.)

BARBOUR, GEORGE
1935 Recent observations on the loess of North China. *Geographical Journal* 86 (1): 54–64.

BARBOUR, GEORGE, EMILE LICENT, P. TEILHARD DE CHARDIN
1927 Geological study of deposits of the Sankanho basin. *Bulletin of the Geological Society of China* 5 (3–4): 263–278.

BIRDSELL, J.
1972 *Human evolution*. Chicago: Rand-McNally.

BOULE, M., H. BREUIL, E. LICENT, P. TEILHARD DE CHARDIN
1928 *La Paléolithique de la Chine*. Archives de l'Institute de Paléontologie Humaine, Mémoire 4.

BREUIL, HENRI [ABBÉ H. BREUIL]
1939 Bone and antler industry of the Choukoutien, *Sinanthropus* site. *Palaeontologia Sinica* 2D (6): 7–41.

CHANG, KWANG-CHIH
1963 Prehistoric archaeology in China. *Arctic Anthropology* 1 (2): 29–61.
1968 *Archaeology of ancient China* (revised edition). New Haven: Yale University Press.

CH'ANG, SHEN-SHUI
1959 Discovery of Late Palaeolithic artifacts in Inner Mongolia and northwest Shansi. *Vertebrata Palasiatica* 3 (1): 47–56.
1960 New materials of palaeoliths from Inner Mongolia. *Vertebrata Palasiatica* 4 (1): 48.
1962 Some problems concerning the Sinanthropus lithic industry. *Vertebrata Palasiatica* 6 (3): 270–279.

CH'ANG, YU-P'ING, et al.
1964 Preliminary observations on the Cenozoic formation of Lantian, Shensi. *Vertebrata Palasiatica* 3 (2): 134–160. (In Chinese.)

CHAO, TZE-KUEI, ERH-CHIEN TAI
1961 Report on the excavation of the Choukoutien Sinanthropus site in 1960. *Vertebrata Palasiatica* 5 (4): 374–378. (In Chinese.)

CHARD, CHESTER S.
1969 Archaeology in the Soviet Union. *Science* 163: 774–778.

CHENG, TE-K'UN
1959 *Archaeology in China I: prehistoric China*. Cambridge: W. Heffer and Sons.

1966   *New light on prehistoric China. Archaeology in China*, supplement
1. University of Toronto Press.

CHIA, LAN-PO

1959a The Palaeolithic site of Hsi-kou, Li-ts'un in Ch'uwo, Shansi. *K'ao-ku*
1: 18–20. (In Chinese.)

1959b Notes on the bone implements of Sinanthropus. *K'ao-ku hsueh-pao*
3: 1–6. (In Chinese.)

1960   The stone artifacts of Sinanthropus and its relationship with the
contemporary cultures in North China. *Vertebrata Palasiatica* 4 (1):
37–38.

CHIA, LAN-PO, P'EI KAI, YEN-HSIEN LI

1964   New finds of Palaeolithic remains from Shuitungkou. *Vertebrata
Palasiatica* 8 (1): 75–86. (In Chinese.)

CHIA, LAN-PO, H. T. LIU

1950   Fossil myriapods from Choukoutien. *Bulletin of the Geological
Society of China* 30: 23–27.

CHIA, LAN-PO, CHIEN WANG

1962   Current status and the outlook of Palaeolithic studies in Shansi.
Wen-wu 4/5: 23–27. (In Chinese.)

CHIA, LAN-PO, TZE-YI WANG

1957   Discoveries of Palaeolithic cultures in Chiao-ch'eng, Shansi. *K'ao-ku*
5: 12–18. (In Chinese.)

CHIA, LAN-PO, TZE-YI WANG, CHUNG-LANG CHIU

1960   Palaeoliths of Shansi. *Vertebrata Palasiatica* 4 (1): 27–29.

1961   *Palaeoliths of Shansi*. Institute of Vertebrate Palaeontology and
Palaeoanthropology, Memoir 4. Peking. (In Chinese.)

CHIA, LAN-PO, TZE-YI WANG, CHIEN WANG

1961a Excavation of early Palaeolithic remains at K'oho, Jui-ch'ang,
Shansi. *K'ao-ku* 7: 395–397. (In Chinese.)

1961b The Lower Palaeolithic site of K'oho, Jui-ch'eng, Shansi. *K'ao-ku*
7: 8. (In Chinese.)

1962   *K'oho*. Institute of Vertebrate Palaeontology and Palaeoanthropology, Memoir 3. Peking. (In Chinese.)

1964   K'oho: an Early Palaeolithic site in south-western Shansi Province.
Arctic Anthropology 2 (1): 105–117.

CHIU, CHUNG-LANG

1958   Discovery of palaeoliths on the Tsinghai-Tibet Plateau. *Vertebrata
Palasiatica* 2 (2/3): 157–163. (In Chinese.)

CHOU, MIN-CHEN

1964   On the mammalian remains from Lantian locality, Shensi. *Vertebrata
Palasiatica* 8 (3): 295–307. (In Chinese.)

CHOU, MIN-CHEN, HSIANG-HSI HSIEN

1958   Late Cenozoic fossils from Chienping, Liaoning. *Acta Palaeontologica Sinica* 6: 51–58. (In Chinese.)

CHOU, PEN-SHEN

1965   Vertebrate remains from the Palaeolithic cave site of Hsiao-nan-hai,
Anyang. Honan. *K'ao-ku hsueh-pao* 1: 29–50. (In Chinese.)

COON, CARLETON S.

1963   *Origin of races*. New York: Alfred Knopf.

HSU, JEN

1965   The climate in North China during the time of Sinanthropus. *Quaternaria Sinica* 4 (1): 77–83. (In Chinese.)

JERNAKOV, V. N., V. V. PONOSOV
1958 Discovery of a fossil rhinoceros in Pan-la-ch'eng-tzu near Harbin. *Vertebrata Palasiatica* 2 (4): 269–275.

KAHLKE, HANS-DIETRICH
1963 Zur chronologischen Stellung der Choukoutien-Kultur. *Alt-Thüringen* 6: 23–41.

KAHLKE, HANS-DIETRICH, PEN-SHEN CHOU
1961 A summary of stratigraphy and palaeontological observations in the lower layers of Choukoutien locality 1 and on the chronological position of the site. *Vertebrata Palasiatica* 5 (3): 212–240. (In Chinese.)

KOWALSKI, K., CHUAN-KUEI LI
1963 Remarks on the fauna of bats (Chiroptera) from Locality 1 at Choukoutien. *Vertebrata Palasiatica* 7 (2): 148–150. (In Chinese.)

KUO, YUNG
1959 Archaeology in Shansi during the last decade. *K'ao-ku* 2: 62–64. (In Chinese.)

KURTEN, BJORN
1961 An attempted parallelization of the Quaternary mammalian faunas of China and Europe. *Societas Scientarium Fennica* 23 (8).
1968 *Pleistocene mammals of Europe.* London: Weidenfeld and Nicolson.

MOVIUS, HALLAM L., JR.
1944 Early man and Pleistocene stratigraphy in South and East Asia. *Papers of the Peabody Museum of American Archaeology and Ethnology* 19 (3).
1948 The Lower Paleolithic cultures of southern and eastern Asia. *Transactions of the American Philosophical Society*, n.s. 38 (4): 329–420.
1956 New Palaeolithic sites near Tingts'un on the Fen River, Shansi Province, North China. *Quaternaria* 3: 13–26.

P'EI, WEN-CHUNG
1932 Preliminary note on some incised, cut and broken bones found in association with Sinanthropus remains and lithic artifacts from Choukoutien. *Bulletin of the Geological Society of China* 12 (1): 105–108.
1934a A preliminary report on the Late Palaeolithic cave of Choukoutien. *Bulletin of the Geological Society of China* 13 (1): 327–358.
1934b On the carnivora from locality 1 of Choukoutien. *Palaeontologia Sinica* C8 (1).
1938 A preliminary study on a new Palaeolithic station known as locality 15 within the Choukoutien region. *Bulletin of the Geological Society of China* 19 (2): 174–187.
1939a New fossil materials and artifacts collected from the Choukoutien region during the years 1937 to 1939. *Bulletin of the Geological Society of China* 19 (3): 207–232.
1939b The Upper Cave industry of Choukoutien. *Palaeontologia Sinica* 2D: 9.
1940 Upper Cave fauna of Choukoutien. *Palaeontologia Sinica*, n.s. C10.
1957 The zoographical divisions of Quaternary mammalian fauna in China. *Vertebrata Palasiatica* 1 (1): 9–24.
1958 More palaeoliths found in the upper Fenho region, Shansi. *Vertebrata Palasiatica* 2 (4): 295. (In Chinese.)

1960 On the problem of the "bone implements" of Choukoutien Sinanthropus. *K'ao-ku hsueh-pao* 2: 1–9. (In Chinese.)
1965 "Professor Henri Breuil, pioneer of Chinese Palaeolithic archaeology and its progress after him," in *Mescelánea en homenaje al Abate
Henri Breuil*. Edited by E. Ripoll Perelló, vol. 2, pp. 251–269.
Barcelona: Diputación Provincial de Barcelona, Instituto de Prehistoria y Argueología.

P'EI, WEN-CHUNG, YIU-HENG LI
1964 Tentative opinions on the Sjara-osso-gol Series. *Vertebrata Palasiatica* 8 (2): 99–119. (In Chinese.)

P'EI, WEN-CHUNG, *et al.*
1958 *Report on the excavation of Palaeolithic sites at Tingts'un, Hsiang-
fen-hsien, Shansi Province*. Institute of Vertebrate Palaeontology and
Palaeoanthropology, Memoir 2. Peking. (In Chinese.)

PIEN, M. N.
1934 On the fossil Pisces, Amphibia and Reptilia from Choukoutien
localities 1 and 3. *Palaeontologia Sinica* C10 (1).

PING, CHI
1929 Fossil terrestrial Gastropods from North China. *Palaeontologia
Sinica* B6 (5).
1931 Tertiary and Quaternary non-marine Gastropods of North China.
Palaeontologia Sinica B6 (6).

SHAW, T. H.
1935 Preliminary observations on the fossil birds from Choukoutien.
Bulletin of the Geological Society of China 14 (1): 77–81.

SUN, MENG-JUNG
1965 On the pollen from the Choukoutien Sinanthropus site. *Quaternaria
Sinica* 4 (1): 84–96. (In Chinese.)

TAI, ERH-CHIEN
1966 Palaeoliths from Kungwangling, Lantian and vicinity, Shensi. *Vertebrata Palasiatica* 10 (1): 30–34. (In Chinese.)

TAI, ERH-CHIEN, HUNG-CH'IANG CHI
1964 Palaeoliths from Lantian, Shensi. *Vertebrata Palasiatica* 8 (2):
152–161. (In Chinese.)

TAI, ERH-CHIEN, YUN-CHE PAI
1966 Investigations in a Palaeolithic cave in Shantung. *Vertebrata Palasiatica* 10 (1): 82–83. (In Chinese.)

TEILHARD DE CHARDIN, P.
1941 *Early man in China*. Institut de Géo-Biologie, Publication 7. Peking.

TEILHARD DE CHARDIN, P., PIERRE LEROY
1942 *Chinese fossil mammals*. Institut de Géo-Biologie, Publication 8.
Peking.
1945 *Les félidés de Chine*. Institut de Géo-Biologie, Publication 11. Peking.

TEILHARD DE CHARDIN, P., WEN-CHUNG P'EI
1932 The lithic industry of the Sinanthropus deposits in Choukoutien.
Bulletin of the Geological Society of China 11: 315–358.

THOMA, A.
1964 Die Entstehung der Mongoliden. *Homo* 15 (1): 1–22.

WANG, YU-P'ING
1962 Cultural remains from Shuitungkou. *K'ao-ku* 11: 588–589. (In
Chinese.)

WEIDENREICH, FRANZ

1939a On the earliest representatives of modern mankind recovered on the soil of East Asia. *Peking Natural History Bulletin* 13 (3): 161–174.

1939b The duration of life of fossil man in China and the pathological lesions found in his skeleton. *Chinese Medical Journal* 45: 33–44.

1943 The skull of *Sinanthropus pekinensis*: a comparative study on a primitive hominid skull. *Palaeontologia Sinica*, n.s. D10 (127).

WU, HSIN-CHIH

1961a Study on the Upper Cave man of Choukoutien. *Vertebrata Palasiatica* 5 (3): 181–203. (In Chinese.)

1961b On the racial types of the Upper Cave man of Choukoutien. *Scientia Sinica* 10 (8): 993–1006.

WOO, JU-KANG

1964a A newly discovered mandible of the Sinanthropus type – Sinanthropus lantianensis. *Vertebrata Palasiatica* 8 (1): 1–17. (In Chinese.)

1964b A newly discovered mandible of the Sinanthropus type – Sinanthropus lantianensis. *Scientia Sinica* 13 (5): 801–811.

1964c Discovery of the mandible of Sinanthropus lantianensis in Shensi Province, China. *Current Anthropology* 5 (2): 98–101.

YOUNG, C. C.

1932 On the Artiodactyla from the Sinanthropus site at Choukoutien. *Palaeontologia Sinica* C8 (2).

1934 On Insectivora, Rodentia and Primates other than Sinanthropus from locality 1, Choukoutien. *Palaeontologia Sinica* C8 (3).

ZDANSKY, OTTO

1928 Die Säugetiere der Quartafauna von Chou-k'ou-tien. *Palaeontologia Sinica* C5 (4).

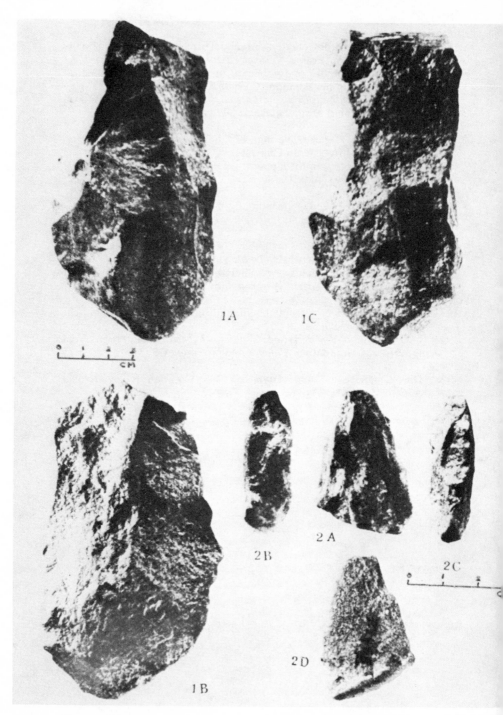

Plate 1.   K'oho (See Figure 6) (Chia, Wang, and Wang 1962)

Plate 2. Tingts'un (see Figure 7) (P'ei et al. 1958)

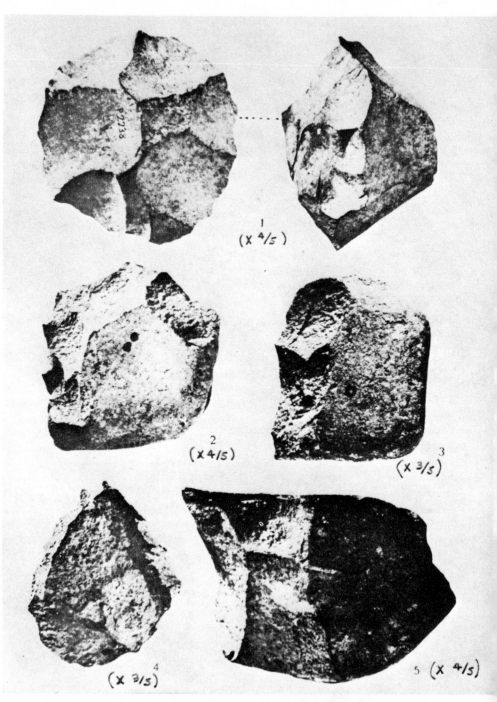

Plate 3. Other paleoliths from Shansi Province (Chia, Wang, and Chiu 1961)

The Early Paleolithic Industries of Sŏkchang-ni, Korea

POW-KEY SOHN

1. Only during the last decade have Paleolithic industries been brought to light in Korea. Thirty-odd sites have now been located through surface finds along the riverine and lacustrine area of the Korean peninsula (Figure 1). Two of the open sites have been excavated; it is reported that at the Kulpo-ri site in the northeastern tip of Korea there is an Early Paleolithic assemblage in the lower horizon and an Upper Paleolithic assemblage in the upper horizon (To 1964; To and Kim 1965).

At Sŏkchang-ni site, excavations conducted between 1964 and 1972 under the auspices of Yonsei University Museum have revealed twelve archaeological horizons and twenty-seven geological layers at Locality 2 and an Upper Paleolithic habitation site at Locality 1 (Sohn 1967, 1968, 1969, 1972a). Excavation of Locality 1 was conducted between 1970 and 1972 (Sohn 1972a, 1973a, 1973b). The site is located on the Kum River terrace 200 kilometers southwest of Seoul.

From Locality 1, we were able to obtain a greater variety and quantity of data including pollen samples, engraved objects, hearth ash, hairs of Sŏkchangniens and animals, mineral pigments and painted cobbles, and chipped animal figures. A radiocarbon test on the ashes collected from the hearth yielded a date for the habitation of $20,830 \pm 1,880$ B.P. (Yang 1972). Below this layer another layer associated with a few quartz tools has been dated $30,690 \pm 3,000$ B.P. (Yang 1970).

2. The correlations between Locality 1 and Locality 2 were established by the presence of geological layers IV (with mud cracks), V (compact clay), and VI (gravel-sand) at both localities (Sohn 1973a, 1973b). Through further correlations, layers 10 to 27 of Locality 2 could be assigned to the Würm I and pre-Würm I periods.

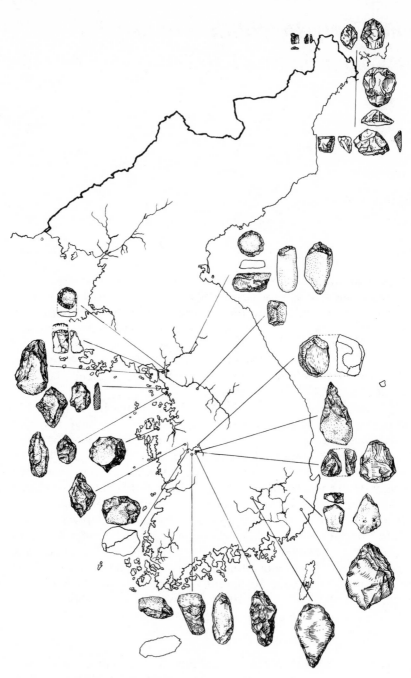

Figure 1. Paleolithic sites in Korea

Geological analysis, including soil and sedimentological analysis, suggests that there had been a cyclical change, albeit with some irregularities (see Figure 2). Clearly, the Sŏkchang-ni sediments have survived the various erosion cycles of the meandering Kum River and have undergone a continuous depression. It has been shown that the western coast of the Korean peninsula has continuously submerged at the rate of 0.426 millimeters per year for the last 4,000 years and 1.4 millimeters per year for at least 2,700 years prior to the last 4,000 years (Park 1969). In other words the western coast has evidently submerged at least 548 centimeters in the last 6,700 years. In view of such a depression, layers 10 to 27 of Locality 2 are comparable to the Shimosueyoshi and pre-Shimosueyoshi formations in Japan (Nakagawa 1967).

The geological layers can be classified into three major categories: (1) a gravel layer, (2) a fine-grain sand layer, and (3) a silty-clay layer. The average ratio of sand to silt-plus-clay of the three categories, as obtained by sieve analysis (conducted after gravel had been removed), is as follows:

	Sand	Silt+clay
gravel layers	89.66%	10.34%
fine sand	31.20%	68.80%
silt-clay	12.85%	87.15%

The identification of each geological layer within the Pleistocene geochronological sequence should await further study.

Table 1 shows the components of clay, silt, and sand.

Table 1. The components of clay, silt, and sand (in percent)

	Layer number	Clay	Silt	Sand	Classification
c^a	10	49.3	21.9	28.8	clay
s^b	11	44.6	16.4	39.0	clay
c	12	12.0	4.3	83.7	gravel-sand
c	13	13.6	19.9	66.5	sandy loam
s	14	52.1	10.1	37.8	sandy clay
c	15, 15a	4.1	3.6	92.3	gravel-sand
s	16	56.5	11.3	32.2	clay
c	17	4.4	7.8	87.8	gravel-sand
s	18	30.4	22.7	46.9	sandy-clay
c	19	29.7	13.6	56.7	gravel-sand
s	20	67.1	18.8	14.1	clay
c	21	5.2	10.4	84.4	gravel-sand
s	22	12.1	12.2	75.7	sandy loam
c	23	1.4	2.1	96.5	gravel-sand
s	24	69.3	19.1	11.6	clay
s	25	4.8	7.9	87.3	gravel-sand
s	26	47.2	22.6	30.2	clay
c	27	4.7	9.2	86.1	rolled gravel-sand
	Bedrock	22.0	14.0	64.0	sandy clay

[a] *c*: cultural layer.   [b] *s*: sterile layer.

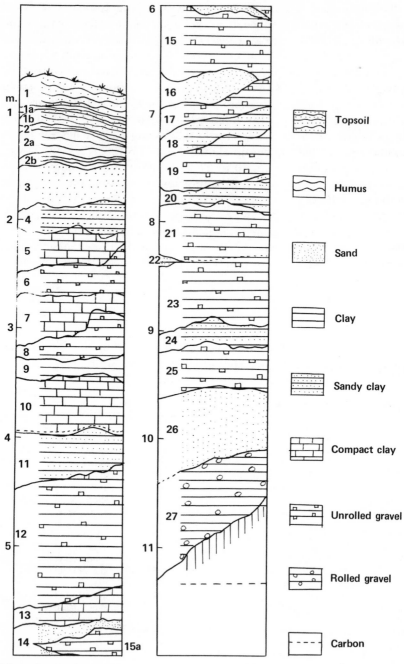

Figure 2. Section

The industries which can be considered to be Early (Middle and Lower) Paleolithic were obtained from layers 10, 13, 15a, 15, 17, 19, 21, and 27 of Locality 2 (Sohn 1972a, 1972b). These layers are at depths between 4 and 11 meters below the surface.

The climate was probably colder when the gravel layers (layers 12, 15a, 15, 17, 19, 21, 23, 25, 27) were formed, while it was wetter and warmer when the sandy-clay layers (layers 10, 11, 13, 14, 16, 18, 20, 22, 24) were deposited; it was somewhat windy at the time of layer 26. We welcome suggestions from Quaternary geologists on the geological and chronological interpretation of the site.

3. Excavations at Locality 2 were limited to a small area, especially in the lower layers. Because the present water level is 6.4 meters and the layers 15 to 17 are below it, the excavation in layers 19 to 27 had to be conducted on an extremely limited scale. The size of the excavation pit was 1.5 by 2 meters. At the depths of 8 meters and below (layers 21 to 27) the pit became even smaller. Although the numbers of tools obtained from the lower layers are accordingly rather small, evolutionary trends in their typology and technology are observable in layers 10, 13, 15a, 15, 17, 19, 21, 23, and 27.

From layer 27, the lowermost layer, at 10.2 to 11.2 meters below the surface, 23 (21 core tools and 2 flake tools) artifacts were recovered. There were 4 unifacial choppers, 4 pointed tools, 6 scrapers, and 3 hammerstones. The materials used in this industry are mostly quartz plaquettes which were easily available in the locality. At Locality 1 the bedrock is mainly of granite gneiss and pegmatite. The rocks often disintegrate in sheet forms. The primitive techniques are observed in the unifacial flaking on the dorsal face of plaquette material. The natural cortex of the plaquette is left on both surfaces and retouch is rarely seen on these tools (Figure 3). Layers 26, 25, 24, 23, and 22 are sterile.

In layer 21, only three tools and some naturifacts were unearthed. One of the tools is a large triangular porphyry pick with flaking around the wider grip end and some retouch along one side (Figure 4). Two other quartz flake tools show some wear from usage which could be mistaken for minute retouch.

In layer 19 there were 25 tools, 13 pieces of waste material, and 2 naturifacts. These included two unifacial double choppers made by alternate or obverse flaking techniques (Figure 5 bottom) and 16 scrapers, 12 of which were equipped with double cutting edges. In this industry 17 out of 25 tools had double cutting edges. In one of the scrapers a small portion is retouched consecutively as if to form denticulate, and obverse flaking becomes prevalent especially on plaquette material. There are 19 convex and 7 transversal scrapers (Figure 5, top) and only one concave scraper.

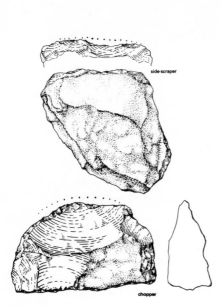

Figure 3.   Layer 27

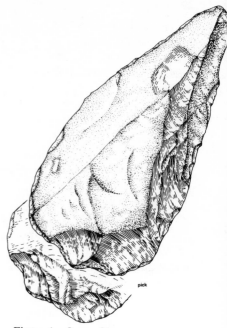

Figure 4.   Layer 21

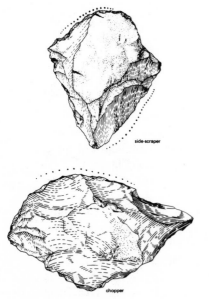

Figure 5.   Layer 19

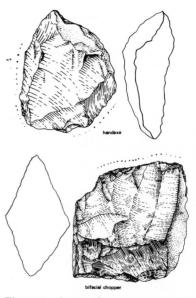

Figure 6.   Layer 17

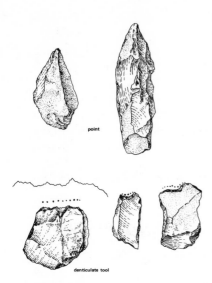

Figure 7.   Layer 17

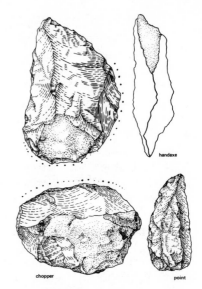

Figure 8.   Layer 15

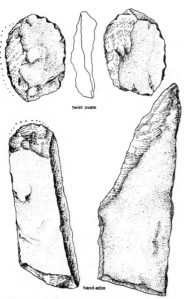

Figure 9.   Layer 15

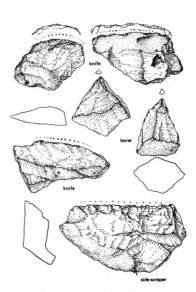

Figure 10.   Layer 15a

In layer 17, a slightly larger area was excavated. From a 25-square-meter area 70 generalized tools, 5 toolmaking tools, 1 core, 1 blank, and 70 waste flakes and chips were unearthed. There were 64 quartz tools, 1 granite gneiss tool, and 1 hornblendite tool. About half of the tools had multiple cutting edges.

One of the significant changes in this layer is the appearance of a proto-handaxe (unifacial) and a core biface. This bifacially retouched tool remarkably resembles an Abbevillian handaxe (Figure 6, top). The bifacial chopper, on the other hand, exhibits parallel flaking scars and retouch (Figure 6, bottom).

There are 26 scrapers, 3 of which are convergent scrapers on two different ventral bases and four of which are alternate double scrapers. The technology shown on these implements appears to represent a better adaptation to the lithic material (plaquette quartz) available to the toolmakers.

There are also tools that can be classified as notched (encoché) tools (Figure 7, bottom) and denticulate. Their cutting edges show wear due to utilization. There are also crudely shaped points (Figure 7, top). Certain tool types and toolmaking techniques that were absent in the lower layers now occur in this layer.

In layer 15, 86 tools were excavated; 2 handaxes, 13 choppers, 17 points, 17 scrapers, 7 end-scrapers, 19 knives, 4 handadzes, and 7 planes.

The handaxes still retain the Abbevillian features (Figure 8, top), whereas the choppers are all bifacial and similar to a handaxe in form (Figure 8, bottom left). There is a chopper-and-scraper in the form of a so-called twist-ovate (Figure 9, top). An improvement in the flaking technique is seen in the removal of a blade-like flake (Figure 8, bottom right) from a quartz core with a prepared striking platform. In addition, the method of handadze production (Figure 9, bottom) has become more standardized through the use of bipolar technique.

The increase in number of alternate scrapers is also conspicuous in this layer. The tool occurring most frequently is a knife; most of these had a convex cutting edge. The majority of the tools were of core tradition; flake industry did not develop as long as the lithic materials available were of poor quality for such flaking.

Layer 15a can be distinguished from layer 15, as seen in the profile (Figure 2). In this layer the tools are smaller and the main tool types are different from layer 15. The back grip of the scraper in this layer is elevated to form a hafted horse-hoof shape (Figure 10, bottom). Couteau-shaped knives become more numerous (Figure 10, top middle left) and perçoirs or borers occur in this layer (figure 10, middle right).

Layer 13 is markedly different from the lower layers in that it is a compact clay, not a gravel-sand layer, and in that chert and felsite, rather that quartz, were utilized for toolmaking (Figure 11). The deposit is very thin and the flakes are small both in number and size. A new tradition of making flake tools with subtle retouch appears in this layer. Although some of the tools are reminiscent of those from Shuitungkou, the full significance of the appearance of this technique could be understood only after a more extended excavation. It should be added that sources of felsite and chert are situated at about 30 kilometers from Sŏkchang-ni.

In layer 12 (Figures 12 and 13) a slightly larger portion was excavated (5.0 by 7.5 meters). There were 280 artifacts among which points account for 33.7 percent, end-scrapers 16.1 percent, and other scrapers 15.4 percent. There were 21 denticulated tools out of the 280. The increase of denticulate tools, together with the increase of single-function tools, seems to be an indication of Mousteroid industry. The increasing trend of double tools is thus arrested in this layer. Of the 280 tools only 13 had double cutting edges. There were anvils of quartz, granite gneiss, amd porphyry, and hammerstones were mostly of heavy biotite schist. The settlement seems to have lasted longer than in other layers, as this layer is approximately 110 centimeters thick.

Although the lithic material is still predominantly quartz, there was a gradual increase in the number of flake tools in this layer. This should be considered as an indication of improvements in flaking technology.

Layer 10 consists of the same compact clay although it has a chocolate color due to the limonitic contents of the soil. In this layer almost all the tools were made of porphyritic water-worn pebble. This pebble chopper industry exhibits the features of Clactonian, Levalloisian, and Mousterian industries (Figures 14, 15).

The total number of tools was 67, with 40 core tools and 27 flake tools. The Levalloisian index is 14.9, index of Levalloisian typology 19.2, and bifacial index 48.4. In this pebble chopper industry, pebble cylinder hammers (20 and 26 centimeters in length) were utilized in flaking, and relatively large flakes were also obtained from cores of porphyritic cobble.

There were 1 proto-handaxe, 12 bifacial choppers, and 3 choppers, 18 side scrapers, 9 end-scrapers, 10 points, 9 knives, 1 borer, and 4 burins. These tools fall into three classifications with respect to their weight: heavy, medium and light. The average weight for each category was 460.9 grams, 197.1 grams, and 68.9 grams respectively. Flaking angles range from 131° to 103°, with the most frequent between 117° and 113°.

Typologically, there are a few choppers of archaic type and bifacial choppers of the Clacton type, but there are also Levalloisian cores, Levalloisian blade-like flakes, and Mousteroid scrapers of quasi–La

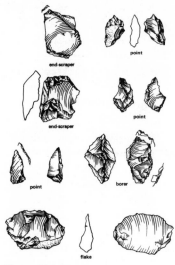

Figure 11.   Layer 13

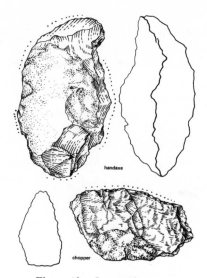

Figure 12.   Layer 12

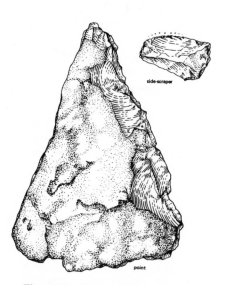

Figure 13.   Layer 12

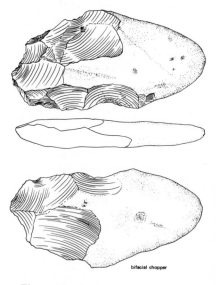

Figure 14.   Layer 10

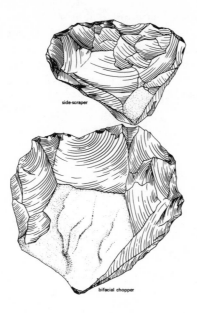

Figure 15.   Layer 10

Quina type as well as denticulates. Judging from typological and tech-nological characteristics, as well as the stratigraphic position, this industry can be considered a Middle Paleolithic industry.

Above this layer at least three Upper Paleolithic industries are present.

4.   At Locality 2 of Sŏkchang-ni, there are nine earlier Paleolithic horizons. In seven of the horizons, quartz, pegmatite, and granite gneiss plaquette materials are mostly utilized for tools, whereas in two other layers (layer 13 and layer 10), pebbles of porphyry, chert, and felsite were brought in for flaking. While the seven layers were composed of gravel, the other two layers were of compact clay. Possibly different environmental conditions are indicated by the seven lower layers as opposed to the two middle layers. The environmental and paleoclimatic conditions for each of the Sŏkchang-ni industries is one of the problems for future investigation.

In addition there are several cave sites in the mid-eastern part of Korea. Three cave sites have been located that yield animal bones in well-fossilized as well as semi-fossilized states. One of the caves has at least three Paleolithic horizons. From pollen analysis it is known that pollens of *Cyperaceae*, *Pinus*, and unknown spores are present in the upper layer. The middle layer contains *Chlorophyta*, *Pinus*, and unknown spores; in the lower layer only *Pinus* pollen is present.

This palynological difference is related to the variability in faunal fossils. The upper layer contained semi-fossilized *Cervus* and numerous bone tools; well-fossilized *Ursus spelaeus*[1] with numerous bone tools were recovered from the middle layer; some well-fossilized *Cervus* and *Macaca* sp. were present in the lower layer.

When excavations are resumed at these caves, more evidence of Early Paleolithic industries, as well as additional information on fauna and flora, will certainly be brought to light. Correlations of the Korean industries with those of the Asiatic continent and insular Japan will then be greatly facilitated.[2]

REFERENCES

NAKAGAWA, HISAO
  1967 Quaternary sea levels of the Japanese Islands. *Journal of Geoscience, Osaka City University* 10: 1–5; 37–42.
PARK, YONG AHN
  1969 Submergence of the Yellow Sea coast of Korea and stratigraphy of Sinpyeongcheon Marsh, Kimje, Korea. *The Journal of the Geological Society of Korea* 5: 57–66.
P'EI, WEN-CHUNG
  1934 On the Carnivora from locality 1 of Choukoutien. *Palaeontologia Sinica*, series C, 8(1).
SOHN, POW-KEY
  1967 Stratified Palaeolithic cultures newly excavated in Korea. *Yoksa Hakpo* [Korean Historical Review] 35: 1–25; 36: 346–352.
  1968 Pebble chopping-tool industry of the stratified Palaeolithic cultures of Sŏkchang-ni, Korea. *Han-guk-sa Yon-gu* [Journal of Korean History] 1: 1–62.
  1969 Surface finds of the Palaeolithic tools in Korea. *Paek-san Hakpo* 7: 1–24.
  1970 The burin-grattoir industry of the stratified Palaeolithic cultures at Sŏkchang-ni, Korea. *Han-guk-sa Yon-gu* [Journal of Korean History] 5: 1–46.
  1972a Lower and Middle Palaeolithic industries of the stratified Sŏkchang-ni cultures. *Han-guk-sa Yon-gu* [Journal of Korean History] 7: 1–58.
  1972b The Palaeolithic industries of Korea. *Paekche Yon-gu* 3: 55–72.
  1973a The Upper Palaeolithic habitation, Sŏkchang-ni, Korea. *Han-guk-sa Yon-gu* [Journal of Korean History] 9: 1–57.
  1973b *The Upper Palaeolithic habitation, Sŏkchang-ni, Korea: a summary report*. Publication of Yonsei University Museum, English Series 1.
TO, YU-HO
  1964 On the Palaeolithic industry of Kulpo-ri, Korea. *Kogo Minsok* [Archeology and Ethnography] 3: 3–7.
TO, YU-HO, YONG-NAM KIM
  1965 Palaeolithic site found in Supohang-dong, Kulpo-ri, Wunggi, Hamgyong pukto. *Kogo Minsok* [Archeology and Ethnography] 1: 54–56.

[1] The *Ursus spelaeus* excavated in Choukoutien was the same species as the one we have discovered in the cave (cf. Pei 1934).
[2] It is of interest to compare some of the industries of China and Japan with those of Sŏkchang-ni, Korea.

YANG, KYUNG RIN
1970   Atomic Energy Research Institute of Korea [AERIK]: radiocarbon measurements I (AERIK-5). *Radiocarbon* 12: 350–352.
1972   Atomic Energy Research Institute of Korea [AERIK]: radiocarbon measurements II (AERIK-8). *Radiocarbon* 14: 273–279.

The History of Early Paleolithic Research in Japan

FUMIKO IKAWA-SMITH

"The Early Paleolithic," in the Japanese context, refers to the archaeological assemblages which actually or purportedly predate the base of the Tachikawa Loam Formation of the southern Kanto Plain. This definition was proposed by Serizawa (1968c, 1969, 1970), and has been widely accepted by Japanese prehistorians. The Tachikawa Loam is one of the formations in the standard sequence on which the Pleistocene stratigraphy of Japan is based, and it appears to have begun its deposition about 30,000 years ago (K. Kobayashi 1965a). Thus the time range of the "Early Paleolithic" of Japan covers the general time range of both the Lower Paleolithic and Middle Paleolithic and continues into the early part of the Upper Paleolithic of Western Europe.

The rapid development of the Paleolithic research since the 1949 excavation of the Iwajuku site, in the northern Kanto Plain, has unearthed an immense amount of archaeological material from Pleistocene formations in Japan. Concomitant geological investigations and applications of the radiocarbon method suggest that almost all of the archaeological remains, from some 1,000 sites all over Japan, come from formations younger than 20,000 B.P., when the depressed sea level of the maximum glaciation would have caused the Japanese Islands to be connected with the mainland of Asia. A few, such as the famous Iwajuku I assemblage, appear to date to the period between 20,000 and 30,000 B.P. Few, if any, archaeologists question the human workmanship of these specimens, even though they may disagree on the details of typological classifications and chronological assignments. It is now well established that the Japanese Archipelago was inhabited by man by the time populations of *Homo sapiens sapiens* were expanding into many corners of the earth, and that many of the archaeological remains left in Japan by these *sapiens* populations share the general characteristics of tools attributed to the *sapiens* type of man elsewhere in Eurasia – that is to say, a variety of cutting, piercing, and scraping tools made on blade blanks. Relatively recent discussion, in English, of this later phase of the Japanese Paleolithic include Hayashi (1968), Ikawa (1964, 1968, 1970), T. Kobayashi (1970), R. Morlan (1967), V. Morlan (1971), Oda (1969), Serizawa (1970), and Sugihara (1969).

But on the question of hominid occupation of Japan prior to 30,000 B.P. there is no agreement in archaeological circles in Japan; heated controversy continues. During the last decade, many claims of the discovery of archaeological remains from pre-Tachikawa formations have been made. Large-scale excavations were conducted at Nyu and Sozudai in Kyushu, and at Hoshino and Iwajuku in the Kanto Plain (cf. Figure 8 for the locations, see p. 263); scores of other localities were investigated and the older claims for the presence of early Paleolithic man in Japan, such as those made by Munro in the 1910's and by Naora in the 1930's, were reevaluated.

In this paper I would like to review the history of Early Paleolithic research in Japan, in the hope of placing the research report presented by Professor Serizawa (this volume) in a proper perspective.

The history of the research into the Early Paleolithic of Japan may be reviewed in terms of three periods: prior to 1949, between 1949 and 1962, and the current period since 1962. The significance of the year 1949 for Paleolithic research in Japan is evident. It was the year when the Iwajuku site was excavated, thus putting an end to the era of speculation about the existence of the Paleolithic in Japan and marking the beginning of vigorous investigations. The year 1962 appears to me to mark the turning point in the burst of research activities which followed the Iwajuku discovery. Two events symbolize the change. First, it was in 1962 that the Nyu site in northern Kyushu was discovered and attracted much public attention. Although the subsequent investigations of the sites proved rather unfruitful, the discovery, nevertheless, is significant as the beginning of the renewed interest in the Early Paleolithic manifestations in Japan. Furthermore, the investigations were conducted under the initiative of Bun'ei Tsunoda of the Paleological Association of Japan, Inc. of Kyoto. Tsunoda was not among the workers who participated in the formulation of the framework of the Japanese Paleolithic during the 1950's. This point is relevant to the second event which also occurred in 1962, that is, the publication of the controversial paper by Yamanouchi and T. Sato (1962) questioning the entire chronology of the Japanese Paleolithic which was widely accepted by the scholars at that time. These events seemed to indicate the breakdown of the consensus which had prevailed up to that time in the field of Paleolithic research. From this point onward, debates and controversies frequently appeared in print. Dissenting opinions were no longer voiced privately, or absorbed and accommodated by the consensual framework, because the research was no longer carried out by a small, select group of people who owed loyalty to one another. This controversial atmosphere continues· to this day and one of the subjects which provokes the most heated debate is the Early Paleolithic problem.

1. EARLY PALEOLITHIC RESEARCH PRIOR TO 1949

The Paleolithic research in Japan prior to the Iwajuku excavation has been characterized as being confined to sporadic discoveries (Serizawa and Ikawa 1960: 1). Most of these discoveries and speculations fall in the category of the Early Paleolithic as defined above. As Kidder (1959: 27) put it: "Before that date [1949] there had been strong proponents of an Old Stone Age, but the scattered and often unconvincing objects, and what seemed to be exaggerated claims, may have actually delayed full cognizance of their significance." The sporadic finds and claims consist of the following:

a. Munro's collection of lithic specimens near Yokohama (1911);
b. Kida's speculation on the Lower Paleolithic status of lithic items from Kô, near Osaka (1917);
c. Sone's claims for "eoliths" from Tsubakiyama in northern Honshu (1929a, 1929b);
d. Nagasawa's finds of stone and bone specimens from Hiyoshidai, Yokohama (1939); and
e. Naora's collection of stone and bone items as well as a hominid skeletal fragment from Nishiyagi, near Akashi (1931).

The locations of the above sites are shown in Figure 1.

1.1. SAKAWAGAWA AND HAYAKAWA. Munro's argument for the six lithic specimens which he illustrated in his *Prehistoric Japan* was none too enthusiastic, for he stated (1911: 41–42): "These specimens are...not sufficient to definitely establish the existence of paleolithic man in this country, though I venture to think they are suggestive." These are only a small proportion of many items which he had collected in the valleys of the Sakawagawa and the Hayakawa in the southern Kanto Plain in 1905. As far as the illustrated specimens were concerned, they were considered by most archaeologists as "nothing but rubble" (Hamada 1918: 30; Serizawa 1954: 67; 1960: 39) until a few years ago. With the resurgence of active interest in the problem of the Early Paleolithic remains, however, efforts are being

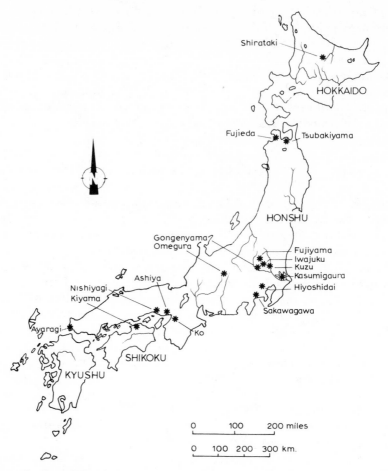

Figure 1. Locations of sites where reportedly early archaeological remains were recovered prior to 1962

made to locate and reexamine the Munro collection (e.g. Suzuki 1968). Such workers as Serizawa, reversing the former stand, now feel it necessary to reevaluate the specimens collected by Munro some sixty years earlier (e.g. Serizawa 1965: 81).

1.2. Kô. Kida (1917) suggested a possible human occupation of Japan in very ancient times on the basis of his observation that, at the Kô site in Osaka Prefecture (Figure 1), large and crude artifacts were obtained from a gravel layer at one to two meters from the surface, while well-made arrowheads occurred in the black soil within 60 centimeters of the surface.

Hamada (1918), however, contradicted Kida by saying that during his own excavation of the site in 1917 the large and crude artifacts were found in the same layer as arrowheads and pottery at about 100 centimeters from the surface. The layers below were evidently not explored. Hamada agreed that some of the "large and crude artifacts" do indeed resemble Acheulian artifacts of Europe, but, finding it difficult to accept a human occupation of Japan in Paleolithic times, suggested that these artifacts are the results of the survival in Japan of the Paleolithic stone-working techniques into the Neolithic times (1918: 30–31). As to other forms, Hamada enumerated several possibilities: that they could be axes manufactured by chipping, rather than by a polishing process, due to the hardness of the stone; they could be unfinished spearheads; some of them could be rejects of spearheads; and certain others could be cores for obtaining small flakes from which arrowheads were manufactured (Hamada 1918: 32–33).

The existence of a preceramic horizon at the site was verified by the excavations in 1957 and 1958, but the "Acheulian-like" artifacts described by Kida and Hamada have not yet been obtained through excavation (Kamaki and Takahashi 1965). Some of the materials recovered by these excavations are shown in Figure 7.

1.3.   TSUBAKIYAMA. In 1929, Sone reported on nine lithic specimens collected from the shore of Tsubakiyama on Natsudomari Peninsula in Aomori Prefecture at the northern end of Honshu (Sone 1929a, 1929b). The specimens, described as "eoliths," were believed to have been derived from a Pleistocene formation under water. The stratigraphic provenance has not been verified and the specimens in question were not, at the time, accepted as Paleolithic artifacts. After the Iwajuku excavations, however, Serizawa (1954: 64) felt at least some of the specimens shown in Sone's illustrations could be typologically Paleolithic. The present location of the specimens, apparently, is unknown.

1.4.   HIYOSHIDAI. The reason for inclusion of the Hiyoshidai finds in this list of early claims for the Early Paleolithic of Japan is stratigraphic. Nagasawa (1939) reported that he obtained these specimens *in situ* from a gravel bed which he considered as a member of the Shimosueyoshi Formation. The Shimosueyoshi Formation, as it is understood today, is a marine formation assignable to the Riss-Würm Interglacial times. The author, however, suggested that the gravel bed was not older than Aurignacian because he felt that one of the specimens, which he termed a bone "spatula" (Figure 2: a), was comparable to Magdalenian artifacts of Europe (Nagasawa 1939: 166–169). The other specimen was a scratched pebble.

There are two possible reasons for this apparent contradiction:

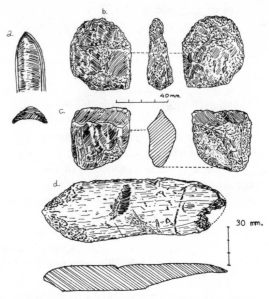

Figure 2.   Bone and lithic specimens; (a) bone specimen from Hiyoshidai, Yokohama (approx. ½ natural size); (b, c) lithic specimens from Nishiyagi (Akashi); (d) bone specimen from Kuzu, Kanto Plain. (All illustrations taken from Naora 1954b)

either Nagasawa's typological comparison of the bone specimen was unwarranted, or his recognition of the gravel bed as a member of the Shimosueyoshi Formation was in error. The first possibility is more likely. The occurrence of *Cervus praenipponicus* and possible *Elephas namadicus naumanni* in the same horizon in a nearby locality (Naora 1954b: 178) suggests that Nagasawa, who was a geologist, correctly assigned the horizon to the Shimosueyoshi Formation. As to the "spatula" itself, I am not fully convinced that the smoothed, pointed end is the result of human workmanship; it certainly does not exhibit a diagnostic enough constellation of attributes to be assignable to Magdalenian or to any other workmanship.

1.5.   NISHIYAGI (AKASHI). Perhaps the most ardent and tenacious advocate of Paleolithic man in Japan, during the last few decades prior to the Iwajuku discovery, was Nobuo Naora, who presented his "definite proof of the existence of the Paleolithic Age in Japan" (Naora 1931: 156). The "proof" came from the shore of Nishiyagi near Akashi, where he collected, between 1927 and 1930, several lithic specimens and one bone fragment with scratches. These were reportedly obtained from the same gravel bed where fossilized and extinct animal and plant remains also occurred (Naora 1931). Two of the lithic specimens that escaped the bomb destruction of 1945 are shown in Figure 2 (b and c).

The academic climate at the time, not unreasonably, was not receptive to Naora's claim of the lithic and bone specimens as artifacts. Fujimori (1965b: 98–99) relates that the hostility and skepticism of the academics prevented Naora from publishing a report on the now famous innominate bone when it was encountered by Naora in 1931 at the same locality. It was not until 1948, after the original pelvic specimen was lost during the war, that Kotondo Hasebe of the University of Tokyo came across the photographs and the cast of the innominate bone and noted its "primitive" characteristics (Hasebe 1948). The investigation of the Nishiyagi locality by a special committee of anthropologists, geologists, and paleontologists, however, did not produce any evidence to confirm Naora's finds (Takai and Tanai 1949; H. Watanabe 1949; N. Watanabe 1950). As far as the search for early man in Japan was concerned, the pre-Iwajuku period ended on a negative note.

Thus Groot's *Prehistory of Japan* (1951), which was probably written about the time of the Iwajuku discovery, pessimistically predicts (1951: 5):

Archaeologically, Japan has been rather thoroughly explored; many thousands of Stone Age sites have been discovered, none of which can be assigned to a Palaeolithic horizon. There is, thus, no great hope that future investigation will turn up Palaeolithic sites. If there were ever Palaeolithic sites in Japan proper, they are now probably sunk below the ocean level.

2. THE PERIOD BETWEEN 1949 AND 1962

When the Iwajuku excavation of 1949 confirmed the existence of artifacts in the Pleistocene formations in Japan, many workers in the field tacitly assumed that the Japanese Paleolithic was comparable in its time depth and in its cultural tradition to the Paleolithic industries in better known parts of East and South Asia. Thus Sugihara (1956a: 34), who considered the earlier assemblage from the Iwajuku site as a "flake culture," noted the high incidences of flakes at Locality 1 and Locality 15 of Choukoutien and Tingts'un, and pointed out the occurrence of pear-shaped handaxes at Tingts'un. Maringer (1956a, 1957b), on the other hand, compared some of the artifacts from the nearby Gongenyama to the Patjitanian artifacts of Java. With the subsequent development in Quaternary geology, application of chronometric methods, and revisions in typological classifications, the assumption of great antiquity for the axe-like artifacts of Japan was gradually abandoned by most of the workers. By the end of the period under consideration, only a few of the increasing number of Paleolithic assemblages were recognized by most scholars as predating the base of the Tachikawa Loam. It is also noteworthy that eminent workers in the field expressed a negative feeling towards most of the earlier claims for the Early Paleolithic specimens as described in the previous section (e.g. Serizawa 1954: 68; Sugihara 1953: 97–98).

In a sense the period under consideration, 1949 to 1962, may be said to be the period of adjustment for the Japanese archaeological profession to the new situation created by the Iwajuku discovery. Up to that time, the professional archaeologists had never been placed in the position to face the problem of the Paleolithic seriously, for the sporadic finds, such as those described in the previous section, could all be dismissed as unorthodox attempts by amateurs (the group did include one eminent professional, Dr. Kida, but he did not pursue the matter of the "Acheulian" artifacts of Kô beyond the casual remarks summarized above). Thus at the time of the Iwajuku discovery, the Japanese archaeologists faced the new situation with the textbook knowledge of Paleolithic cultures and with the unconscious assumption of an orthogenetic course of development. The assumption of the uniform sequence of cultural development, with index fossil artifacts as indicators, was abandoned by many of the Japanese archaeologists when stratigraphic and chronometric evidence suggested that the Paleolithic remains from Japan do not conform to the standard European sequence described in textbooks.

It may be worth noting here also that archaeology in Japan has been a subfield of history, which belonged to the Faculty of Arts, while anthropology (meaning physical anthropology of North America) has traditionally been housed in the Faculty of Science or School of Medicine, with ethnological sciences usually attached to the Department of Sociology or Political Science. Thus an attempt to understand the prehistoric cultural development in terms of the biological theory of evolution has been, and still is, completely alien to most Japanese archaeologists, who are also unaccustomed to any attempt to understand it as a process of sociocultural change. The dominant preoccupation of Japanese archaeologists is to formulate regional and areal sequences of assemblages, and to establish historical relationships between cultural sequences, in an attempt to extend the chronology of Japanese history into the past without written records.

Within a few years after the Iwajuku discovery, tentative chronological syntheses of the Japanese Paleolithic were presented by several of the workers in the field. The earliest attempt was by Sugihara (1952, 1953), who simply arranged the known assemblages, only a handful in number at that time, in a chronological order. The "flake culture" of Iwajuku I was considered to be one of the first manifestations of the preceramic development of Japan, followed by the backed blades of Moro, Tokyo. With the increase in the number of Paleolithic assemblages, students of the Paleolithic began using a chronological framework consisting of a series of "industries" or "cultures" (Kamaki 1954, 1957, 1959, 1960; Serizawa 1954, 1956, 1957, 1959; Serizawa and Ikawa 1960; Sugihara 1956b; Sugihara and Tozawa 1960). Although the authors differ in certain details, they conform in the general outline in recognizing the industries characterized by handaxes, blades and backed blades, points, and microliths. The industry characterized by handaxes was considered to be the earliest. Serizawa (1957: 107) felt "there is a possibility that they may pre-date the Tachikawa Loam," while Sugihara and Tozawa (1960: 4, 23) suggested that Iwajuku I dated to "the first half of the Upper Pleistocene" and Gongenyama, though uncertain, may be as early as "the upper part of the Middle Pleistocene."

During the latter half of the 1950's, the handaxe industry of Japan was thought to include the specimens from the following sites (see Figure 1 for the locations of the sites):

a.   Iwajuku (Kanto), discovered by Tadahiro Aizawa in 1948, and excavated by Meiji University in 1949 and 1950 (Sugihara 1956a);

b.   Gongenyama (Kanto), discovered by Aizawa in 1949 (never excavated) and reported by Maringer (1956a, 1956b, 1957a, 1957b);

c.   Shirataki (Hokkaido), known from surface collections;

d.   Omegura (Chubu), investigated by the Shinshu Loam Research Group (Kodama 1957);

e.   Kiyama (Shikoku), investigated by Kamaki (1959).

2.1.   IWAJUKU. The assemblage widely known as "Iwajuku I" consisting of three "handaxes" (two obtained by the 1949 excavation, the other collected by Aizawa), two scrapers, and several blades (Figure 3: B), was regarded as the type assemblage for the handaxe industry of Japan. In fact it continues to be considered the only reliable group of materials for the "Axe-Tool Culture" of Japan by Sugihara (ed. 1965). However, by the close of the 1950's there was a growing realization that its age was not as great as had once been assumed. Thus, although Sugihara and Tozawa (1960) ascribed an early Upper Pleistocene age to the assemblage, Serizawa and Ikawa (1960) wrote that the Iwajuku I horizon was to be correlated "with the lower part of the Tachikawa Loam or the uppermost part of the Musashino Loam" (p. 31). Since then, a detailed geological study by Arai (1962) has been made available, and the same author also suggested, on the basis of a radiocarbon determination, the age of the Iwajuku I horizon to be somewhat greater than 23,000 B.C. (Arai 1967). The term "handaxes" continued to be applied to the heavy implements of Iwajuku I throughout the period under consideration, but in 1962 Serizawa adopted a term "ovate artifacts" which he also applied to a newly obtained specimen from Isoyama, also in northern Kanto Plain (Serizawa 1962: 88).

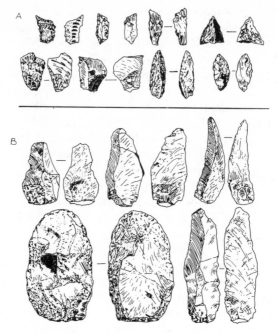

Figure 3. Artifacts from Iwajuku Site, Guma Prefecture, Kanto: (a) Iwajuku II; (b) Iwajuku I (scale: approx. 3/10 natural size; after Sugihara 1956a)

2.2. GONGENYAMA. One of the three handaxe assemblages from Gongeyama (Maringer 1956a, 1956b, 1957a, 1957b) is the only assemblage of the handaxe industry in the 1950's that survived the growing skepticism regarding the antiquity of Japanese Paleolithic manifestations (Figure 4). The artifacts shown in Figure 4 belong to the assemblage known as Gongenyama I. Although the artifacts were not recovered under a controlled condition, Aizawa (1957) reported that they occurred below the Hassaki Pumice, which is now dated to 40,500±3,500 B.P. by the radiocarbon method (Arai 1971b). On the other hand, the Gongenyama II assemblage, which was also compared to the Patjitanian of Java by Maringer (1956b), probably occurred in the buried humus zone in which the Iwajuku I assemblage was found (Arai 1971b): if so, a probable age of this assemblage is in the neighbourhood of 24,000 B.C.

2.3. SHIRATAKI. The vast number of extremely large, bifacially flaked specimens collected from Shirataki Village in Hokkaido was only briefly considered to belong to the handaxe industry of Japan. Serizawa (1957) referred to them as specimens prepared by the baton technique (p. 59), nevertheless placing Shirataki in parentheses in his

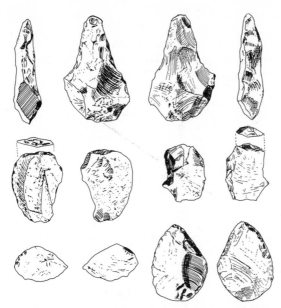

Figure 4. Artifacts of Gongenyama I (scale: approx. ¼ natural size; after Maringer 1956a)

chronological chart (p. 133). In a joint paper prepared during 1958 (Serizawa and Ikawa 1960), however, it is stated: "the obsidian bifaces from Hokkaido are now known to belong to a much later assemblage " (p. 32). Since then, Yoshizaki (1961) convincingly argued that these bifacial specimens are blanks to be used for preparing microblade cores or the Shirataki core-burins by means of what he calls "Yubetsu technique" (cf. Ikawa 1968 and R. Morlan 1967 for description in English of the Yubetsu technique). The measurement of obsidian hydration layers places the appearance of the Yubetsu technique in Hokkaido at 15,200 B.P. or ca. 13,250 B.C. (Katsui and Kondo 1965).

2.4. OMEGURA. The large obsidian bifaces obtained during the 1957 excavations of the Omegura site in Central Honshu were once regarded as the possible manifestations of the handaxe industry in this region (Serizawa 1957: 59), but like the Shirataki specimens, they were shortly withdrawn by the same author (Serizawa 1959; Serizawa and Ikawa 1960). These bifaces have never been stratigraphically isolated from other artifacts obtained at the site, which included smaller bifacial foliates, steeply retouched blades, and end-scrapers (Fujimori 1965a: Kobayashi 1960; Kodama 1957). More recently, Otsuka (1968) suggested that, like the Shirataki bifaces, the Omegura

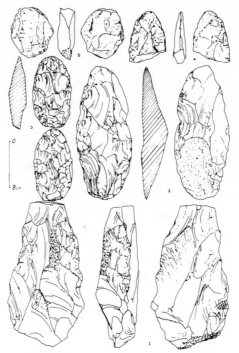

Figure 5.   Artifacts from the Kiyama Site, Shikoku, I (after Kamaki 1959: 301)

specimens may have been the blanks to be utilized in a process similar to the Yubetsu technique of Hokkaido. In any event, Kunio Kobayashi's geological study (1960) clearly shows that the Omegura bifaces are younger than the base of the Tachikawa Loam, since the artifacts occur in the surface humus and the Hata Loam, the latter being correlatable with the Tachikawa Loam of the southern Kanto Plain (K. Kobayashi 1965a).

2.5.   KIYAMA. In 1955 and for a few years thereafter, Kamaki and his associates collected a number of artifacts from the surface of a hill named Kiyama which has since been made into a golf course. No excavation was conducted and there is no possibllity, it seems, of conducting one now. Kamaki (1959) stated that sanukite fragments were scattered in several places over the hill, and that the six bifacial specimens (Figure 5), as well as scores of others (Figure 6), were obtained from one of them, at the top of the hill. Thus, although Kamaki (1959) divided the artifacts into six chronological periods, this is based entirely on typological grounds. The heavy artifacts shown in Figure 5 were described as "handaxe-like artifacts," and were divided into three chronological groups: Kiyama I-A (represented by

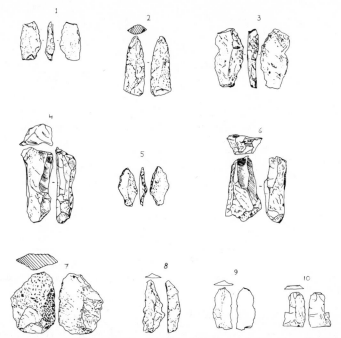

Figure 6. Artifacts from the Kiyama Site, Shikoku, II (after Kamaki 1959: 303)

Figure 5: 1), Kiyama I-B (consisting of Figure 5: 2 and 3), and Kiyama I-C (Figure 5: 4 and 5, associated with Figure 6: 7).[1] The resemblance of the ovate specimen (Figure 5: 3) to the Iwajuku I artifacts was noted (Kamaki 1959: 302), and since "handaxe-like tools of Japan, with certain exceptions such as those of Hokkaido, belong to a period as early as, or earlier than blades," it was felt that the axe-like tools of Kiyama should also be given a similar chronological position (Kamaki 1959: 305).

I have expressed a certain reservation towards Kamaki's chronological division based on typology as it was applied to Washuzan artifacts (Ikawa 1964: 109). The same feeling is entertained regarding the Kiyama artifacts. The large bifacial forms of Kiyama may well be a part of the assemblage which also included the side-blow flakes. In this connection it is interesting to note that side-blow flakes (Figure 7: 5 and 6) and retouched knives made from these flakes (Figure 7: 1, 2, 3, 4) also occur at the Kô site, where the elusive "handaxes"

[1] The rest of the artifacts were also divided into three chronological groups: Kiyama II, represented by blades and blade cores (Figure 6: 4, 6, 9, 10), Kiyama III, represented by boat-shaped artifacts (Figure 6: 8) and side-blow flakes (Figure 6: 5), and Kiyama IV, consisting of narrow bifacial forms (Figure 6: 2). In a later publication, however, it is stated that the narrow bifacial forms may not belong to the preceramic period at all (Kamaki and Takahashi 1965: 292).

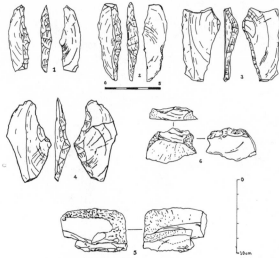

Figure 7.   Artifacts from Kô Site, Osaka (1–4: after Kamaki 1959: 305; 5, 6: after Kamaki and Takahashi 1965: 293)

have been reported. Admittedly, it is also possible that at both localities, the handaxe-using people were followed by the manufacturers of side-blow flakes. The problem, of course, cannot be solved at this time without stratigraphic verification.

In addition to the materials from the five sites discussed above, the 1949–1962 period saw the reports on specimens from several other sites as possible indications of very early human occupation of the Japanese islands. Most of these, however, were not widely accepted, and in one case (Fujieda), the investigator himself (Sugihara) retracted the claim.

2.6.   FUJIYAMA. Two specimens had been extracted in 1949 by Aizawa from a roadside exposure at this locality, not far from Iwajuku and Gongenyama, but it was not until 1960 that these specimens were mentioned in archaeological literature (Serizawa 1960). Serizawa (1960: 48) called one of the specimens a "handadze" and the other a "chopper," and felt they might be the oldest artifacts from the northern Kanto Plain, with possible relationship to the Lower Paleolithic of continental Asia. Arai (1971b), in the light of more recent geological investigation and chronometric information, confirms his earlier observation (Arai 1962) concerning the considerable antiquity of the specimens. He cautions, however, against facile acceptance of the specimens as artifacts since the basal stratum of the Fujiyama site is a mud-flow deposit and the dark brown clay, in which the specimens occurred, may well contain rock fragments derived from the mud-flow deposit.

2.7.   FUJIEDA. In 1953, Sugihara directed a large-scale investigation of the Fujieda Reservoir area of Kanagi Town in northern Honshu. This investigation involved an organization and financial support which had never been realized for archaeological fieldwork in Japan up to that time. The specimens were referred to as the "flake culture" of Fujieda and were considered by Sugihara to represent the earliest stage in the preceramic development of Japan in his first chronological synthesis (Sugihara 1952): this cultural stage, however, was removed from the revised version of the synthesis (1953) as a result of the investigations. According to Serizawa (1966–1968, in *Kokogaku Janaru* 9) and Tozawa (1963), who were both participants in the investigations, it was concluded that these specimens were not man-made for the following reasons: (1) there was no regularity in the manner of modification; for example, the flaking angles on pieces failed to conform to a definite pattern; (2) although some of the specimens appeared to be retouched, such "retouching" was located in places where it could have served no purpose; furthermore, there was no directional uniformity in the small scars that made up the "retouch"; (3) the specimens were included in the Kanagi Gravel Bed, composed of angular shale rubble and rounded pebbles of rhyolite; these lithic materials were derived from the mountains behind Fujieda area; (4) many fractured pieces of hard shale, some with bulbs of percussion, and others with apparent retouch, occurred in the present riverbed about one kilometer north of Fujieda. It was concluded therefore that the flaking scars on the Fujieda specimens resulted from the process in which hard and soft rocks hit against each other as they were transported by water.

A formal retraction of the Fujieda specimens by Sugihara appeared in the following year (Sugihara 1954). It is conceivable that the extreme reluctance on the part of Sugihara to accept claims of Early Paleolithic artifacts, as will be reviewed later, may originate in this experience.

2.8.   KUZU. Naora, in the meantime, continued his efforts to obtain the evidence for early man in Japan, and excavated the caves of Matsugae (Tsunemi Cave) in Kyushu and Kuzu in the Kanto Plain. Although the Matsugae investigations were unfruitful by his own admission (Naora 1954a), the Kuzu caves produced what he considered to be human skeletal remains and several artifactual remains (Naora 1952a, 1952b, 1954b). It seems to me that the skeletal materials from Kuzu exhibit too many unusual features to be accepted as human skeletal remains and that the evidence of human workmanship in the so-called artifacts is extremely tenuous. One specimen made on a limb bone of an elephant, which Naora (1954b: 96) describes as "axe-like," is reproduced here (Figure 2: d).

2.9.   H A N A I Z U M I. Naora (1959) then cautiously proposed that some of the bone and antler pieces from the fossiliferous formation of Hanaizumi in Iwate Prefecture could possibly be artifacts. These included lengths of deer antlers, a scapula of bison (which Naora thought could be used as an earth-digging tool), and a number of rib bones, all about thirty centimeters long, of *Bison, Bos,* and *Megaceros.*

Although Naora implied an Upper Pleistocene age for these specimens by his identification of the fauna, Matsumoto and his associates (Matsumoto et al. 1959), who also described a number of stone, bone, and antler specimens as artifacts, called the fauna "Villafranchian" and of "Upper Pliocene" age. Since radiocarbon determinations place the Hanaizumi Formation in the late Upper Pleistocene, Matsumoto's characterization of the fauna as "Villafranchian" appears to be in error. Some of the specimens, however, are acceptable as artifacts.

2.10.   K A S U M I G A U R A. Kiyono (1952, 1953) reported on his recovery of stone and wooden specimens from the southern shore of Kasumigaura Lake in the eastern Kanto Plain. These were reported to have been obtained from the "Narita Bed," which would correlate with the Shimosueyoshi Formation of the Riss-Würm Interglacial. The heavily rolled stone specimen was compared to "Chellean" or "pre-Chellean" artifacts, while the wooden specimen was considered to exhibit a groove on one surface. Kiyono's description of the specimens was admittedly inadequate, but, even taking this into consideration, he has failed to present a convincing case.

2.11.   A Y A R A G I. Several "handaxes" and pebble tools were collected from part of a village site of the Yayoi Period at Ayaragi, in Shimonoseki City in the westernmost part of Honshu (Ono 1957, 1958). The specimens are reported to have been encountered in storage pits and other features pertaining to the Yayoi Period (300 B.C. to 300 A.D.), as well as in a reddish soil layer overlying the terrace gravel (Ono 1958; Ono and Kawano 1964; Kokubu 1967). The terrace gravel, which was once assigned by the investigators to the Riss-Würm Interglacial Stage, is now considered to be of an early Würm age; the lithic specimens accordingly have been assigned to the "Paudorf Interstadial" times (Ono 1969, 1971a).

In a sense the reaction to the activities at the Ayaragi site was symptomatic of the end of the 1949–1962 period in the development of Japanese Paleolithic research. Although these finds were almost completely ignored by the active workers of preceramic archaeology at the time (such as Serizawa, Sugihara, Kamaki, and Yoshizaki), they received a full acceptance by certain other anthropologists, as

HOKKAIDO

Koshinyama
Kamiyachi
Nagaki
Amidachi

Shimonoseki City (Ayaragi, etc.)
Toyoura Town (Isogami, etc.)
Minogahama
Sorayama, Yakabe,
Shimamuradani,
Yumachi

HONSHU

Iwajuku
Akabori
Oizumi
Hoshino
Mukoyama
Ushiroyama
Iwadeyama
Wadayama
Horigome - cho
Shimofuji
Kamifuji
Shimohikoma
Machiya
Okubo
Nishifune
Azumasaka

Kasheizawa
Tajimi

Fukui

SHIKOKU

Sozudai
Nyu
Izuruha

KYUSHU

| 0 | 100 | 200 miles |

| 0 | 100 | 200 | 300 km. |

Figure 8.   Locations of sites where early Paleolithic materials have been reported since 1962

evidenced by Kokubu's treatment of the Ayaragi site in his review of Japanese prehistory (Kokubu 1966). By this time a rift was also developing between Serizawa and Sugihara, the two archaeologists who were instrumental in organizing the Iwajuku excavation and who continued to be prominent figures in preceramic archaeology. The disagreement resulted in Serizawa's departure from Meiji University in 1959. Yoshizaki, on the other hand, left Japan in 1962 to accept a fellowship at the University of Wisconsin; on his return to Japan a year later, he took a post in the northern island of Hokkaido.

Thus Meiji University, the most important institution during the first decade after the Iwajuku discovery, was no longer the sole center of preceramic research. Indeed it was by the archaeologists outside the Meiji University circle that the main thrust of the research activity

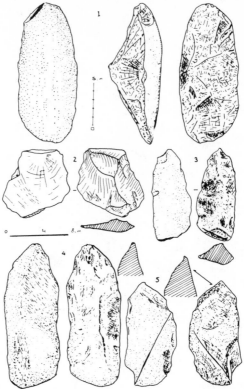

Figure 9.   Artifacts collected from Locality I-B of the Nyu site, Kyushu (after Nippon Kyusekki Bunka Kenkyu Iinkai 1966: 70–71)

in search of the Early Paleolithic of Japan was provided during the period after 1962.

3.   THE PERIOD SINCE 1962

The year 1962 is often described as a year full of "turbulence" and controversy as far as archaeology was concerned (e.g. S. Nakagawa 1963). In the field of Paleolithic research two sets of events contributed to the disturbance.

3.1.   THE NYU EXCAVATIONS. The first set of events concerns the report of the discovery of the "Lower Paleolithic" tools at Nyu in northeastern Kyushu (Figure 9). It began when pebble tools collected from the terrace surface in the Nyu area were brought to the attention of Takeo Kanaseki, who in turn notified several of his colleagues. The keen competition over this seemingly promising site culminated in stormy sessions of a Japanese Archaeological Association meeting in the spring of 1962. Several eyewitness accounts (Fujimori 1965b; S. Nakagawa 1963; Tozawa 1963) describe how survey reports were presented by two competing groups of researchers, how the reports met criticisms from the chairman of the session (Sosuke Sugihara) as well as from the audience, and how the meeting failed to endorse a motion to organize a special committee of the Association to investigate the site.

While the results of the preliminary investigations were being published in rapid succession (Sato 1963; Sato, Kobayashi, and Sakaguchi 1962; Sato and Sakaguchi 1962–1963; Sato, Sakaguchi, and Kobayashi 1962; Tsunoda 1962b), the "Research Committee of Paleolithic Culture of Japan," organized by Bun'ei Tsunoda of the Paleological Association of Japan, conducted the first of its series of excavations at Nyu. The excavations were to continue until 1967, with their findings published in the name of the Committee (Nippon Kyusekki Bunka Kenkyu Iinkai 1964, 1965, 1966, 1968).

During the same year (1962), the Nyu discovery was followed by a series of reports of "Early Paleolithic" sites. Certain pebble specimens from Nagaki on Sado Island in Japan Sea were considered to resemble "Kafuan" artifacts of Africa (Homma et al. 1962), while Kokubu, Sato, and Kanaseki (1962) reported on the discovery of some one hundred sites in Yamaguchi Prefecture, mostly from the Shimonoseki area. Although most of these sites have yet to produce truly convincing evidence stratigraphically or artifactually, these are the beginning of the serious efforts to obtain the evidence for the Early Paleolithic occupation of Japan.

3.2. EXPRESSIONS OF DISSENT. The second set of events which contributed towards the "turbulence" of the year 1962 began with the publication of an article by Yamanouchi and Sato in a popular science magazine (1962). In this article, that is sometimes described as a "bombshell" (Fujimori 1965b: 200), the authors rejected the validity of the radiocarbon method altogether, and the chronological framework based on radiocarbon determinations. They emphasized the importance of typological comparisons as the only valid "archaeological dating method," and argued that all but a few preceramic assemblages of Japan should be considered "nonceramic Neolithic" dating to the fourth and fifth millennia B.C. The bases for this startling argument, as I have discussed in more detail elsewhere (Ikawa 1964), are that the ovate axe-like tools of Iwajuku I and Isoyama, for example, are partially ground on the working edges and therefore they should be considered the products of a Neolithic culture; and that certain other ground stone artifacts from northern Honshu are similar in form to those from the Isakovo period of the Lake Baikal Neolithic and therefore they could not be older than 3,000 B.C.

It was perhaps the stature of the late Dr. Yamanouchi as the outstanding scholar of Jomon archaeology that made this article so influential; in any case, the suspicion concerning the radiocarbon method still lingers among many of the professional archaeologists (e.g. Ohyi 1965, 1968). The Yamanouchi–Sato article, at any rate, was the first of a series of provocative articles openly challenging the established system of nomenclature and conceptual and chronological frameworks.

Among the other dissenting opinions voiced about this time were Tsunoda's fivefold periodization of the pre-Jomon cultures and Takizawa's criticisms of the presumed function and chronological significance of major categories of tools. Tsunoda (1962a) proposed to divide the pre-Jomon cultures (which he insisted on calling "Iwajuku Culture") into five periods: (1) the Initial Period, characterized by the absence of proto-handaxes; (2) the Early Period, when assemblages are primarily composed of choppers and proto-handaxes; (3) the Middle Period, when handaxe-like tools, blades, and scrapers made on flakes appear; (4) the Late Period, when points, knives, burins, and scrapers made on blades occur; and (5) the Final Period, when small blades and microliths are characteristic. Tsunoda (1962a: 70) states that this periodization was presented merely as a "working hypothesis" and that empirical evidence is yet insufficient. The empirical evidence available at that time was tenuous at best for his "Middle Period," and nonexistent for his "Initial" and "Early" periods. These periods were proposed for Japan because choppers and handaxes are known to occur in the early phase of prehistory elsewhere in the world. Tsunoda's "hypothesis," it seems to me, is based on his belief that the development of the Paleolithic cultures in Japan "follows the same trends as the early cultural developments in Eurasia and Africa" (Tsunoda 1962a: 72). One of the major points of disagreement between Tsunoda, on the one hand, and the archaeologists who constituted the main stream of Paleolithic archaeology (e.g. Chosuke Serizawa and Sosuke Sugihara), on the other, seems to lie in the fact that the latter group of archaeologists abandoned, shortly after the Iwajuku discovery, the belief that Paleolithic cultures everywhere follow the same course of development. Tsunoda's adherence to this belief is also evident in his proposed chronology for the Nyu assemblages, which are divided into thirteen groups on the basis primarily of typology.

Takizawa's criticism of the accepted framework comes from the entirely opposite direction. In a series of articles, Takizawa (1963a, 1963b, 1964a, 1964b) expressed a serious doubt as to the cultural succession accepted by most archaeologists, where knives (backed blades), points, and microliths follow one after another, and proceeded to show that there is no "microlithic culture" as such, because in every case where microliths were reported other tool types occurred and stratigraphic isolation of the microliths from other tools was inadequate. It was also argued by the same author that some of the "knives," for example, were not cutting tools but arrowheads. Takizawa's views, representing the most radical departure from the assumption of the orderly and unilinear progression of cultural stages, were never accepted by the established archaeologists.

In the meantime, Yamanouchi and Sato followed up their attack on the prevailing chronological framework of the preceramic cultures, this time in the opening chapters of the handsomely produced *Nippon genshi bijutsu* [Primitive art of Japan]. In these chapters (Yamanouchi and Sato 1964a, 1964b), the authors maintained that the artifacts from Nyu, Fujiyama, Gongenyama and possibly those from western Honshu investigated by Kokubu and Kanaseki, constituted the "Paleolithic" of Japan, the rest being "nonceramic Neolithic."

This was countered by Serizawa, who had been the main target of the attacks, in the form of a review of *Nippon genshi bijutsu* (Serizawa 1964b). It was pointed out, among other things, (a) that the evidence for the Paleolithic status of the Nyu artifacts is insufficient, both stratigraphically and typologically, and (b) that the presence of a few ground stone tools does not make the nonceramic assemblages "Neolithic." This biting review of the book was read with astonishment by many archaeologists in Japan, especially in view of the fact that Serizawa had been a student of Yamanouchi's for many years.

Serizawa also defended the past achievements of the students of nonceramic archaeology and the principle of stratigraphy against the typological emphasis given by Yamanouchi (Yamanouchi and Sato 1962) and Tsunoda (1962a; also in NKBKI 1964) in a comparative review of twenty chronological schemes presented up to that time (Serizawa 1964a). This extremely useful review traces the development of the preceramic chronology from the earliest attempts by Sugihara (1952, 1953, 1956c) through several versions of his own (Serizawa 1954, 1959, 1963), Yoshizaki's proposals on Hokkaido (1956, 1958, 1961; Shirataki Dantai Kenkyukai 1963), Aizawa's observation of north Kanto stratigraphy (1957), Arai's study of the same area (1962), several versions of Kamaki's chronology for western Japan (1954, 1957, 1959) and for Japan as a whole (Kamaki 1960) to Tsunoda's "tentative chronologies" (1962a; NKBKI 1964) and finally Yamanouchi's provocative proposal (Yamanouchi and Sato 1962). With critical comment on each of these schemes, written by one of the most outstanding contributors to the achievements of preceramic archaeology for the preceding decade and a half, this review is as much

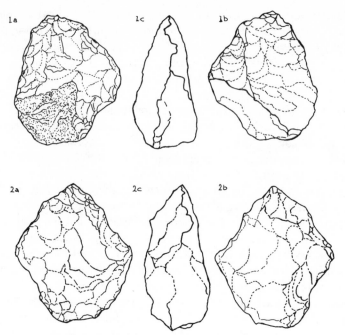

Figure 10.   "Proto-handaxes" from Sozudai, Kyushu (scale: approx. ½ natural size; after Serizawa 1965)

a document of self-analysis and self-criticism as it is a defense of the achievements. The author appears to be groping for a new avenue of development, both for himself and for Japanese archaeology, for he states, "I think it is about time that we looked back on the chrono-logical schemes presented in the past, and determined a new direction of progress" (Serizawa 1964a: 16).

What followed since then does not indicate a complete reorientation of research goals. Serizawa turned to François Bordes' statistical methods for interassemblage comparison (e.g. Serizawa 1965; ed. 1968) and became actively involved in the investigation of "Early Paleolithic" remains (e.g. Serizawa 1965; ed. 1966, 1968, 1969). He also expanded the scope of cultural comparisons to areas outside Japan – a reversal of his former stand (e.g. Serizawa 1955a, 1955b, 1958, 1964b), as will be noted below. His research goals, however, remained the same: that is, to bring the chronology of the Japanese Paleolithic into perfection (e.g. Serizawa 1966–1968, 1967b, 1969, 1970).

3.3.   THE SOZUDAI AND HOSHINO EXCAVATIONS. In 1964 Serizawa conducted the first of what turned out to be a long series of excavations of controversial Early Paleolithic sites. This was the

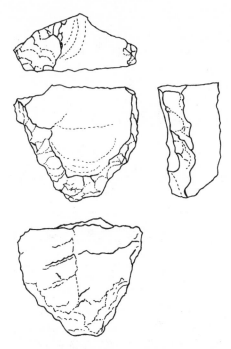

Figure 11. A triangular core from Sozudai, Kyushu (scale: approx. ½ natural size; after Serizawa 1965)

excavation of the Sozudai site, directly opposite Nyu across Beppu Bay, where quartzite specimens of Early Paleolithic appearance had been encountered during the excavation of the Jomon site at the same locality earlier in the year. A total of 425 specimens were obtained by the excavation and this assemblage was described as exhibiting certain traits which are also present in the assemblages from Choukoutien Locality 1, Koho, and Patjitan (Figures 10 and 11). Even though the artifact-bearing horizon was considered to postdate the Shimosueyoshi Transgression, which is commonly equated with the Riss-Würm Interglacial, the investigators felt the horizon might date to an earlier interglacial, inasmuch as the correlation of Japanese Pleistocene formations with the Alpine sequence was not yet firmly established (Serizawa 1965; Serizawa and H. Nakagawa 1965).

In the following year (1965), Serizawa began his investigations of the Hoshino site in the northern Kanto Plain, where a Levallois core had been collected from the surface by a local collector (Figure 12). The investigations continued for three years until 1967, and again in 1973, and Serizawa and his associates isolated eleven nonceramic cultural horizons, ten of which were considered by the investigators (Serizawa, ed. 1966, 1968, 1969) to predate the Tachikawa Loam. One of the assemblages (Horizon 3) was compared with the upper part of

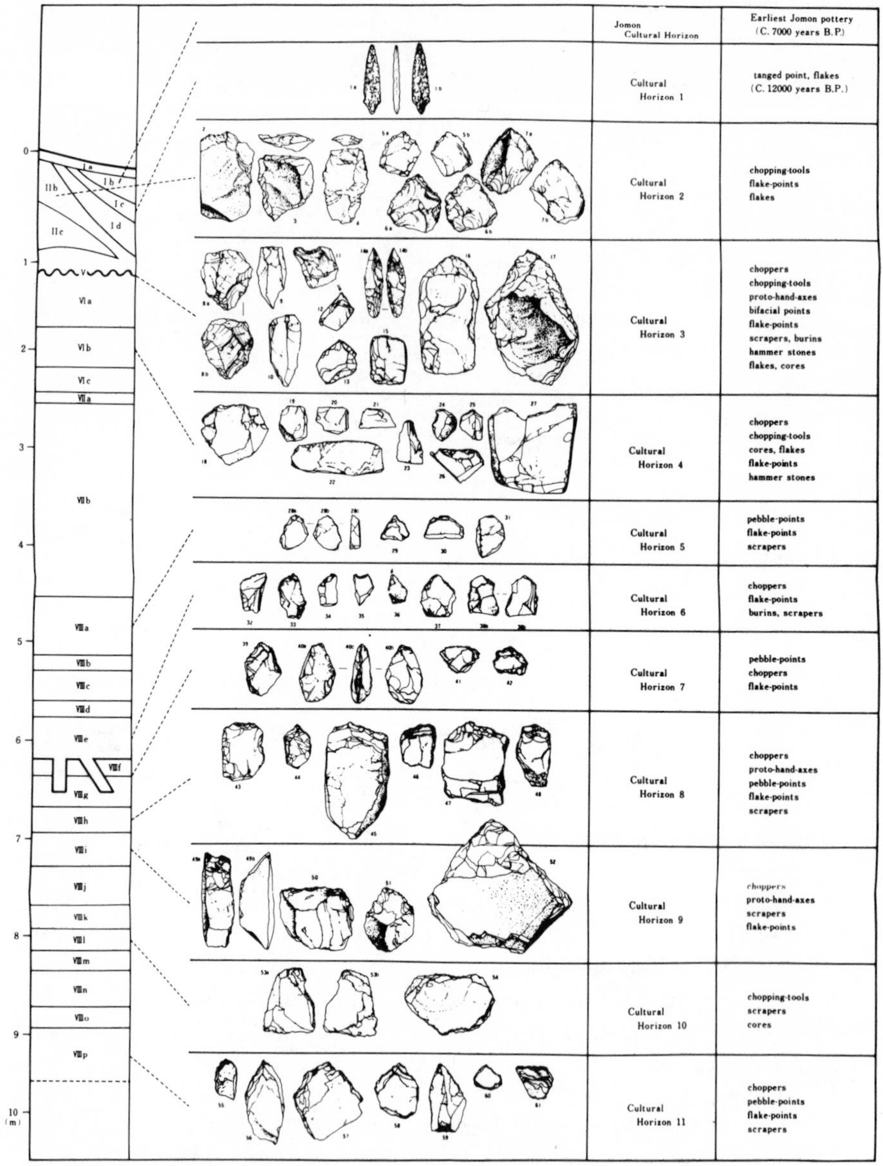

Figure 12. Stratigraphic sequence at Hashino (after Serizawa 1969)

Choukoutien Locality 1, while another (Horizon 4) was suggested to resemble Locality 15 of Choukoutien. High incidences of Levallois technique at various horizons of the Hoshino site were also noted.

The investigations of these two sites, initiated by such an established figure in Japanese Paleolithic archaeology as Serizawa, now conferred a certain respectability on the search for early man in Japan. However, the findings from these sites were not to be accepted readily by many archaeologists.

3.4. REACTIONS TO THE NYU, SOZUDAI, AND HOSHINO INVESTIGATIONS. The strongest objections came from archaeologists of Meiji University. Sugihara, in a very useful handbook on preceramic Japan edited by himself (Sugihara, ed. 1965), stated that the question of the Lower Paleolithic for Japan is still a problem for the future, inasmuch as neither Nyu, Sozudai, nor Nagaki presented convincing evidence (pp. 21–22, 130). It was maintained that the oldest reliable archaeological assemblage from Japan was that of Iwajuku I, which, together with less reliable materials from Fujiyama and Gongenyama, constituted the "Axe-Tool Culture" of Japan (Sugihara, ed. 1965: 126). It is interesting to note that Sugihara at this time characterized Iwajuku I as "very early Upper Paleolithic or final Middle Paleolithic"[2] and suggested an age of between 30,000 and 50,000 for this assemblage (Sugihara 1965: 369; ed. 1965: 22). If the 30,000 to 50,000 B.P. time range for the Iwajuku I assemblage were accepted, this assemblage should be considered to belong to the Early Paleolithic within the framework of this paper. However, as I have pointed out (Ikawa 1966), the 30,000 to 50,000 time range for Iwajuku I is too early to be compatible with the statements given by geologists contained in the same volume (Kaizuka 1965: 82; K. Kobayashi 1965b: 92).

In a paper presented to the 1966 Japan–United States conference on "Microevolution and Population History of the Northern Pacific" held in Sapporo, Hokkaido (later published in part as Sugihara 1967a and in full as Sugihara 1969), Sugihara stated that few archaeologists recognize the so-called Lower Paleolithic specimens from Nyu, Sozudai, Nagaki, and Hoshino as artifacts.

More specific criticisms of the Nyu, Sozudai, and Hoshino findings were voiced by two of Sugihara's students at Meiji University. Tasaka (1966), reviewing the Sozudai reports (Serizawa 1965; H. Nakagawa 1965) and the report of the first three seasons' work at Nyu (NKBKI 1964, 1965), felt that in both cases the research methods relied too heavily on typological comparisons with Lower Paleolithic artifacts outside of Japan, and that the stratigraphic evidence for the Japanese specimens was unsatisfactory and their artifactual nature unconvincing. Similarly, Yokota (1967), in the review of the report of the 1965 season's work at Hoshino (Serizawa, ed. 1966), noted that (1) the assemblages probably belonged to the Tachikawa Loam, since knives,

[2] A few years later, Sugihara (1967b) strongly argued that Middle Paleolithic did not exist in Japan.

points, and blades were present; (2) the crude chert "artifacts" did not appear to have been made by man; and (3) the Levallois technique probably did not exist at this site.

Sugihara's position on the Early Paleolithic problem was spelled out in a tongue-in-cheek article, entitled "I wish 'Sugihara's Hypothesis' would be disproved" (Sugihara 1967b). The "hypothesis" states that the Lower and Middle Paleolithic did not exist in Japan. The hypothesis seems to be based on two premises: (1) Sugihara's judgment on the available empirical evidence, and (2) his belief in the relationship between cultural and biological evolutionary stages of man.

The first, and by far the more reasonable, premise maintains that there are no reliable materials pertaining to the Lower and Middle Paleolithic from Japan. The materials from Nagaki, Nyu, Sozudai, and Hoshino were discussed. The case of the Nagaki materials, Sugihara felt, was exactly the same as his own experience with Fujieda materials. A few of the Nyu materials encountered *in situ* appeared to Sugihara to be natural rocks, while those with clear signs of human workmanship lacked stratigraphic evidence and were probably of Jomon age. Neither did the Sozudai materials present to Sugihara convincing enough evidence of human manufacture, especially since quartz rhyolite, of which some of the specimens were said to be made, was probably unsuitable as the material for stone tools. Sugihara agreed that some of the specimens from Cultural Horizons 3 and 4 of Hoshino, including the Levallois core, were manufactured by man, but he could not accept the others as products of human manufacture. However, Sugihara suggested that the Horizons 3 and 4 were assignable to the Tachikawa Loam, not to the much earlier Shimosueyoshi Loam as had been suggested by the investigators. Incidentally, this interpretation of the Hoshino stratigraphy has been convincingly advanced by a geologist, Fusao Arai (Arai 1968, 1971b).

Concerning the second premise, Sugihara subscribes to the view that there are clearly demonstrated and universally applicable, relationships between the Lower Paleolithic and the Pithecanthropine physical type, the Middle Paleolithic and the Neanderthals, and the Upper Paleolithic and the anatomically modern man respectively. The presence of the anatomically modern man in Pleistocene Japan, Sugihara felt, was attested by the numerous artifacts of the Upper Paleolithic age in the Tachikawa Loam. The presence of the Pithecanthropines and/or the Neanderthals, Sugihara argued, must be assumed, if there had been the Lower and/or Middle Paleolithic cultures. If so, the author continued, one must further assume that the anatomically modern man evolved *in situ* in Japan from either of the earlier forms or that the Pithecanthropines, the Neanderthals, and the *sapiens*-type of man arrived in successive waves, by way of the land bridge which materialized at three different periods. The first alternative, in Sugihara's words, is "unthinkable," while the second alternative presumes the circumstances to be so accommodating as to be extremely unlikely.

In a rebuttal of Sugihara, Serizawa (1966–1968, in *Kokogaku Janaru* 8) presented counterarguments on the workability of quartz rhyolite, and on the nature of the fracture on Sozudai specimens. It was also pointed out that the problems of land connection with the mainland, the equation of Japanese coastal terraces with the Alpine glacial sequence, and the existence of the Asiatic counterparts of the European Neanderthals are still open questions that could not be used in argument against the possibility of human occupation of Japan during the Middle and early Upper Pleistocene.

Tsunoda and Mikami (1967) also responded to Sugihara's remarks (1967a, 1967b) concerning the Nyu investigations, as well as to an earlier critical review of the Nyu report (NKBKI 1966) by Serizawa (1967a). The authors reiterated that (1) the "artifacts" are indeed manmade; (2) contrary to the observations by Serizawa and by Sugihara, none of the axes were polished, and they were typologically distinct from Jomon axes; and (3) the lack of stratigraphic contexts for most of the Nyu specimens was not unique, since Lower Paleolithic artifacts were rarely found in the primary depositional contexts. The authors then went on to criticize Serizawa's stratigraphic interpretations of the Sozudai and the Hoshino sites.

S. Kato's critical remarks (1967) on the Hoshino Horizon 3 specimens were of a somewhat different nature because Kato did not categorically deny the existence of Levallois technique nor did he doubt that the specimens were artifacts. Instead he argues that it would be more appropriate to compare the Horizon 3 assemblage of Hoshino with the Ust-Kanskaia assemblage of Siberia than with Choukoutien; the Hoshino assemblage would then be assigned to the Middle Paleolithic and to the Early Würm rather than to the Lower Paleolithic.

From the summaries of exchanges given above, the issues involved in the "Early Paleolithic problem," which has developed during the last decade, clearly emerge. Debate centered on issues such as:
1. the presence or absence of stratigraphic context for the specimens,
2. interpretation of stratigraphy and geology,
3. the manmade nature of the specimens themselves, and
4. appropriateness of comparative reference materials.

There was a clear, though implicit, agreement on research goals (the reconstruction of culture history) even though the authors differed on such matters as the reliability of the radiocarbon method and the relative importance of stratigraphy vs. typology.

Needless to say, not all the archaeologists reacted negatively to the

Nyu, Sozudai, and Hoshino finds. Thus Kokubu (1966) fully accepted the findings at Nyu and at Sozudai, as reported by the investigators, and went on to describe several assemblages from Toyoura Town and from Shimonoseki City of Yamaguchi Prefecture in western Honshu. Yoshizaki (1967), on the other hand, maintained silence on Nyu, but listed Sozudai and Hoshino as the earliest archaeological evidence for human occupation of Japan, probably by the Pithecanthropines. Evidence of the Neanderthal presence in Japan, Yoshizaki felt, had not been obtained.

Implicit indications of positive reactions to the Early Paleolithic finds, of course, are to be found in the increasing number of sites producing possible Early Paleolithic artifacts, which were investigated during the latter half of the 1960's up to the present date.

3.5. RECENT RESEARCH. In Kyushu, where the "Early Paleolithic problem" began with the investigations at Nyu and Sozudai, Izuruha Cave was investigated by Shigeharu Suzuki (1967a, 1967b) in 1965 and 1966. The investigations produced artifacts which were considered by the investigators to be reminiscent of the materials obtained from Sozudai and Hoshino, but there has been no geological or chronometric verification of their early age. In addition, a radiocarbon determination in excess of 31,900 B.P. (GaK-592) for the Horizon 15 materials from Fukui Cave, previously investigated by Kamaki and Serizawa (1967), places this assemblage within the time range of the "Early Paleolithic" (Serizawa 1966–1968, 1967b, 1970).

In western Honshu, Ono (1968, 1969, 1970, 1971a, 1971b, 1971c) and his associates continued their investigations of sites producing specimens with an Early Paleolithic appearance. Although some of the specimens do present a convincing appearance, the depositional contexts of the specimens, unfortunately, have been less than satisfactory to provide firm evidence of the extraordinary antiquity which has been claimed for some of the specimens by the investigators.

In Chubu District of central Honshu, Komura and his associates excavated the Kasheizawa site, near Nagoya City, in 1965 (Komura et al. 1968), while many chert specimens were collected by the members of an archaeological club in Tajimi City from the surface of some dozen localities in the city (Tajimi-shi Kokogaku Kenkyukai 1969).

In northern Honshu, M. Kato and his associates investigated the Kamiyachi site in Yamagata Prefecture in 1968, which appears to have produced evidence of Early Paleolithic man in this northern region (M. Kato 1969; Yoneji and M. Kato 1969). It has been suggested that a few other assemblages may also belong to the Early Paleolithic period (M. Kato 1969; Yokoyama 1970).

By far the largest number of possible Early Paleolithic sites were reported from the Kanto Plain in Central Honshu. Serizawa (1968a) described chert specimens from fourteen sites in the northwestern foothill region of the Kanto Plain, arguing that these represent the cultural remains of a population characterized by "chopper/chopping-tool culture," which settled along the coast of an enlarged Tokyo Bay during the Shimosueyoshi Transgression (usually equated with the Riss-Würm interglacial). The materials described came from the following sites (see Figure 8):

1. Hoshino, Tochigi City
2. Mukoyama, Tochigi City
3. Ushiroyama, Tochigi City
4. Iwadeyama, Tochigi City
5. Wadayama, Ohira Town, Tochigi Prefecture
6. Horigome-cho, Sano City
7. Shimofuji, Sano City
8. Kamifuji, Sano City
9. Shimohikoma, Tanuma Town, Tochigi Prefecture
10. Machiya, Tanuma Town, Tochigi Prefecture
11. Okubo, Ashikaga City
12. Nishifune, Ashikaga City
13. Azumasaka, Ashikaga City
14. Oizumi, Iwase Town, Ibaragi Prefecture.

Of the fourteen sites listed above, the Hoshino site was investigated between 1965 and 1967. The Okubo site has been investigated since 1968, and the Mukoyama site since 1970, both by Serizawa. In addition, reinvestigation of the well-known Iwajuku site was conducted by Serizawa and Aizawa in 1970 and 1971. The materials obtained by the new investigation for the southern side of the Iwajuku hill was named "Iwajuku 0 (zero)" (Serizawa 1971b; Serizawa and Aizawa 1970). Aizawa is also investigating the Akabori Iso site near Iwajuku. Aside from brief reports (Serizawa 1968b, 1971a; Toda 1969; Arai 1971a, 1971b) details of these new activities have not yet been made public.

It is evident from this brief survey of recent research that the most prominent worker in the field of Early Paleolithic research in Japan at this time is Chosuke Serizawa of Tohoku University. Unlike Nobuo Naora of earlier years, Serizawa, with his academic position and with his reputation based on several decades' contribution to archaeology, has been able to organize a series of excavations and to give effective support and encouragement to other interested workers. His eagerness to establish the existence of the Early Paleolithic in Japan has, in some instances, led him to disregard geological opinion and to rely primarily on typological comparisons with the Lower Paleolithic assemblages from abroad, mainly from China.

It is somewhat ironic to recall that Serizawa has always been critical of those who rely heavily on morphological comparisons at the expense of stratigraphy and evidence provided by natural sciences. It was precisely for this reason, as has been remarked earlier, that Serizawa (1964a) criticized the chronological schemes proposed by Tsunoda (1962a) and by Yamanouchi and T. Sato (1962). A few years earlier, in an article highly critical of Maringer's treatment of the Gongenyama assemblages, Serizawa (1958) strongly argued for the need to understand the Japanese preceramic assemblages in their own terms, before making comparisons with materials abroad. When a microblade assemblage was discovered at Yadegawa, Serizawa (1955b) cautioned against facile comparisons with continental materials by saying: "the most urgent task is to determine the nature and chronological position of the Yadegawa culture within Japan; it is a dangerous practice to be unduly concerned with similar artifacts abroad." One of his brief surveys of the Japanese preceramic development written about this time concluded with the observation that the chopper/chopping-tool tradition as formulated by Hallam L. Movius, Jr. does not appear in Japan, and that research on preceramic culture in Japan should proceed independently, without being influenced by preexisting theories (Serizawa 1955a).

The arguments advanced by Serizawa in recent years (e.g. Serizawa 1965; ed. 1966) appear to represent a complete reversal of this stand. It may be argued that additional materials have been recovered in the intervening years and that circumstances are right for undertaking what had once been considered premature. I felt that the Early Paleolithic materials being brought to our attention during the past decade were qualitatively new kinds of materials (just as the Yadegawa microblades were in the 1950's) calling for the cautious approach advocated by Serizawa (1955b), and that it was necessary to evaluate and assess the Early Paleolithic materials from Japan in their own terms. Therefore, I undertook to examine the stratigraphic and artifactual evidence from ten sites which had been excavated by 1971 and twenty-eight additional sites from which surface collections of "Early Paleolithic" specimens had been made (Ikawa-Smith 1974). I cannot go into the details of my findings here, but it was my conclusion that there was a very small number of assemblages (Gongenyama I, Hoshino Horizon 8, and Kamiyachi among them) which presented convincing enough evidence of human workmanship and positive stratigraphic contexts predating 30,000 B.P. There are many other assemblages, however, which consist of implements definitely different from the "Late Paleolithic" assemblages: but some of these lack the evidence for a finite geologic age (as at Sozudai) and others are clearly indicated to be quite late (e.g. Hoshino Horizons 2–4, and

Gongenyama II). It is my feeling therefore that the "Early Paleolithic" technological tradition lasted in Japan until about 20,000 years ago, if not later. By this time, the "Late Paleolithic" cultures with the classic blade technique were certainly present in the northern island of Hokkaido and possibly in the island of Honshu as well. If the "Early Paleolithic" and "Late Paleolithic" assemblages were at least partially coeval, we could not speak of the "Early Paleolithic Period." I think our task now is to try to understand the nature of the relationship between the two kinds of assemblages and to "explain" how and why the seemingly crude chopper/chopping-tool technology persisted in Japan for so long.

REFERENCES

AIZAWA, TADAHIRO
  1957 Akagisanroku ni okeru Kanto romu chu shosekki bunka no ichi ni tsuite [The sequence of various stone industries found in Kanto Loam Beds, near Mount Akagi]. *Daiyonki Kenkyu* 1 (1): 17–22.
ARAI, FUSAO
  1962 Kanto Bonchi hokuseibu chiiki no daiyonki hennen [The Quaternary chronology of the northwestern Kanto District, Japan]. *Gumma Daigaku Kiyo, Shizenkagaku-hen* 10 (4): 1–79.
  1967 Maebashi Deiryu no funshutsu nendai to Iwajuku I bunkaki [The age of the Maebashi Mudflow and the Iwajuku I Culture]. *Chikyu Kagaku* 21: 46–47.
  1968 Hoshino iseki ni okeru bunkaso no soi ni tsuite [On the stratigraphic positions of the cultural horizons at the Hoshino site]. *Chishitsugaku Zasshi* 74: 123.
  1971a Kita Kanto no iwayuru zenki kyusekki hoganso ni kansuru ni-san no mondai [Problems concerning the so-called Early Paleolithic horizons in northern Kanto]. *Daiyonki Kenkyu* 10 (1): 44–45.
  1971b Kita Kanto romu to sekki hogan-so – tokuni zenki kyusekki bunkaso no shomondai [Stone implement-bearing layers in the Kanto loam in North Kanto: Problems on the so-called Early Paleolithic in view of geology]. *Daiyonki Kenkyu* 10 (4): 317–329.
FUJIMORI, EIICHI
  1965a "Chubu chiho nambu no sendoki jidai [The preceramic period in the southern part of Chubu District]," in *Sendoki jidai*. Edited by Sosuke Sugihara, 264–283. Tokyo: Kawade Shobo.
  1965b *Kyusekki no kariudo* [The hunters of the Paleolithic]. Tokyo: Gakuseisha.
GROOT, G. J.
  1951 *The prehistory of Japan*. New York: Columbia University Press.
HAMADA, KOSAKU
  1918 Kawachi no kuni Ko shinsekki jidai iseki hakkutsu hokoku [A report on the excavation of a Neolithic site at Ko in the province of Kawachi]. *Kyoto Teikoku Daigaku Bunka Daigaku Kokogaku Kenkyu Hokoku* 2: 29–35.

HASEBE, KOTONDO
1948 Akashi-shi fukin Nishiyagi saishinsei zenki taiseki shutsudo jinrui yokotsu (sekkogata) no genshisei ni tsuite [A human coxal bone from Lower Pleistocene deposit at Nishiyagi]. *Zinruigaku Zasshi* 60 (1): 32–36.

HAYASHI, KENSAKU
1968 The Fukui microblade technology and its relationships in northeast Asia and North America. *Arctic Anthropology* 5 (1): 128–190.

HOMMA, YOSHIHARU, et al.
1962 *Sado Nagaki hakken no zenki kyusekki yoho 1* [A preliminary report on the Early Paleolithic artifacts from Nagaki, Sado]. Sado Haku-butsukan Ho 10.

IKAWA, FUMIKO
1964 The continuity of nonceramic to ceramic cultures in Japan. *Arctic Anthropology* 2 (2): 95–119.

1966 Review of *Sendoki jidai*, edited by Sosuke Sugihara. *American Anthropology* 68 (2): 583–584.

1968 "Some aspects of Palaeolithic cultures in Japan," in *La préhistoire: problèmes et tendances*, 237–244. Paris: Centre National de la Recherche Scientifique.

1970 "The Japanese Palaeolithic in the context of prehistoric cultural relationships between northern Eurasia and the New World," in *Proceedings of the VIIIth International Congress of Anthropological and Ethnological Sciences*, Tokyo and Kyoto, 1968, volume three, 197–199. Tokyo: Science Council of Japan.

IKAWA-SMITH, FUMIKO
1974 "Early Palaeolithic Cultures of Japan: an appraisal." Unpublished Ph.D. thesis, Harvard University.

KAIZUKA, SOHEI
1965 "Kanto romuso [The Kanto Loam Bed]," in *Sendoki jidai*. Edited by Sosuke Sugihara, 71–87. Tokyo: Kawade Shobo.

KAMAKI, YOSHIMASA
1954 Setouchi engan ni okeru mudoki bunka no sompi ni tsuite [On the existence or nonexistence of nonceramic culture in the coastal areas of the Seto Inland Sea]. *Nippon Kokogaku Kyokai Iho*, supplement 3: 2–4.

1957 Nishi Nippon no mudoki bunka ni tsuite – toku ni Setouchi o chushin to shite [On nonceramic cultures in western Japan – with special reference to the Seto Inland Sea area]. *Watakushitachi no Kokogaku* 13: 15–22.

1959 Kagawa-ken Kiyama iseki shutsudo no sekki – yokujo hakuhen sekki o shuto suru [Stone implements, especially the wing-shaped flake-tools, found at the site of Shiroyama [sic], Prefecture of Kagawa, Japan]. *Kodaigaku* 8 (3): 300–307.

1960 Sen-Jomon bunka no hensen [Changing trends in the pre-Jomon culture]. *Zusetsu Sekai Bunkashi Taikei* 20 (Japan I): 35–42. Tokyo: Kadokawa.

KAMAKI, YOSHIMASA, CHOSUKE SERIZAWA
1967 "Nagasaki-ken Fukui dokutsu [The Fukui Cave, Nagasaki Prefecture]," in *Nippon no Dokutsu Iseki*. Edited by Nippon Kokogaku Kyokai Dokutsu Chosa Iinkai, 256–265. Tokyo: Heibonsha.

KAMAKI, YOSHIMASA, MAMORU TAKAHASHI
   1965   "Setonaikai chiho no sendoki jidai [The preceramic period in the Seto
          Inland Sea area]," in *Sendoki jidai*. Edited by Sosuke Sugihara,
          284–302. Tokyo: Kawade Shobo.
KATO, MINORU
   1969   Tohoku chiho no kyusekki bunka [The Paleolithic cultures of Tohoku
          District]. *Yamagata kenritsu Yamagata Chuo Kotogakko Kenkyu
          Kiyo* 1: 1–17.
KATO, SHIMPEI
   1967   Nippon ni okeru Rubarowa giho no mondai – Hoshino dai-san chiten
          shutsudo ibutsu no ichi [The problem of the Levallois technique in
          Japan – the position of the artifacts from Locality 3 of the Hoshino
          site]. *Shien* 27 (3): 8–17.
KATSUI, YOSHIO, YUKO KONDO
   1965   Kokuyoseki no suiwaso sokutei ni yoru sekki-gun no nendai kettei
          [Dating of stone implements by using a hydration layer of obsidian].
          Hokkaido Kokogaku 1: 1–18.
KIDA, TEICHIKI
   1917   *Shiseki Chosa Iinkaiho* [Reports of the committee for the investiga-
          tion of historic remains] 4. Osaka: Osaka Prefectural Government.
KIDDER, J. EDWARD, JR.
   1959   *Japan before Buddhism*. London: Thames and Hudson.
KIYONO, KENJI
   1952   Nippon ni okeru shoki sekki jidai no bunka to jumin [The culture
          and inhabitants of Japan early in the Stone Age]. *Kokogaku Zasshi*
          38 (2): 109–127.
   1953   Kasumigaura engan no kyuzo kaseki to kyusekki [Elephant fossils
          and Paleolithic implements from the Kasumigaura shore]. *INQUA
          Renrakushi* 4: 3–4.
KOBAYASHI, KUNIO
   1960   Bearing of "Shinshu Loam" on the Pleistocene geology of Matsu-
          moto Basin in Central Japan. *Journal of Faculty of Liberal Arts and
          Sciences, Shinshu University* 10 (2): 23–69.
   1965a Late Quaternary chronology of Japan. *Chikyu Kagaku* 79: 1–17.
   1965b *Shinshu romu-so* [The Shinshu Loam Bed], in *Sendoki jidai*. Edited
          by Sosuke Sugihara, 88–100. Tokyo: Kawade Shobo.
KOBAYASHI, TATSUO
   1970   Microblade industries in the Japanese archipelago. *Arctic Anthro-
          pology* 7 (2): 38–58.
KODAMA, SHINOBU
   1957   Shinano Omegura iseki mudoki bunka ryakuho [A brief report on the
          nonceramic culture at the Omegura site in Shinano]. *Shinshu Romu*
          2: 2–5.
KOKUBU, NAOICHI
   1966   Shina-kai shochiiki to senshi Nippon bunka [The China Seas areas
          and prehistoric Japan]. *Minzokugaku Kenkyu* 30 (4): 277–300.
   1967   Shimonoseki-shi Ayaragigo-daichi iseki [The Ayaragigo-daichi site
          in Shimonoseki City]. *Kokogaku Janaru* 12: 17–19.
KOKUBU, NAOCHI, SATOSHI SATO, TAKEO KANASEKI
   1962   "Seibu Nippon ni okeru zenki kyusekki iseki – gaiho [A brief report
          of the Early Paleolithic sites in western Japan]." Paper delivered to
          the November meeting of the Nippon Kokogaku Kyokai.

KOMURA, HIROSHI, et al.
1968 Aichi-ken Kasheizawa kyusekki jidai iseki [The Paleolithic site of Kasheizawa, Aichi Prefecture]. Tokyo: Genbunsha.

MARINGER, JOHANNES
1956a Einige faustkeilartige Geräte von Gongenyama (Japan) und die Frage des japanischen Paläolithikums. Anthropos 51: 175–179.
1956b A core and flake industry of Palaeolithic type from Central Japan. Artibus Asiae 19: 111–125.
1957a Some stone tools of Early Hoabinhian type from Central Japan. Man 57: 1–4.
1957b A stone industry of Patjitanian tradition from Central Japan. Kokogaku Zasshi 42 (2): 1–8.

MATSUMOTO, HIKOSABURO, et al.
1959 On the discovery of the Upper Pliocene fossiliferous and culture-bearing bed at Kanamori, Hanaizumi Town, Province of Rikuchu. Bulletin of National Science Museum 4: 287–324. Tokyo.

MORLAN, RICHARD E.
1967 The preceramic period of Hokkaido: an outline. Arctic Anthropology 4 (1): 164–220.

MORLAN, VALDA J.
1971 The preceramic period of Japan: Honshu, Shikoku and Kyushu. Arctic Anthropology 8 (1): 136–170.

MUNRO, NEIL G.
1911 Prehistoric Japan. Yokohama: Fukuin Printing.

NAGASAWA, JOJI
1939 Kanagawa-ken Hiyoshi no kyusekki jidai jinrui ibutsu [On the remains of Paleolithic man found at Hiyoshi, Kanagawa Prefecture]. Shigaku 18 (1): 165–169.

NAKAGAWA, HISAO
1965 Sozudai kyusekki hogan-so no soiteki yosatsu [A preliminary report on the stratigraphic horizon of the Paleolithic implements from the Sozudai site, Hijimachi, Kyushu, Japan]. Tohoku Daigaku Nippon Bunka Kenkyusho Kenkyu Hokoku 1: 121–141.

NAKAGAWA, SHIGEO
1963 Showa sanju-shichi-nen no Nippon kokogakkai o kaerimite [Review of Japanese archaeology in 1962]. Rekishi Kyoiku 11 (3): 49–55.

NAORA, NOBUO
1931 Harima-no-kuni Nishiyagi kaigan koseki-so-chu hakken no jinrui ihin [On the discovery of Paleolithic relics in the Province of Harima]. Zinruigaku Zasshi 46: 155–165, 212–223.
1952a Kuzu Maegahara dokutsu to dosho shutsudo no jinrui kasekikotsu [Cave of Kuzu Maegahara and the fossil human bones]. Kokogaku Zasshi 38 (2): 79–100.
1952b Tochigi-ken Kuzu hakken kosekisei jinrui no igai [On the fossil men discovered at Kuzu]. Zinruigaku Zasshi 62 (3): 115–119.
1954a Fukuoka-ken Moji-shi Tsunemi dokutsu [The Tsunemi Cave in Moji City, Fukuoka Prefecture]. Nippon Kokogaku Nempo 2: 69.
1954b Nippon Kyusekki Jidai no kenkyu [The Old Stone Age in Japan]. Waseda Daigaku Kokogaku Kenkyushitsu Hokoku 2. Tokyo: Waseda University.
1959 Iwate-ken Hanaizumi-cho Kanamori no kasekirui to jinrui ibutsu to koso-sareru kokkaki ni tsuite [On the fossils found in Hanaizumi, Iwate Prefecture]. Daiyonki Kenkyu 1 (4): 118–124.

NIPPON KYUSEKKI BUNKA KENKYU IINKAI (NKBKI)
1964   Oita-ken Nyu iseki dai-ichiji dai-niji hakkutsu chosa gaiho [Nyu
        sites: preliminary report on the excavations of the primeval sites on
        the Nyu Plateau, Oita Prefecture, on the east coast of Kyushu].
        Kyoto: Kodaigaku Kyokai [The Paleological Association of Japan].
1965   Oita-ken Nyu iseki dai-sanji hakkutsu chosa gaiho [Nyu sites: pre-
        liminary report on the excavations of the primeval sites on the Nyu
        Plateau, Oita Prefecture, on the east coast of Kyushu, the third
        season]. Kyoto: Kodaigaku Kyokai.
1966   Oita-ken Nyu iseki dai-yonji hakkutsu chosa gaiho [Nyu sites: pre-
        liminary report on the excavations of the primeval sites on the Nyu
        Plateau, Oita Prefecture, on the east coast of Kyushu, the fourth
        season]. Kyoto: Kodaigaku Kyokai.
1968   Nyu: Oita-ken Nyu iseki hakutsu chosa gaiho – sokatsu hen (Les
        fouilles des stations primordiales sur le plateau de Nyu à la Préfecture
        d'Oita, côte est de Kyushu). Kyoto: Kodaigaku Kyokai.

ODA, SHIZUO
1969   Some aspects of Japanese preceramic age: the microlithic tendency
        in the southwestern parts of Japan. Zinruigaku Zasshi 77 (5–6):
        224–245.

OHYI, HARUO
1965   "Senshi-Genshi I [Prehistory and proto-history I]," in 1964-nen no
        rekishi gakkai – Kaiko to tembo [Historical studies in Japan 1964],
        Shigaku Zasshi 74 (5): 507–511.
1968   Nippon no sendoki jidai sekki-gun no keito ni tsuite [On the tradi-
        tions of the preceramic industries in Japan]. Hoppo Bunka Kenkyu
        [Bulletin of the Institute for the Study of North Eurasian Cultures,
        Hokkaido University] 3: 45–93.

ONO, TADAHIRO
1957   Honshu-to seitan chiho ni okeru mudoki bunka no sekki to sono
        hakkenchi – yoho [Nonceramic stone implements and sites at the
        western end of Honshu Island: a preliminary report]. Watakushitaki
        no Kokogaku 4 (1): 27–33.
1958   Yamaguchi-ken Shimonoseki-shi Ayaragi Yayoi-shiki iseki [The sites
        of Yayoi culture, Ayaragi, Shimonoseki City]. Kokogaku Zasshi
        43 (4): 235–249.
1968   Yamaguchi-ken Isogami iseki no suisho shusekishi to kyusekki –
        ryakuho [Quartz piles and the Paleolithic implements from the
        Isogami site, Yamaguchi Prefecture – brief report]. Kokogaku
        Kenkyu 14 (4): 69–77.
1969   Koko-chiri-gaku kara mita kaigan sakyu no keisei – nishi Nippon no
        baai [Sand dune formation as seen from archaeogeography: a case
        of western Japan]. Chirigaku Hyoron 42 (3): 163–168.
1970   Yamaguchi-ken Toyoura-cho Isogami iseki no suishosekki to sono
        iko [The quartz artifacts and the features at the Isogami site, Toyoura
        Town, Yamaguchi Prefecture]. Kokogaku Janaru 46: 15–21.
1971a   The Early Palaeolithic spots discovered in the western Japan and their
        stone implements. Faculty of Education, Yamaguchi University.
1971b   Izumo no meno-sei kyusekki [Paleolithic stone tools in agate from
        Izumo]. Kokogaku Janaru 58: 4–9.
1971c   Shuisho, meno-sei kyusekki hakkenchi no zoka [Additional finds of
        Paleolithic implements of rock quartz and agate]. Daiyonki 16: 35–40.

ONO, TADAHIRO, MICHIHIRO KAWANO
1964   Honshu seitanbu no kaigan dankyu [The coastal terraces in the westernmost part of Honshu, Japan]. *Daiyonki Kenkyu* 3 (5): 249–263.

OTSUKA, KAZUYOSHI
1968   Honshu chiho ni okeru Yubetsu giho ni kansuru ichi kossatu [An observation on the Yebetsu technique in Honshu]. *Shinano* 20 (4): 233–242.

SATO, TATSUO
1963   Shukoten bunka ni kankei aruka Nyu iseki [The Nyu sites: their possible relationship with the Choukoutien culture]. *Kagaku Yomiuri* 13 (4): 69.

SATO, TATSUO, TATSUO KOBAYASHI, YUTAKA SAKAGUCHI
1962   Oita-ken Nyu shutsudo no zenki kyusekki – yoho [The Lower Paleolithic implements from Nyu, Oita Prefecture – a preliminary report]. *Kokogaku Zasshi* 47 (4): 293–311.

SATO, TATSUO, YUTAKA SAKAGUCHI
1962–1963   The Nyu industry and other Palaeolithic remains in Japan. *Quartär* 14: 115–131.

SATO, TATSUO, YUTAKA SAKAGUCHI, TATSUO KOBAYASHI
1962   Nyu bunka no sekki [Stone implements of the Nyu culture]. *Museum* 138: 24–27.

SERIZAWA, CHOSUKE
1954   Kanto oyobi Chubu chiho ni okeru mudoki bunka no shumatsu to Jomon bunka no hassei to ni kansuru yosatsu [Preliminary observation on the end of the nonceramic culture and the beginning of Jomon culture in Kanto and Chubu districts]. *Sundai Shigaku* 4: 65–106.

1955a   Nippon ni okeru mudoki bunka no seikaku [Nature of the nonceramic culture in Japan]. *Kanto Romu* 3: 1.

1955b   Yadegawa bunka no imi suru mono [The significance of the Yadegawa culture]. *Mikurorisu* 11: 7.

1956   Nippon ni okeru mudoki bunka [On the nonceramic culture in Japan]. *Zinruigaku Zasshi* 64 (3): 31–43.

1957   Senshi Jidai I: mudoki bunka [Prehistoric Period I: nonceramic culture]. *Kokogaku Noto*, volume one. Tokyo: Nihon Hyoron Shinsha.

1958   Nippon no me to gaikoku no me [Japanese viewpoints and foreign viewpoints]. *Kaizuka* 72: 1–2.

1959   Romuso ni hisomu bunka – sen-Jomon jidai [Culture in the Loam – pre-Jomon period]. *Sekai Kokogaku Taikei*, volume one. *Japan I*, 17–38. Tokyo: Heibonsha.

1960   *Sekki Jidai no Nippon* [The Stone Age of Japan]. Tokyo: Tsukiji Shokan.

1962   "Kyusekki jidai no shomondai [Problems of the Paleolithic period]," in *Nippon Rekishi*, volume one, 79–109. Tokyo: Iwanami Shoten.

1963   Kazanbai-chu no jinrui ibutsu [Archaeological materials from volcanic ash layers]. *Daiyonki Kenkyu* 3 (1–2): 67–71.

1964a   Mudoki bunka no hennen ni tsuite [On the chronology of the nonceramic culture]. *Kokogaku Kenkyu* 11 (3): 16–28.

1964b   Review of *Nippon genshi bijutsu I – Jomon-shiki doki* [Primitive arts of Japan I: Jomon pottery]. *Bunka* 28 (3): 441–446.

1965   Oita-ken Sozudai ni okeru zenki kyusekki no kenkyu [Lower Paleolithic industry from the Sozudai site, Oita Prefecture]. *Tohoku*

Daigaku Nippon Bunka Kenkyusho Kenkyu Hokoku [Reports of the Research Institute for Japanese Culture, Tohoku University] 1: 1–119.
1966–1968 Nippon no kyusekki [Paleolithic tools of Japan]. *Kokogaku Janaru* 1: 9–12; 2: 6–10; 3: 7–10; 5: 7–11; 8: 7–11; 9: 11–14; 11: 10–11; 12: 10–12; 13: 5–8; 14: 4–5; 20: 6–7.
1967a Kyusekki jidai [The Paleolithic period]. *Kokogaku Janaru* 7: 3–8.
1967b Nippon ni okeru kyusekki no soiteki shutsudorei to 14C nendai [The chronology of Paleolithic industries and carbon-14 dates in Japan]. *Tohoku Daigaku Nippon Bunka Kenkyusho Kenkyu Hokoku* [Reports of the Research Institute for Japanese Culture, Tohoku University] 3: 59–109.
1968a Keigan-sei kyusekki gun to Ko-Tokyo-wan [A Paleolithic industry made from chert and paleo-Tokyo Bay]. *Tohoku Daigaku Nippon Bunka Kenkyusho Kenkyu Hokoku* [Reports of the Research Institute for Japanese Culture, Tohoku University] 4: 1–45.
1968b Keigan-sei kyusekki o shutsudo suru Ashikaga-shi Okubo iseki – sokuho [The chert artifacts and the Okubo site, Ashikaga City – a brief report]. *Kokogaku Janaru* 22: 2–5.
1968c Kyusekki jidai [The Paleolithic period]. *Kokogaku Janaru* 19: 3–10.
1969 *Nippon no kyusekki* [The Paleolithic period of Japan]. *Kagaku* 39 (1): 28–36.
1970 "The chronological sequence of the Paleolithic cultures of Japan and the relationship with mainland Asia," in *Proceedings of the VIIIth International Congress of Anthropological and Ethnological Sciences, 1968, Tokyo and Kyoto*, volume three, 353–355. Tokyo: Science Council of Japan.
1971a Kita Kanto no romuso yori shitsudo suru kyusekki ni tsuite [Paleolithic artifacts from the loam formations of northern Kanto Plain]. *Daiyonki Kenkyu* 10 (1): 45.
1971b *Showa 45-nendo Iwajuku iseki hakkutsu chosa gaiho* [Preliminary report of the 1970 excavation of the Iwajuku site]. Kasagake-mura Koiku Iinkai.

SERIZAWA, CHOSUKE, *editor*
1966 *Hoshino iseki – Tochigi-shi Hoshino iseki daiichi-ji hakkutsu chosa hokoku* [The Hoshino site – report of the first excavation of the Hoshino site, Tochigi City]. Tokyo: Nyu Saiensusha.
1968 *Tochigi-shi Hoshino iseki – daini-ji hakkutsu chosa hokoku* [The Hoshino site, Tochigi City – report of the second excavation]. Tochigi: Tochigi-shi Kyoiku Iinkai.
1969 *Tochigi-shi Hoshino iseki – Daisan-ji hakkutsu chosa hokoku* [The Hoshino site, Tochigi City – report of the third excavation]. Tochigi: Tochigi-shi Kyoiku Iinkai.

SERIZAWA, CHOSUKE, TADAHIRO AIZAWA
1970 Iwajuku iseki no saihakkutsu o megutte – "zero bunka-so" hakken no igi [The re-excavation of the Iwajuku site – the significance of the discovery of the "zero-horizon"]. *Kagaku Asahi* 30 (7): 114–117.

SERIZAWA, CHOSUKE, FUMIKO IKAWA
1960 The oldest archaeological materials from Japan. *Asian Perspectives* 2 (2): 1–39.

SERIZAWA, CHOSUKE, HISAO NAKAGAWA
1965 "New evidence for the Lower Palaeolithic from Japan: a preliminary report on the Sozudai site, Kyushu," in *Miscelánea en Homenaje al Abate Henri Breuil*, volume two. Edited by E. Ripoll Perelló,

363–372. Barcelona: Diputación Provincial de Barcelona, Instituto de Prehistoria y Arqueología.

SHIRATAKI DANTAI KENKYUKAI
1963   *Shirataki iseki no kenkyu* [The study of the Shirataki Site]. Tokyo: Chigaku Dantai Kenkyukai.

SONE, HIROSHI
1929a   Mutsu Tsubakiyama kaigan yori hakkutsu seru eorisu-yo no sekihen ni tsuite [The stone pieces, probably Eolithic, from the Tsubakiyama coast, Province of Mutsu]. *Chishitsugaku Zasshi* 36: 392–400.
1929b   Mutsu-no-kuni Natsudomari-hanto fukin sekki jidai jinrui iseki no kenkyu [Research on the Paleolithic sites in the vicinity of Natsu-domari Peninsula in the Province of Mutsu]. *Saito Hoonkai Gaku-jutsu Kenkyu Somubu Jigyo Nempo* 4: 119–122.

SUGIHARA, SOSUKE
1952   Nippon sekki bunka no dankai [Stages of Stone Age culture in Japan]. *INQUA renrakushi* 1: 15–17.
1953   Nippon ni okeru sekki bunka no kaitei ni tsuite [On the stages of Stone Age culture in Japan]. *Kokogaku Zasshi* 39 (2): 97–101.
1954   Aomori-ken Kanagi sareki-so no gisekki [Pseudo-artifacts from the gravel layer at Kanagi, Aomori Prefecture]. *Mikurorisu* 10: 27–29.
1956a   *Gumma-ken Iwajuku hakken no sekki bunka* [The Stone Age remains found at Iwajuku, Gumma Prefecture]. Meiji Daigaku Bungakubu Kenkyu Hokoku, Kokogaku Dai-issatsu [Reports of the Research by the Faculty of Literature, Meiji University: Archaeology 1].
1956b   "Jomon bunka izen no sekki bunka [The Stone Age culture prior to Jomon culture]," in *Nippon Kokogaku Koza* 3: 2–24. Tokyo: Kawade Shobo.
1956c   "Nippon no shigen bunka [The earliest culture of Japan]," in *Zusetsu Nippon Bunkashi Taikei 1 – Jomon, Yayoi*, 78–88. Tokyo: Shogakkan.
1965   Nippon no genshi jidai no kaimei to shizenkagaku [Natural sciences and the investigations into the earliest period of Japanese history]. *Kagaku* 35 (7): 336–370.
1967a   Nippon sendoki jidai no shin-hennen ni kansuru shian [A proposal of a new chronology for the preceramic period of Japan]. *Shinano* 19 (4): 245–248.
1967b   "Sugihara's hypothesis" o yabutte hoshii [I wish "Sugihara's hypo-thesis" would be disproved]. *Kokogaku Janaru* 8: 2–3.
1969   Similarity and difference between the prehistoric cultures of Japan and Alaska. *Kokogaku Shukan* 4 (3): 1–14.

SUGIHARA, SOSUKE, *editor*
1965   *Sendoki jidai: Nippon no Kokogaku I* [Preceramic period: Japanese archaeology I]. Tokyo: Kawade Shobo.

SUGIHARA, SOSUKE, MITSUNORI TOZAWA
1960   Preceramic age in Japan. *Acta Asiatica* (*Bulletin of the Institute of Eastern Culture*) 1: 1–28.

SUZUKI, SHIGEHARU
1967a   Miyazaki-ken Izuruha dokutsu no hakkutsu chosa – zenki kyusekki o shutsudo shita dokutsu iseki [The excavation of the Izuruha Cave, Miyazaki Prefecture – A cave site producing Lower Paleolithic remains]. *Kokogaku Janaru* 4: 12–15.
1967b   Miyazaki-ken Mitate Izuruha dokutsu [The cave of Izuruha, Miyazaki Prefecture]," in *Nippon no Dokutsu Iseki*. Edited by

Nippon Kokogaku Kyokai Dokutsu Chosa Iinkai, 298–314. Tokyo: Heibonsha.

1968   Manro-shi kyuzo no sekiei-sei kyusekki [A Paleolithic tool of quartzite from the Munro collection]. *Kokogaku Janaru* 25: 9–10.

TAJIMI-SHI KOKOGAKU KENKYUKAI
1969   Tajimi no chato-sei kyusekki [The Paleolithic tools in chert from Tajimi]. *Kokogaku Janaru* 28: 13–16.

TAKAI, FUYUJI, TOSHIMASA TANAI
1949   Yuwayuru "Nipponantoropusu " no sanshutsu chiso ni tsuite [On the so-called Nipponanthropus-bearing formation]. *Zinruigaku Zasshi* 54 (3): 117–120.

TAKIZAWA, HIROSHI
1963a   *Kanto Chubu chiho ni okeru naifugata sekki bunka to sono shumatsu* [The study of knife blade culture and the end of it in central Japan]. Tokyo: H. Takizawa.
1963b   Naifu-gata sekki no kino [The function of the knife blade]. *Shimofusa Kokogaku* 1.
1964a   Honshu ni okeru saisekki bunka no saikento [Reexamination of the microlithic culture in Honshu]. *Bushitsu Bunka* 3: 1–24.
1964b   Sentoki [The points]. *Kokogaku Techno* 23: 2–5.

TASAKA, MIYOKO
1966   Nippon ni okeru "Zenki Kyusekki " kenkyu – Nyu iseki to Sozudai iseki no hokoku ni kanshite [Early Paleolithic research in Japan – with reference to the reports on the Nyu and the Sozudai sites]. *Sundai Shigaku* 18: 167–190.

TODA, MASAKATSU
1969   Tochigi-shi Kamifuji iseki no senki kyusekki [The Early Palaeolithic tools from the Kamifuji site, Tochigi Prefecture]. *Jodai Bunka* 38: 43–51.

TOZAWA, MITSUNORI
1963   Nippon ni okeru iwayuru "zenki kyusekki " no shomondai [Problems of the so-called "Early Paleolithic " in Japan]. *Rekishi Kyoiku* 11 (3): 8–14.

TSUNODA, BUN'EI
1962a   Iwajuku bunka kenkyu no mondaiten [Problems concerning the research on Iwajuku culture]. *Kodai Bunka* 8 (4): 64–73.
1962b   Oita-ken Nyu iseki – yosatsu gaiho [The Nyu site, Oita Prefecture – a brief report of the preliminary survey]. *Kodai Bunka* 8 (4): 74–92.

TSUNODA, BUN'EI, TEIJI MIKAMI
1967   Iwayuru "Nyu hihan" no mondaiten [Problems of the "Nyu criticism"]. *Kokogaku Janaru* 11: 4–9.

WATANABE, HITOSHI
1949   Nipponantoropusu-so no shizenhasaireki [Natural fracture of pebbles from the fossil-bearing deposits near Akashi]. *Zinruigaku Zasshi* 60 (3): 121–122.

WATANABE, NAOTSUNE
1950   Akashi seiko gankasekiso ni okeru hone no hozon kanosei [On the possible preservation of bone in the fossil-bearing formation near Akashi]. *Zinruigaku Zasshi* 61 (4): 183–190.

YAMANOUCHI, SUGAO, TATSUO SATO
1962   Jomon doki no furusa [The antiquity of Jomon pottery]. *Kagaku Yomiuri* 14 (12): 21–26, 84–88.
1964a   "Kyusekki jidai [The Paleolithic period]," in *Nippon genshi bijutsu*

I – Jomon-shiki doki. Edited by S. Yamanouchi et al., 135–137. Tokyo: Kodansha.

1964b   *Mudoki bunka* [The nonceramic culture]," in *Nippon genshi bijutsu I – Jomon-shiki doki.* Edited by S. Yamanouchi et al., 137–140. Tokyo: Kodansha.

YOKOTA, YOSHIAKI
1967   Review of *Hoshino iseki* [The Hoshino site] by Chosuke Serizawa. *Kokogaku Kenkyu* 53: 56–69.

YOKOYAMA, EISUKE
1970   Nippon no zenki kyusekki jidai ni okeru hakuri gijutsu no jittai to koki kyusekki jidaei e no kanrensei ni tsuite no yosatsu [A preliminary observation on the nature of the flake production technique in the Early Paleolithic, and the relationship with the Late Paleolithic]. *Kokogaku Kenkyu* 19 (2): 17–36.

YONEJI, FUMIO, MINORU KATO
1969   Yamagata-ken Nakatsugawa Kamiyachi no zenki kyusekki jidai iseki to sono shuhen no chisei [The Early Paleolithic site at Kamiyachi, Nakatsugawa, Yamagata Prefecture, and the geomorphology of the area]. *Tohoku Chiri* 21 (3): 136–142.

YOSHIZAKI, MASAKAZU
1956   Hokkaido no *blade industry* ni tsuite [Blade industry in Hokkaido]. *Hokkaido Daiyonki Kenkyukai Renrakushi* 7: 2–6.

1958   Hokkaido no mudoki bunka ni tsuite – kyusekki to chusekki jidai no sekki [On the nonceramic cultures of Hokkaido – Paleolithic and Mesolithic tools]. *Kyodo no Kagaku* 19: 3–7.

1961   Shirataki iseki to Hokkaido no mudoki bunka [The Shirataki site and the preceramic culture in Hokkaido]. *Minzokugaku Kenkyu* 26 (1): 13–23.

1967   Kokogaku kara mita Nipponjin [The Japanese people as seen from an archaeological point of view]. *Iden* 21 (1): 14–18.

The Early Paleolithic in Japan

CHOSUKE SERIZAWA

THE KANTO LOAM AND CHRONOMETRIC DATES

In the vicinity of Tokyo, in the southern Kanto Plain, Central Honshu, there are four terraces which are believed to have been formed during the latter half of the Pleistocene. These are named, in chronological order, the Tama Terrace, the Shimosueyoshi Terrace, the Musashino Terrace, and the Tachikawa Terrace. The volcanic ash overlying the terrace deposits is collectively known as the Kanto Loam, which, in southern Kanto, is divided into four parts: the Tama Loam (which occurs only on the Tama Terrace), the Shimosueyoshi Loam (which occurs on the Shimosueyoshi Terrace and overlies the Tama Loam on the Tama Terrace), the Musashino Loam (which occurs directly above the gravel on the Musashino Terrace and over the older loam on the Shimosueyoshi and Tama Terraces), and the Tachikawa Loam (which occurs on all of the four terraces). To the north of Tokyo, in the northwestern Kanto Plain near the mountain range, are three terraces known as the Lower, Middle, and Upper Terraces which in turn are covered with the Lower, Middle, and Upper Loam Beds. The Upper Loam of the northern Kanto Plain has been correlated with the Tachikawa Loam of the southern Kanto Plain, the Middle Loam with the Musashino Loam, and the Lower Loam with the Shimosueyoshi Loam.

Molluscan fossils from south Kanto suggest that the Tama Terrace was formed during a period of marine transgression called the Tama-Byobugaura Transgression; the Shimosueyoshi Terrace was formed during the Shimosueyoshi Transgression. The Musashino and Tachikawa Terraces appear to have been formed during a period of marine

This paper was translated by Fumiko Ikawa-Smith.

regression which preceded the Yurakucho Transgression. While the Yurakucho Transgression is clearly a postglacial transgression during which Jomon shellmounds were formed, the Shimosueyoshi and Tama-Byobugaura Transgressions could not definitely be correlated with specific interglacial episodes. Many geologists, however, feel that the Shimosueyoshi Transgression is probably attributable to the warm period known as the Eemian Interglacial in Europe, and that the Tama-Byobugaura Transgression is probably attributable to the Holsteinian.

Although correlation with the European sequence is not altogether clear, a number of chronometric dates are being obtained thanks to an increasing number of investigators interested in this field of research, and this helps define the temporal ranges of various Kanto Loam beds (Machida and Suzuki 1971). Radiocarbon determinations on samples obtained from the Tachikawa Loam fall between 30,000 and 10,000 B.P., suggesting that this youngest unit of the Kanto Loam is assignable to this temporal range. The age of the Musashino Loam, according to radiocarbon and fission track dates, is approximately 40,000 to 50,000 B.P., and the age of the Shimosueyoshi Loam is indicated by fission track determinations as being 66,000 to 132,000 B.P. The age of the Tama Loam, therefore, must be in excess of 130,000 years (Figure 1).

STRATIGRAPHY AND ARTIFACTS OF THE SOZUDAI SITE

The Sozudai site in northeastern Kyushu[1] was investigated in 1964 by the Archaeology Laboratory of Tohoku University. The site, over-looking Beppu Bay, is located on a thirty-five-meter marine terrace which Nakagawa (1965) attributes to the Shimosueyoshi Transgression. The stratigraphy of the site is as follows:

1. Humus.
2. Black soil, containing Joman shards.
3. Dark brown soil, containing blades and cores.
4. Yellow clay (sterile).
5. Andesite gravel, containing numerous artifacts of vein quartz and quartz rhyolite.
6. Sandy clay, containing some artifacts.
7. Andesite breccia tuff (bedrock).

The artifacts obtained from layer 5, some 500 in number, included choppers, chopping tools, proto-handaxes, pointed tools, proto-burins,

[1]   For the location of the site see Ikawa-Smith (this volume), Figure 8. – *Editor.*

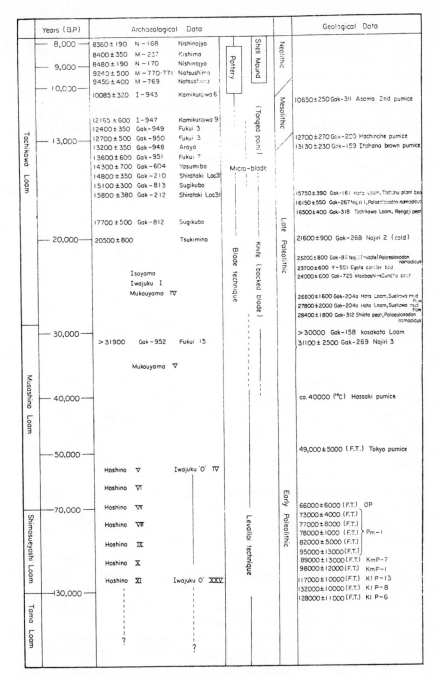

Figure 1.   C¹⁴ and F.T. dates of the Stone Age in Japan

scrapers, cores (proto-Levallois type), and flakes.[2] Unlike Paleolithic assemblages previously known from Japan, this assemblage contains almost equal proportions of core and flake tools. And again unlike other Paleolithic assemblages, choppers and chopping tools are predominant in this assemblage, and the proto-Levallois and bipolar techniques appear to have been utilized. (For experimental replication of bipolar flakes, see Kobayashi 1975.) For these reasons, I felt that this assemblage predates the assemblages in which blades and knives occur. The blades and knives obtained from layer 3 of Sozudai are similar to those which had been obtained from the Tachikawa Loam. Since a sterile layer (layer 4) occurs between this layer (layer 3) and the andesite gravel layer (layer 5), it appeared that the assemblage recovered from layer 5 was considerably older than the layer 3 assemblage. On the other hand, the site is located on a topographic surface which Nakagawa equates with the Shimosueyoshi Terrace of southern Kanto: in view of the fission track date of this terrace, the layer 5 assemblage of Sozudai should be younger than 130,000 B.P.

STRATIGRAPHY AND ARTIFACTS OF THE IWAJUKU 0 (ZERO) ASSEMBLAGES

The Iwajuku site, in the northwestern Kanto Plain, was discovered by Tadahiro Aizawa in 1949 and is well-known as the first Paleolithic site ever recognized as such in Japan. The 1949 excavation, conducted at Locality A, revealed two Paleolithic horizons named Iwajuku I and Iwajuku II. Both are situated in the Upper Loam, which can be correlated with the Tachikawa Loam of the southern Kanto Plain (Figure 1). During the reinvestigation of the site in 1970 and 1971, however, entirely different assemblages were recovered from both the Middle and Lower Loam beds. Since these assemblages occur below the Iwajuku I assemblage, they have been referred to as the assemblages of the Iwajuku 0 (zero) horizon (Serizawa 1970, 1971). Almost all the artifacts of Iwajuku Zero are of chert, with the exception of hammerstones which are made of quartz porphyry pebbles. The assemblages include pointed tools, scrapers, choppers, chopping tools, proto-handaxes, proto-ovates, cleavers, picks, proto-burins, hammerstones, cores, and flakes (Figure 2). Choppers and chopping tools tend to be more numerous in lower strata, while points and scrapers increase in the upper strata within the Iwajuku Zero horizon. In terms of technological characteristics of the assemblages, we feel that the bipolar technique is present but the alternate flaking method

[2]   Some of the Sozudai specimens are shown in Ikawa-Smith (this volume), Figures 10 and 11. – *Editor.*

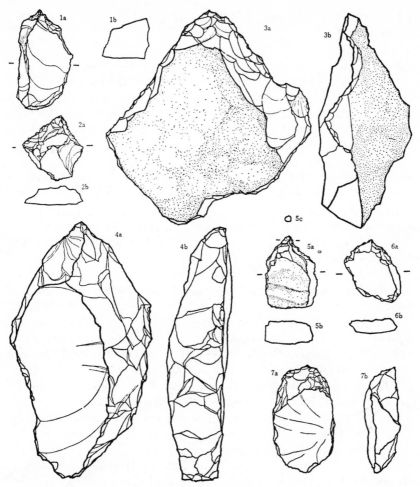

Figure 2.   Artifacts from the Iwajuku Zero horizon

is rarely employed. Instead many of the specimens are unifacially modified or unifacially worked along alternate sides of both surfaces.

Stratigraphically, an Iwajuku Zero assemblage recovered at Locality B occurred in a stratum below the Hassaki Pumice, dated to 40,000 B.P., which is situated below the Iwajuku I horizon. At Locality D, Iwajuku Zero assemblages were encountered not only in strata below the Hassaki Pumice, but continued further down to strata below the Yunokuchi Pumice. Thus it appears that the Iwajuku Zero assemblages are older than 40,000 B.P. at least and some of them could be between 60,000 B.P. and 130,000 B.P.

STRATIGRAPHY AND ARTIFACTS OF THE HOSHINO SITE

Since 1965 four excavations have been carried out at the Hoshino site in the northeastern part of the Kanto Plain, but the bedrock is yet to be reached. Although some of the localities were dug to the depth of 9.5 meters, a thick layer of loam appears to be present below this level. While eleven Paleolithic horizons have been distinguished at Hoshino,[3] my comments here are based on the materials obtained from Cultural Horizons 5, 6, 7, 8, 9, 10, and 11 only, because a dispute arose among geologists over the ages of Cultural Horizons 3 and 4. Cultural Horizon 5 occurs just below a two-meter layer of pumice, which, according to Fusao Arai of Gumma University, is the Kanuma Pumice, approximately 30,000 to 40,000 years old. Thus the assemblages of Cultural Horizons 5 to 11 are certainly older than 30,000 to 40,000 B.P. Arai also identifies the pumice just above Cultural Horizon 6 as the Hassaki Pumice and the pumice deposit just above Cultural Horizon 7 as the Yunokuchi Pumice. Therefore, Cultural Horizons 5 and 6 of Hoshino are in the Middle Loam and Cultural Horizons 7 to 11 in the Lower Loam of the northern Kanto Plain. Correlation with the southern Kanto sequence would suggest that Cultural Horizons 5 and 6 are in the neighborhood of 40,000 to 50,000 B.P. and Cultural Horizons 7 to 11 are anywhere between 60,000 and 130,000 B.P. (Figure 1). More precise chronological assignment of the assemblages may be possible when Masao Suzuki of St. Paul's University, Tokyo, completes fission track age determinations of the samples from the 1973 excavation.

Since the artifacts recovered during the 1973 excavation are not yet fully analyzed, the assemblages from Cultural Horizons 5, 6, 7, 8, 9, 10, and 11 can only be described in general terms. All the artifacts are made of chert and they range in size from about two to fifteen centimeters. Small tools appear to be more numerous in the assemblages of Cultural Horizons 5 to 8. The assemblages include pointed tools, scrapers, choppers, burins, proto-ovates, proto-handaxes, chopping tools, knives, flakes, and cores. Most numerous are implements made on tabular flakes and angular chunks of chert. Some of the noteworthy characteristics of the assemblages are the occurrence in Cultural Horizons 7 and 8 of specimens remarkably similar to the *kiridashi*-shaped artifacts of later Paleolithic assemblages, lower frequencies of chopping tools, and infrequent use of the alternate flaking method (Figures 3–6). It is hoped that further investigation of the site will produce significant information on the Early Paleolithic of Japan.

[3] See Figure 12 of Ikawa-Smith's paper (this volume) for a schematic representation of the Hoshino stratigraphy. – *Editor.*

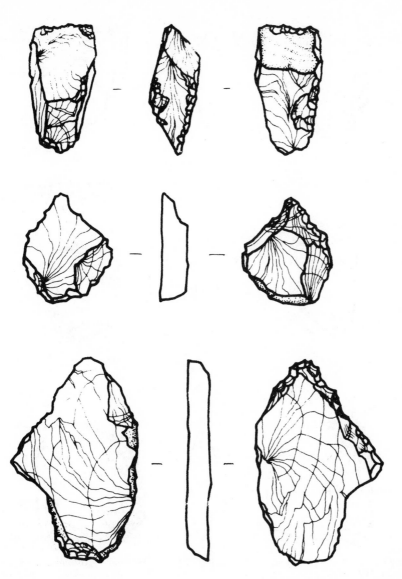

Figure 3.   Artifacts recovered from Cultural Horizon 7 of the Hoshino Site, Kanto Plain (1973 season)

PROBLEMS FOR FUTURE RESEARCH

Early Paleolithic research in Japan, which began as late as 1964, has not yet produced a great deal of results. I believe, however, that records of early man in Japan have been demonstrated at the three

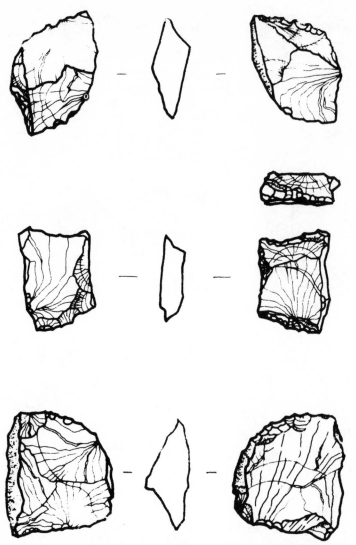

Figure 4.   Artifacts recovered from Cultural Horizon 7 of the Hoshino Site, Kanto Plain (1973 season)

sites mentioned above: Sozudai, Iwajuku, and Hoshino. Although the relative chronological positions of the assemblages from these sites are not yet clear, it appears, on the basis of typology and technology, that the Sozudai assemblage is the oldest of the three, followed by the Iwajuku assemblages and by the Hoshino assemblages. Our first objective is to establish the chronology of the Early Paleolithic in Japan by utilizing fission-track and other chronometric methods. Another important problem for future research is understanding the

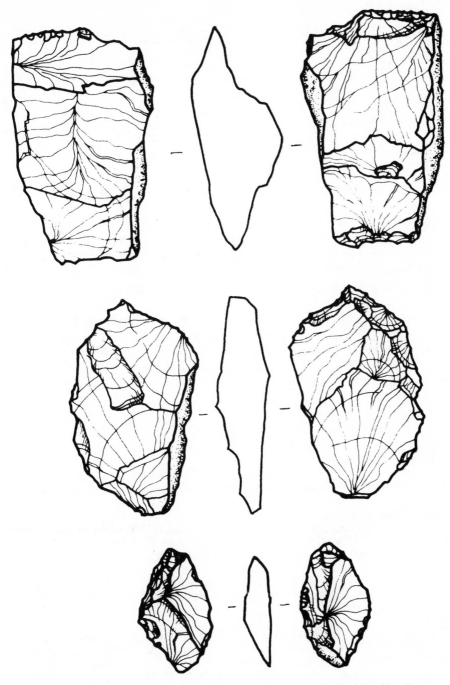

Figure 5. Artifacts recovered from Cultural Horizon 8 of the Hoshino Site, Kanto Plain (1973 season)

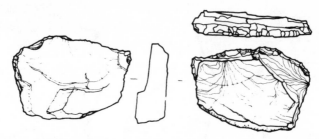

Figure 6.   Artifacts recovered from Cultural Horizon 8 of the Hoshino Site, Kanto Plain (1973 season)

nature of continuity to, or replacement by, the Late Paleolithic cultures of Japan.

Although virtually no human or animal bones have been found in association with Paleolithic artifacts in Japan, the recovery in 1973 of mandibular and limb bones of the Mongolian wild horse (*Equus hemionus*) from a stratum comparable to Cultural Horizons 5 and 6 of Hoshino greatly increases our hope of obtaining more faunal information in the future.

Negative opinions have been voiced by some archaeologists and geologists (e.g. Arai 1971; Sugihara 1967) on our investigations of Early Paleolithic remains.[4] The difference of opinion, however, results from recognition of lithic specimens as artifacts; it will be resolved when detailed technological studies of artifacts are presented.

REFERENCES

ARAI, FUSAO
1971   Kita Kanto romu to sekki hoganso [Stone implement-bearing layers in the Kanto Loam in north Kanto, Japan]. *Daiyonki Kenkyu* 10 (4): 317–329.

KOBAYASHI, HIROAKI
1975   "The experimental study of bipolar flakes," in *Lithic technology: making and using stone tools.* Edited by Earl Swanson, 115–127. World Anthropology. The Hague: Mouton.

MACHIDA, HIROSHI, MASAO SUZUKI
1971   Kazanbai no zettai nendai to Daiyonki koki no hennen [A chronology of the late Quaternary period as established by fission-track dating]. *Kagaku* 41 (5): 263–270.

NAKAGAWA, HISAO
1965   Sozudai kyusekki hoganso no soiteki yosatsu [A preliminary report on the stratigraphic horizon of the Paleolithic implements from the Sozudai site, Hiji-machi, Kyushu, Japan]. *Tohoku Daigaku Nippon Bunka Kenkyusho Kenkyu Hokoku* 1: 121–141.

[4]   Ohyi (this volume) presents a negative opinion of Serizawa's findings. Also see Ikawa-Smith (this volume) for background of the controversy. – *Editor.*

SERIZAWA, CHOSUKE

    1970   Zenki kyusekki no shomondai [Problems of the Early Paleolithic in Japan]. *Daiyonki Kenkyu* 9 (3–4): 192–200.

    1971   Zenki kyusekki ni kansuru shomondai [On the Early Paleolithic in Japan]. *Daiyonki Kenkyu* 10 (4): 179–190.

SUGIHARA, SOZUKE

    1967   "Sugihara's hypothesis" o yabutte hoshii [I wish "Sugihara's hypothesis" would be disproved]. *Kokogaku Janaru* 8: 2–3.

Some Comments
on the Early Paleolithic of Japan

HARUO OHYI

A serious discussion of the Early Paleolithic in Japan began during the last decade. As for the history of the investigation, I have almost nothing to add to the paper presented by Ikawa-Smith (this volume). In my opinion, however, there have been two sets of heated controversies over the Paleolithic and Mesolithic cultures in the Japanese Archipelago; they began about the same time and are not logically related to each other. One of these concerns the dates and cultural affiliations of the so-called preceramic cultures and is related to the question of reliability of the radiocarbon method of dating. The other centers on the problem of the Early Paleolithic cultures in the Archipelago. With the exception perhaps of Sosuke Sugihara, no scholar in Japan would categorically deny the existence of early man in the Archipelago during the Lower and Middle Pleistocene; most archaeologists feel that the so-called preceramic cultures of Japan were probably preceded by Early and/or Middle Paleolithic cultures.

It would be impossible to discuss the problem of the Early and/or Middle Paleolithic cultures in Japan without reference to Serizawa's investigations in the last decade and a half at such sites as Sozudai, Hoshino, and Iwajuku, the results of which were summarized by him for this volume. At these sites, the layers from which Serizawa and his associates recovered the "stone implements" are clearly older than those containing the so-called "preceramic" cultures. As seen in Serizawa's paper in this volume, the dates, ranging from 40,000 to 130,000 years, were given to these layers by means of the radiocarbon and the fission-track methods. Although the dates may be correct, a question remains as to the identification of the lithic specimens as artifacts.

The specimens recovered from Sozudai, Hoshino (Cultural Horizon 5 and lower), and the Iwajuku 0 (zero) horizon, as presented in Serizawa's publications, reveal remarkable resemblance between them. It is the crudeness of the specimens that strikes one at first sight. Perhaps the crude appearance of these specimens is, at least in part, due to the nature of the lithic materials. Vein quartz and quartz rhyolite are the most frequent lithic materials at Sozudai, while siliceous rocks are reportedly used at Hoshino and Iwajuku exclusively. These rocks no doubt are among the most unsuitable for toolmaking because it is most difficult to control flaking. One of the simple questions, then, is why such difficult materials were chosen. In the upper layers of all the three sites there occur preceramic assemblages which consist of tools made of other, more suitable materials. In other words these materials were available, if the toolmakers wished to utilize them.

Accepting, for the moment, Serizawa's argument that the choice of lithic materials in itself is one of the characteristics of this group of assemblages, we come to another question: whether the specimens are really artifacts and whether there are any technological regularities. Serizawa has classified the specimens into eight to twelve categories of implements and described their technological characteristics in detail. He presented many beautiful line drawings of the specimens in his publications. However, the drawings were made by people who firmly believe in the artifactual nature of the specimens and therefore some plausible features have been drawn into the illustrations. Thus it is rather dangerous to base one's judgement on the line drawings only. Some photographic illustrations are also shown in Serizawa's publications. From these photographic illustrations it is rather difficult to arrive at the same conclusions as Serizawa: in fact it is quite impossible to see any evidence of intentional flaking or retouching on the specimens. Serizawa himself has stated that he and his associates spent nearly six months studying the specimens before they discovered technological characteristics and were convinced of the artifactual nature of the specimens. It seems that as much or even more time would be necessary for us readers of his publications to share his conviction. I believe that the published accounts of the assemblages of Sozudai, Hoshino, and Iwajuku 0 (Zero) failed to present convincing enough evidence of human workmanship.

Further questions may be raised about these assemblages. One of them concerns the extraordinary numbers of "implements" and the large variety of tool types in these assemblages. Another is about the large numbers of "cultural layers" – twenty-nine at Iwajuku Locality D and eleven at Hoshino – which happen to be present at the very spots where Serizawa's trenches were cut. All of these lead us to suspect that some natural agency was responsible in producing quantities of rocks with certain fractures on them.

A detailed and exhaustive discussion on the nature of these "Early Paleolithic" specimens appears to be the first task which should be undertaken by those who are interested in the problem of the Early Paleolithic in Japan. As Serizawa suggests in his paper, a thorough technological study of the lithic specimens may satisfactorily answer questions such as those raised here.

There is no question, however, that there are several assemblages which consist of unmistakable artifacts and which exhibit technological characteristics different from those of later "preceramic" assemblages. Among them are the materials known as the Gongenyama I assemblage and the Cultural Horizon 3 and 4 assemblages of the Hoshino site. These assemblages clearly occurred in horizons below those of "preceramic" assemblages. Since geochronological information on the earliest group of "preceramic" cultures (i.e. Iwajuku I and Shirataki Locality 31) points to the chronological position being within or just before the last expansion of the Würm Glaciation, assemblages such as Gongenyama I and Hoshino Cultural Horizons 3 and 4 must date to the initial stage of the Würm if not earlier. It would then appear that Shimpei Kato's argument (as summarized by Ikawa-Smith in this volume) for the correlation of the Hoshino Cultural Horizon 3 with the Ust-Kanskaia Cave materials is a plausible one. As to the Gongenyama I assemblage, it does appear to be older than the others typologically, even though a precise cultural affiliation of this assemblage is difficult to determine. The Gongenyama I assemblage, therefore, appears to be the oldest undeniable evidence of human occupation in Japan and is possibly related to such Early Paleolithic assemblages of the Asiatic continent as Tingts'un.

In summary, then, I believe that there certainly were Early and/or Middle Paleolithic cultures in Japan and these probably underwent changes both through internal development and through external influences. Each of these assemblages may indicate certain close relationships with specific continental assemblages. Therefore, it would be necessary, for full understanding of the Early and/or Middle Paleolithic cultural sequence in Japan, to trace their cultural traditions in a wider context, including the entire continent of Asia.

In this sense, Chosuke Serizawa's investigations of the "Early Paleolithic" assemblages provided an important impetus in the right direction. In spite of certain serious questions about his arguments, such as those mentioned above, the significance of Serizawa's investigations, in the history of Paleolithic research in Japan, must be recognized.

The Problem of the Lower Paleolithic in the South of the Soviet Far East

A. P. DEREVIANKO

Only fifteen or twenty years ago the Far East was believed to be an outlying province of man's homeland where man had appeared comparatively late. This belief persisted despite the discovery of Acheulian-type stone knives in the area by Eliseev, a well-known Russian traveler, in the late nineteenth century (Eliseev 1890). Almost thirty years later Farcache found a point in the south of Maritime Territory. In the opinion of Breuil it exhibits a typological similarity with the Aurignacian while chronologically he placed it in the Pleistocene (Breuil 1925).

This idea of the Stone Age of the Far East changed radically beginning with the 1950's after Okladnikov discovered a camp near Osinovka village and a number of other Paleolithic sites in the Maritime Territory (Okladnikov 1959). But even these finds could not shake the general belief that the Soviet Far East was populated by man comparatively late, somewhere around the end of the Paleolithic and the beginning of the Mesolithic.

A real revolution in this field was wrought by Okladnikov who discovered exceedingly archaic stone artifacts near Filimoshki village in the Zeya basin (Figures 1–3). According to the mode of occurrence, typology, and technique of manufacture he placed them in an unexpectedly early period, the first half of the Middle Pleistocene; by archaeological chronology in the Lower Paleolithic, pre-Mousterian time (Okladnikov 1964). This also led to the conclusion that the pebble-tool tradition of the Paleolithic of Siberia and the Far East must have had its own deep roots.

The hypothesis that primitive man lived in the Far East in the Lower Paleolithic was further supported by the discovery of a pebble-tool assemblage by Shavkunov near Kumary village, in the basin of the

Upper Amur, in 1957. He amassed a collection of stone tools that undoubtedly belonged to the Paleolithic.

In 1968, I continued the work started in Kumary. Excavations and a careful examination of the river terrace helped uncover several culture horizons in the area of the village: Paleolithic, Mesolithic, and Neolithic (Derevianko 1970). Of special interest are three Paleolithic assemblages. One of them included several dozen implements dating back to the Lower Paleolithic. The implements were found lying in the riverside pebble bed while individual tools were being recovered from the water. The stretch of pebble bed containing tools exceeded 800 meters. Three types of artifacts were found – choppers (Figure 4), chopping tools, and beaked scrapers (Figure 5) – as well as several shapeless pebbles from which crude flakes had been struck.

The mode of occurrence is also noteworthy. All the tools were found in an ancient pebble bed with a ten to fifteen meter overlap of sandy loam. The loose strata, gradually rising, run up to a chain of rocky hills which lie within 200 to 300 meters of the present-day Amur Valley. In some places the rocks end abruptly by the waterline to form a steep bank. A similar picture is to be seen on the right bank of the Amur. It is quite possible that in the Lower Paleolithic the breadth of the Amur Valley showed seasonal variations in rainy and dry periods with the stream channel expanding and receding. As the river valley narrowed, the pebbles left exposed by the receding water provided an excellent material for tool manufacture. A similar regularity is also to be seen in Mongolia where most of the Lower Paleolithic remains were discovered in the stream channels of old rivers. The loose deposits of the Amur's flood terrace are all referable to the Upper Pleistocene and were formed much later than the pebbles.

A third site with equally archaic stone artifacts was discovered on the Zeya River in 1969. It lies near the mouth of the Ust-Tu River. Crude pebble tools (Figure 6) occur in a pebble bed resting on bedrock. Overlying the pebble bed is an eight-meter terrace composed of loose stratified deposits of slimy sand and sand loam. The terrace, gently rising for two or three kilometers, approaches a medium-sized mountain range. Over 200 pebble tools were discovered there during excavations in 1969–1970.

Two more sites with similar pebble tools were found at a distance of four to five kilometers from this locality.

All the three sites are characterized by identical geomorphological conditions: a rocky left bank and a right bank beginning with an eight-to-twelve-meter-high terrace which abuts on a not very high rocky ridge. The loose deposits of this terrace are young and date back to the Upper Pleistocene. The terrace was evidently formed during an intensive thawing of mountain valley glaciers on the Upper Zeya

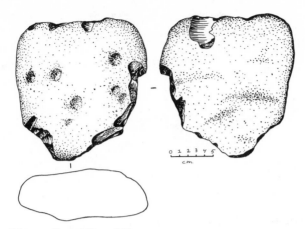

Figure 1. Chopper from Filimoshki

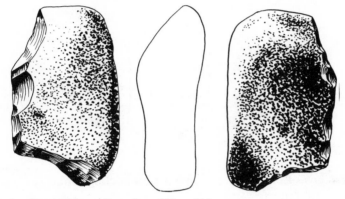

Figure 2. Scraper-like artifacts from Filimoshki

when the river carried a mass of sand and slime particles; little valleys which are extremely rare in the upper and middle reaches of the river were quickly filled with loose deposits. This is convincingly evidenced by thin slimy bands which may be traced up almost to the very top as well as by oxbow lakes on all the three sites where chipped pebbles occur. The situation on the Zeya is similar to that on the Amur and in the area of Kumary. In the dry season, when the water level was low, pebbles in the riverbed were exposed and ancient man came to the river valley to make his tools.

All the sites indicated above yielded identical forms of stone tools with choppers being the predominant type (Figures 1, 4, and 6). Some of the tools have edges fifteen centimeters wide and up to twenty-five centimeters long. These were chipped almost at a right angle (70°–90°). The working end is not retouched. All the tools have massive backs

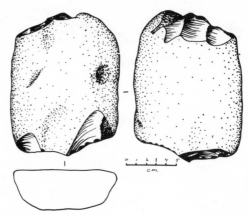

Figure 3.   Nucleus from Filimoshki

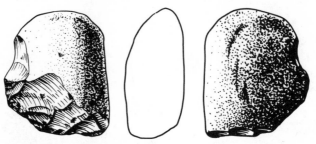

Figure 4.   Chopper from Kumary I

with no signs of chipping for convenient handling. Some tools weigh up to five kilograms.

Next come the scrapers (Figure 2). They are made of less massive pebbles and their working edge runs lengthwise and not along the narrow end. The edge is chipped, just as in the case of choppers, by massive strikes without secondary working. Typologically and technically the scrapers have much in common with choppers but have steeper edges (50°–70°).

There are also handaxes of chopping-tool type chipped to an edge on both sides at one end. But these are few in number. Beaked scrapers make up a distinctive group of artifacts (Figure 5). They were made from pebbles which were chipped on one side in such a way as to form in the middle a pointed projection up to two centimeters long. All the sites on the Amur River yielded pebbles from which crude flakes were chipped at a right angle on an unprepared striking platform. All the pebble tools found on the Amur are archaic in form and primitive in manufacture technique.

The pebble-tool industry of the Amur and Zeya is among the

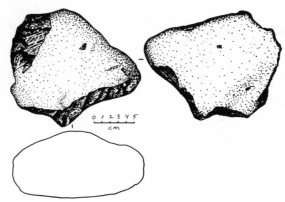

Figure 5.   Beaked implement from Kumary I

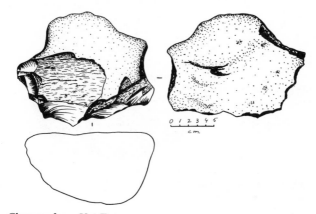

Figure 6.   Chopper from Ust-Tu

earliest in man's history, both typologically and technically. None of the sites has the definite stable forms of stone artifacts characteristic of the Upper Paleolithic. This is apparently a very ancient stage in the evolution of stone-working technique and hence in the history of man himself. This is shown not only by the technique of stone-tool manufacture but also by places where the pebbles tools occur. All the previous Paleolithic finds in the neighboring regions of Siberia and Mongolia were made in loess-like and sandy loam, which resembled the slimy sand and sand loam of Filimoshki without its underlying pebble bed. Hence, according to the places where they occur, the pebble tools from Filimoshki, Kumary, and the Ust-Tu are older than all the known Upper Paleolithic remains of East Siberia.

It is very difficult so far to date the pebble beds which yielded crude implements on the Zeya because we have insufficient knowledge of the history of formation of the surface shape in the area in the

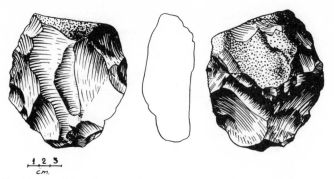

Figure 7.   Nucleus from Kumary II

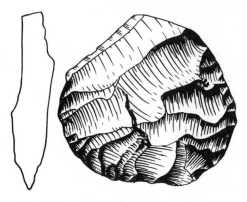

Figure 8.   Nucleus from Tambovka

Anthropogenic period. We can only set out some general considerations. The fluvial pebble bed which contained the tools must evidently be similar to the redeposited pebble-gravel-sand deposits of the Byelogorsk Suite and conditions of alluvium facies (*Geologija...* 1962).

The upper Lower Quaternary fluvial pebble beds of the Byelogorsk Suite were down-cut only in the first half of the Middle Pleistocene. The pebble tool assemblages in Filimoshki, on the Ust-Tu River, and in Kumary may be placed in this period. The places where these chipped pebble tools occur give grounds for assuming that they lie in redeposited horizons of Lower Quaternary deposits and that this process evidently could not take place later than the first half of the Middle Pleistocene.

The hypothesis on man's appearance in the Amur basin as early as the first half of the Middle Pleistocene naturally encounters many objections because not so long ago the most ancient remains of man and his culture in regions closest to Siberia and the Far East were those found in Choukoutien, North China.

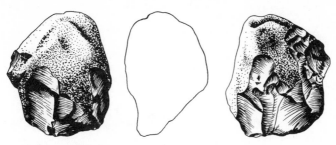

Figure 9.   Nuclear cutting implement from Osinovka

Figure 10.   Disc-like nucleus from Osinovka

Could ancient man, in the natural, geographic, and historical conditions prevailing at that time in eastern, southeastern, and central Asia, penetrate as far to the north as up to the Amur?

Three horizons corresponding to three climatic periods are now recognized in the Amur-Zeya depression (Miachina 1961). The lowest horizon, which is placed chronologically in the Eopleistocene, has been found to contain the pollen of conifers with a considerable addition of the pollen of deciduous species from the catkin group. But alongside these representatives of the temperate climate there are often fair amounts of the pollen of warmth-loving subtropical plants such as caria and magnolia. Mixed forests consisting of coniferous and deciduous species were growing at that time in the Amur-Zeya depression. The conifers were represented by pine which grew together with spruce and hemlock, while alder and birch were dominant among the deciduous species. There were also nut tree, hickory, oak, beech, hornbeam, elm, maple, linden, and hazel nut, with evergreen and subtropical plants growing in the underwood. The forests in the Maritime area, which at that time were mixed, included relics of Tertiary fauna.

In the Lower Quaternary and Middle Quaternary periods, the climate throughout the territory of the Far East grew colder, which caused some change of flora, particularly in the north of the Far East. But this was, however, not a sharp and catastrophic change of climate that could induce a profound alteration of vegetation in the area in the Lower Quaternary period.

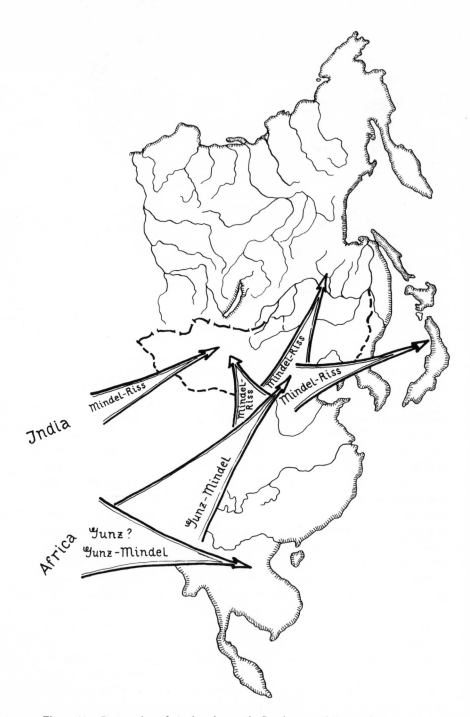

Figure 11.   Penetration of *Archanthropus* in Southeast and East Asia

The Early Quaternary glaciation even in the mountain systems in the northeast of the Soviet Union is considered problematic by certain scientists (Giterman and Golubeva 1965) while a majority of researchers point directly to the Middle Quaternary glaciation as the first and maximum ice in the area (Ganeshin 1959).

It should be noted that throughout the Quaternary period, the fauna and flora of the Far East as a whole underwent rhythmic changes exhibiting a certain tendency. These changes bore many features of local specificity (Eroshenko and Aleksandrova 1968). Throughout the Quaternary period, the vegetation and the fauna of the area retained many relics of earlier ages. As distinct from northwestern Eurasia, which was deeply affected by catastrophic changes of climate, the Far East experienced little change in natural conditions in the Anthropogene. A majority of researchers explain the difference by the surface glaciation of the northwest and its absence in the Far East (Markov et al. 1965). The climate in the Amur region and the Maritime Territory was still comparatively warm and humid in the Lower Quaternary and the early Middle Quaternary periods. So, climatic conditions in the Amur basin and the Maritime Territory were quite favorable in the Pleistocene; man could easily live there in the Lower and Middle Paleolithic. The Middle Quaternary Aldan (Riss) glaciation, which was maximum ice for the area, had a considerable effect on the formation of the flora and fauna in the Far East as a whole. The spore-and-pollen spectra of deposits synchronous with glaciation periods point to a considerable presence of birch forests and open woodlands in the vegetative cover. Large areas were occupied by moss and sphagnum bogs with shrubby birch and alder growing on them. It is noteworthy that there were no catastrophic changes in fauna and flora there even during the glacial epoch; this is apparently due to maritime climate. The presence of a great number of Tertiary relics in the present-day flora of the Maritime Territory, Amur region, and Sakhalin indicates that they survived glacial epochs in more favorable habitats with their area shrinking greatly during glacial times and expanding during interglacial periods (Giterman and Golubeva 1965: 368).

The milder climate there during glacial times seems to account for the fact that the present-day flora in the Amur and Ussuri taiga includes such ancient subtropical plants as cork, Manchurian nut tree, Virginia creeper and shizandra, ginseng, and aralia.

Natural conditions for man's settlement in the south of the Far East were most favorable early in the Middle Pleistocene or the Mindel-Riss Interglacial period according to the European scheme.

A comparison between palynological spectra from Choukoutien and the Zeya-Bureya Depression shows that North China and the Amur Region had similar vegetation in the first half of the Middle

Pleistocene. Among the arboreal plants were spruce, pine, birch, and linden; among the grasses were arrow-grass, sedge, gramineous and orach grasses. Both the specific composition and the percentage of each species can be correlated. This shows that natural conditions in the Amur region and northern China where Peking man lived were almost identical in the first half of the Middle Pleistocene. It is significant that the finds of *Elephas trogontherii* Polh, which is identical to *Elephas namadicus* Falconer and Cautley from Choukoutien deposits, are assignable to Maximum Aldan Glaciation in the south of the Soviet Far East (second half of the Middle Pleistocene). It seems logical to assume that in later periods, too, the two areas did not differ much from each other in natural conditions.

The Amur basin lies about 1,500 kilometers from Choukoutien. But since the movement to the north was a slow one, primitive man could naturally cover such a distance only in the course of thousands of years, given favorable natural conditions. The earlier belief that Lower Paleolithic man inhabited chiefly tropical and subtropical regions is quite wrong. In the time of the early Peking man northern China had a colder climate than today.

The fact that Peking man or other related species continued to live in northern China in the period of maximum ice testifies to great potentialities of our remote ancestors. Man at that time was no longer a passive being fully dependent on his environment. He was successfully making the first attempts to make nature serve his needs. He settled in new areas further to the north and adapted himself to changing ecological conditions as the climate grew colder instead of moving to the south where conditions were more favorable.

It was evidently by chance and in small numbers that man penetrated to northern areas such as the Amur region.

The similarity of stone tools found in the basins of the Zeya, Amur, and Choukoutien I indicates that man from northern China settled in the Amur region in the Mindel-Riss period (according to the European scheme).

The ancient assemblages of northern China – K'oho, Lantian, and Choukoutien I – are characterized by distinctive pebble tool traditions; choppers, chopping tools, and pebble cores. The presence of less specialized implements in the Amur, compared with the finds in northern China, is to be explained not by their being older but, more likely, by the mode of occurrence: the pebbles were repeatedly washed by water and a great number of smaller objects and flakes were carried away by the stream.

Man apparently came to the Amur region from East Asia before the maximum Aldan (Riss) Glaciation in this area, some 300,000 to 200,000 years ago.

The discovery of prehistoric occupation sites and camps in Central Asia (Okladnikov) and other regions of Asia, including the Japanese islands (Serizawa and Nakagawa 1965; Sato, Kobayashi, and Sakaguchi 1962), provided fresh evidence in support of the theory on the possibility of man's penetration to the north at such an early time.

In Central Asia, a Soviet-Mongolian expedition led by Okladnikov discovered Lower Paleolithic complexes of pebble tools (in the area of the town of Sain-Shand, near Mandakh settlement) and handaxes (Mount Yarkh, sixty-three kilometers from the Ghurban-Saikhan settlement). On Mount Yarkh the expedition discovered a profusion of bifacial tools, not just individual artifacts of this type, which points to the presence of a well-developed bifacial-tool manufacture technique close to the Madras tradition of India and the Abbevillian tradition of the European-African region. These two traditions in tool manufacture occur in pure, unmixed form in Central Asia; it is only later, in the Acheulian-Mousterian time, that a merger of the pebble-tool technique and Levalloisian tradition occurs in Mongolia.

The discovery of a well-stratified site with traces of fauna near the city of Gorno-Altaisk (Altai), datable to the late Riss Glacial, opens up new prospects before archaeologists in the search for such tools in south Siberia (Okladnikov 1970).

The newly discovered Lower Paleolithic complexes in East and Central Asia are classed typologically and by tool manufacture technique with pebble tool cultures. It was evidently in the Günz-Mindel time or even earlier that *Archanthropus* penetrated to southeast Asia from Africa and, in the subsequent periods, became distributed in Eastern and Central Asia in territories which later separated from the mainland (the Japanese Islands) as a result of a rise of sea level, as well as in the south of the Soviet Far East.

To validate more thoroughly the hypothesis of such an early penetration of man to central Asia, Siberia, and the Far East, new sites will have to be discovered and the known ones will have to be studied in greater detail. But even at this stage, available facts give us grounds to claim that man first appeared in the south of the Soviet Far East in an unexpectedly early period – in the first half of the Middle Pleistocene.

The discovery of early Paleolithic complexes in Central Asia, Siberia, and the Far East allows a new approach to be taken to such a problem as the peopling of America. It is quite possible that the New World was first inhabited not by *Homo sapiens* but by a more ancient being in the Paleoanthropus stage who already possessed pronounced features of *Homo sapiens*.

Further investigations in the south of the Far East and in Siberia will help shed more light on the problem of the populating of the northern regions of Asia by ancient man and the place held by these regions in the general process of man's evolution.

REFERENCES

BREUIL, H.
1925   Pierre taillée présumée paléolithique de Skotovo (Sibérie Orientale). *L'Anthropologie* 3–4.
DEREVIANKO, A. P.
1970   *Novopetrovskaja kul'tura Srednego Amura* [The Novopetrovsk culture of the Middle Amur]. Novosibirsk.
ELISEEV, A. V.
1890   Otchët o poezdke na Dal'nij Vostok [Account of a journey to the Far East]. *Izvestija Russkogo Geograficheskogo Obshchestva* 26.
EROSHENKO, N. V., A. N. ALEKSANDROVA
1968   "Stratigrafija chetvertichnykh otlozhenij Dal'nego Vostoka i ikh korreljatsija [Stratigraphy of Quaternary deposits in the Far East and their correlation]," in *Problemy izuchenija chetvertichnogo perioda*. Khabarovsk.
GANESHIN, G. S.
1959   Chetvertichnoe oledenenie Sikhote-Alinja [Quaternary glaciation of Sikhote-Alin]. *Materialy VSEGEI*, vyp. 27; *Materialy po chetvertichnoj geologii i neomorfologii SSSR* 2.
Geologija i inzhenernaja geologija Verkhnego Amura
1962   [Geology and geological engineering of the Upper Amur]. Izdatel'stvo MGU.
GITERMAN, R. E., L. V. GOLUBEVA
1965   Isoroja razvitija rastitel'nosti Vostochnoj Sibiri v antropogene [History of the development of the flora of East Siberia in anthropogenesis] *Osnovnye problemy izuchenija chetvertichnogo perioda*. Moscow.
KURTEN, B., Y. VASARI
1960   On the data of Peking Man. *Soc. Scientarium Fennica Comment. Biol.* 23 (7).
MARKOV, K. K., G. I. LAZUKOV, V. A. NIKOLAEV
1965   *Chetvertichnyj period* [The Quaternary period]. Izdatel'stvo MGU.
MIACHINA, A. I.
1961   K voprosu o granitse tretichnykh i chetvertichnykh otlozhenij Amuro-Zejskoj depressii [On the question of the boundary of Tertiary and Quaternary deposits in the Amur-Zeya depression]. *Materialy Vsesojuznogo soveshchanija po izucheniju chetvertichnogo perioda* 3: 307–308.
NIKOL'SKAJA, V. V.
1951   O nakhozhdenii kostej trogonterievogo slona v chetvertichnykh otlozhenijakh juga sovetskogo Dal'nego Vostoka [On the discovery of bones of *Elephas trogontherii* in Quaternary deposits of the southern Soviet Far East]. *Problemy fizicheskoj geografii*. Institut geografii, vyp. 17.

OKLADNIKOV, A. P.
1959   *Dalëkoe proshloe Primor'ja* [Distant past of the Maritime Territory].
       Vladivostok: Publishing House of the Maritime Region.
1964   O pervonachal'nom zaselenii chelovekom Sibiri i novykh nakhod-
       kakh paleolita na reke Zee [On man's original settlement of Siberia
       and new finds from the Paleolithic on the Zeya River]. *VII Mezh-
       dunarodnyj kongress antropologicheskikh i etnograficheskikh nauk.*
       Moscow.
1970   "Ulalinka – drevnejshee paleoliticheskoe mestonakhozhdenie Sibiri
       [Ulalinka – the oldest Paleolithic site in Siberia]," in *Arkheologi-
       cheskie otkrytija 1969 goda.* Moscow.
n.d.   *Pervobytnaja Mongolija* [Primitive Mongolia].
SATO, T., T. KOBAYASHI, Y. SAKAGUCHI
1962   The Lower Palaeolithic implements from Nyu, Oita Prefecture – a
       preliminary report. *Journal of the Archaeological Society of Nippon*
       47 (4): 293–311.
SERIZAWA, CH., H. NAKAGAWA
1965   "New evidence for the Lower Palaeolithic from Japan: a preliminary
       report on the Sozudai site, Kyushu," in *Mescelánea en homenaje al
       Abate Henri Breuil.* Edited by E. Ripoll Perelló, vol. 2, pp. 363–371.
       Barcelona: Diputación Provincial de Barcelona, Instituto de Pre-
       historia y Arqueología.

The Paleolithic of Mongolia

A. P. OKLADNIKOV

Central Asia comprises a large part of the Asian continent, with its southern borders delineated by the Himalayas and its northern borders defined by the Vitimo-Patomskiy and Sayan uplands. This territory, known nowadays for its severe continental climate and its abundance of steppes and deserts, including mountain deserts, has long attracted scholars who wished to determine the place of central Asia in the ancient history of mankind and the role it played in the development of man and his dispersion over our planet.

As far back as 1900, Osborn put forward some ideas that provided a theoretical foundation for a new, Central Asian hypothesis of the original homeland of man. Nevertheless, for quite some time no reliable documentary evidence was found that would incontrovertibly prove that the original Paleolithic man had sprung from this area. Even special research, such as that of Andrews' Central Asia–United States expedition and Sven-Hedin's Chinese–Swedish expedition, failed to find any material that would prove this assumption. If evidence was found, it has remained unpublished and inaccessible to scientific analysis, as is the case with the huge collections of the Andrews expedition.

Nelson, the Andrews expedition archaeologist, summarized the enormous quantity of material collected by the Americans in this way: "I have found nothing; anyway nothing that would correspond by type to the West European Lower Paleolithic." He finally came to the following conclusion about the importance of the Mongolian archaeological finds for the theory of the central Asian original homeland of man: "There is definitely no ground to the argument that East Central Asia had been close to the original focus [where the hominids emerged] or to the centre of cultural dispersion."[1] This came at a time when a number of leading scholars accepted Central Asia as the most probable "original homeland" of man.

The first specially oriented search for the remains of Paleolithic culture over the territory of Central Asia that culminated in a measure of success was carried out in 1949 by this author, who was assisted on behalf of the Mongolian party by Ser-Ojav (then a student at Moscow University), and which was initiated by Kisselyov, an eminent scholar in Siberian and Mongolian archaeology. The special Paleolithic group of the Soviet–Mongolian expedition, comprising Okladnikov and Ser-Ojav, made several trips: in the west of Mongolia along the banks of the River Orkhon in the vicinity of Kharakhorin (Erdeni-Dzu); east of Ulan-Bator all the way to Choibalsan and further east up to the River Khalkhin-Gol. In the south of the country in the vicinity of Dalan-Dzagagad we studied the famous Neolithic settlements of "The Flaming Cliffs" (Baindzak, or Shabarak-Ussu according to American scholars). These expeditions resulted in numerous finds related to the Stone Age, both Neolithic and Paleolithic. From among the Neolithic cultural materials, mention should be made of such important settlements as Tamtsak-Bulak in the eastern part of the Mongolian People's Republic as well as a number of settlements abounding in rich finds in the River Kerulen basin at the town of Choibalsan.

As for the Paleolithic, the most significant finds were those in the multilayered settlement of Moiltyn-am [Bird-Cherry Valley], found in 1949 on the left bank of the River Orkhon opposite the town of Kharakhorin. A series of Paleolithic settlements was found also in 1949 on the banks of the River Tola in the immediate vicinity of Ulan-Bator and on the northern slopes of the holy Mount Bogdoul. At the same time a very interesting Upper Paleolithic find was made 126 kilometers from Ulan-Bator on the road to Kyakhta, at what is now the vicinity of the town of Darkhan.[2] No less interesting was a remarkable find on the left bank of the River Khalkhin-Gol at Mount Khere-ul which yielded an excellent collection of stones including "Gobi cores."

Commencing in 1960 and continuing later in cooperation with the archaeologists of the Academy of Sciences of the Mongolian People's Republic, we furthered our efforts in the search for and partial excavation of the Paleolithic finds on the territory of Mongolia. During two field seasons, Troitskij, a geologist specializing in the Quaternary

[1]   The review of theories on the Central Asian original homeland of man derives from the works of M. F. Nesturkh (1964).
[2]   See the general review of the results of the Soviet-Mongolian archaeological expedition in Okladnikov (1964a: 3–23).

period, took part in the work along with the archaeologists (Okladnikov and Troitskij 1967: 4–30). These expeditions resulted in an
extensive amount of new material placed in charge of the Institute
of History of the Academy of Sciences of the Mongolian People's
Republic. Thorough analysis of this material collected in the south,
west, and east of the Mongolian People's Republic gives an idea about
the general outline of Mongolia's ancient past, including its Stone Age
culture and its relationships with the cultures of neighboring and more
distant territories of the Asian continent.

At present, not only can we assert the presence of Paleolithic sites
in Central Asia, but we are also in a position to trace its history
beginning with very early and archaic materials from the pre-Upper
Paleolithic period. Of special interest in this respect are the finds of
primitive pebble implements in 1969 and 1970 in the eastern part of
Mongolia, in the vicinity of the town of Sain-Shand and west of it.
These artifacts, extremely archaic and very similar to the most ancient
pebble implements found in Africa and western Europe, are associated
with gravels in vast basins which had possibly been covered by lakes.
Such gravels form what is known in Siberia as *manes*, that is, residual
outcroppings of obscure origin. Among the worked pebbles, almost
exclusively quartz or quartzite, there are split blank pebbles having
one or two dents on a side, as well as pebbles with crudely cross-cut
blade-choppers.

There are also chopping tools which have been bifacially worked
in such manner as to form a sharpened tip resembling the handaxe
tip of a Chelles type. These implements may be called proto-handaxes.
There are two well-defined places with finds of this sort in the vicinity
of Sain-Shand west of the town. In all probability there are other
similar sites of the same age and answering the same geomorphological
description in this area.

In 1971 in Somon Huld, while investigating the territory between
the Gurban-Saikhan mountains and Lake Khara-Us-Nur west of the
town of Dalan-Dzagagad, we again found ancient gravels and flaked
pebbles similar to those found in the Sain-Shand area. There are
reasons to believe that such an ancient pebble industry will be found
south and west of the places mentioned. In 1948 a prospecting party
of Mongolian and Polish geologists found in the Gobi-Altai area, not
far from Dalan-Dzagagad, what they referred to as "proto-handaxes";
it is likely that what they uncovered, in fact, were primitive pebble
implements close to those in question. We, too, found similar artifacts
in the west of Mongolia in the area of Bayab-Ulga and Kobdo-
Zhargalant, including split pebbles, choppers, and chopping tools
often covered with desert varnish or patina, testifying to their great
age. All these implements have been found on the surface, yet the

manifestly archaic manner of stone working and equally archaic forms of tools are evidence of their antiquity.

Of particular importance in this connection are the similar finds made in a specific stratigraphic situation in the Altai mountains, not far from the town of Gorno-Altaisk. Here we found two sites containing primitive pebble tools: Ulalinka and Kizil-Ozek [the River Maima]. Stratigraphically, these sites with pebble tools are the oldest in northern Asia. Thus, according to the geologists who investigated these monuments with us, they date back at least to the end of the Middle Pleistocene or possibly the Lower Pleistocene. A similar pebble industry is found in the Soviet Far East at Filimoshki and Ust-Tu on the River Zeya and Kumary on the left bank of the Amur. There also exists one more very ancient site with pebble tools on the River Amghuni below the Polina Osipenko settlement (Okladnikov 1964b: 251–257; Okladnikov and Derevianko 1968, 1969: 114).

It follows then that the pebble industry and pebble technique were widely represented over a vast expanse of Asia in the Paleolithic, and even before the Upper Pleistocene. This consideration is especially important now that we know of generally analogous assemblages of the pebble-tool culture not only in northern Asia, but also in south-eastern Asia, in various areas of Indochina, in Thailand, and particularly in eastern Cambodia. Characteristically, pebble tools are found here too; among them we find specific tools with a tip similar to those found in Ulalinka in the Altai area, in the sites of Filimoshki and Ust-Tu in the Zeya basin, or in the Kumary site on the Amur.

The problem of the Lower Paleolithic pebble culture in these vast areas of Asia is all the more important because it is connected with the place of the pebble industry in the subsequent development and with the further fate of the ancient population of this section of the world. Specifically, we mean that certain features of a characteristic pebble-tool technique of stone working can be traced in later epochs as well. Moreover, the Upper Paleolithic of Siberia and Mongolia was marked by a genuine upsurge of this technique, which is evidenced by extensive series of pebble tools and core blanks in such well-known settlements as Afontova Gora on the Yenisei, Verkholenskaya Gora on the Angara, or Nyanga on the River Selenga. It follows then that, in certain groups of the local population, the pebble-tool tradition was stable and continuous from the Lower and Middle Paleolithic up to the end of the Upper Paleolithic, i.e. through hundreds of millennia.

Another serious point is that this pebble-tool technique is genetically associated with the Levallois technique of flake production known in the Upper Paleolithic of Siberia (including Cape Canny on the River Udhe in the Selenga basin), the Altai and Mongolia (Moiltyn-am on the Orkhon; Zaisan-Tologoi, Aeroport, and other sites on the River Tola close to Ulan-Bator). The finds of an archaic pebble-tool culture in the Soviet Altai, and the fact that pebble tools constitute an important component of each Paleolithic industry in Siberia (not excepting Mal'ta and Buret) have prepared us somewhat for the discovery of pebble-tool industry sites in Central Asia, in the east of the Mongolian People's Republic. We were taken unaware, however, when a Lower Paleolithic workshop, enormous in area and abounding in finds, was discovered in 1970 in the eastern part of Mongolia, west of Sain-Shand, between Saik-han-Dulan and Ghurban-Saikhan, near Mount Yarkh. This workshop is connected with siliceous bedrock (in this case yellow, jasper-like rock) rather than gravels, a typical phenomenon for Mongolia and partly for Soviet Central Asia (Kapchigai and Okhna in Fergana valley, Uch-Tuch in the lower reaches of the Zeravshan).

This workshop presents excellent specimens of Acheulian-type tools, drastically different in typology and technique of production from the pebble tools, i.e. choppers, chopping tools and proto-handaxes. Handaxes of the classical shapes are oval (limands) and subtriangular. There are also simple cores found here, as a rule with one striking platform. They can be labeled proto-Levalloisian as they lack the characteristic marginal trimming of the long edges. Subtriangular or triangular cores are not found. The "wastes" of the stone tool production are absolutely dominated by flakes, mostly solid and subtriangular ones. But there also occur, though comparatively rarely, Levalloisian blades which are elongated-triangular in outline, without retouching of the striking platform. Marginal flakes from cores are also found.

It should be noted that in terms of the typological expressiveness of shapes of the Acheulian type, let alone their number, this site is not comparable with such sites as Tingts'un in China. There, according to some authors, "handaxes" of Western shape are found, but in our opinion Tingts'un is a peculiar phenomenon which cannot be fitted in with Western typology; it contains no handaxes or points of a Western nature. In the case of our workshop, however, there are reasons to believe that not only the Acheulian technique but its carriers had penetrated from the areas of the classic Abbevillian and Acheulian cultures of Afro-European origin to the central regions of Asia. Thus, a new problem arises concerning the development of the ancient technique of tool-making in two cultural traditions: the east and the north of the Asian continent.

The first tradition, most definitely manifest in the finds of such settlements as Ulalinka and Kizil-Ozek in the mountainous Altai area, is represented by pebble tools and is indigenous to these areas. As has been pointed out, this tradition existed here at a much later period, too, in the subsequent Upper Paleolithic epoch.

The second tradition may be labeled Acheulian. Apparently its origin can be traced to those areas of the Old World where the corresponding technique of production of bifacially worked tools of the Abbevillian-Acheulian type had developed from time immemorial. In all likelihood, this technique was brought to Central Asia by a group of archanthropes who penetrated deep to the east at the most favorable interglacial time, most probably the Riss and pre-Riss stages.

This group of western migrants was moving through sparsely populated, though definitely not empty, territories which abounded in game. It is believed that the aborigines of these vast tracts of land were precisely the same as the bearers of the indigenously Asian pebble-tool technique who had left their traces in the mountainous areas of the Altai in Ulalinka and farther east – in the Amur basin, in Filimoshki, Kumary, and Ust-Tu.

Hence, there took place a disordered and spontaneous displacement of "atoms" – prehistoric communities, human groups that followed their game, rather than a process of resettlement of large and compact masses of ancient populations. Each such group had its own peculiar technical tradition inherited from its ancestors: in some cases these were the traditions of the East Asian pebble-tool technique; in other cases, more rare and exceptional, the human groups carried the Abbeville or Acheulian traditions.

As regards the subsequent Middle Paleolithic epoch, we found a scant number of important implements with similar characteristics around Bogd-Somon (Gobi-Altai) as well as three sites in eastern Mongolia, on the road from Barun-Oort to Sain-Shand. These are elongated-triangular blades made mostly from heavy, deeply patined flint with a thick white patina, similar to those which are characteristic of the Mousterian culture of Soviet Central Asia, including the upper layers of Teshik-Tash and Obi-Rakhmat.

The remarkable assemblages, such as the settlements in the vicinity of Otson-Mant in the south of the Mongolian People's Republic as well as similar sites which we found in the west of Mongolia, are connected with the Bogd-Somon finds but in all probability must be referred to the next stage of Mongolia's Middle Paleolithic. These are characterized by cores in the Levalloisian fashion, including triangular ones, and also Levalloisian blades corresponding to these cores. By the period and character of the finds, these Mongolian assemblages come close to the Ust-Kanskaia Cave in the Altai and also to its analog – Strashnaya Cave which was recently found and partly excavated in the very same Altai in the Tighirek mountains. The Levallois technique of flake production is clearly evidenced by the finds in these Altai caves.

It can therefore be asserted that there was a common element in the development of the most ancient population of this part of our planet, in what is now Soviet Central Asia, Mongolia, and the Altai, which persisted through hundreds of millennia.

At this juncture we must mention that the Levalloisian materials of the interior of Asia are definitely related to the analogous materials of Soviet Central Asian Uzbekistan (for instance, Khodjikent grotto near Tashkent) and Tajikistan, and, via these to the Near and Middle East, especially Iran and Palestine (the caves on Mount Carmel, and Bisitun in Iran) (Okladnikov 1949; 1961: 68–76).

The history of development of the Upper Paleolithic culture of Mongolia is most vividly illustrated by the multilayer settlement of Moiltyn-am in the River Orkhon basin. The lower cultural layers of this site feature clearly defined Levalloisian cores, blades, and also individual finds of Aurignacian and Solutrean end-scrapers with radial retouching. Also found are choppers and points of the "Mousterian type." Eventually, the Moiltyn-am layers start exhibiting crude implements of the "Gobi-core" type (wedge-shaped cores, core-scrapers, etc.). These core-like tools then acquire a more regular form, diminish in size, and become the most characteristic element in the stone industry. The upper layers of Moiltyn-am also contain rather numerous pebble choppers. Characteristically, Moiltyn-am, like most other Paleolithic settlements of Mongolia, contains no semilunar, straight-margined, and notched pebble scrapers, so typical of Siberian finds and imparting so peculiar a character to the stone industry of the Siberian Upper Paleolithic (Afontova Gora, Oshurkovo, and the like) (Okladnikov and Troitskij 1967).

As shown by observations in the River Tola basin as well as on the Orkhon (Moiltyn-am), the Upper Paleolithic Mongolian settlements in question are connected with the blanket deposits of the second terrace, labeled as the Sanginskaya terrace in the Tola basin by Troitskij. This terrace has two levels: an upper level at fifteen to seventeen meters, and a lower one at twelve to thirteen meters. The Paleolithic remains are found in the upper level of the terrace. Apparently these remains date from a time when Mongolia had a more humid and milder climate than now, as is evidenced by the geography of Paleolithic settlements which are found in what are now arid places, far from large rivers or lakes. In the subsequent period, the country became progressively more and more arid, so that in the period immediately following the Mongolian Upper Paleolithic in the Tola and Orkhon basins settlements arose which are associated with the river terraces of the lower level, as shown by our investigations performed in cooperation with Troitskij. At this level there is an abundance of chopper-like pebble tools and pebble cores. In the Orkhon area we have also found bifacially worked leaf-shaped cleavers. The last ones resemble the leaf-shaped Solutrean knives or points of Verkholenskaya Gora and Ushkanka on the Angara, of the upper layer of Ustinovka on the River Tadshi in the Primorye area, and in the preceramic settlements of the Japanese Isles.

On the whole, the archaeological materials found on the terraces of the lower level may be associated with a transitional period which marked Mongolia's passage from the Paleolithic to the subsequent Neolithic. By analogy with the corresponding European materials, they can be referred to as Mesolithic or epi-Paleolithic.

Particular mention should be made of the small stone implements including toothed or notch-toothed scrapers found in the western part of Mongolia and closely resembling the finds of the upper layer of the River Kouyum settlement in the Altai. These probably represent a specific version of the Mesolithic culture spreading through the Altai, Western Mongolia, and Northern Kazakhstan.

This is the picture of the development of ancient preceramic cultures of Central Asia as it emerges in the light of many years of joint research of Soviet and Mongolian scholars. It is clear that this picture is far more complicated and far richer in events than could have been supposed earlier. At this stage it is obvious that there could be no single "Siberian–Chinese" Paleolithic province, as Zamyatnin suggested, basing his hypothesis on the knowledge available in the 1930's. And yet, what happened here in the ancient Stone Age has a direct bearing on the history of Paleolithic man and his culture in both neighboring and distant territories.

REFERENCES

NESTURKH, M. F.
  1964 *Problema pervonachal'noj prarodiny chelovechestva. U istokov chelovechestva* [The problem of the original homeland of mankind. At the origins of mankind]. Moscow.
OKLADNIKOV, A. P.
  1949 Issledovanija must'erskoj stojanki i pogrebenija neandertal'tsa v grote Teshik-Tash Juzhnyk Uzbekistan (Srednjaja Azija) [Investigations of the Mousterian site and the burial of Neanderthal Man in the grotto of Teshik-Tash South Uzbekistan (Central Asia)]. *Teshik-Tash. Paleoliticheskij chelovek.* Moscow.
  1961 Khodzhikentskaja peshchera – novyj must'erskij pamjatnik Uzbekistana [Khodjikent cave – a new Mousterian monument of Uzbekistan]. *Kratkie soobshchenija Instituta arkheologii AN SSSR*, vyp. 82.
  1964a K voprosu o drevnejshej istorii Mongolii. Pervobytnaja Mongolija [On the question of the earliest history of Mongolia. Primitive Mongolia]. Ulan-Bator.
  1964b O pervonachal'nom zaselenii chelovekom Sibiri i novykh nakhodkakh paleolita na reke Zee [On man's original settlement of Siberia and new finds from the Paleolithic on the Zeya River]. *VII Mezh-*

dunarodnyj kongress antropologicheskikh i etnograficheskikh nauk. Moscow.

OKLADNIKOV, A. P., A. P. DEREVIANKO

1968   Paleolit Dal'nego Vostoka (tipologija i stratigrafija) [Paleolithic of the Far East (typology and stratigraphy)]. *Problemy izuchenija chetvertichnogo perioda. Tezisy.* Khabarovsk.

1969   Paleolit Amura [Paleolithic of the Amur]. *Izvestija SO AN SSSR, serija obshchestvennykh nauk,* vyp. 1.

OKLADNIKOV, A. P., S. L. TROITSKIJ

1967   K izucheniju chetvertichnykh otlozhenij i paleolita Mongolii [Toward the study of quaternary deposits and the paleolithic of Mongolia]. *Bjulleten' komissii po izucheniju chetvertichnogo perioda* 33.

1970   *VII Mezhdunarodnyj kongress antropologicheskikh i etnograficheskikh nauk* (MKAEN) 10 [VIIth International Congress of Anthropological and Ethnographic Sciences 10]. Moscow.

PART FOUR

New World Implications

An Approach to the Prehistory of the Far East, From Farther East

W. N. IRVING

The theoretical clamor arising from American archaeology these days and the large numbers of people engaged in making it suggest that one might be justified in hoping to make an interesting and perhaps worthwhile contribution to this conference on the Early Paleolithic in the Far East simply by enumerating the earliest cultures in the Americas and extrapolating them westward toward their presumed point of origin. Surely it must be a worthwhile exercise to postulate that the earliest American cultures are extensions from the Far East and then seek evidence for the validity of the postulate. In fact, this is very difficult to do.

Let me illustrate the difficulty by reviewing some of the fundamental questions of New World prehistory that have teased generations of scholars and, perhaps because they have gone unanswered for so long, now seem unanswerable.

American Indians and their ancestors for which we have skeletal evidence are most like Mongoloids. Logic and common sense tell us that they came originally from Asia by way of Bering Strait. But no one in recent times has proposed a particular Asian population as the ancestor of any American population except the Eskimo, so we must assume that the biological relationship, although real, is not sufficiently close or well understood to support other useful taxonomic or phylogenetic statements. There seems to be little justification for using our present biological knowledge to estimate a time and place in Asia from which the New World population came. This is consistent with the general impression that the earliest of our dated skeletal remains (e.g. Laguna Beach Man: see Berger et al. 1971) are not very different from the latest. My reading of the biological record leads me to think that it neither confirms nor refutes the hypotheses of multiple migrations into the New World. In short, the human biology of American Indians as it is known at present has little to tell us about Pleistocene populations (see also Laughlin [1967] who estimates some 15,000 years as the minimum time needed to produce observable genetic variation).

New World archaeological cultures of 11–12,000 years ago bear little obvious resemblance to any known Asian cultures of that, or any, age. Moreover, evidence for older New World cultures is sparse and but grudgingly accepted by many. But by and large, even those of us who do accept some of the older New World dates are hard put to describe the relationships of the associated cultures to Asian cultures. The reasons for these dilemmas are, in my view, primarily the dearth of material with which to work and our lack of experience in the New World with analytical techniques that can be used on such "Early Paleolithic" materials as I think we have here. Such techniques are developing, but few of us, in North America at least, are yet aware of them. Thus it is difficult to begin either with Clovis of 11–12,000 B.P., or with any older culture, and from this to extrapolate backward in time and eastward in geography to ancestral cultures in the Far East. This situation is about to change, but before I suggest how and why, I would like to review briefly some of the developments in recent years.

Not so long ago it was customary to attribute the earliest New World culture to some sort of Neolithic ancestor in the Far East, because Clovis and Folsom biface points, which were thought to be the oldest, could not be traced in any known Paleolithic ancestral form in Asia. Then Krieger (1962), Chard (1959), and Bryan (1965) hypothesized and vigorously defended an earlier stage than Clovis in the New World, with or without bifaces, from which Clovis developed. Chard for a time derived this stage from Movius' Lower Paleolithic of East Asia, and time may yet prove him right. More recently, on the one hand, America and the Far East have discovered blades and burins and, on the other, Europe and the Far East have discovered that Solutrean bifaces are not a freak of nature or culture, but just one example of a technological development that took place in many parts of the world. These developments have thrown American archaeologists into a tizzy, as anyone who follows our journals knows, and the confusion has elicited some rather startling statements about the New World from abroad.

When a scientist observes that some of his colleagues (and perhaps he himself) show signs of irrational behavior, he does not despair. If he is well disciplined, he looks about for evidence which is upsetting old paradigms and which might be used to erect new ones. With obeisance to Kuhn, whose terminology I have borrowed, and to

Kipling who said something similar for the nonscientist as well, I suggest that our convenor has hit the mark with the title of our conference on the "Early Paleolithic of East Asia"; the conventional meanings of the terms Lower, Middle, and Upper Paleolithic are not useful in the organization of data from the Far East, any more than they are useful in the New World. And in the New World we find that terms such as Paleo-Indian can be used to designate a field of study, but not a cultural phenomenon or event.

In an international conference it is especially important to strive for a common understanding of the significance of formal terms, so I shall pursue this matter further at the risk of appearing to be more of a nominalist than I am, before I consider the new evidence.

There is no evidence in the New World of a typologically recognizable Lower Paleolithic (whether one understands by this the Pebble Tool tradition or something else) that indicates an historical relationship with a specific, plausible Old World ancestral culture. And it is very difficult to perceive in well-documented New World collections anything that would pass for Middle Paleolithic in terms of typology. There are, indeed, some technological resemblances between Clovis and the Mousterian of eastern Europe, and these permit experts to say that a man with Mousterian technical training could have made most or all of the Clovis stone tools. Probably the same man could have made the biface from Wilson Butte Cave, Idaho, 14,500 years ago (Gruhn 1965) and the edge-retouched flake implements from Valsequillo, Mexico, some 21,000 years ago (Irwin-Williams 1977). But this is very different from saying that a Mousterian man in fact made these specimens. The "Mousterian" and the "Middle Paleolithic" are concepts that were defined in Europe, initially on the basis of typology and only secondarily on the basis of technology. To apply these concepts in remote areas such as the New World, using only technological criteria, is to obscure rather than to clarify the historical position of early New World cultures with respect to those of the Old World.

With this in mind I question the wisdom of using early bifaces in the New World to demonstrate a derivation of Clovis, for example, from some sort of East European Mousterian, or Mousteroid (Müller-Beck 1966; Chard 1969; and, less specifically, Bryan 1965). If we classify New World cultures in terms of the European sequence of technologies and types, we deny ourselves the opportunity to make full use of the Far Eastern evidence, which ought to be more relevant and more easily understood because it is geographically closer to the New World. A more philosophical reservation against this practice arises from its evolutionary implication: if the terms for major cultural stages devised in Europe can be applied in the Far East and the New

World, then we cannot expect to make significant discoveries bearing on the major features of cultural evolution in the New World or in the Far East. On this same basis I would issue caveats with respect to Müller-Beck's concept of "Aurignacoid" and Bandi's concept (1969) of Epi-Gravettian when they are applied to New World blade and burin industries. These may be world-wide cultural stages or developmental phenomena, and the authors I cite may perceive them accurately, but if so their definition is of paramount importance and it must take account of evidence from the Far East and the Beringian area that lies between Asia and North America. Until this has been done, it is rash to extrapolate these concepts into the Americas.

Of several attempts by Americanists to compare early or putatively early Alaskan collections with the Late Paleolithic of Siberia and Europe (e.g. Campbell 1963; Wilmsen 1964; Giddings 1949; and Mac-Neish 1964), each offers useful insights and guides to future research, but none shows a command of the Old World material that convinces me that they have identified an Asian or European ancestor for a New World culture. Perhaps Mochanov (1973) is on the right track with his suggestion that the Duktai culture is ancestral to the biface-point cultures of the New World, but this is hard to evaluate at present and it may not bear directly on problems of the Early Paleolithic.

By demolishing some of the most provocative current hypotheses about relationships between the Old World and the New during the Pleistocene – if in fact, this is what I have done – I have either given my intellectual landscape an unobstructed horizon or I have left it barren. In northern Yukon Territory when I first tried to cope with newly discovered cultures of Pleistocene age the outlook was bleak and the horizon obscure. We confronted evidence that apparently contradicts the hypotheses I have just criticized, and other evidence that does not conform with any hypothesis devised for northern regions. In general the evidence shows the presence of man in north-western North America between 25,000 and 30,000 years ago, with a sophisticated technology in which bone was the most common raw material used for implements (Irving and Harington 1973). We remain confident that our basic evidence for this is clear, unambiguous, and technically sound; if our confidence is well placed then this evidence may point to a way out of the dilemma it helps to create.

A very brief review of the evidence will clarify this optimistic statement. From along the Old Crow River, which runs through an intermontane basin in the unglaciated Beringian Refugium, a large quantity – perhaps 20,000 fossil vertebrate animal bones of Upper Pleistocene age have been collected by the National Museum of Canada, the University of Alaska, and the University of Toronto. They come from at least 114 collecting localities; prominent in the collections are *Mammuthus primigenius*, *Bison crassicornis*, and *Equus* sp., but at least a dozen other extinct forms of Upper Pleistocene age are present. In 1967 (Harington and Irving 1967) we reported that bones of the three named species showed definite evidence of modification by man, and in 1973 we described the material in more detail and reported radiocarbon dates on three implements of 25,000, 27,500, and 29,000 B.P. (Irving and Harington 1973). Our continuing study of the collections, and the technological studies of Robson Bonnichsen, confirm and elaborate our findings that man was responsible for the distinctive fractures on hundreds of bones from 20 or more of the collecting localities. Of special interest here is our observation that the bones of mammoth and possibly also horse and bison have been deliberately fractured in such a way as to produce flakes, which in our opinion were used as cutting implements. The single finished implement is a serrated scraper or flesher made on a tibia of *Rangifer tarandus*; it was dated to 27,500 B.P. and constitutes a special problem inasmuch as it shows technological refinement far beyond what we might expect at this date.

These large collections and our observations on them raise many questions, most of which we think will be answered in due course. But a point I wish to emphasize here is that we have found almost no stone implements that might be associated with the bones, and few or none on lookout sites that appear to be of similar age (Cinq-Mars and Irving, unpublished research). This apparent anomaly may well be not an anomaly at all: the extraordinary preservation of bone in the frozen ground along the Old Crow River may afford us a glimpse of a Paleolithic industry which we would not normally get in more temperate latitudes where preservation is not as good, and where the raw material for stone implements is easier to find.

This raises the specter that haunts every prehistorian, that of the culture that leaves behind no durable evidence of itself. But we have encountered this one before, in the Barren Grounds where the Caribou Eskimo left little but boulder tent rings to record their presence, and even in Old Crow Flats where the Vunta Kutchin have left just a few flakes for us to find. We ought therefore to be prepared already, psychologically if not methodologically, to cope with Pleistocene cultures in which stone implements are numerically unimportant. Others, for example Solheim (1972) and Menghin (1957) have said substantially the same thing in other parts of the world. My associates and I, having coerced our psyches, are now working on the methodology.

At the very least, these findings at Old Crow show that paleontological collections from Siberia and the New World that may be more than 20,000 years old should be studied systematically for evidence of human activity. Of course, it must be borne in mind that in the past collectors of vertebrate fossils have been inclined to leave behind broken fragments of long bones – which are just what the archae-ologist can use most effectively.

But for this conference and for the Early Paleolithic in the Far East, the primary present significance of our findings is that they do not fit neatly into any widely accepted model or paradigm. And this seems to be true also of Robert Fox's materials from Palawan and Luzon (this volume), and of Yoshizaki's from Lower Shukubai in Hokkaido (1974). The latter may well conform to the outlines presented by Serizawa (this volume) and Ikawa-Smith (this volume) inasmuch as it demonstrates the presence of an industry characterized by edge-retouched flakes at about 21,000 B.P. which was succeeded very soon thereafter by a blade and burin industry. The Philippine evidence for Middle and Upper Pleistocene implements that are edge-retouched flakes – as opposed to blade or core tools – is consistent with that from Japan, and perhaps also with Bartstra's attempt to revise the Patjitanian (this volume). On the basis of what we have seen and heard at Montreal it seems not unreasonable to hypothesize a late Far Eastern Early Paleolithic industry characterized by skillful production and use of flakes, but not of blades or burins, which began perhaps as early as Middle Pleistocene time and continued to be recognizable, for example in Japan, until long after the appearance of blade and burin industries.

From the foregoing, if such a late Far Eastern Early Paleolithic is a real historical phenomenon, the questions arise: What are its other characteristics and what contribution did it make to the later prehistory of the Far East, of the New World, and of, for example, Australia? Can it be seen as the source of the bone industry at Old Crow, and some or all of our early New World sites farther south? At this point it seems a far more promising candidate than any Paleolithic previously defined, however they may be named, for example the "Middle" or "Upper Paleolithic."

In any event, on the basis of North American evidence alone we should hypothesize Upper Pleistocene cultures in the Far East with the technical capability of specializing in flaked and carved bone implements. Additionally – and this is most important – they required the ability to cope with the northern coniferous forest. It seems to me that the northern forest with its deep snow and sparse resources must have been the most formidable obstacle to tropical and temperate adapted man expanding his territory toward Alaska and the New World.

We have learned recently that man got to Australia by boat and probably occupied the Boreal Forest and the Tropical Rain Forest at about the same time. I think that these events are related to one another. Perhaps when we understand them better they will be seen to mark the end of the Early Paleolithic in the Far East. They signify the attainment and spread of a level of technology that could be adapted to use in the most challenging environments.

REFERENCES

BANDI, HANS-GEORG
  1969 *Eskimo prehistory*. College, Alaska: University of Alaska Press.
BERGER, R. R., PROTSCH, R. REYNOLDS, C. ROZAIRE, J. A. SACKETT
  1971 New radiocarbon dates on bone collagen of California Indians. *Contributions of the University of California Archaeological Research Facility* 12: 43–49. Berkeley.
BRYAN, ALAN L.
  1965 *Paleo-American prehistory*. Occasional Papers of the Idaho State Museum 16. Pocatello.
CAMPBELL, JOHN M.
  1963 Ancient Alaska and Palaeolithic Europe. *University of Alaska Anthropological Papers* 10: 20–49.
CHARD, CHESTER S.
  1959 New World origins: a reappraisal. *Antiquity* 33: 44–48.
  1969 *Man in prehistory*. New York: McGraw-Hill.
GIDDINGS, JAMES L.
  1949 Early Flint Horizons on the north Bering Sea coast. *Journal of the Washington Academy of Science* 39 (3): 85–90.
GRUHN, RUTH
  1965 Two early radiocarbon dates from the lower levels of Wilson Butte Cave, south-central Idaho. *Tebiwa* 8 (2): 57.
HARINGTON, C. R., W. N. IRVING
  1967 "Some Upper Pleistocene middens near Old Crow, Yukon Territory." Paper presented at the annual meeting of the Society for American Archaeology, Ann Arbor, Michigan.
IRVING, W. N., C. R. HARINGTON
  1973 Upper Pleistocene radiocarbon-dated artefacts from the northern Yukon. *Science* 179: 335–340.
IRWIN-WILLIAMS, CYNTHIA
  1977 "Summary of archaeological evidence from the Valsequillo Region, Puebla, Mexico," in *Cultural continuity in Mesoamerica*. Edited by David L. Browman. World Anthropology. The Hague: Mouton.
KRIEGER, ALEX D.
  1962 The earliest cultures in the western United States. *American Antiquity* 28 (2): 138–144.
LAUGHLIN, W. S.
  1967 "Human migration and permanent occupation in the Bering Sea area," in *The Bering land bridge*. Edited by D. L. Hopkins, 409–450. Stanford: Stanford University Press.
MACNEISH, R. S.
  1964 Investigations in the southwest Yukon. *Robert S. Peabody Foundation for Archaeology Papers* 6: 201–488.

MENGHIN, O. F. A.
   1957   Das Protolithikum in Amerika. *Acta Prehistoria* 1: 5–40. Buenos
          Aires: Centro de Estudios Prehistoricos.
MOCHANOV, Y. A.
   1973   "Early migrations to America in the light of a study of the Duktai
          Paleolithic culture in northeast Asia." Paper presented at the
          IXth International Congress of Anthropological and Ethnological
          Sciences, Chicago.
MÜLLER-BECK, HANSJÜRGEN
   1966   Paleohunters in America: origins and diffusion. *Science* 152 (3726):
          1191–1210.
SOLHEIM, WILHELM G., II
   1972   An earlier agricultural revolution. *Scientific American* 226 (4): 34–41.
WILMSEN, EDWIN N.
   1964   Flake tools in the American Arctic: some speculations. *American
          Antiquity* 29 (3): 338–344.
YOSHIZAKI, MASAKAZU, *editor*
   1974   *Shukubai Sankakuyama chiten* [Sankakuyama locality, Shukubai].
          Chitose: Chitose Kyoiku Iinkai.

Comments on Irving's "Approach to the Prehistory of the Far East, From Farther East"

ALAN L. BRYAN

The comments here are addressed to the general paper regarding the status of research on early man in America. I must agree that there is currently no well-regarded, or at least accepted, theory to account for the early cultures as enumerated by Irving. I do believe that the core of an adequate explanatory theory exists in the literature (e.g. Chard 1959; Bryan 1965, 1973; Krieger 1964; Müller-Beck 1966; Wormington 1962); however, this theory, which will be outlined below, is in direct conflict with the theory of rapid immigration of "specialized big-game hunters" (e.g. Martin 1973). Unfortunately, as a result, the significant questions of when man first arrived in America and what he brought with him remain very much a matter of personal opinion. Hopefully, this state of flux and indecision will soon change, as Irving predicts; but it will not change until better-substantiated and better-dated remains of man before about 12,000 years ago are found in clearly defined stratigraphic contexts. In another paper (Bryan 1973) I have argued that the presence of several significantly different flaked-stone assemblages in America between 11,000 and 14,000 B.P. means that so-called "specialized big-game hunters," such as those who fashioned Clovis fluted or Fell's Cave fishtail projectile points, were not the original Americans as Martin (1973) and others have argued. Rather, the many distinctively different assemblages by 12,000 B.P. implies that a considerable amount of time must have elapsed for such differentiation to have occurred. A few of these assemblages will be mentioned here in my reply to Irving's provocative but, I feel, unnecessarily negative paper concerning the present status of theory and research on the problem of early man in America.

No one could disagree with Irving when he states that Amerindians are biologically most like Mongoloids, and that well-documented evidence for American man is amply demonstrated from about 12,000 B.P. to the present. It is also true that New World cultures bear little obvious resemblance to any known Asian cultures of any age, but it is necessary to add that archaeological assemblages older than about 12,000 years ago bear little obvious resemblance to any *specific* known Asian cultures of any age.[1]

The fact that diligent and prolonged search for such specific similarities between American and Asian assemblages has repeatedly resulted in failure is the key to the problem and to the conflict of opinion. The fact that *specific* similarities in total assemblages, though much sought after, have not been found is usually glossed over. Most significantly, no truly fluted point has ever been found anywhere in the Old World. The Clovis fluted-point assemblages or other early assemblages associated with big-game hunters in America are only generally similar to Eurasian Upper Paleolithic assemblages. That is, similarities can be found between general tool types, such as end scrapers or bifacial projectile points, but the total assemblages are always quite different. Nevertheless, many archaeologists have actively searched for fluted-point sites in Alaska with the implicit idea in mind that the Alaskan fluted points should be earlier than the established 11,500 B.P. dating for Clovis sites on and adjacent to the Great Plains. As long as people continue to think that Clovis hunters or their immediate ancestors must have come from Asia, the alternate possibility that Clovis fluted points developed somewhere in North America south of the Wisconsin ice sheet seems somehow unreasonable because of the disturbing implication that the technological (and therefore cultural) antecedents to fluted-point assemblages must already have been present for a long time somewhere in America. This implication is disturbing because there are no acceptable published reports of pre-Clovis occupation floors excavated under carefully controlled conditions, well dated, and in clear stratigraphic contexts.

---

[1]   Actually, of course, this statement is true for all of prehistoric time except for late Eskimo sites on both sides of the Bering Sea. It would seem that this fact alone would be sufficient for people to accept the concept of essentially independent cultural development in America, but as it is obvious that the ancestors of all Amerindians must have come from Asia sometime, the proposal that all of the presently verified "early man" assemblages developed indigenously has led some critics to state the ridiculous conclusion that such an hypothesis means that man and his culture evolved independently in America. No archaeologist would ever seriously propose such an idea. The basic hypothesis I have argued for a long time is that the immediate technological antecedents of all presently verified "early man" assemblages or cultures in America are to be found in America. Also, this hypothesis does not mean that no further contact was made with the Old World after initial colonization. Among others, the microblade tradition appears to have entered America from Asia about 10,000 B.P. The indigenous development hypothesis states simply that all the essential technological traditions for the independent development of "specialized big-game hunting" economies were available in America long before 12,000 B.P.

In my opinion, the major reason why this unfortunate situation has remained a fact for so long is because the majority of American archaeologists retain the limiting theoretical orientation that the earliest occupants of America must have been specialized big-game hunters with an "Upper Paleolithic"[2] kind of tool assemblage – in other words, an assemblage like that used by Clovis hunters, consisting of bifacially flaked stone projectile points, large bifaces, blades, and end scrapers. Tacit acceptance of this limiting theoretical orientation which leads to circular reasoning has resulted in the situation that very few American archaeologists are actively looking for new sites in stratigraphic contexts which could predate Clovis occupation, i.e. before 12,000 B.P. (cf. Bryan 1973 for further discussion of this factor).

Obviously, I agree that American assemblages cannot be classified in Asian taxonomic schemes because no specific Asian cultures are relatable to any specific American assemblages; but the fact remains that "typologically recognizable" general artifact classes are present in America as well as in Eurasia and I hypothesize that all or most of these artifact classes were introduced to America from Asia. These general classes of flaked-stone tools, all of which were already present in Eurasia in "Early or Middle Paleolithic" contexts, include pebble tools, large bifaces (some of which have been called "handaxes"), Levallois cores and flakes, burins, and blades. In addition, basically similar bone-working techniques of flaking, whittling, scraping, and grooving are present in both hemispheres. It should be clearly understood that all of these similarities should be thought of primarily as distinctive technological traditions which in most, if not all, cases were developed quite early in the Old World and persisted quite late in many parts of the world simply because knowledge of these techniques allowed the production of many different and highly efficient tool types. With this concept in mind, there can be no imputation of great antiquity put on any artifact or assemblage of artifacts containing these technological traditions in America, even if an assemblage of typologically "real" handaxes is found on the surface somewhere. Such assemblages may indeed be early but they must be demonstrated to be early on stratigraphic grounds.

Because in various parts of America there are many assemblages containing some of these basic classes, but lacking diagnostic bifacially flaked stone projectile points, such traditions seem to be significant. The problem is that these industries are rarely demonstrably

[2]   As pointed out by Irving, until relatively recently many archaeologists attributed fluted-point assemblages to some Asian Neolithic ancestor. Tolstoy (1958) demonstrated that such linkages do exist but that the direction of influence was from America to the Lake Baikal Neolithic and Bronze Age.

early on stratigraphic grounds. A few such industries include the Snake River Levallois and large biface industry, particularly a series of localities in southwestern Idaho which are stratified quarry/ workshop sites, but as yet unexcavated (Muto 1973). A remarkably similar industry has been reported from northwestern Argentina (Cigliano et al. 1962). In northeastern Argentina and adjacent parts of Paraguay and Brazil, the Altoparanaense industry (Menghin 1955–1956) appears to be a derived form of this biface tradition.

Another biface tradition is apparently correlated with the Río Pedregal terrace sequence in the desert of northwestern Venezuela (Rouse and Cruxent 1963). Here, the higher levels above the dissected terraces yielded only large, thick, crude bifaces while the high terraces also yielded some thinner bifaces made with better control. No projectile points were found by Cruxent on these higher levels. The main terrace forming most of the valley floor yielded thick willow-leaf-shaped El Jobo bifacial projectile points in addition to the same kinds of bifaces. Tanged projectile points were added to the total assemblage only on the floodplain terrace. The apparent significance of this reported sequence is enhanced by the presence of El Jobo points at those sites in direct association with the fossilized bones, some worked and burned, of extinct animals. The stratigraphy at one of these sites, Muaco, was confused by spring activity, but the stratigraphy and associations at the other two nearby sites are much clearer. At Cucuruchu, fossil bones and an El Jobo point were associated in a stream channel deposit. The most convincing associations are at Taima-Taima where three El Jobo points were excavated from a layer just above bedrock with undisturbed overlying deposits. The layer itself, as well as the bones, were repeatedly dated to about 13,000 years old. One El Jobo point was removed *en bloc* to show its close proximity to a Mastodon bone. At Taima-Taima and Muaco there were no large flaked-stone artifacts (see Bryan 1973 for a more detailed report on these important localities).

Among the many "typologically early" assemblages collected from the surface of the Atacama Desert in northern Chile is an assemblage of Acheulian-like handaxes at a locality known as Altamira (Padre Gustavo le Paige, personal communication 1970). Apparently there is no way to date these deflated surface assemblages. The large bifaces recovered in an old beach deposit of Pleistocene Lake Manix in the Mohave Desert of California could also be called "handaxes" (Simpson 1960). In this case, the presence of tufa dated 19,300 B.P. (UCLA-121) at a slightly higher level than the excavated area gives some indication of antiquity. Unfortunately, however, the dated tufa was not located directly over the cultural zone, and as the lake probably refilled to the same high level many times, the "handaxe" assemblage remains undated.

"Morphologically early" human skulls have also come to light recently. A burial with a skull exhibiting a very heavy browridge was found in northern Minnesota, but as the deposit in which it was found overlies the latest till, apparently the individual must have been interred sometime after 12,000 years ago. T. D. Stewart of the U.S. National Museum is studying the skull (John Brink, personal communication 1973).

In 1970 I encountered a human calvarium with enormous brow ridges packed away with a collection of fossil bones of large mammals recovered from caves in the Lagoa Santa region of Brazil (Plates 1–3). Several bones of extinct mammals had been chopped and cut (Plate 4). I did not have time to study the cut bones or the calvarium but noted that the vault was apparently of more or less normal size and height for modern man. Other than the huge supraorbital torus, the only suggestions of antiquity were the extreme thickness of the skull wall and the fact that it was fossilized. After the initial excitement of discovery I retreated to a temporary hypothesis that the calvarium must have been brought to Brazil from the European. I have now abandoned this hypothesis because the supraorbital torus does not really look like a Neanderthal or any other Old World skull I know of. In addition, I recently encountered a picture of another similar calvarium reportedly recovered from a cave in Santa Catarina, about 500 miles south of Lagoa Santa (Bleyer 1913: 50–53, Plate 4). Although the torus of the second calvarium is not as large as on the Lagoa Santa specimen, the similarity suggests that at some time there was a population of people with very large supraorbital tori living in southern Brazil. The fact that the oldest radiocarbon-dated artifacts (10,000 B.P.) in the Lagoa Santa region are associated with modern unfossilized animal bones (Hurt and Blasi 1969) is the only other indication of relative antiquity ascribable to these calvaria. Professor T. Jacob pointed out to me later, that a series of burials with skulls of enormous proportions had been recovered recently at Kow Swamp in Australia (Thorne and Macumber 1972) and radiocarbon dated to about 10,000 B.P. Extremely late persistance of the *Homo erectus* type is suggested by the authors, but as much older Australian skulls are of modern type, Professor Jacob suggested to me that the masticatory apparatus of the Kow Swamp people could have been very heavily used, causing development of enormous supraorbital tori, a thick skull wall, and a mandible larger than the Mauer mandible. If such "devolution" can occur, it seems clear that typological dating, even for human skulls, simply cannot be accepted as a substitute for dating under stratigraphic controls. Nevertheless, the evidence seems suggestive enough to warrant pursuit of early man in Brazilian caves.

A new method of dating the extent of aspartic acid racemization of bone has recently been announced along with dates on four separate

Plate 1.   Frontal view, approximately in Frankfort plane, of human calotte in the
H. V. Walter collection from Lagoa Santa Caves, Brazil

Plate 2.   Lateral view of same calotte

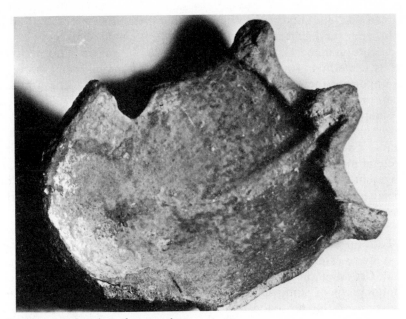

Plate 3.   Interior view of same calotte

Plate 4.   Example of mineralized ground sloth bone exhibiting series of chopping marks
(below 40–80 cm. on scale) in H. V. Walter collection from Lagoa Santa Caves, Brazil.
This specimen is now on exhibit in the Museu de Historia Natural in Belo Horizonte,
Minas Gerais

human skeletal finds from the southern California coast (Bada, Schroeder, and Carter 1974: 791–793). The Laguna skull, previously radiocarbon dated 17,150±1470 (UCLA 1233A) was used to calibrate the two methods for the region, as the mean annual temperature is an important factor in determining aspartic acid ratios. Los Angeles man, previously radiocarbon dated at > 23,600 (UCLA 1430) yielded a comparable 26,000-year racemization date while bone fragments from two sites near La Jolla yielded dates of 28,000, 44,000, and 48,000 years. The method requires reconfirmation and recalibration with skeletal material of known age for each local area, but as only small fragments of bone are necessary and as the method is most useful for an age range from 5,000 to 100,000 years, several other putatively early remains from various sites should be tested to see if the method can be validated.

To return to specific comments on Irving's paper, I agree that it is best not to extend terms like Middle Paleolithic, Mousteroid, Aurignacoid, Cro-Magnon or Neanderthal to America because of the implicit connotations of some sort of genetic relationship. With regard to the question of the presence of bone industries, some of which lack flaked-stone tools altogether, I am prepared to accept and to reinforce Irving's idea that certain people simply did not leave much imperishable material behind, and the chances of recovering the little that was left is reduced drastically with increasing antiquity because of the greater possibility of disturbance by erosion and redeposition. The material remains of early occupations are significantly less abundant in America than in Europe. For example, I have just returned from excavating a Clovis campsite in highland Guatemala. It was only during this third and last season at the site that we discovered the base of a fluted point and knew for certain what kind of site we were excavating. Incidentally, this was the only projectile point recovered in our 224-cubic-meter excavation. In addition to hundreds of retouched flakes, we recovered 79 other artifacts, only about a quarter of which remain whole, and many of these had been discarded because they were completely worn out. The other artifacts include biface fragments, end scrapers, unifacial "scrapers," blades, and burins; in other words, they represent a large proportion of the critical technological traditions I previously listed as being sufficient for the indigenous development of American tool assemblages.

At Jaguar Cave, Idaho, several bone artifacts were shaped by scraping and whittling and many thousands of bones were broken and flaked (Sadek-Kooros et al. 1972; Sadek-Kooros, personal communication). Limestone rubble with sharp edges and rough surfaces was readily available in the cave and could easily have been utilized without any obvious modification to work the bone.[3] If one accepts Breuil's hypothesis (1939), a bone breaking and flaking industry was already present at Choukoutien Locality 1, and certainly a sophisticated bone industry was present in the Upper Cave. The point that man living near Peking in North China must have been adapted to cold has been made several times before but needs repeating because it does imply that man could have become adapted to even colder areas, such as the maritime coast of Siberia, long before we have any indication of his entry into Alaska.

Although I believe that adaptation to a forested environment must have been a factor before man could have spread throughout the far north, I would like to point out that recent palynological work in central Alaska indicates that during the Last Glacial maximum most of the Yukon Valley was open steppe and not boreal forest (Charles Schweger, personal communication 1973). The dense and very extensive boreal forest with its deep fluffy snow cover as we know it today may not have existed before postglacial times, or at least not in full glacial times when the Bering land bridge existed.

I have reached the opinion that it is largely a waste of time to try to guess just when man may have come into America simply by trying to reconstruct the presence and absence of Beringia, the timing of the opening and closing of the Cordilleran "ice-free corridor," or the former presence of a vast, dense, boreal forest cover. We must have a great deal more information from the Quaternary geologists and palynologists who are working in the critical areas. Rather than guessing, archaeologists must get out and search in likely places for earlier sites.

---

[3] I have had the opportunity to examine a large part of the Old Crow fossil bone material which Irving mentions, and I agree with him that the bone must have been worked – cut, polished, whittled, scraped, and flaked – while the bone was green, and not after the bone reached its present fossilized and weathered condition.

346   ALAN L. BRYAN

REFERENCES

BADA, JEFFREY L., ROY A. SCHROEDER, GEORGE F. CARTER
  1974   New evidence for the antiquity of man in North America deduced from aspartic acid racemization. *Science* 184: 791–793.
BLEYER, GEORGE CLARKE
  1913   Ueber die Anthropophagie Prähistorischer Ureinwohner des Hochplateaus von Santa Catharina in Brasilien. *Proceedings of the 18th International Congress of Americanists* part one, pp. 50–53. London.
BREUIL, HENRI
  1939   Bone and antler industry of the Choukoutien, *Sinanthropus* site. *Palaeontologia Sinica*, Series D, 6: 7–41.
BRYAN, ALAN L.
  1965   *Paleo-American prehistory*. Occasional Papers of the Idaho State Museum 16. Pocatello.
  1973   Paleoenvironments and cultural diversity in Late Pleistocene South America. *Quaternary Research* 3 (2): 237–256.
CHARD, CHESTER
  1959   New World origins: a reappraisal. *Antiquity* 33: 44–48.
CIGLIANO, E. M., et al.
  1962   *El Ampajanguense*. Instituto de Antropología de la Facultad de Filosofía y Letras, Publicación 5. Rosario: Universidad Nacional Litoral.
DAVIES, D. M.
  1973   Fossil man in Ecuador. *Spectrum* 106.
HURT, WESLEY, OLDEMAR BLASI
  1969   *O Projecto Arqueologica "Lagoa Santa", Minas Gerais, Brasil.* Arquivos do Museu Paranaense, Arqueologia 4. Curitiba.
KRIEGER, ALEX D.
  1964   "Early man in the New World," in *Prehistoric Man in the New World*. Edited by Jesse Jennings and Edward Norbeck, 23–81. Chicago: University of Chicago Press.
MARTIN, PAUL S.
  1973   The discovery of America. *Science* 179: 969–974.
MENGHIN, OSWALDO
  1955–1956   El Altoparanaense. *Ampurias* 17: 171–200.
MÜLLER-BECK, HANSJÜRGEN
  1966   Paleohunters in America: origins and diffusion. *Science* 152 (3726): 1191–1210.
MUTO, GUY
  1973   "Levallois blades in the Old and New World." Paper given at the 38th annual meeting of the Society for American Archaeology, San Francisco.
ROUSE, IRVING, J. M. CRUXENT
  1963   *Venezuelan archaeology*. New Haven: Yale University Press.
SADEK-KOOROS, HIND, et al.
  1972   The sediments and fauna of Jaguar Cave. *Tebiwa* 15 (1): 1–45.
SIMPSON, RUTH
  1960   Archaeological survey of the Eastern Calico Mountains. *Masterkey* 34 (1): 25–35.

THORNE, A. G., P. G. MACUMBER
  1972 Discoveries of Late Pleistocene man at Kow Swamp, Australia. *Nature* 238 (5363): 316–319.

TOLSTOY, PAUL
  1958 The archaeology of the Lena Basin and its New World relationships, Parts I and II. *American Antiquity* 23 (4): 397–418; 24 (1): 63–81.

WORMINGTON, H. M.
  1962 The problem of the presence and dating in America of flaking techniques similar to the Paleolithic in the Old World. *Atti del VI Congresso Internazionale delle Scienze Preistoriche e Protoistoriche*, I: 273–283. Rome.

PART FIVE

Review

Southern and Eastern Asia: Conclusions

HALLAM L. MOVIUS, JR.

I am convinced that any attempt to draw together the core and flake archaeological assemblages considered thus far from South and East Asia into an integrated scheme must necessarily fall far short of its mark, at least at the present state of our knowledge. The reasons for this failure are at least as varied as are the regions studied. In each area Paleolithic research has proceeded at a different rate. To begin with, those who have applied themselves to studies in the various territories under consideration have had unequal resources at their disposal, as well as unequal capacities for observation, excavation, and interpretation. And, like the sites themselves, the published reports (if published at all) are of very disproportionate values. Thus it goes, until ultimately there is little common ground remaining on which to stand.

The only standard measure which still persists seems to be the fivefold categorization of the toolkits themselves which I first devised and published in 1944 (Movius 1944). This has been widely employed with surprisingly little question of its applicability in areas far removed from Burma and Java, where it was originally developed and applied. Attempts to refine it have been infrequent and of a relatively minor order (cf. Sieveking and Walker 1962) as have challenges against it (cf. Mulvaney 1970). Probably the main reason for its popularity is that it is both simple and basic. Yet, for these same reasons, it is patently obvious that it is inadequate at present. Even in 1937, when I was studying G. H. R. von Koenigswald's collection from Patjitan, I soon became aware of the shortcomings of the scheme: in essence the categories were too broad and there was too much overlap (Movius 1944: 92). It is difficult, however, to propose workable alternatives. In the first place, there is the question of how much would be gained by dividing and subdividing these major categories to produce a finely tuned typology of pebble tools. For one thing the limitations and influences imposed upon the tools by the raw material from which they were manufactured are very great; certainly a high degree of correlation of specific artifact types to raw material has been noted for the Anyathian, the Tampanian, the Changpinian, and other assemblages reported to date. Therefore, it appears that some options were closed to the actual toolmaker using these materials even before he began. Then too the size of the chunk of stone determines to a considerable extent the size of the tool which can be manufactured from it. In the case of the Patjitanian, one can see that the size of the boulders of silicified tuff had a direct effect on the number of cores vs. flakes. Hence it becomes clear that a more refined typology would be virtually useless if it only reflected the actual properties inherent in the raw material.

For substantially the same reasons, attribute analysis would encounter similar difficulties. This method has an enormous potential when the tools in question can be studied in terms of some common denominator, such as parallel-sided blades of Upper Paleolithic type. But it is virtually impossible to produce anything except tabular, steeply retouched tools from the fossil wood of Upper Burma. Consequently it is impossible to compare such objects with forms fashioned from a more tractable stone. What is needed is to find a classificatory procedure which truly reflects, or expresses, those choices which the toolmaker was required to cope with as he worked. If the "type concept" has any reality for these ancient tools – and one must assume that it has or the assemblages in question would fall back into chaos – the tool-maker's ideal form, or mental template of it, should become evident as certain trends recur.

These trends or modes might consist of such general features as unifaciality, bifaciality, maximum dimensions of the tool, length of the "working axis," chord of the cutting edge, straight-edginess, wavy-edginess, length/breadth ratio, long-axis orientation, "scar ratio," techniques of manufacture, etc. But most of these attributes have little direct bearing on limitations imposed by the raw material. If one combines seven or eight of them into a type, however, one should immediately note that the shorthand quality of the present fivefold categorization has been sacrificed for somewhat more precision.

An unachievable ideal, of course, would be a typology which would reflect the actual use of a given tool in the context of the assemblage in association with which it was collected, but it seems unlikely that this can ever be convincingly accomplished. Present terms, such as knife, scraper, chopper, etc., should not be presumed to describe function, although in certain instances the proper one is perhaps indicated for experimental purposes. Wear pattern studies, such as those of Semenov (1964), might to a certain extent be useful, but many of these ancient artifacts with which we have been dealing are presumably either too heavily weathered or they were not used for a given purpose consistently enough to produce any characteristic wear patterns. One need only read the article by Gould, Koster, and Sontz (1971) to despair utterly of ever being able to determine anything approaching the actual function of many tools. For, in studying tool usage among a living group of aborigines in Central Australia, these researchers found that some tools were even subjected to ritual restrictions. One of the most commonly used tools was an unaltered pebble, which was used once and then discarded.

Archaeology is admittedly incapable of recovering cultural manifestations of this sort or even of considering tools which do not exhibit any indication of ever having been used. If a more rigorous typology could be developed, however, it would certainly be useful in reconstructing culture areas, thereby reducing the vast chopper/ chopping-tool complex to manageable units. On a somewhat limited basis this has in fact been attempted by Chang for the Lower–Middle Paleolithic of China (Chang 1968: 40–65). And, in point of fact, I had even earlier suggested a broader division into western, northern, central, and southern regions (Movius 1948: 408ff). Now, with the addition of several new sites in the western Pacific, demonstrating the survival of this ancient tradition to within comparatively recent times, one would be justified in suggesting an eastern region as well. Certainly it will require a systematic reexamination of much of the material before any such broad, areal differences and relationships can be substantiated. With regard to most of the material which has already been collected, however, the construction of a more realistic and up-to-date typology is all that can be hoped for.

Insofar as future sites are concerned, the most pressing and fundamental need of all is for better and more up-to-date fieldwork and for improved reporting. In these respects it is unfortunate that the outlook is far from promising. The impoverished nations of Asia – which includes most of the Asian nations – understandably have not been allocating their very meager and limited funds to Paleolithic research. If available at all, archaeological funds are spent on visible and nationalistic monuments in the interests of attracting tourists. Furthermore, in some countries foreign investigators would be either unwelcome or unsafe under present circumstances. But the salient fact remains that those assemblages which have been randomly collected without reference to either geological or cultural context are of virtually no value and it is misleading to base interpretations upon them, e.g. the Sembiran of Bali or the materials found on Mount Do in North Vietnam. In the final analysis there is no substitute for the discovery of living floors, but then much is dependent on good excavation technique (e.g. Niah Cave in Borneo). The next best alternative is, of course, the finding of tools in good geological context or faunal association in open sites. For, particularly in the tropical regions of Asia, patination and other physical or chemical alterations of the implements themselves are very poor indicators of antiquity. And any student of the subject can clearly see that the artifact forms themselves provide just as little information concerning age, especially since tools of remarkable similarity persisted in use for hundreds of thousands of years in South and East Asia.

The underlying reasons for this remarkable conservatism still remain unfathomed. I have suggested (Movius 1948: 408) that in some manner it may be connected with the long persistence of a primitive form of man in this area. But perhaps man was not such a particularly static quantity in the East and Southeast of Asia as we once believed; this is supported by the discovery of so many contemporary species in Java alone in beds that are believed to be of the same geologic age. Then too the restrictions imposed by the raw materials might be invoked here, although even in cases where flint was available, the typology of the artifacts inevitably remained within the strictures of the general pebble tool category. Another possible answer may be offered by climatic or environmental (ecological) factors. But no research along these lines has even been attempted.

Sieveking ([and Walker] 1962: 127–132) considers what may be called the psychological effects of climate upon early man. She suggests that the lack of climatic variability offered little stimulus and led to a general cultural stagnation. One might also posit an even more plausible climatic tie-in by correlating the existence of flake and core assemblages with a monsoon climate. The heavy-duty tools found in all assemblages under consideration were perhaps necessary for dealing with the dense forests of such environments.

As a final observation one should note that, with the exception of G. J. Bartstra's current excavations in the Puning regions of the Baksoko Valley and those of R. B. Fox in the Philippines, the past three decades of research have produced relatively little other than a few thousand more artifacts, some from new localities. But scarcely anything substantive has been added to our general understanding of the fundamental problems of the core and flake assemblages of South and East Asia. When one realizes that the same old methods have been employed in most instances in gathering and analyzing the data, perhaps this is not surprising.

REFERENCES

CHANG, KWANG-CHIH
  1968   *The archaeology of ancient China* (revised edition). New Haven: Yale University Press.
GOULD, RICHARD A., DOROTHY A. KOSTER, ANN SONTZ
  1971   The lithic assemblage of the Western Desert Aborigines of Australia. *American Antiquity* 36 (2): 149–169.
MOVIUS, HALLAM L., JR.
  1944   Early man and Pleistocene stratigraphy in southern and eastern Asia. *Papers of the Peabody Museum of American Archaeology and Ethnology* 19 (3).
  1948   The Lower Palaeolithic cultures of southern and eastern Asia. *Transactions of the American Philosophical Society*, n.s. 38 (4): 329–420.
MULVANEY, D. J.
  1970   The Patjitanian industry: some observations. *Mankind* 7 (3): 184–187.
SEMENOV, S. A.
  1964   *Prehistoric technology: an experimental study of the oldest tools and artifacts from traces of manufacture and wear.* Translated and with a preface by M. W. Thompson. Bath, England: Adams and Dart.
SIEVEKING, ANN DE G., D. WALKER
  1962   The Palaeolithic industry of Kota Tampan, Perak, Malaya. *Proceedings of the Prehistoric Society* 28 (10): 103–139.

Biographical Notes

JEAN S. AIGNER (1943–) is Associate Professor of Anthropology at the University of Connecticut. At the University of California, Los Angeles and the University of Wisconsin (Ph.D., 1969), she studied archaeology, environmental sciences, and Chinese. Major research interests and active publication in the areas of Pleistocene Chinese hominid adaptations and subarctic human maritime adaptations, particularly in the Aleutian Islands, emphasize the theoretical paradigm of the Asiatic-New World Continuum. Since 1970 Aigner has been co-principal investigator for the research program, "Aleut Adaptation to the Bering Land Bridge Coastal Configuration."

GERT-JAN BARTSTRA (1940–) studied anthropology and sociology at the University of Amsterdam (1964–1967) and prehistory and geology at the University of Groningen (1967–1971). He is now at the Biologisch-Archaeologisch Instituut in Groningen and is primarily concerned with the study of Paleolithic archaeology and Pleistocene geology of East Asia. He has done fieldwork on Celebes and Java.

FRANCOIS BORDES (1919–) was born in Rives (Lot et Garonne, France). He studied at the universities of Bordeaux, Toulouse, and Paris, where he received his Sc.D. in Geology in 1951. From 1945 to 1956 he worked at the Centre National de la Recherche Scientifique; since 1956 he has been Professor at the University of Bordeaux. In 1959 he was Visiting Professor at the University of Chicago; in 1969, at the University of Arizona (Tucson); and in 1970, at the University of Montreal. He was Research Associate at the University of California at Berkeley in 1965. His main interests include man and his environment in the Pleistocene, and the typology and technology of Paleolithic cultures.

PAVEL I. BORISKOVSKY (1911–) has been Chief of the Department of Palaeolithic Studies since 1961 at the Institute of Archaeology (Leningrad Branch) of the Academy of Sciences, U.S.S.R. From 1952 to 1972 he was Professor of Archaeology at the University of Leningrad, and during that time he spent one year (1960–1961) in Vietnam as Professor of Archaeology at the University of Hanoi. He is particularly interested in research on the Paleolithic and Mesolithic of the U.S.S.R. and on the prehistory of Southeast Asia, especially Indochina.

ALAN LYLE BRYAN (1928–) is Professor of Anthropology at the University of Alberta, Canada. He has done extensive research on early man at sites located throughout North, Central, and South America, has worked on paleoenvironmental reconstruction of archaeological sites in Essex, England, and is interested in primate communication. His publications include: *Paleo-American prehistory* (Occasional Papers of the Idaho State University Museum 16: 1965) and "Early man in America in the light of Late Pleistocene chronology of western Canada and Alaska" (*Current Anthropology* 10 (4): 1969).

A. P. DEREVIANKO. No biographical data available.

ROBERT B. FOX. No biographical data available.

TOM HARRISSON (1911–76), born in Buenos Aires, was Government Ethnologist and Curator, Sarawak Museum (Borneo) from 1947 to 1967, during which time he conducted major cave and open-site excavations supported by the Gulbenkian Foundation, the Shell Group of companies, and the British Government. On retirement he became Visiting Professor in Anthropology at Cornell University and Research Professor at Sussex University, U.K. His numerous publications include *The peoples of Sarawak*, *The prehistory of Sabah* (*North Borneo*), and (1974) *Prehistoric wood*. He also acted as a consultant to H.H. the Sultan of Brunei in Borneo, with the rank of Datu Seri Leila.

FUMIKO IKAWA-SMITH (1930–) is Associate Professor and the Chairman of the Department of Anthropology at McGill University, Canada. She studied at Tsuda College, Tokyo Metropolitan University, Radcliffe College, and Harvard University, where she received her Ph.D. with a dissertation on the Paleolithic of Japan. She became a resident of Canada in 1960 and taught at the University of Toronto before coming to McGill in 1968. She has done fieldwork in Japan, the United States, Mexico, Egypt, and Iran. Her current research interest is in prehistoric sociocultural changes, from the Paleolithic to the formation of the state in Japan.

WILLIAM N. IRVING (1927–) is Professor of Anthropology at the University of Toronto. He has done archaeological and ethnological research throughout the United States and Canada, especially in Alaska, the Yukon Territory, and the Mackenzie and Keewatin Districts. Some major fields of interest are the study of early man in northern North America and the Arctic Small Tool tradition in Alaska and northern Canada.

TEUKU JACOB (1929–) is Professor of Anthropology at Gadjah Mada University College of Medicine, Yogyakarta. Educated in medicine and physical anthropology in Indonesia, the United States, and the Netherlands, he is a member of several anthropological and related societies. His research interest is primarily paleoanthropology, and in this pursuit he has studied almost all of the original pithecanthropine specimens from Java. Since 1962 he has been occupied with fossil man research in Central and East Java. His publications include works on craniology and dentition, the living Javanese, the Pleistocene hominine fossils, and Mesolithic and Paleometallic skeletal remains from Southeast Asia.

HALLAM L. MOVIUS, JR. (1907–) was born in Newton, Massachusetts. He graduated from Harvard College in 1930, and now is Professor Emeritus of Anthropology and Curator of Palaeolithic Archaeology in the Peabody Museum of Harvard University. From 1958 to 1964 he excavated the Abri Pataud at Les Eyzies, Dordogne, and is now engaged in writing a monograph on this very large and important Upper Paleolithic site. Before World War II he worked with Professor T. D. McCown at Mt. Carmel in Palestine, was a member of the Harvard-Irish expedition in Ireland, and searched successfully for traces of early man in Burma.

HARUO OHYI (1934–) was born in Tokyo. He studied at the University of Tokyo, and received his M.A. there in 1960. He taught at the University of Tokyo, Faculty of Letters (Lecturer in Archaeology, 1965–1966) and since 1966 has been Associate Professor of the Research Institute for Northern Cultures (Section of Archaeology), Faculty of Literature, Hokkaido University. His special interests include the growth and succession of the cultures in northern parts of the Asiatic continent and northern North America, from Paleolithic time to recent ages.

ALEXEI PAVLOVICH OKLADNIKOV (1908–), Academician of the Academy of Sciences of the U.S.S.R. and Director of the Institute of History, Philology, and Philosophy of the Siberian Department of the Academy of Sciences of the U.S.S.R., was born in Siberia on the Lena River. Since 1925 he has studied the archaeology of the Paleolithic, Neolithic, Bronze, and Iron periods in Siberia, Mongolia, and Middle Asia. During his work in the field, he discovered the skeleton remains of a neanderthal boy in the Teshik-Tash Cave, Uzbekistan, and Paleolithic dwellings and sculptures in Buret, near the Angara River. He is author of a series of works on Paleolithic and Neolithic art. Currently he is Professor at the Novosibirsk University, Fellow Member of the British Academy, Honourable Member of the Academy of Hungary, and Foreign Member of the Academy of Mongolia.

H. D. SANKALIA (1908–), M.A. (Bombay) and Ph.D. (London), was Professor of Proto-Indian and Ancient Indian History at the Deccan College Postgraduate and Research Institute from 1939 to 1973. At present, he is Professor Emeritus of Archaeology at that same institute. Initiator of excavations and explorations carried out by several universities, he is primarily interested in research in prehistory and protohistory, and has conducted excavations in several parts of India. He is also interested in historical geography (based on inscriptions) and a critical study of traditional literature, such as the epics and the Puranas, from an archaeological point of view. Author of fourteen books, his two most recent works are: *Prehistory and protohistory of India and Pakistan* and *Ramayana: myth or reality?*

CHOSUKE SERIZAWA (1919–) was born in Shizuoka City, Japan. He studied at Meiji University and has been Professor of Archaeology at Tohoku University since 1963. His present research interests include the Stone Age of Japan and its adjacent area, and Ceramics of Japan.

POW-KEY SOHN (1922–) is Professor of History and Prehistory at Yonsei University, Seoul, Korea. He is also Director of the Museum there and of the Centre d'Etude Franco-coréenne of Yonsei University. From 1952 to 1954 he was Assistant Professor of History at Seoul National University. From 1960 to 1963 he was a Fellow of the Rockefeller Foundation and received his Ph.D. in History from the University of California at Berkeley in 1963. Since 1964, he has initiated Paleolithic studies and excavations in Korea. His recent publications include: *Early Korean typography* (1970), *The history of Korea* (1971), *The Upper Paleolithic habitation at Sŏkchang-ni, Korea* (1973), and "L'analyse palynologique et l'environment paléolithique de la Corée" (1974).

GUSTAV HEINRICH RALPH VON KOENIGSWALD (1902–) was born in Berlin. He studied geology and paleontology in Berlin, Tübingen, Cologne, and Munich. Between 1930 and 1948 he was paleontologist for the Geological Survey of the Netherlands East Indies in Bandung, Java. From 1948 to 1968 he was Professor of Palaeontology at the State University of Utrecht, the Netherlands. Since his retirement in 1968, he has been connected with the Senckenberg Museum, Section of Palaeontology, Frankfurt/Main. His fieldwork over the years has covered a large portion of the globe. In Java he worked primarily on Pleistocene stratigraphy and early man. He visited China in 1935, 1936, 1937, 1939, and 1973 to study and collect fossil mammalian remains from Chinese drugstores. From 1946 to 1948 he worked in collaboration with Prof. Franz Weidenreich at the American Museum in New York. His other fieldwork locations have included East and South Africa, the Philippines, and Pakistan. His special interest is early man.

Index of Names

Index of Subjects